TIN HATS, OILSKINS & SEABOOTS

Other Books by L.B. Jenson

WRITTEN AND ILLUSTRATED

Vanishing Halifax (Petheric Press, 1968)

Nova Scotia Sketchbook (Petheric Press, 1969)

Wood and Stone, Pictou (Petheric Press, 1972)

County Roads, Pictou County (Petheric Press, 1974)

Bluenose II (large folio) (Hosmer Enterprises & L.B. Jenson, 1975)

Fishermen of Nova Scotia (Petheric Press, 1980)

Saga of the Great Fishing Schooners (Nimbus Publishing, 1992)

ILLUSTRATED

H.F. Pullen, *Atlantic Schooners* (Brunswick Press, 1967)

Lester Sellick, *Canada's Don Messer* (Kentville Publishing, 1969)

H.F. Pullen, *Shannon and Chesapeake* (McClelland and Stewart, 1970)

Claude Darach, *From a Coastal Schooner's Log* (Nova Scotia Museum, 1980)

H.F. Pullen, *Sea Road to Halifax* (Nova Scotia Museum, 1980)

J.C. Burke, *Treasury of Newfoundland Humour and Wit* (Kingfisher, 1981)

Jessie Coade, *Messdeck News* (Ragweed Press, 1985

Murray Barnard, *Sea, Salt and Sweat* (Nova Scotia Department of Fisheries, 1986)

H. Chapman, *Sketches of Old Dartmouth* (Dartmouth Museum Society, 1991)

L.B.J.

based on a sketch by James Holland

LATHAM B. JENSON

Tin Hats, Oilskins & Seaboots

A NAVAL JOURNEY,

1938–1945

Foreword by
W.A.B. DOUGLAS

ROBIN BRASS STUDIO
Toronto

Published 2000 by Robin Brass Studio Inc.
10 Blantyre Avenue, Toronto, Ontario M1N 2R4, Canada
Fax: 416-698-2120 • e-mail: rbrass@total.net
www.rbstudiobooks.com

Distributed in the United States of America by
Midpoint Trade Books
27 West 20th St., Suite 1102
New York, NY 10011, U.S.A.
Fax: 212-727-0195 • e-mail: midpointny@aol.com

Printed and bound in Canada by AGMV-Marquis,
Cap-Saint-Ignace, Quebec

Canadian Cataloguing in Publication Data

Jenson, L. B., 1921–
     Tin hats, oilskins & seaboots : a naval journey, 1938-1945

Includes index.
ISBN 1-896941-14-1

1. Jenson, L. B., 1921–   . 2. World War, 1939-1945 – Naval operations,
Canadian. 3. World War, 1939-1945 – Personal narratives, Canadian.
4. Canada. Royal Canadian Navy – Biography. I. Title. II. Title: Tin
hats, oilskins and seaboots.

D811.J46 2000   940.54'5971'092   C00-931109-2

For my dear wife, Alma. Words cannot express my appreciation of her assistance, encouragement and patience.

Magnetic compass rose

The Lookout

Contents

Georges Island — Halifax Harbour

LBJENSON

Foreword

One of the qualities that ensures the sanity of a sailor is a sense of humour. Commander L.B. "Yogi" Jenson, as this memoir attests, must be one of the sanest sailors alive. The humour is understated and self-deprecating, rather like a Thurber cartoon. Having escaped an outbreak of dysentery on board HMS *Renown*, for example, he writes, "Happily, I was not afflicted, being from Alberta".

Those of us lucky enough to have served with Commander Jenson encountered his sense of humour by the day and by the hour. Some years after the war a seaman in his ship managed, while in a state of intoxication, to steal a mobile crane in Bermuda. For the officer of the day it was the last among a series of dreadful mishaps that had taken place ashore during the night, and which had to be reported to the captain at a very early hour in the morning. Yogi relieved the tension by exclaiming, "It's all my fault. I only told them not to steal bananas." On more serious occasions, when the ship was under way, and as often happens beset by possible dangers, such as heavy weather or thick fog, he was always reassuring, always funny, and always professional to the core. The ships he commanded, as the people who served in them will tell you, were happy and efficient. So is this memoir.

Yogi used to keep in his cabin a shelf of scrap books recording the events of his naval career. It was a constant reminder of the varied life and the wonderul experiences that a seafaring man can experience, and he has here recorded the fun and excitement that those scrap books symbolised. As he tells us, he has always "had some ability to draw pictures." Tragically, all his wartime drawings were lost in HMS *Renown*, HMS *Hood* and in HMCS *Ottawa*, torpedoed southeast of Newfoundland on the night of Sunday, 13 September 1942, an episode that marked his life for ever.

The findings of the Board of Enquiry into the loss of that ship drew special attention "… to the commendable devotion to duty … of the following officers and men: The Commanding Officer, Acting Lieutenant Commander

Clark A. Rutherford, RCN and the medical officer, Surgeon Lieutenant George A. Hendry, RCNVR. These officers lost their lives largely through exhaustion caused by little or no rest for some days previous. Also to Sub-Lieutenant L.B. Jenson, RCN, who for a young officer displayed considerable initiative and power of command, Acting Gunner (T) L.T. Jones, Petty Officer Gridel, Leading Stoker McLeod, and Sub-Lieutenant Arnold of HMS *Celandine.*"

The late Captain T.C. Pullen, who was the First Lieutenant of *Ottawa*, has described the scene as the ship suffered its last agonies: "… for a moment, it seemed the stern section might break free and remain afloat. It appeared buoyant. However, this was not to be. The stern tilted higher and higher. As it too approached the vertical there came a mighty clatter, clouds of dust, and the entire after superstructure, X Gun included, as well as nearly seventy depth charges, broke loose and plummeted into the sea. What remained of the hull, dripping propellers and all, soon followed, leaving nothing in its wake but a bewildered collection of oil-covered swimmers and crowded carley floats." Among them was Sub-Lieutenant Jenson, and Yogi's illustration on page 139 captures brilliantly that terrible sight.

The illlustrations that adorn the pages of this book are indeed a special treat. Not only do they reflect a sailor's love of his profession, but they comprise a most useful set of references about the details of naval life, and the realities of war at sea in the Second World War.

It was Yogi's great ambition to attain command of a ship. Some time after the adventures he has here recounted, he achieved that ambition, and nothing else mattered. Readers of this memoir will find out why.

W.A.B. "ALEC" DOUGLAS
Official Historian, Canadian Armed Forces, 1973–1994
Navigating Officer, HMCS Fort Erie, *1962–1964*

Preface

Far called our navies melt away,
On dune and headland sinks the fire;
Lo, all our pomp of yesterday
Is one with Nineveh and Tyre.

Kipling, "Recessional"

Among my reasons for writing the following memoir is the desire to record how many young Canadians saw the world in the 1930s and 1940s. It was a very different view from the present. The British Empire, of which Canada was a dominion, included so many parts of the world that the sun never set upon it. The Royal Navy was the largest and most powerful on the oceans and protected all the British dominions and colonies from whatever problems might arise.

When my overwhelming desire to go to sea led me to join the Royal Canadian Navy, that service was still very much a junior partner of the Royal Navy, and my schooling as an officer took me to Great Britain and into the training organization of the British navy. It was a time of rapid adjustment and change to meet the looming threat of Hitler's Germany. After World War One, the British had concentrated on a conventional navy, one capable of engaging in a fleet action (such as Jutland in 1916) against any other fleet or combinations of fleets. Although they had a number of aircraft carriers, there was no serious appreciation of the threat to its large ships by aircraft. Anti-submarine detection was assumed by most officers to be almost infallible thanks to the newly invented Asdic (sonar). It was honestly believed that this spelled the end of the submarine menace, and in fact I and my classmates were taught very little about anti-submarine warfare before the war .

As a consequence, when war broke out our ships were badly prepared against enemy aircraft, and we were not suitably prepared for submarine attacks on our shipping. However, right from the start the convoy system was inaugurated, as slow merchant vessels sailing independently

The Battle of the Atlantic raged from 1939 to 1945. This was the testing time for the young Royal Canadian Navy, the time when our heritage of courage, skill and endurance was established. Starting with only a few ships, Canadian sailors fought on one of the world's stormiest, coldest and bleakest oceans, playing a vital role in the struggle. To commemorate our ships and seamen of those brave days, the last remaining corvette, HMCS *Sackville*, was preserved and lovingly restored, using the donations of thousands of Canadians to create a living, floating Canadian Naval War Memorial.

could be easily torpedoed and sunk without danger to the attacking U-boats. The idea was to battle the submarines with the escorting destroyers. The British Admiralty immediately decided to order large numbers of small warships designed after the very seaworthy Antarctic whalers. Small shipyards in the United Kingdom and Canada were able to build such vessels cheaply and quickly. These were the corvettes, which formed the backbone of the wartime Royal Canadian Navy.

A year after I joined the navy we went to war with Germany and for just under six years we were engaged in a deadly game of hunting and being hunted. When the war

THE CANADIAN NAVAL CORVETTE TRUST

HEREBY CERTIFY THAT

L. B. JENSON

HAS CONTRIBUTED TO THE PRESERVATION & RESTORATION
OF THE LAST REMAINING CORVETTE

H.M.C.S. SACKVILLE

IN HONOUR OF THE MEN AND SHIPS OF THE

ROYAL CANADIAN NAVY

IN

THE BATTLE OF THE ATLANTIC

1939–1945

MAY 3, 1984

DATE

CAMPAIGN CHAIRMAN

AGASSIZ
+ ALBERNI +
ALGOMA
AMHERST
ARNPRIOR
ARROWHEAD
ARVIDA
ATHOL
ASBESTOS
BADDECK
BARRIE
BATTLEFORD
BEAUHARNOIS
BELLEVILLE
BITTERSWEET
BOWMANVILLE
BRANDON
BRANTFORD
BUCTOUCHE
CALGARY
CAMROSE
CHAMBLY
+ CHARLOTTETOWN +
CHICOUTIMI
CHILLIWACK
COBALT
COBURG
COLLINGWOOD
COPPER CLIFF
DAUPHIN
DAWSON
DRUMHELLER
DUNDAS
DUNVEGAN
EDMUNDSTON
EYEBRIGHT
FENNEL
FERGUS
FORESTHILL
FREDERICTON
FRONTENAC
GIFFARD
GUELPH
GALT
HALIFAX
HAWKESBURY
HEPATICA
HESPELER
HUMBERSTONE
HUNTSVILLE
KAMLOOPS
KAMSACK
KENOGAMI
KINCARDINE
KITCHENER
LACHUTE
LA MALBAIE
LEASIDE
LETHBRIDGE
+ LEVIS +
LINDSAY
LONGBRANCH

+ LOUISBURG +
LOUISBURG II
LUNENBURG
MATAPEDIA
MAYFLOWER
MERRITTONIA
MIDLAND
MIMICO
MONCTON
MOOSEJAW
MORDEN
NANAIMO
NAPANEE
NORSYD
NORTH BAY
OAKVILLE
ORANGEVILLE
ORILLIA
NEW WESTMINSTER
OWEN SOUND
PARRY SOUND
PETERBOROUGH
PETROLIA
PORT ARTHUR
PICTOU
PRESCOTT
QUESNEL
RIMOUSKI
RIVIERE DU LOUP
REGINA
ROSTHERN
SASKATOON
SACKVILLE
ST. LAMBERT
ST. THOMAS
+ SHAWINIGAN +
SHEDIAC +
SHERBROOKE
+ SPIKENARD +
SMITH FALLS
SNOWBERRY
SOREL
STELLARTON
STRATHROY
SUDBURY
SUMMERSIDE
THE PAS
THORLOCK
TILLSONBURG
TIMMINS
TRAIL
+ TRENTONIAN +
TRILLIUM
VANCOUVER
VILLE DE QUEBEC
WEST YORK
WETASKIWIN
+ WEYBURN +
WHITBY
+ WINDFLOWER +
WOODSTOCK
+ LOST

SACKVILLE

H.M.C.S. SACKVILLE

L.B. JENSON

ended, our world had been changed beyond our imaginings.

This book relates my experiences before and during the Second World War. Just as the war with Germany concluded, I was appointed senior term lieutenant at the college for naval cadets at Royal Roads, near Victoria, British Columbia. This was followed by appointment to HMCS *Cayuga,* a Tribal Class destroyer under construction in the Halifax Shipyard. When *Cayuga* was completed, I served as her executive officer both in Atlantic waters and in the Pacific, which became her home station.

After shore duties in Halifax and Ottawa, I was appointed to command of HMCS *Crusader,* a recently acquired destroyer, and promoted to the rank of commander. This was followed by command of HMCS *Micmac,* one of the earlier Tribal Class destroyers. From *Micmac* I went as a student to the NATO Defence College, at that time in Paris, then returned to Ottawa for a variety of duties. My next and final sea appointment was to HMCS *Fort Erie* as commander of the Seventh Escort Squadron of seven frigates, as well as of *Fort Erie.* I retired from the Royal Canadian Navy as a commander in 1965, having had an adventurous and rewarding career.

All the drawings that I made during the war were lost due to enemy action. I sent home little sketches on my letters and some that were saved were traced and appear in this book. My main drawings were done after I retired and had the time to devote to research. A number are based on photographs taken by Dr. Neil Chapman, Lieut. RCNVR (Rtd), a wonderful shipmate in *Niagara, Long Branch* and *Algonquin.* These drawings are not of a permanent nature and are just sketched out on tracing paper. A few drawings are based on ones from other books of mine.

ACKNOWLEDGEMENTS

I would like to acknowledge my reference to the Reports of Proceedings for *Algonquin* by Rear Admiral D.W. Piers, DSC, CD, notes provided by Captain R.M. Steele, DSC, CD, Commander I.A. Macpherson, CD, details concerning uniforms by Commander E.L'Heureux, CD, all RCN (Rtd), the intrepid Kenneth Garrett, ex-Leading Seaman RCNVR, and by kind permission of the Atlantic Chief and Petty Officers Association an article by C.R. Skillen, RCNVR (Rtd) from their book *Fading Memories.* The Directorate of History in Naval Headquarters, in the late 1960s, kindly provided much help from German naval records.

For the guidance and editing of my publisher, Robin Brass, and the kindness of Dianne and Donald Graves and of Michael Whitby of the Department of National Defence Directorate of History in reviewing the text and providing invaluable comments and suggestions, I cannot sufficiently express my appreciation.

LATHAM B. JENSON
12 April 2000

1

Getting under way

My father was born near Preston in Lancashire, England, in 1889. The Jensons were supposed to have been among the Danes driven from Ireland by Brian Boru, the King of the Irish, in 1014. First they went to the Isle of Man, but when that became crowded they settled in Lancashire. My father as a boy was shown by an aunt where our people, who had rowed up the River Dee, pulled their boats ashore. Like most people of those times, they were farmers. In later years, some Jensons went to Archangel in Russia in the fur business; others went to St. Petersburg to set up cotton mills.

Our family was converted by the preaching of John Wesley and joined the Brereton and Molineux families in building a Methodist Chapel which is now preserved by the National Trust. In the early 1800s they established a business, Jenson's Hams, which prospered. Later they established a jam factory and then a soap factory in Manchester.

My grandfather married a Margaret Peake of Preston, whose parents had Peake's Pot Shop. Her mother was French Huguenot. Other relations were Lathams, involved in dyes and colours for pottery. After the depression of 1897 my grandfather, with his brothers and sisters, sold the factories and immigrated to western Canada to homestead on the prairies.

Homesteading was not at all what my grandparents imagined. Grandmother had thought that servants would be available, as she could not cook and had never done housework. Of course there was no such help and she struggled at being a farm wife. The first bread she made provided the hired man with targets for rifle practice. Once the farm was established, at Knee Hill Valley, near Innisfail, Alberta, it was rented and my grandparents moved to Calgary. My grandfather became active in politics before Alberta became a province in 1905. He was an accountant and had studied chemistry at Manchester University. He also was a Liberal and was given money by Lord Derby to distribute as seemed appropriate on behalf of the Liberal Party in western Canada. He ran unsuccessfully against R.B. Bennett in federal elections. Because of Grandfather's short stature, his high riding boots and little beard, Bennett referred to him as "Puss in Boots," not a political advantage. Bennett became Prime Minister of Canada in the 1930s.

Later on, Grandfather became executive assistant to a millionaire named Freddy Lowe, a real estate developer in Edmonton. In the depression of 1911, Lowe's fortune vanished, he went insane and eventually committed suicide. Grandmother hated living in Canada and died in the 1920s. After that Grandfather lived with us for a time, then moved to Vancouver, where he became a speech writer for Gerry McGear, the flamboyant mayor of Vancouver. He died in 1938.

When the family moved to Canada, Father had been left behind in Manchester Grammar School to complete his education, and he came to Canada about 1904 or so. In Calgary the family lived in Rideau Park on the banks of the Elbow River. Sarcee Indians camped on a hill behind the house. All night long drums would beat. He had a go at the University of Alberta in Edmonton and then went on to Vancouver, where he had an interesting job collecting taxes on Lower Hastings Street, a red light district.

In 1914 he applied to join the North West Mounted Police, but when war broke out, he immediately enlisted in the 15th Alberta Light Horse and was in France in 1915. Relatives in England had obtained a commission for him in a Lancashire regiment but he declined, preferring to remain a private soldier with his friends in a Canadian regi-

ment. He was fortunate because shortly the Lancashire regiment was sent to Gallipoli, where they were practically wiped out by the Turks.

Father was present at the first gas attack on the Western Front. He and the others stood fast, holding their socks soaked in urine over their faces while the French and French Colonials retreated through their lines. He served in several regiments during this dreadful conflict and took part in all the major actions involving Canadians, including the Somme and Vimy Ridge. He was never wounded, but the war left its mark on him in other ways. In the middle of a cold, still night I would awaken to a sort of discordant singing which would be followed by yells, shouts and cries, all hair-raising, settling in to muttering and snores. However, all in all I think he enjoyed military life. He served in the army of occupation in Bonn and Cologne in 1919 but declined to serve with the Canadians against the Bolsheviks and the Red Army in Russia. When his regiment returned to Calgary, a recruiter for the post office was waiting on the station platform as the postal workers were on strike. A good many of the regiment marched directly to the post office and began work, still in uniform, Father among them.

Shortly after returning to Calgary he married my mother. In 1921 he joined the militia as a lieutenant, back in the cavalry. Each year he trained at Sarcee, the Indian Reserve near Calgary, or at Work Point Barracks near Victoria. When war broke out in 1939, he went on active service, serving in Newfoundland until the war ended. He was 91 when he died of old age.

CALGARY STAMPEDE
JULY 1938
BOB HOLGATE WAS MOTHER'S
BROTHER

CHECK YOR HARDWARE

BURY YOR OWN DEAD

BOB HOLGATE'S CALGARY OUTFIT

COOKIN' FLAPJACKS
FRONT OF ROYAL HOTEL

My mother remembered crossing Canada by train as a child about 1900 and, in particular, the red plush seats in the coaches. Her next memories were of Indian children, in their birthday suits, playing in the yard and looking in the windows. An elderly neighbour, Mrs. Sam Livingstone, an American widow of an NWMP guide, slept with two Navy Colt Six Shooters under her pillow.

Mother was born in Lancashire, a Holgate descended supposedly from Robert Holgate, the Archbishop of York at the time of Henry VIII. Like Luther, the Archbishop married a nun. He had redistributed church lands for Henry and on the king's death was lucky to have his life spared by Bloody Mary, Queen Mary I. My mother's mother was born in Calcutta, India. Her family had been in India since before the Mutiny; her hair was black, like a raven's wing, said my grandfather. She died when my mother was nine and the five children lived with relatives in Calgary who were Indian Army veterans.

My mother's father, old Mr. Holgate, had a stable, selling and buying horses. He was from a Yorkshire farming family and Mother thought he had gone to Edinburgh University and studied medicine. Grandfather's accent was broad Yorkshire and he used "thee, thou and thine." One ear had been bitten off by a horse and he smoked a pipe steadily. One of Mother's brothers, Bob, became the chuckwagon champion of the world in the 1930s at the Calgary Stampede with "Bob Holgate's Chuckwagon." Another brother, Doug, was a cowboy and lived in a caravan drawn by a team of horses, hiring out himself and his team. One of Mother's sisters married Iver Iverson, a machinist in the CPR shops at Ogden who bought a number of acres of property near Bowness where he cut trees and built a Norwegian log cabin for himself and family. Later on in the 1950s and 1960s Calgary expanded to become the second largest city (in area) in the world and Iverson's property became valuable beyond their wildest dreams. Life is full of surprises.

Our family lived in a large c.1890 farm house near what became 17th Avenue and 14th Street West. The lady who owned it had been a nurse and was addicted to drugs, which were perfectly legal then. She explained very seriously that a large black dog materialized through the walls from time to time. I was fascinated, aged four, but our dog

1935
INTRODUCTION TO
THE DELIGHTS OF LIFE
ABOARD SHIP

"BANSHEE" ON SYLVAN LAKE
ALBERTA
30 ft. CABIN CRUISER OWNED
BY MR PERCY ADAIR, A ONE-
LEGGED VETERAN, LONDON DERRY,
AND BUILT BY MR. HIMMELMAN,
AN ALBERTAN FROM LUNENBURG,
NOVA SCOTIA.

spread our picnics. In the summer holidays we went to Banff, often climbing small mountains in a gentle sort of way. We watched the bears feeding by the Bow River and swam in the Banff hot springs.

In later years we went to Sylvan Lake. It was there that I first encountered Percy Adair, a tall moustached gentleman, a native of Londonderry, Ireland. His wounded right leg had been amputated at the hip during the Great War. He did well with just one crutch, drove a car, swam, and even dived off a high board. He possessed a lovely 30-foot Bermuda-rigged yacht with a built-in engine. She was named *Banshee* and had been built to his order by a transplanted Lunenburger named Himmelman. I used to hang around the wharf when *Banshee* was alongside and eventually Mr. Adair took me for long sails. We grew to be good friends, discussing everything under the sun, particularly when driving about southern Alberta. He often came to our home and sometimes I stayed with him either in a caravan he had or in his boat.

A great influence on my life was our minister, Archdeacon Cecil Swanson of Saint Stephen's Church. He was a Londoner by birth who had been a missionary in the Yukon and preached most inspiring sermons. He had great sympathy for the Indians and Eskimos and told us many of their legends, pointing out how similar they were to ideas in the Bible. He was the chaplain of the Naval Reserve Division, HMCS *Tecumseh*.

Another influence on my life was Calgary's fine Carnegie Public Library. My favourite magazines were British, particularly *Triumph*, which was full of horrors.

must have driven the black dog away. We then bought a nice house at the foot of Mount Royal and this was the family home until the 1950s.

I went to Earl Grey School, which was blessed with excellent teachers, mainly from Nova Scotia and New Brunswick. Few adults in those days had been born in the West. My earliest recollections are of picnics and hikes. The heat of the prairie summer is intense and often we would go with Mother to Reilly Park or St. George's Island. At the park there was a wading pool surrounded by tall cottonwood and willow trees set in spacious lawns where we

My parents gave me the *Chums Annual* each Christmas for several years and it was a great mixture of science, adventure, life in the colonies and so on. All these made me feel sorry to live in a place that had no history, or so I thought. Little did I know.

Calgary, at the junction of the Bow and Elbow rivers, is beautifully situated where the prairie, the great central plain of North America, meets the Rocky Mountains. It is blessed with the most sunshine in Canada and the harsh winters are made more bearable when warm Chinook winds from the Pacific descend from over the mountains and melt the snow and ice. Wild flowers of every kind grow in profusion and small wild creatures are abundant. How is it possible to account for the fact that from my earliest years, four or five, I had one main ambition, to leave Calgary and go to sea? Some might say that he who would go to sea for a living would go to hell for a pastime. Others would agree with Dr. Johnson, who asked why anyone would go to sea when there were perfectly good prisons on shore. I read everything I could find about life at sea and drew pictures of ships and the sea. Over my bed I had a painting of merchant ships in the Pool of London, lovely ships in a soft haze with the sun filtering down.

A friend and I built a sort of boat which we launched in the Elbow River. It filled with water and sank immediately. Swimming was my chief sport, in the Elbow all summer and at the YMCA in winter. I aimed to get in the water on 24 May, Queen Victoria's birthday, and generally succeeded. Another interest was fossil collecting. The Elbow

had cut through the prairie, forming cliffs with layers of rock clearly exposed. Generally my dog went with me on these expeditions and I collected many excellent fossil shells. Some years ago I went back to the top of the cliffs and was surprised that I had escaped falling and breaking my neck. On several expeditions hiking over the prairie I encountered squadrons of the Lord Strathcona Horse galloping along, a breathtaking sight especially in fall or winter with the breath of men and horses showing in the clear, cold air. It was a visible reminder of the great British Empire.

The Sea Cadets with their smart uniforms, bugle band and drill appealed to me. I begged my parents to let me join them. They had a reputation for toughness and Mother and Dad were dubious. However, I finally got permission to join and my whole life changed. The Sea Cadet Corps *Undaunted* trained at the Calgary Armouries twice a

Sea Cadets – cutlass drill

week or more. The boys were a different mixture from the boys at my school. My part of Calgary was mostly Anglo-Saxon/Scottish, predominantly Protestant. The boys in the Sea Cadets were a mixture of all the races and religions of southern Alberta: English, German, Ukrainian, Rumanian, Greek and so on. Discipline, unquestioning obedience, perfection in dress and appearance and perfect attendance were the watchwords of *Undaunted.* Anyone who would not conform to the rules was dismissed at once and could not rejoin.

Every meeting night we began with Divisions (the naval equivalent of Parade) and inspection of uniform and general appearance. We wore the standard dress of the Royal Navy with its collars, dickies, ribbons, lanyard, flap trouser fronts, all the traditional things carried over from the last century and very fussy. We had drill of the standard style, dressing, forming fours, marching, wheeling and so on. Often we drilled with rifles, and we had cutlass drill in a form which must have been laid down in the 1700s. It was "Cut! thrust! parry! advance! guard! and step back!" almost like a series of ballet movements, very pretty to watch. Our cutlasses were made of wood and were much lighter than the real thing. Another exercise was boarding drill: grapnels were thrown from one set of benches to another, dragging them together. We did not get into board-

Sea Cadet "Undaunted"

ing pikes and tomahawks; it would have been mayhem with such lively boys. Seamanship training in the form of magnetic compass, knots and splices, anchor work and nautical terminology occupied the rest of the evening. We had a band of bugles and drums which used to make my spine tingle. I would march home, my head filled with thoughts of the battles of Jutland, Trafalgar, Copenhagen and the Nile with their great naval heroes.

On Saturday mornings we used the armoury rifle range and shot for our bronze, silver and gold Dominion Rifle Association badges. There must have been a hundred or so boys serving in *Undaunted.* The working leader of *Undaunted* was an example of the true British bulldog. Such men in our youthful eyes made the British Empire synonymous with courage, honour and justice, which many consider to be the foundation for decency and civilization. William Mitchell was a retired chief petty officer, torpedo gunner's mate, of the Royal Navy. Short, stocky, with great bushy eyebrows, very strong, tireless and just but fair, he was always available for instruction, advice or whatever was required. He had joined the Royal Navy as a boy seaman in the 1890s. Some of his officers had served under officers who in turn had served with Lord Nelson. He was ably assisted by retired three-badge Able Bodied Seaman Arthur Liddal, a shy, quiet man who also was a tower of strength. The quarters in the armoury basement reeked of tobacco, Stockholm tar, hemp rope and human sweat, like parts of many of the ships in which I sailed in later years.

Our commanding officer was Lieutenant Commander Bromley, RNR (Rtd). A tall, gentlemanly man with grey hair and distinguished features, he had commanded patrol vessels in the Orkney Islands and Faeroes area in the First World War. The duty of these vessels was to detect disguised German raiders breaking into the Atlantic to prey on our ocean trade. One innocent-looking vessel which he boarded and which fooled him completely was *Sea Devil,* commanded by the famous Count von Luckner. *Sea Devil* went on to sink many of our ships but in every case an effort was made to spare human life. Subsequently, when von Luckner visited Calgary in the 1930s, he was received as a man who had done his duty and behaved with honour. I believe he lectured at the Alberta Military Institute.

Mr. Mitchell and Mr. Liddal both worked for the Canadian Pacific Railway, while Mr. Bromley was the meteorologist at the Calgary Airport. Mr. Bromley permitted me to see all the meteorological instruments and to help with the readings. Getting to the airport and back home in winter often was a long, windy and bitterly cold walk from

DUST STORM DURING THE 1930's DROUGHT
APPROACHING CALGARY FROM THE NORTH

northeast Calgary to southwest Calgary, over prairie and down the North Hill to the Centre Street bridge, then home. I shudder at the memory.

The cadets originally had a camp at Sylvan Lake which was pleasant but not well fitted out. We had two cutters for boat pulling and smaller rowboats. We moved to a permanent camp site at Chestimere Lake, a large slough a few miles east of Calgary, where I helped Mr. Mitchell and Mr. Liddal lay the camp out, setting up the mast in a cement base and so on. There we were camping on the bald prairie as opposed to the mixed woodlands around Sylvan Lake. The wind blew all the time and sailboats travelled the length of Chestimere and back in a jiffy. The water was warm and full of weeds, with a few leeches, but there was lots of room to swim. Each morning in camp after "Call the Hands" we would run down to bathe or just wash. My Christian name is Latham, which neither I nor anyone else had every heard before. I had the habit of wrapping my towel around my head and dashing in my otherwise state of nature right into the water. One morning another cadet called out, "Here comes the Yogi!" and that has been my nickname all these years. (Mahatma Gandhi was much in the news at the time.) I have to say that I personally like the name Latham; a distant ancestor whose surname was Latham was shot dead in battle by an arrow. After three or four years and examinations by Lieutenant Reginald Jackson, RCNVR, the commanding officer of HMCS *Tecumseh*, the local Naval Division, I passed for petty officer.

My great ambition had been to go to sea for a living, but I had not really considered in what capacity or in what service. I supposed that probably it would be as a merchant seaman as the Canadian navy was not well known, being almost minuscule in size. Father had heard of *Conway* in England and wrote off for a prospectus. It looked interesting but expensive. Most sea cadets had no thought of joining the navy, and when Lieutenant Commander Bromley heard of my ambition he advised Father to write to Naval Headquarters in Ottawa about cadet entry.

It turned out that every year competitive examinations were written by boys like myself. Paymaster Captain Cossette, the Naval Secretary, sent us specimen papers and my father saw the principal of Western Canada, my high school, to arrange my curriculum to cover the subjects of examination. Mr. Woodman obliged and I settled in for two years of very hard study. In May 1938 I sat for the exams at the Normal School under Dr. Coffin and shortly afterwards learned to my astonishment that I had passed. There were 125 candidates and seven were accepted.

I was fortunate in being guided in the direction of Special Entry Cadet. Apart from the money required to purchase uniforms and other clothing at Messrs. Gieves of 21 Old Bond Street, London, there were no other expenses for my family. The other method of entry was via two years at the Royal Military College at Kingston, where the training was largely of a military nature as opposed to naval, though some of our finest officers followed that route. My father had met a retired Royal Navy Lieutenant Commander Tampkins, released as a result of cutbacks, who had come to Calgary to supervise the settlement of British orphans on Canadian farms. He kindly suggested that he chat with me once or twice a week until I left to join. He discussed all the social mores of being an officer in the Royal Navy (to which the Royal Canadian Navy was closely connected). This gentleman was typical of many officers and men in the service, who were unsparing of themselves in helping younger servicemen and asked for nothing in return. "Tammy" was a member of Toc H, a religious society in the armed forces which was formed in the trenches of the Great War by a chaplain named "Tubby" Clayton. The idea was to conduct all one's activities according to divine guidance. Toc H would offer mutual support in all circumstances of life and death.

The Great Depression was at its height in 1938. My father was fortunate to have employment and also to be an officer in the militia. Funds for Reserves were very low so officers did not retain their pay. Instead they turned it in to their regiment for the good of all. I believe the men did the same. My father also suffered a substantial reduction in pay as a government employee, as did many in other employment. In Western North America drought reigned for a number of years. The wind blew mercilessly and every month or so in the sickeningly hot summers, we would

have terrible dust storms that would appear in the form of a great, black wall, hundreds of feet high, approaching from the north. Our house would be filled with fine dust and my great-uncle's farm was totally buried. Fortunately he had sufficient money to buy a house and retire in Calgary. In the nearby Rocky Mountains, forest fires raged and the sun became a bloody eye. Russian thistle or tumbleweed blew about everywhere, scattering its seeds as it rolled. On one occasion a prairie fire swept a huge area between Cochrane and Calgary killing livestock in large numbers. Mr. Adair, who had first interested me in sailing, drove me through the devastated landscape, a sad sight with many dead animals.

Most of the freight trains passing through Calgary had large numbers of hoboes on board, on the roofs and between the cars. In all the cities, in old quarries and such places, the hoboes had settlements of ramshackle huts – the hobo "jungles." A Calgary high school principal named William Aberhart started a fundamentalist movement called "Back to the Bible." He had a tabernacle where he preached but he also had his own radio program, which had a large following. "Bible Bill," as he was called, was influenced by the teachings of Major C.H. Douglas, an

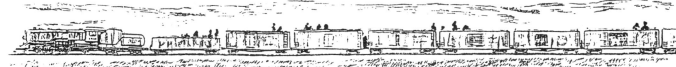

HOBOES RIDING THE RAILS 1935

Englishman with startling economic theories, and formed a political party to establish a new economic order, Social Credit. The main promise was $25 a month in Social Credit money for every Albertan. It was a sort of answer to the orthodox lunacy where there apparently was no way to get desperate men working at jobs which needed to be done and for which all the resources were readily available. Aberhart was elected premier; Social Credit didn't do any of the things it promised but the war came, the rains came and Alberta prospered once more.

I have always had some ability to draw pictures. Perhaps this is because I am ambidextrous to a degree and therefore have difficulty in catching or kicking a ball; I can't decide which hand or foot to use. I write left-handed, shoot right-handed and so on. Perhaps it is compensation or sublimation but I draw and enjoy people's comments on my work. Mr. Cotteral, the superintendent of the CPR for Western Canada, lived opposite us, and my sister, Margaret and his youngest daughter, Betty, were best friends. Mr. Cotteral suggested that he might be able to further my art studies at, say, the Chicago School of Fine Art. In any case, I passed the naval cadet entrance exams, so no art school. However, drawing has been an interest in my life and became a full-time activity after I retired from the service.

Although the prairie drought was terrible, the city of Calgary itself did not suffer so much. The Bow and Elbow rivers are fed by melting glaciers in the Rocky Mountains and there never is a water shortage. In winter we had lovely outdoor rinks, and a particular pleasure was skating when a warm Chinook wind was blowing. In summer we had great swimming in a large, slightly warmed public pool in Bowness Park or in the refreshing and beautiful Elbow River.

All these things were put behind me now and I was off to join the navy.

2

Joining the navy

In August 1938, at the age of 17, I boarded the train in Calgary, bound for Ottawa and eventually England, the "Old Country" as my people called it. The Sea Cadets with a bugle band came down to see me off, singing "All the Nice Girls Love a Sailor" and so on, much to my mortification. The long trip on the train was a magnificent experience. The meals were elaborate and quite outside my normal experience. The waiters were helpful, quietly saying which knife, fork or spoon to use for a particular course. A near-disaster occurred in Sudbury, in a landscape like the moon, when a young lady suggested we walk on the platform. To my horror the train pulled out without me. The station master called a taxi and the train waited for me in the next hamlet, thank God! When I arrived in Ottawa I stayed at the YMCA overnight.

The next morning I reported to Naval Headquarters in an old building over a grocery store. Lieutenant Commander Rollo Mainguy greeted me and I have been an admirer of his ever since. He seemed to me to incorporate all the qualities one would expect in a naval officer. My judgment was justified because he went from one important appointment to another to become Chief of the Naval Staff in 1951. His most important contribution came after the war as chairman of the commission looking into every aspect of the treatment and aspirations of naval personnel. The result formed the basis of the excellent morale and efficiency with which our navy continues to serve Canada.

The "interview" with Mainguy I suppose was the whole experience. I remember one question: "Why do you wish to join the navy?"

Answer: "My uncle is a captain in the Royal Navy and has had a very interesting life. I do not want to stay in Calgary and see the grain elevators every day. I love the water and want to see the world."

He invited me for lunch and his wife, Kita, a tiny lady of great charm, collected me and took me to their pleasant home. I declined cigarettes and liquor, and all I remember is how nervous I was and how my soup spoon trembled.

That evening I went out with an RCNVR midshipman named Brown, another young man and their ladies. We had a wonderful evening driving around, my date and I in the rumble seat of a sports car.

Back on the train the following morning, I was on my way to Quebec to catch RMS *Ascania* (Cunard White Star Line), a beautiful passenger liner. We cruised for many hours down the Saint Lawrence River and through the Strait of Belle Isle into the North Atlantic. What a wonderful experience for a boy from the prairies! Now I met fellow cadets Chadwick, Harvey, Robbins and Moore from British Columbia, Morris from Regina and Roberts from Ontario. Other passengers included some Molsons from Montreal, a lieutenant commander RN returning to the U.K. from the China Station and an attractive American girl embarking on a European tour with her aunt. The trip across the Atlantic was mostly calm, I was fascinated by the phosphorescence in the water at night – I had never even heard of this phenomenon. The other strong first impression was of the Gulf Stream, encountered a couple of days after losing sight of land. The air became more languid and pleasant and it was delightful to stroll the upper deck with the American girl. We touched at Ushant in France, made a brief stop in Southampton and finally docked at Tilbury near London. I saw my first Royal Navy sailors in a picket boat in Southampton, just as smart as one could imagine and how proud that made me feel. We caught a train to London, where we registered at the Lancaster Gate Hotel near Marble Arch. The next day we reported to Canada House in Trafalgar Square, where we were met by a Mr. MacLeod and were told about getting our uniforms at Gieves and other arrangements.

We had two or three weeks in London. I called on my uncle, Captain Cedric Naylor, and my aunt. The captain had been decorated for his service in command of a Q Ship, a successful trap for German submarines, in the First World War. Now he was the administrator of a pensioners' residence on Fulham Road in Chelsea. My aunt said that she had become tired of him sitting around after he retired in 1937 and suggested he get a job. This was the first one he saw in *The Times,* so here they were, enjoying it very much. I believe he ran the residence much like a ship, with quartermasters and so on. He told me not to be easily satisfied with Gieves and not to take any nonsense from them. He also told me to look up some senior officers in Portsmouth and give them a kick in the behind and his regards – I never did. My American friend and I "did" the British Museum and visited a music hall. She moved on and, sadly, I never saw or heard from her again. As the days passed in London our money supply ran down and we spent a lot of time just walking around. The Irish Republican Army blew up a public washroom at Marble Arch nearby but no one was injured.

One of the cadets, not me, ran a bath on the second floor of our hotel, forgot about it and went out for a walk. When I returned to the hotel, I found all the residents and many staff standing out in front looking at the building. It was quietly astonishing. Water was cascading down the front steps in a series of waterfalls that came from inside, tumbling down the main staircase from a closed bathroom

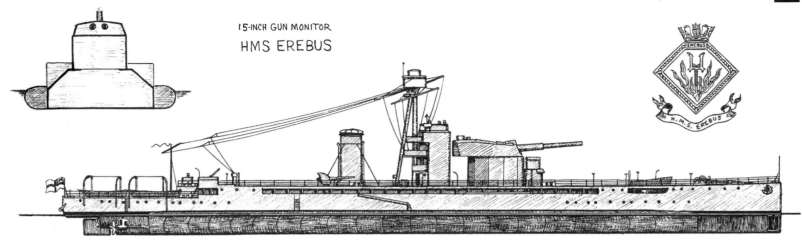

15-INCH GUN MONITOR
HMS EREBUS

door at the head of the stairs. The heavy bathroom door had to be broken open to turn the water off. When we left the hotel a few days later the staff lined up outside to say goodbye and receive tips. I don't think any of us had any money left, but the staff must have been relieved to see us depart.

Early in September 1938, we joined HMS *Erebus*, moored in Portsmouth Harbour in a sort of backwater called Fountain Lake. Close by is Whale Island, the main gunnery school for the Royal Navy. *Erebus*, a monitor, was designed to control bombardment and built in the First World War for shelling the western end of the German lines in Belgium. She had a large turret on her fo'c's'le, with two 15-inch guns. Also on her fo'c's'le was a large gymnasium for the cadets. A remarkable feature of this ship was the large pontoons on each side which could be flooded with seawater, causing the ship to sink. In the shallow water off Belgium, the ship would settle on the bottom, providing a stable platform for the guns and thus greater accuracy.

In no time we were indoctrinated in the ways of the navy. Item number one was slinging, getting into and sleeping in a hammock. This has to be one of the most comfortable beds devised by mankind. In harbour it is delightful, at sea, the worse the weather, the snugger the hammock. A thin mattress stuffed with straw, a couple of blankets, perhaps a pillow and with a measure of tiredness, one could not be more comfortable. Alas, before daylight, "Wakey, wakey," Call the Hands, with petty officers shaking the "micks" (hammocks) and perhaps a couple of taps with a "starter," a rope's end, broke the spell. A bucket of hot cocoa with a box of broken sea biscuits waited in the flat to wake us up before we "fell in" to clean the decks.

"Six days shalt thou labour and do all that thou art able, and on the seventh thou shalt holystone the decks" was the old naval proverb. Wet decks were sprinkled with sand and the cadets, on hands and knees, would rub the sand on the wood with a brick-sized lump of sandstone. Next the petty officers would hose down the decks with seawater and the cadets, forming a row, would squeegee the water away. The decks would dry up, the sun would rise and shine and the decks would turn a gleaming white. One might think the decks would be holystoned right through, but I never heard of such a happening.

What heaven it was to stir to wakefulness hearing the wind crying in the rigging and dashing rain against the ship's side! Then you might have a "guard and steerage" and sleep in a bit. In either case, next came a hot shower and shave, and what lovely hot showers there were in *Erebus*. We were told that in the "old days," whatever those were, the youngest cadets had the task of warming the toilet seats for the older ones. For us the toilet seats were extremely cold. All cleaned up and dressed, we had breakfast at wooden tables in the open messes: porridge, a kipper or bacon and eggs, toast, jam and tea. "Cooks of the mess" were detailed to wash up the dishes in fannies of hot water with pusser's soap. Next was Morning Divisions where we were inspected by our divisional officer and had morning prayers.

Divisions were the means of dividing the cadets up in Parts of Ship. These were Forecastle (FX), Foretop (FT), Maintop (MT), and Quarterdeck (AX) (AX stood for Aftercastle). Most of our day was devoted to instruction in navigation, engineering, gunnery, torpedo and signalling (using Morse code, semaphore and flag signals). We had boat pulling, sailing, swimming in the Pitt Street Baths and rifle and parade ground drill on Whale Island. We were busy from morn to night.

Whale Island, the gunnery school, was named HMS *Excellent*, originally a Victorian hulk. Over the years, from a garbage dump for Portsmouth, the island had grown to be beautiful with lovely trees, lawns and gardens. There was even a zoo with animals that had been ships' mascots at one time. Peacocks wandered at large. It even included a pen where happy pigs lived on leftovers from the messes, with a keeper, an old three-

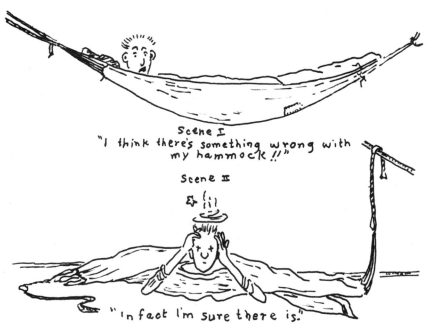

Scene I
"I think there's something wrong with my hammock!!"

Scene II

"In fact I'm sure there is."

badge able seaman, a "stripey," who gathered food remnants in a hand cart. He was reputed to be more fond of his pigs than he was of his fellow men.

Some common terminology of the World War Two RN and RCN is meaningless today. For example, a killick was a leading seaman. His rank was shown by a single anchor on his left sleeve. "Killick," from the old Norse, means a small anchor. Maritime fishermen used to make a boat's anchor from a rock bound with branches with four arms sticking out as flukes, which was also called a killick. A stripey was an older seaman with three good-conduct badges but still an able seaman. Stripeys were generally respected by younger hands because of their experience.

The sailing was superb, particularly the cutters. A frequent exercise was to lower the cutters, the crews jumping in as the boats passed the deck, and "slip" the boats by the Robinson's disengaging gear (a spectacular experience if "slipped" from too great a height). The crews would then pull (row) to a buoy a mile or so distant, boat their oars, erect the mast and hoist the sails to sail to the next buoy a mile or two off, then down mast and sails, out oars and pull back to *Erebus*. We learned to sail without a rudder by shifting our weight and finally to sail in formation, manoeuvring together just as capital ships did in days of old. We sailed and pulled in all weather: snow, rain, wind, sun and fog. We also went to the Boys' Training Establishment, HMS *Saint Vincent*. Here was the tallest mast in the British Empire (captured from the Germans in the First World War, I believe) and this we climbed to the top. I can still recollect hanging nearly upside down on the futtock

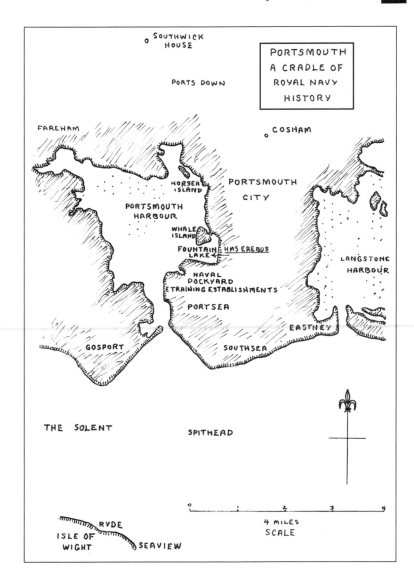

shrouds to get to the topmast and from there surveying the Isle of Wight and the coast of Hampshire. All this was the stuff of my dreams and the dream was coming true.

Seamanship was the easiest subject for me, Mr. Mitchell and Mr. Liddal at *Undaunted* having been excellent instructors. Petty Officers Gibbs and Walbridge in *Erebus* were patient men and excellent instructors. My terrible weakness was spherical trigonometry for celestial navigation. I hadn't the vaguest idea of the derivation and use of Inman's Tables. The trouble lay in my lack of education in mathematics and indeed my ignorance of the basic concepts. All my other subjects were excellent. I failed navigation the first three months but it was decided to let me have another term.

We all went on leave for Christmas. I went to London and stayed at the Seamark Junior Officers Club, 7 The Crescent, Tower Hill, right by the Tower of London. I have never felt so miserable as I did on the first day of that leave.

There was snow and fog, dawn came about eight in the morning and it was dark around four in the afternoon. However, gradually I began to feel better. Harry Chapell was the rector of All Hallows Church and he also ran Seamark, which was a Toc H Club. I met Reverend "Tubby" Clayton, the founder, who lived nearby. The crypt of All Hallows contained the remains of Roman shops, and artifacts such as perfume bottles, clay pots and tiles lay around in quite a casual way. The basement of Seamark itself was a lesson in history. At the very bottom was a crude British wall. Above that was the Roman wall, distinguished by the neat Roman bricks laid in perfect order, and above that was more crude and irregular British brickwork from the time after the Romans returned to Italy. Georgian and Victorian brickwork completed the wall. All the other members staying there were young officers of the Merchant Service who were waiting to be examined for their next

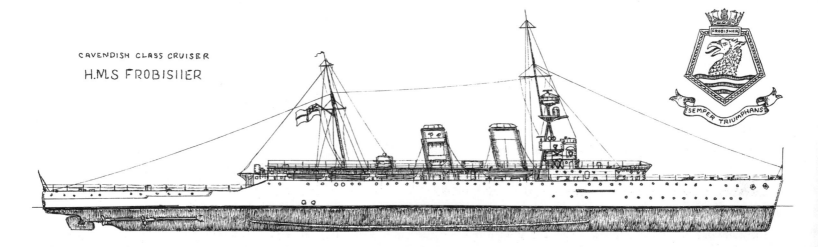

CAVENDISH CLASS CRUISER
H.M.S FROBISHER

ticket or attending courses. One such studying for his Extra Masters' Certificate was a splendid man, Richard Stannard, who went on to win the Victoria Cross at Namsos, Norway, in a desperate naval engagement. My leave concluded, I went to the replacement for HMS *Erebus,* which was HMS *Frobisher.*

The badge of *Erebus* was a pitchfork surrounded by flames, but it really did not symbolize my state of mind. I guess I said to myself that I was to enjoy myself less and work more seriously and that is certainly what I did. *Frobisher* was an old cruiser and had been a seagoing cadet training ship until recently when she reverted to being laid up in Fountain Lake. Portsmouth in those days must have been little changed from late Victorian times. There was a particularly quaint section with narrow streets, a music hall and street vendors. A lot of the city was made up of small brick houses, mostly the same, on rather grimy streets. On the afternoons we were allowed ashore – Wednesday "make and mend" and Saturdays and Sundays – I sometimes felt a bit homesick and walked down these streets thinking how nice it would be if one of the houses were my home with my family. Often I walked past the house where Charles Dickens was born, but I found it difficult to relate past to present.

Frobisher was slightly different from *Erebus* in the composition of the naval cadets. My new term, like the last, was mostly made up of boys from the great public schools –

For my little sister

This is what the geese all looked like at Whale Island GUNNERY SCHOOL

Eton, Winchester, Harrow and so on – plus the Nautical Training Establishments, ships in themselves such as *Conway, Worcester* and *Pangbourne.* "Colonials" also were there. Australians, New Zealanders and Indians as well as a chap from Siam joined us Canadians. I think Canadians were regarded as Yanks but certainly we were accepted in a friendly fashion. The *Frobisher* difference was that there were also Short Service Naval Cadets (seven years engagement) selected differently from the Public School Cadet Entry. They were destined for the Fleet Air Arm. What an asset they turned out to be when war broke out! Was it my imagination or was it a fact that these boys were different from my group? They seemed more aggressive, louder, less thoughtful than our group – qualities that would serve them better in the dangerous branch they had selected.

It was evident to anyone who read the papers that we would soon be at war with Germany. We all were provided with gas masks, drilled in them and even briefly played games wearing our masks.

In the 1920s a Royal Navy ship went aground in the Mediterranean and sank in full view of shore. There were insufficient boats and many sailors drowned. The Admiralty resolved that every man and boy in the navy should be able to swim fully clothed and to stay afloat for half an hour or so. We were checked out at the Pitt Street Baths. Dressed in heavy white canvas seamen's jumpers and bell bottoms, we paddled around the deep end for the required time. The rig was not comfortable for swimming and you became tired in short order. If you headed for the side of the pool, the "springers," the physical and recreational training hands, were waiting with long boathooks to fend off delinquents. Hideous were the scenes as gasping, floppy white creatures begged to come alongside but were fended off with brutal laughter by the springers. Now and again a pathetic creature would grab the end of the boathook and frantically cling there until the brute at the other end called another sadist with a boathook to poke him free, to perish if necessary.

There was a lovely open public bathing pool towards Portsdown Hill and here I swam in great happiness until one day I went down the slide, ripping the seat out of my bathing suit. Back to Pitt Street, I still remember the cry of the springers, "Don't pump ship in the water!" One last memory of the Pitt Street Baths was an exercise that involved swinging from a trapeze at one end of the pool to a trapeze launched from the other end. Most accomplished this feat, going by air from one end to the other. Not me! I missed the first time, landing in the pool, which was all right with me. Next try I caught the other in the middle over the pool but didn't let go of the first trapeze. After a

Why is it we always feel weakest before the three mile run around "Whaley" ???

minute of embarrassed suspension, back to the pool! Last try, I transferred to the second trapeze and roared on towards the other platform, but not quite making it. Into the pool once more.

Once a week the cadets were landed on Whale Island for a run around the place. It was about a mile and everyone tried to do it as quickly as possible. The course was a dirt road passing by well-cared-for lawns and instructional buildings. Over the entrance to the main building containing a variety of types and calibres of guns was a large statue of a lion. It was a British lion, I suppose, and under it was the motto of HMS *Excellent*, "Si vis pacem para bellum," meaning "If you wish peace, prepare for war." Good advice in those times. The lion's tail stood straight up like a pussy cat saying hello. The only trouble was that the lion was facing our line of travel so we looked up the wrong end for a long time.

When we were being landed for rifle and bayonet drill on the island we always had a lecture from the petty officer in charge of the boat that if we dropped our rifle overboard we might as well go with it. Otherwise our fate would be beyond description.

At anchor or at moorings in Fountain Lake were a number of World War I destroyers, mostly of the V and W Class. They had been maintained in good condition and served long and well in the coming conflict. Of the three armed forces of the United Kingdom, the Royal Navy was the most ready. The reason was that ships take so long to build and officers and men take as long or longer to train. With machinery and weapons being so technical, training and skill were vital. Anyone from the top to the most junior could endanger the ship. It was vital, therefore, that our people be volunteers without grievances.

The cadets went to sea in one of the V Class destroyers and we scuffed about the Isle of Wight for a day. Conditions in those ships were primitive. Water for washing faces, bodies, dishes and so on had to be brought from a central tap. Officers' baths were small, round, metal tubs. I think the hands had the luxury of cold seawater showers. Sailors were on a form of messing which could be bad for their health. Each man was given a sum of money for food. Cooks of messes were given the money to buy the food, a small quantity at a time. By 1938 the Royal Navy had suffered a substantial pay reduction. The worldwide depression was so serious that many men simply had tea and tobacco for breakfast, perhaps potatoes and bread and jam for lunch and then something very light for supper. In this way they saved money to send home for their wives and children. The result was that some of the seamen suffered from malnutrition. Most carried on cheerfully and without resentment, thankful to have employment and proud of being in the "Service". However, some duties required constant vigilance and if a man was not alert, something important could be missed or neglected. On this day our destroyer attained 28 or 30 knots and gave us a great thrill. We also had short trips in a motor torpedo boat, again a tremendous experience.

The cadets visited the various training schools which were in Portsmouth Dockyard: HMS *Vernon*, the Torpedo School, the Signal School and the Royal Naval Tactical School. It is interesting to reflect that despite the near strangling of Britain by German submarines in the Great War, the subject of anti-submarine warfare was not touched upon in the lectures we attended at the tactical school. The only thing I remember being taught was the "A to K Line" of cruisers screening the battle fleet. Nor was there any mention of the role of aircraft carriers in naval warfare.

HMS *Victory* lay in a dry basin in the Dockyard. It was a memorable experience for a young naval officer to walk the decks upon which Lord Nelson had walked and where he was shot from aloft and mortally wounded. From this ship at the Battle of Trafalgar, a boy seaman wrote his mother about his concern with the approaching action with the French, but when the first shots were fired, he "bid fear kiss my ass goodbye." And it did.

From time to time distinguished personages spoke to us. Especially memorable was "Ginger" Boyle, Admiral of the Fleet, the Earl of Cork and Orrery. A short, lean, redheaded man with a florid complexion, he began his talk with a startling, "Blood! Blood! Blood! You young gen'lmen have got to like the sight of blood!" What else he said escapes my memory but we heard that he seemed to follow this pattern himself. He was supposed to have been court-martialled seven times for what might have been described as atrocities in the suppression of piracy in Chinese waters. Villages of the pirates were burned and everyone,

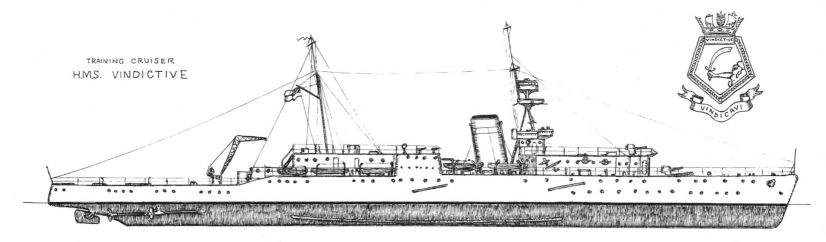

TRAINING CRUISER
H.M.S. VINDICTIVE

men, women and children, ruthlessly killed. Perhaps this was just a legend. During the German invasion of Norway he rode in a Swordfish aircraft and personally dropped bombs near Narvik on the entrances to railway tunnels between Sweden and Norway. These were important for the export of iron ore to Germany.

We visited a new aircraft carrier, HMS *Ark Royal*. The father of one of our cadets, Arthur Power, was captain of this magnificent vessel and we saw his cabin and met him; he looked just like his son, only older. We also visited one of the new destroyers of the Tribal Class. What a beautiful ship and how sparkling clean she was! The engine room was spotless, polished brass and perfection. One of the cadets, not me, kicked over a full pot of white paint in the engine room. The paint splashed and dribbled through the gratings into the bilge. I expected we all might be flogged and put over the side but there was not a murmur from

anyone. The stokers were speechless with horror. By the way, in these reflections I never admit to personally doing anything as dumb as that was, even if I did.

Cadets were required to have weekly dances, dancing with each other to a small Royal Marine Dance Orchestra. The idea was that dancing was one of the social graces expected of naval officers and our dances, even with male partners, although not socially graceful, were great fun. Tunes of the day were "The Lambeth Walk," "The Beer Barrel Polka" and "Little Sir Echo." Crashing about in "The Lambeth Walk" especially was hearty exercise.

This term I applied myself with the utmost effort and passed out as well as I could have wished. Leave in London was a delight and I made some good friends at Seamark. The club was close to Lambeth and the popular song fitted the Lambeth natives perfectly. Bermondsey, the Elephant and Castle, Lambeth, the Embankment, Tower Hill, the bustling, cheerful crowds, the pretty girls, the ships in the London docks – what good fortune it was to see that world before the terrible bombing.

Too soon my leave was over and I returned to Portsmouth to join my next ship, the Cadet Sea Training Cruiser HMS *Vindictive*. She was a light cruiser built in 1918 to replace her predecessor, sunk as a blockship at Zeebrugge. She was fitted out with classrooms on the upper deck. Cadets lived in open messes, coming in from the quarterdeck. The cruise that I had missed had been across the Atlantic to the West Indies. The ship had visited Havana in Cuba and also Bermuda, and I heard that two cadets had died of fever. I believe now that was rubbish although it was dramatic. The Public School entry cadets were joined in *Vindictive* by cadets from the Royal Naval College in Dartmouth, about equal in number. There didn't seem to be any difference in appearance, quality or education between the two groups except the "Darts" were more chummy with each other, having been together for a number of years.

On reflection, the joy of being a naval cadet was that at last I was with a group of serious-minded, healthy young men who had many common ideals and principles, common ambitions, common education and common interests, that is, to be at sea and serving the British Empire. We represented a number of races, white, black and yellow and, of course, a number of world religions. I never heard a word of scorn for anyone: all were trusted equally. Religious limitations of diet were followed exactly. Cigarettes and pipe tobacco were absurdly inexpensive, the only restrictions being no smoking when working or in spaces with inflammables or explosives. Liquor for cadets was confined to a glass of sherry and a glass of port a week.

The routine when the ship was at sea was pretty well the same as when we were alongside or at anchor. The

DECENTRALIZATION

"Vindictive" Magazine

most exciting difference was that we stood watch as quartermaster at the wheel, steering the ship, and at the engine room telegraphs. Others were lookouts and life-buoy sentries. We continued our daily studies in navigation, gunnery, torpedo, engineering, ship construction, Morse code, key and flashing, semaphore and flag signals. We also had lectures on naval customs, discipline and divisional work as well as all sorts of practical seamanship and boat work, both sailing and pulling. All this went on regardless of weather and I cannot imagine better training for war and for peace than we received. The officers, chief and petty officers, leading seamen and able seamen were unfailingly respectful and helpful to the cadets, and I never heard of any unfair conduct or picking on anybody. It is in everyone's interest in a ship to have the best of all ranks, from the captain to the most junior hand, each trained to the best of his ability. The whole attitude as I understood it was "liberty working within a framework of discipline." If only it were possible to conduct all our affairs in this manner!

Cadets were paid one shilling per day. We also were allowed to receive one pound per week from our parents. This applied to boys from the richest backgrounds to those of modest means. Thus there was no hierarchy of wealth among the cadets; we were of equal status in every way. We were paid once a week, and when a cadet took his turn at standing in front of the paymaster's desk (on the upper deck) he was obliged to call out his number in a loud voice. On one such occasion I was drawing my pittance and called out my number.

"I didn't hear his number," said the paybob. "Let him practice it from the masthead."

I spent the afternoon at the top of the mast calling out my number. Finally, the officer of the watch said to the quartermaster, "I hear that cadet singing out his number. Call him down." So down I came, somewhat numb and resolved not to be so shy.

The world situation was becoming heavier and we all were certain that war with Germany could start any time. *Vindictive* had been scheduled to visit Denmark, Norway, Sweden and Finland. Probably we also would have gone to Germany

EVENING "ROUNDS"   YOGI

"Vindictive" Magazine

and Poland, but the thought of a couple of hundred British naval cadets being captured or killed or even trapped in the Baltic was too horrible for the Admiralty to contemplate, and our cruise plans were altered to keep us in the open Atlantic. Some years before, a German sail training vessel for naval cadets had capsized during a gale in the Baltic off the German coast. Most of the cadets were drowned and this sad incident must have had a dreadful effect on the officer structure of the German navy. Horrible to say, this was of ultimate benefit to the Royal Navy.

I am recieving my "education."

It was with the best of spirits that *Vindictive* set sail for Scapa Flow in the Orkney Islands north of Scotland. Almost all the old RN types who served during the Great War talked about this huge anchorage which dominated the North Sea, the Irish Sea and the Faeroes/Orkney passage. This old Viking haunt had been given as a part of the dowry by the king of Denmark to the king of Scotland when his daughter married the latter. It had been the scene of battles between hundreds of Viking longboats and the point of departure for Jellicoe's fleet at the Battle of Jutland.

The Orkneys also had a direct connection with Canada for it was here that the Hudson's Bay Company Ships stopped en route to Hudson's Bay to recruit Orkneymen to work in their North American empire. We steamed into Kirkwall and went alongside. I was impressed by the burly islanders in their black pullovers and caps. Many wore an earring in one ear, an old Viking preventative measure against deafness. Kirkwall was fascinating. The stone houses, the remains of the bishop's palace, the lone tree on

CHATTING WITH
THE CHAPLAIN

the main street, protected by a wrought-iron fence, and the sombre Saint Magnus Cathedral all had a romantic charm.

We moved around into Scapa Flow, a large body of water surrounded by islands and practically the first things we observed were the upside-down hulks of German battleships of the Great War. The German navy, riddled with mutinies, had steamed from Germany to Scapa to surrender. It was still a large navy and what was to be done with it was undecided by the Allies. The problem was solved when one morning, just as daylight returned, the German crews scuttled and abandoned their ships. The British tried to keep them from sinking, shooting a few Germans and boarding ships still afloat, but their efforts were in vain and soon the entire remaining naval might of Germany sank beneath the waves. Several of the large ships just turned upside down and remained in that state looking like small islands swept by waves. When we arrived one battleship was about to be towed away to Rosyth to be broken up. One of the executives of the salvage group gave us a lecture on how they recovered these vessels.

Some years later I was having tea with a lady in her cottage overlooking the Flow. I asked her if by chance she had seen the German ships sinking. Indeed she had. She described how she saw them going down one by one as the crews rowed off in cutters, and then she saw the British moving about. She didn't convey the impression of wonderment I would have expected at having witnessed

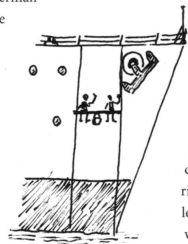

PAINTING VINDICTIVE'S
BOW

one of the most remarkable events in the history of naval warfare. My personal view was that it was an ideal solution. It was completely and utterly final – that was it.

One of our officers told us how during the Great War, the Americans based in Scapa built a golf course on one of the islands. By 1939 it must have been overgrown with heather and gorse. There also are remains of some of the earliest settlements in the British Isles. I was never to see these, though strangely my son had a good look at them 50 years later.

We sailed from Scapa to Iceland. It was a lovely passage with waves of deepest blue rising high over the quarterdeck. On one occasion, *Vindictive* was pooped; that is, a large wave came over our stern, poured across the quarterdeck and raced into the messdeck through the open doors. The cadets were having tea when the great flood arrived. Bread, butter, jam, tea, sugar, milk, cutlery, cups, saucers, plates and cadets were all washing about on the deck with the cadets whooping and shouting to add to the confusion. It was all received with good humour, a part of the adventure of going to sea. From then on when the ship was about to alter course, a warning pipe would be made and necessary measures taken such as guarding things on tables, shutting scuttles and closing doors to the upper deck. In a few months' time most watertight doors, scuttles and deadlights would always be closed on going to sea and everything possible battened down or secured against unexpected alterations of course and speed.

The south coast of Iceland soon became visible and I stood on the upper deck in a state of reverie, imagining that I had seen all this before in a previous life. We steamed into the harbour of Reykjavik, a very neat ancient settlement. The inhabitants seemed a bit distant, and we were aware that there were a number of Germans there, working on the piping of steam from the underground vents into the city for heating water and perhaps other useful purposes. There was an English bookshop, where I bought a couple of Icelandic sagas translated into English. The most striking experience was being bussed to Thingvellir where the Althing, the oldest parliament in the world, originated. This valley floor was crossed by crevices filled with water and the blacks, greys, reds and greens of the valley and surrounding craggy hills, all under a lowering dark sky, was a sight I shall not forget. Here in 1932, beneath the Speakers' Rock, the kings of Denmark, Norway and Sweden had met to commemorate the founding of the Icelandic settlement. Here the preaching by a Christian missionary from Denmark had converted a whole island of pagans. One lady, who had questioned whether Jesus Christ could beat Thor in physical combat, was returning home when she fell off her horse, broke her neck and died. God's punishment? In any case, a convincing event.

From Iceland we sailed to the Irish Sea, where we anchored off Bangor, near Belfast in Northern Ireland, a summer resort with attractive residential hotels filled with affluent, elderly people. The cadets were entertained at

JOIN THE NAVY AND BE ON TOP OF THE WORLD (THE POSTER THEY DON'T SHOW)

6.15 IN THE MORNING !!!!!!

such a hotel, all of us in gray flannel trousers, blazers with a naval crown on the breast pocket and topped with a brown fedora. Then we were off to Oban, northwest of Glasgow in the highlands of Scotland, a scenic, rugged place, where the cadets claimed that the local girls had one leg longer than the other from walking on the sides of hills. Some of us sailed a ship's whaler to an island some miles away, where we had a picnic. Although this part of the

United Kingdom is far north, even north of Churchill, Manitoba, the Gulf Stream has a warming effect on the climate. Our picnic spot to my Canadian eyes was a sort of Eden with rich, lush, deep green vegetation, almost tropical. I had never seen anything like it.

There was an interesting story in *Vindictive* that on the last RN visit to Oban a Royal Marine had killed a man with his bayonet and put his body in a garbage bin. Before this time the Royal Marines always wore a bayonet at their belt when they walked ashore. As a consequence of this murder the practice was rescinded forever. Young people revel in such terrible tales and enjoy ghosts. *Vindictive* had a ghost, the ghost of B Gun Deck. One night at anchor the officer of the watch was doing his rounds when he stumbled on something. He bent down to find out what it was and to his horror found it was a body. He rushed to get assistance and noticed his hands were dripping with blood. They returned; there was no body. Years before a stoker had killed another with a shovel at this spot. This was the ghost of B Gun Deck.

We slipped from Oban and sailed down to the Isle of Man, coming alongside at Douglas. Horse-drawn streetcars were the first curiosities. To make life complete, one could purchase foot-long cigars. For experienced old cigar smok-

we are clad in oversized oilskins and seaboots at the slightest excuse!

ers such as myself they were ideal, but they were difficult to stow in any quantity in a sea chest, and they tended to cloud the atmosphere more than the "ticklers" to which many were addicted.

As we steamed down the Irish Sea I enjoyed one of the finest views of marine life that could be imagined, a group of basking sharks. These huge, harmless creatures, bigger than many whales, lie on the surface apparently soaking up the sunshine. I was sorry that we did not close in for a better look.

Brest was a surprise. I had expected a picturesque city, a small Paris. The Brest I saw consisted of modern concrete office blocks, warehouses and apartments, the whole place rather stained and shabby and not romantic at all. At the Hotel Atlantic I drank cups of coffee and accumulated a little stack of saucers while I wrote to my parents. The cadets of the French Naval Academy challenged us to dinghy races. *Vindictive*'s boats did not bring credit to the ship. Many capsized and I imagine the French must have felt very superior to the English. The French sailed skilfully whereas most of the English boys had not sailed nearly as much. It seemed that my messmates could not have cared less about the French except that everyone wanted a striped shirt such as French sailors wore. Stocking caps also were popular.

In Brest I went to a rural fair. There was a dancing bear and a dentist who pulled teeth without anaesthetic while his assistant beat a drum to drown out the agonized cries of the patient. There was a tent with exhibits such as a two-headed baby in a large bottle of formaldehyde, calves with five legs and so on.

We sailed off into the Bay of Biscay and had a gunnery shoot, with a 4-inch gun, our real introduction to the life and death days that lay ahead. Our next destination was Quiberon near the site of a great naval battle in the old wars with France. This was much more the France I had expected. The small villages must have looked much the same for centuries and many of the women, young and old, wore their local costume. Many wore wooden shoes and I bought a pair to send to my young sister. The beach was lovely, I never had swum in such warm water and I stayed in for long periods. I was soaking up the sun on Bastille Day when a lady asked if I would mind if her daughter sang for me. Of course I agreed and this young girl, aged about 12 or 13, sang the Marseillaise. I can still see her standing in the sand, the waves breaking just behind her, the Bay of Biscay in the background. Of all the national anthems, this surely is the most stirring and this young voice, sweet and powerful, still lives in my memory.

TACKLING A TANGLED TACKLE

Although I have described our various port visits, these were but brief interludes in the routine of studying the elements of what was to be our profession for life. The strength of the Royal Navy was that officers and men generally lived in their ships and spent a good deal of their time actually at sea. It gradually became more natural to be at sea than not to be at sea. British ships were not necessarily better than ships of other nations, our weapons were not much better or worse, our people were not more intelligent or more dense than others, but they were used to being at sea and keeping their ships in working order. RN routines were much the same in peace as they were in war, and warlike exercises were frequent.

We were in the Bay of Biscay when it was time for our final exams. These went on for several days and, of course, providence decreed that we would now get the worst weather of the cruise. How we pitched and rolled while the wind howled and the waves piled up. Our chairs went skidding about our studies, cabins on the upper deck. Pails were lashed to the table legs so that cadets who were ill would not have to leave the exam. Seasickness spreads rather as yawns do, so one sick cadet could set off a whole miserable chain reaction. What fascinated me was that *Vindictive*'s own officers and men regarded this as perfectly normal. Seasickness has never bothered me, but I am well aware of this being a special blessing.

The cruise carried on to St. Peter's Port in Guernsey in the Channel Islands. These have been English since ancient times, and although the inhabitants speak a kind of old French, the appearance of the place is English, not French. Again, this was another place of special beauty, with old buildings, rows of noble trees and peaceful fields with grazing cattle. Onward, up the English Channel steamed *Vindictive.* In those days the Channel was filled with dirty little coasters, *à la* John Masefield, and also fine passenger and cargo vessels, all of us passing the famous white cliffs of Dover. Onward, up the Thames estuary, which was filled with barges, great sailing vessels presenting a spectacular sight. Who would have imagined that within a few years the Thames barge would become an extinct species? Finally we berthed in Chatham. This was the birthplace of my grandmother's father, who ended up in Calcutta, where my mother's mother was born. Chatham at a glimpse seemed to be made up of red brick houses rather like Portsmouth. *Vindictive* was berthed at the end of a basin and one of the petty officers advised us to be careful returning to the ship as the path was narrow and one could fall into the basin. If

Naval Cadet

that happened, he said, you would be fished out, taken to hospital and quarantined for a period to see what terrible disease you might have caught. The basin water looked the part – sooty black, almost muddy. No one fell in.

We all graduated and were able to put on our midshipmen's white patches. We were given forms on which to indicate the station where we would like to serve our midshipman's time. I put down the China Station as I had heard so much about it. It was supposed to be the place for the lighter hearts and less ambitious in the service, with lots of sports and interesting ports. For those of ambition the choice was the Mediterranean Station, where ships exercised the most in weapons and tactics. For the frivolous in nature, the America and West Indies Station was the choice. At one time, this fleet's headquarters was Halifax, Nova Scotia, but in the 1850s the admiral at Admiralty House was told to get rid of his pigs; they were not to be kept within the town limits. He told the city fathers that he preferred to keep his pigs and would move to Bermuda, which he did.

We were sent on leave to await our appointments so I went back to the Seamark Junior Officers Club. It was a lovely summer and it seemed a pity to stay in the heart of London. I met a pair of South Africans, third officers, graduates of the *General Botha* training ship. We thought it would be nice to go punting on the Thames at Oxford. A Miss Parsons, or Auntie as she was known at Seamark, where she was a sort of secretary, gave us a picnic hamper. We went to Oxford, hired a punt and headed up river. This is not as easy as it sounds because the punt does not necessarily go in the direction one wishes. However, we got as far as Wolvercote, where a fair was in progress and in the evening there was a dance. The fair and the dance were very rural and I am sure we seemed as odd to the inhabitants as they did to us.

The weather was lovely, the river calm and refreshingly cool flowing through the beautiful countryside. After lunch this day, we decided to open Auntie's hamper and have some gin. I went to sleep in the soft meadow grass to be awakened by a gentle cow grazing near by. I observed that the punt was rocking back and forth as one of the South Africans was looking around for something. The punt then tipped and all our gear tumbled into the Thames. The rest of the day was spent diving to recover the lost articles from the shallow bottom. Unseamanlike conduct generally, but life is a learning experience and no harm resulted from the affair.

Back to London, I reported daily to Canada House in Trafalgar Square but no appointments came. During the day I did a great deal of sightseeing, including observing a small riot between Blackshirts of Sir Oswald Mosley's British Fascist Party and British Communists. Mounted police broke it up – armed men on horseback trotting in your direction soon occupy your full attention and you get out of the way quickly. The Irish Republican Army was busy – all luggage had to be opened and searched for explosives (my baggage merely contained dirty underwear, socks, shirts, collars and handkerchiefs). They left bombs in public lavatories from time to time, but I don't recollect any public panic on this account.

One lovely late summer day, 3 September 1939, Mr. Chamberlain said on the radio that the country was at war. I read later that this was a surprise to Hitler, but it was not a surprise to millions of Britons.

AMBITION

MY OWN QUARTERDECK

Holystoning Decks

3

The war gets under way

Europe was still at peace on that brisk evening of Friday, 1 September, but little did I care whether she was at peace or war for I had just been to the Admiralty and had received an appointment to my first real fighting ship, HMS *Renown*. The orders were that I should join her on the following Monday, but I received a telegram the next morning saying, "Join ship immediately at Portsmouth."

When I arrived she had just gone and was lying in Stokes Bay for a few hours. Was she bound for China? After making many inquiries, I was given train fare to Scapa Flow in the Orkney Islands, where I was to join her. I left Portsmouth that evening and, after an intolerable taxi ride across London in the blackout, finally got into a crowded train bound for the north of Scotland. Sunday, 3 September, found me still on the train and that morning we heard the news we had been expecting for so long: "Great Britain has commenced hostilities against Germany."

Sleeping in a hotel in Thurso that night, I embarked the next morning upon a small, one-funnelled tramp steamer, the *St. Ninian* and arrived at Kirkwall, the capital of the Orkneys, just as night was falling. Many years later *St. Ninian* turned up in Canada, travelling back and forth between Sydney, Nova Scotia, and Saint Pierre and Miquelon, the French Islands off Newfoundland.

Renown was not in Scapa Flow when I arrived. No one seemed to know where she was or what she was doing. A drifter took me to the *Iron Duke* at anchor near Flotta. She had been the flagship at the Battle of Jutland but was just a depot ship now. I had quite a nice little cabin, very pleasant for a midshipman. What interested me was the thickness of the paint everywhere in the ship, which must have amounted to about a quarter of an inch. Also her watertight compartments didn't seem very watertight, being full of holes for wires and pipes of all kinds. Tuesday forenoon, I was sent to the store ship SS *Voltnire*, a Lampert and Holt Co. liner, and there spent the night.

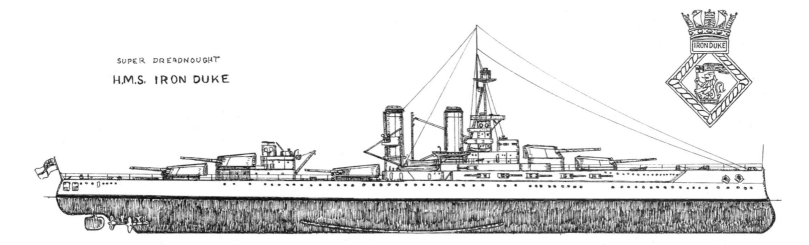

SUPER DREADNOUGHT
H.M.S. IRON DUKE

I received a shake early Wednesday morning and was told to pack as *Renown* had arrived. I boarded the drifter, and while I was on it there were two air raid warnings in which nothing happened. At long last, mid-morning found me aboard my ship. *Renown* had been in Sullom Voe (Home of the Sun) in the Shetland Islands.

The first person I noticed was one of my term mates, a rascally Irishman and a good friend who was midshipman of the watch. Without doubt he was the dirtiest looking creature I've ever seen; pimply, not properly shaven, unpressed uniform and a filthy starched collar. He explained that washing clothes had been impossible and made other excuses. Once aboard, I met a gunroom full of old shipmates of the *Vindictive*, equally unkempt. Except for the sub-lieutenants, we all were midshipmen of the same term. Midshipmen were generally called "snotties" and were supervised by a lieutenant-commander, the "snotties' nurse."

The *Renown* had commissioned in Pompy (Portsmouth) on 29 August 1939 after a two-year refit. She was supposed to have done three months more in dock, but owing to the threat of war this was suspended. The actual commissioning took place in the hangar of the *Argus*. The next few days had been crammed with the taking in of ammunition and supplies and on 2 September she set out for Scapa Flow via the west coast of Ireland. A few miles away from *Renown* on the coast of Donegal, ss *Athenia* was torpedoed and sunk without warning, showing to the world emerging German brutality.

Renown had not had a chance to work up. All her people were permanent force of course, and knew their professional jobs well. Most of the ABs and above had served in battleships or battlecruisers before, so really all that was required was time for our people to get to know each other. Our captain was Simeon. Rather absent-minded, he sometimes would appear on the bridge wearing his steward's cap, a quaint sight. The commander (the executive officer, second in command) was a seemingly ferocious gentleman named Terry. I was appointed to the Torpedo Division and my action station was at the torpedo sights on the bridge, port and starboard. In my division a number of the ordinary seamen had names like Hans Schmidt, Wolfgang Swartz and so on. I asked them how this was. It turned out that they were German orphans from the Great War who were adopted by British families, many from the north of England. They had volunteered for the navy, happy to have employment. My impression of them was very favourable.

Our first cruise was into the Skagerrak, the entrance to the Baltic Sea. Soon we saw floating mines, stopped our engines, went astern and backed off out of it. Whether the mines were German or Danish I don't know. I had a close look at one. They presented much the same appearance as British mines, round with four or five horns sticking out. The British mines that I had seen were black and the horns were not painted, but these were gray, horns and all. They were awash, quite visible in fairly calm weather but they would be dangerous in bad weather. How awful it would have been for *Renown* to have been mined off Denmark. At that stage of the war we were quite unprepared for such an event and it could have been a terrible first blow against our side.

Back in Scapa we were lying at our buoy off Flotta, it was teatime and suddenly there was a tremendous explosion on the starboard side of the quarterdeck. The Sound Reproduction Equipment was playing "Oh Johnny, Oh Johnny, How You Can Love" as we rushed to our action stations. Our second gunnery officer, Lieutenant Walmsley, whose father was a retired admiral and governor of Newfoundland, rushed by with his hands protecting his head, just as I was doing. No more bombs, thank goodness. It was a lovely day with blue sky and a few clouds, what a

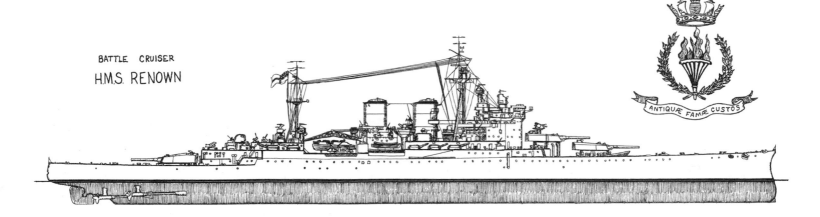

BATTLE CRUISER
H.M.S. RENOWN

ANTIQUÆ FAMÆ CUSTOS

time to be endangered by bombs! The strangest thing, however, was to hear "Oh Johnny" going on and on while guns were firing away. Perhaps the message was "make love, not war." The midshipman of the watch said that the German pilot had flown so low that he could see him smiling, with gold teeth and a white silk scarf, waving cheerfully. The quarterdeck was well splashed with seawater, so we had been lucky.

A few days later a couple of us were invited by midshipmen friends in the cruiser *Norfolk* to have dinner with them in their gunroom. I declined as I had a bad cold and my friend didn't go either. How fortunate. Just at dinner *Norfolk* was bombed, hit in the gunroom, and our friends while escaping in the dark fell into the bomb hole and drowned in oil fuel.

I think it was when *Renown* was in Rosyth, near Edinburgh, for a few days that we heard over the ship's loudspeakers that "Winston is back," meaning Churchill was again First Lord of the Admiralty. A sort of groan went up from the older officers and men who remembered Gallipoli in the First World War.

Finland was being invaded by Russia; the Russians were not doing well and were meeting considerable resistance. The Germans were allied with the Russians so the Finns seemed to stand very little chance. The Swedes and Norwegians appeared indifferent to the fate of the Finns. Our gunroom, however, felt considerable sympathy for Finland and our midshipmen's journals were filled with ideas as to how we could help these unfortunate people. As Russia was an ally of Germany, supplies were coming by ship from Siberia via the Barents Sea and down the Norwegian coast. There was a spot on the coast where ships had to leave the protection of the islands and come out in the open. *Renown* went to the Leads, as they were called, but we never had the good fortune to catch anything.

German aircraft raided Scapa Flow sporadically. As the anti-aircraft defences improved, so the Germans gradually shifted to night raids. These became more spectacular as time went on and tracers and shell bursts filled the skies while searchlights swept back and forth. *Iron Duke* was bombed at her berth at Lyness, but was not damaged. On that occasion I had asked Midshipman Earnshaw if he would take my picket boat to the *Iron Duke* as I had a dinner guest. Poor Midshipman Earnshaw had a ringside seat for this incident. I made a painting for my journal of this scene but Earnshaw did not appreciate my efforts.

I had been asked by the "snotties' nurse" if I wanted to run a picket boat. This was my idea of heaven. The boat was 50 feet in length and had a coxswain, a stoker, a bowman and a sternsheetsman. With its three powerful Meadows engines, the boat could attain 20 knots. There were racks on the stern for four depth charges and two machine guns could be mounted forward. The coxswain generally was a petty officer or acting petty officer; the midshipman was in command, did all the navigation and was the one who got in trouble if anything went wrong. Picket boats were put in the water as soon as the ship anchored or secured to a buoy. Sitting in the tossing vessel to start the engines was not a good experience for anyone given to seasickness. Often, when secured to the stern in stormy weather, I would be joined by a seal who would lie in the water beside the boat looking at me while I looked at her, or him or it.

Our boats officer was the mate of the upper deck, a tough little salt horse Lieutenant Commander Jennings. Once he sent for me at six in the morning. I leaped out of my hammock and rushed to the boat deck eager to please. I hadn't brushed my teeth and he made quite a show of my bad breath, fanning his nose and making a face. His breath was not great either. When I was leaving for my destroyer time he said, kindly, "I have given you the rough side of my tongue Jenson, but I must tell you that it has been meant for your good." I learned a great deal from him. He had an ironic sense of humour. On one occasion when we had been at sea for some time, we could not get into Scapa as the anchorage had been mined by an aircraft. Jennings commented with disgust, "It's like coming home and finding a turd on your doorstep."

The job for the midshipman of the watch at sea was on the bridge; in harbour it was at the accommodation ladder. It included calling the relieving officer of the watch. This could be a dangerous mission because one was not supposed to touch a person senior to oneself. One would stand in the darkened cabin calling, "Lieutenant So and So, sir," and there might be no reply, not even a grunt, but woe betide the wretch who finally gave in and touched the sleeping (or pretending to sleep) senior. Like an uncoiled spring the creature would explode from his bunk and the poor midshipman would have to flee for his life. Lieutenant Commander Jennings was good at being difficult to awaken.

Another duty for the middy was brewing up a mug of kye (cocoa) for the officer of the watch. One would pound up a square lump of Admiralty Unsweetened Cocoa, crumble it into the mug and pour boiling water on it, adding five or six large spoons of sugar. One of our gunroom lunatics used Ex-Lax with the cocoa and thoroughly cleaned out a lieutenant who had incurred his displeasure. His motto was "don't get mad, get even." He was not found out.

Of course, from the day war broke out, all naval ships were blacked out at sunset. Deadlights were screwed down and heavy black canvas curtains screened all the entrances from the decks to the interior of the ship. Smoking outside at night was forbidden, as a U-boat might see the glow. The chart table on the open bridge had a low, metal canopy from which hung a blackout curtain. Usually a human rear end stuck out from the chart table as the navigator, officer of the watch or midshipman of the watch checked the chart, read signals or wrote up the ship's log. One very dark midnight, I was mid of the watch waiting to be relieved by Midshipman Earnshaw. The navigator was checking our position, his behind protruding from the chart table.

H.M.S. ARK ROYAL

I was fascinated to see the dark form of Earnshaw appear and go to the chart table and give the navigator a good kick in his stern. There was a sharp crack as Pilot banged his head on the canopy and emerged to ask Earnshaw why he had kicked him.

"I thought you were Jenson, sir."

"Is Jenson a friend of yours?" asked Pilot.

"Yes, sir," mumbled Earnshaw.

"Well if you do that to your friends, you soon won't have any," said Pilot as he went below to his cabin. Earnshaw immediately gave up the practice and retained his many friends.

Often word of what was planned for the ship would pass around the messdecks, wardroom and gunroom as a "buzz." How these started I cannot imagine, but they were often correct. The "buzz" was that we were bound for West Africa. One day when my boat went to Kirkwall I went to a jewellery store and bought a watertight watch. I read somewhere years later that this jeweller, a Swiss perhaps, actually was a German spy. Could I have revealed West Africa? On the way back to my picket boat I passed by St. Magnus Cathedral, the bleak Gothic structure on the edge of Scapa Flow. A piper in full dress, totally alone, was playing a lament. I got into my boat and returned to my ship. It was one of those magic moments.

Shortly afterwards we slipped from our buoy and steamed through Hoxa Gate to form up behind our screening destroyers. *Ark Royal*, the aircraft carrier, joined us and we set course southerly for West Africa. A day or two out of Scapa, lookouts in *Renown* thought that they had seen a torpedo pop out of the water past the stern of *Ark Royal*. My impression was that no one paid much attention to the report, as it seemed too unlikely. It is easy indeed to imagine that you have just seen something happen, and speaking for myself, I believe that I can even construct a picture in my mind of what I thought I saw, imagining that I saw the fish pop right out of the water a couple of cables astern of the *Ark* and then fall back. In my mind it had a red warhead. Anyway, the captain of a U-boat actually did fire a tin fish (torpedo) at what he believed was the *Ark* and then did an emergency dive. He thought he heard the fish explode and so reported to U-boat Command that he had sunk the *Ark Royal*. Hitler was delighted and presented him a special medal on his return to port.

The midshipmen used to listen to the German radio (Polish midshipmen who had been appointed to serve with us thought we were demented) and, in particular, to Lord Haw Haw, an Irishman with the Germans who became well known for his gloating, unctuous, sneering manner. Every night this creature would ask, "British people, where is the *Ark Royal*?" The German hope was that she had been sunk but they also hoped British public outcry would force the navy to either reveal her presence or confirm her loss. There she was, bouncing along with us as visible as could be.

By now we were sailing due south, from time to time refuelling our destroyers as they ran low on oil. Eventually we developed a very efficient and safe procedure for fuelling alongside while under way at sea. This became the pattern for all the extended operations at sea undertaken by the RN and USN for the remainder of the war. The weather grew warmer and we passed from winter uniforms to shorts and shirts, white knee stockings and white shoes. A lot of people found places to sleep on the upper deck. I stayed below and practically had the whole chest-flat to myself, cool and well-ventilated. Midshipmen were issued with sailors' tropical helmets or solar bowlers. By carefully wrapping white tape around the things, one could produce a facsimile of an officer's solar bowler.

In southern waters

One evening our force altered course to port and steamed into Freetown in Sierra Leone. Above us the Mountains of the Lion growled and rumbled perpetually while clouds swirled about them. Once in the river estuary, we dropped anchor off King Tom's jetty and not far away lay the city of Freetown shimmering in the seemingly endless sun, a scene right out of Conrad's *Heart of Darkness*.

After the slave trade was made illegal in the early 1800s, the Royal Navy attempted to intercept and capture any ships still engaging in this dreadful business. A number of these vessels were taken to Nova Scotia and the enslaved people released. Many of these had no idea where they were captured so that they could not be returned "home." The British gave them the choice of remaining in Nova Scotia or being returned to West Africa. A town was built for the reception and establishment of those who returned – it was Freetown. Many of the inhabitants to whom I spoke were well aware of their Nova Scotian heritage and seemed proud of it.

I went ashore on leave with one or two other mids to the City Hotel. In a small bar on the second floor run by a seedy-looking mulatto we enjoyed warm gin and tonics. The windows had no glass and one gazed out on posts, wires, rails and large, tattered leaves. Here were perched vultures, with scabby red heads and great hooked beaks. They were the local garbage collectors. Few English or other Europeans lived in the town. The businesses, such as they were, were mainly run by Lebanese and some Chinese. The streets were tree-lined with modest houses and large numbers of people were everywhere.

Soon we midshipmen each had a small retinue of young Freetowners who looked after our interests. My young man was George Washington, the son of a fireman, and I found him to be polite, well spoken and helpful. He always addressed me as Captain, pleasant for a lowly snotty. The life of a white person stationed here was said to be five years at the most because of fevers. Civilian dress seemed to be much as in England, and it was said that important people like bank managers were carried about in hammocks. Papers such as *The Times* arrived by steamship and were read in sequence, day by day, the first being read on the day of arrival and so on. It was considered very bad form to read ahead of the other chaps. There was a desert-like golf course which was used by some of our officers. The perils there included snakes which swallowed the golf balls, thinking they were eggs. My chief recreation was swimming at Lumley Beach, a short distance from

Freetown. This was a most beautiful beach with swimming safe from sharks and surf, a rarity in West Africa. The greatest fears were creatures of our own mythology, namely nacker snatchers. It was considered wise to keep on one's trunks in the water.

Bananas, cocoa beans, oranges, limes, nutmeg and all the other tropical fruits were in great abundance. The people generally seemed to be well fed, healthy and friendly, modest and well disposed. In the settlements off Lumley Beach, cool and pleasant in the jungle, people wore very little especially when doing laundry.

One evening shortly after we arrived in Sierra Leone, the paymaster midshipman, Charley Allen, and I were sitting at the gunroom table after dinner. It had been our weekly mess dinner and we had enjoyed our Stilton cheese soaked in port (the stewards described it as alive, it certainly smelt strongly in the tropical heat) as well as a glass of port. Charley started striking his glass with a spoon, making it ring. I pointed out to him that there is a superstition that if a glass

rings, a sailor dies. If someone stops the ringing, his wife dies. Allen just laughed and rang his glass more.

"Please stop," I asked but on he went, ring, ring, ring. I didn't want to kill any wives so I finally said, "For Christ's sake pack it up" and he did. The next morning we learned that Lieutenant Gunther Prien had sunk the battleship *Royal Oak*, at anchor in Scapa Flow. There was a terrible loss of life, 800 or so fellow seamen drowned. Readers are cautioned not to ring glasses. Lieutenant Prien became a great hero in the German U-boat service, decorated by Hitler

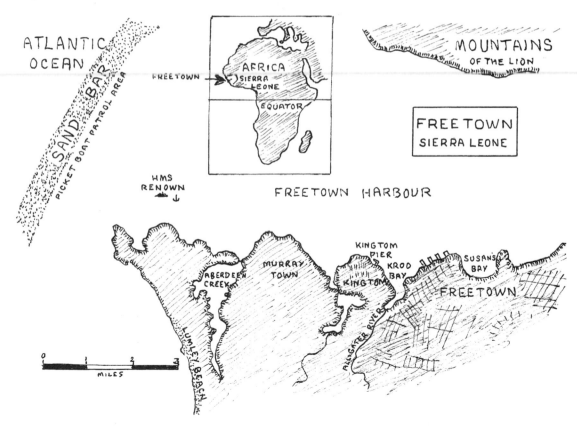

and going on to be a U-boat ace. Certainly sinking *Royal Oak* was a brave and skilful feat and he was admired by both sides (also see map on page 48).

The one thing I associate most with Freetown is the smell of charcoal burning. In the evenings, the women would take their braziers out to the front of their houses, light them up and cook dinner. A grey haze would ascend above the town, and the smell will always be a haunting, pungent reminder of West Africa.

A REMARKABLE FEAT OF ARMS
833 LIVES LOST
TORPEDOING OF HMS ROYAL OAK 13 OCT. 1939
KIRKWALL
ST. MAGNUS CATHEDRAL
MAINLAND
HMS ROYAL OAK
TORPEDO ATTACK
TWO BLOCK SHIPS WITH A SMALL GAP BETWEEN
SCAPA FLOW
KIRK SOUND
HOLM SOUND
NORTH SEA
TOWARDS MAIN ANCHORAGE WHICH WAS EMPTY!
TRACK OF U47
BURRAY
LT. GÜNTHER PRIEN

their hammocks running their red, raw, itching toes up and down the hammock clews for ecstatic relief. We each took one malarial pill a day, a bright yellow thing generally believed to make our skin yellow. We also were supposed to eat a salt tablet two or three times a day to make up for the profuse sweating and salt loss which left us weak or with swollen legs. Some men had skin infections of their arms.

Those who met ladies ashore sometimes ac-

One of the interesting complaints to which most of us were subject was "prickly heat," sometimes all over the body but often mostly between the legs and running down towards the inner thigh. Crotch rot it was called, and there didn't seem to be a simple remedy. Someone said that the trouble was caused by our "dhobi" (Indian for laundry). The laundry women who took our dhobi ashore were reputed to use urine in the rinse water before the clothes were hung out in the hot sun. This would make them sparkling white, but it was thought that the little crystals of uric acid irritated our skin. Athlete's foot was constant and victims would lie in

quired pediculosus pubis, the patter of little feet on one's private parts – crabs. The treatment was to shave off the hair on the private parts. One of our stalwart Royal Marines went ashore for a run and vanished for three or four days. He was found at King Tom's Jetty passed out, stark naked except for his large, heavy boots. As midshipman of the watch I noted that when he was carried aboard his private parts were shaved clean, so at least he protected himself against crabs. This marine later went to a destroyer to back up the young crew and won the Distinguished Service Medal in action. When going ashore men could always qui-

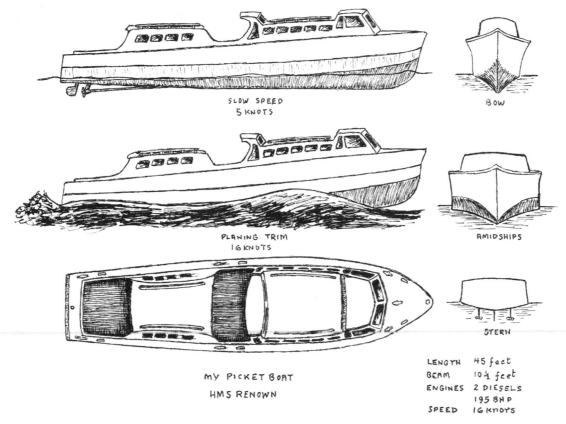

SLOW SPEED
5 KNOTS

BOW

PLANING TRIM
16 KNOTS

AMIDSHIPS

MY PICKET BOAT
HMS RENOWN

STERN

LENGTH 45 feet
BEAM 10½ feet
ENGINES 2 DIESELS
195 BHP
SPEED 16 KNOTS

etly pick up a condom from the quartermaster. This practice reduced the danger of venereal disease.

Unknown to us all, a terrible disease lurked below in the stokers' mess. One man had "galloping consumption" and in the confined atmosphere and close quarters of the mess, the disease spread quickly. When we got back to home waters months later, we heard that 30 in the mess were hospitalized and died. There was no cure then. Everyone, officer, man or boy, received a daily ration of lime juice to prevent scurvy. Captain Cook had proved that this remedy worked, and if his men refused their lime juice

they were flogged. Perhaps the Royal Navy was most famous for its lime juice, hence "limeys" or "juicers." No one had to be flogged in *Renown*.

Of necessity wartime routine was different from peacetime routine for midshipmen. We still had hours of instruction in our gunroom from our schoolmaster officers every day. We also stood watches, night and day, at sea and at anchor, and had important action stations. My harbour duties continued to be my picket boat, running various errands. What fun it was in the glassy waters of Freetown

Harbour! My crew and I delighted in appearing smart and perfecting our boathook drill. Nights often were the best, when the boat would be armed and a lieutenant with six seamen with rifles and cutlasses would clamber aboard. All night long we would patrol over the shallow entrance to the harbour. It was here that a submarine must surface to enter, and we would be ready for them. The lightning flashed and the growling thunder rolled down from the Mountains of the Lion, fish splashed, and everything was as if out of an adventure story. On that coast there lived a marine tribe called the Kroomen, whom we would encounter in their boats of hollowed-out logs, which were very seaworthy. They often would be seen a hundred miles from land, a little fire going in their boat all the time as they went along under a small sail or simply paddling.

Commander Terry took this opportunity to clean the ship up after her long voyage south. He declared that *Renown's* march from now on would be (from Snow White) "Heigh-Ho, Heigh-Ho, It's Off to Work We Go." He also was fond of "I Don't Want to Set the World on Fire," which he hummed constantly. It is not one of my favourites. Great numbers of seagulls, or their southern relatives, hampered the hard work of the ship's company as they scrubbed, chipped and painted under the tropical sun. Commander Terry decided to station a Royal Marine armed with a loaded rifle beside each lower boom. When the Royal decided that gulls were about to desecrate the woodwork, he would fire and the gulls would take off. It was a matter of fine judgement. "Bang!" would go the rifle, "Skwawk, shriek, cry!" would go the gulls and they would

fly up in the air, position themselves over the ship and bomb us with terrible accuracy. It turned out not to matter too much as the rains would come, torrential downpours that lasted a few minutes. Then the sun would come out. On several occasions, the midshipmen stripped off clothing and stood in the rain, as if in a shower, soaping down to be cleansed by the rain. Almost every time, the rain would stop just as we got covered with soap and we would dry off, soap and all, only to be more itchy and uncomfortable than before.

The commander of a capital ship had a "doggie," as his midshipman was called. The doggie's duty was to follow the commander everywhere, running messages, making notes, fetching people, etc. as the commander required. Terry's doggie was a little Dartmouth midshipman whom the sailors called "Spiderlegs." His legs were remarkably insect-like, and he also had bad acne and always wore a troubled expression. This midshipman fascinated me in that he ate his peas off the blade of his table knife. Alas, my ignorance! It was only recently that I learned that some old table knives have a ledge on the blade to hold the peas.

One day when ashore with a couple of friends we asked a taxi driver to take us inland as far as he could go. Very quickly the road deteriorated to a rough trail, and after 10 miles or so even that petered out and we found ourselves in a wild area, with large rocks and high hills with few trees. Beside a small torrent were three or four round grass huts with near-naked people standing or seated about on the ground all holding spears. Their manner was friendly but they did not seem to speak English. We stayed only a few minutes and then returned to Freetown.

In Freetown there was not much to buy in the ordinary sense. Freetowners were clever at covering with skin and decorating such things as old cigarette tins and boxes. Spears were sold, the long blade made of iron ore picked up in lumps off the ground and hammered into shape and fitted on a wooden shaft. The iron was quite soft and bent easily but it could puncture or cut quite well.

There was great excitement one day in harbour when a hospital ship arrived from England. It was fuelling, bound for Singapore, and filled with nurses. We all had visions of pretty, young nurses having cocktails on the quarterdeck with all the officers (except the midshipmen). One evening one of their boats came alongside and all these ladies came aboard, but most of them had medal ribbons from the First World War, ruddy complexions and sturdy frames, so we who had to watch from a distance were not too envious of our seniors.

HMS RENOWN AND HMS ARK ROYAL SEARCHING FOR THE GERMAN RAIDER GRAF SPEE

The reason that *Renown* and *Ark Royal* had been sent to work out of West Africa was that the German pocket battleship *Admiral Graf Spee* was in the South Atlantic sinking our merchant shipping. Our force spent a good deal of time patrolling the area between Africa and South America, going back and forth across the Equator. The first time, in accordance with ancient traditions, Father Neptune clambered on board with his staff to hold court. Everyone, officers and men, who had not crossed before had to appear before the court, then after being roughed up by Neptune's

Bears, Neptune's Barbers shaved the victims and threw them into a large tank of water. It was all a great "skylark."

Generally it was lovely steaming in these waters – blue skies, brilliant blue sea, flying fish and refreshing breezes. Now and again we would encounter a deluge but then the sun would come out and the puddles would dry up. Sometimes we encountered waterspouts, five or six at once, dark, sinister columns going up into black clouds. The officer of the watch conned the ship to avoid them; what would have happened if we had run into one? Other unforgettable sights were pairs of great whales leaping high, right out of the water, then splashing back presumably in a courtship routine.

From time to time word would be received that another British ship had been sunk, and we would rush off toward the reported position only to hear another had been sunk miles away in the opposite direction. We perfected fuelling our destroyers at sea from *Renown* at high speed, a worthwhile skill to develop. It certainly looked exciting and it is a wonder that accidents were rare.

On one occasion massive dysentery afflicted the ships' company. It lasted one night. Officers' and men's heads had been full all night and some used the upper deck as a substitute. The sight of such filth can only be imagined. All sympathy vanished, however, when it was found that persons had used the officers' canvas bath, or bathing pool. Happily I was not afflicted, being from Alberta.

The men remained closed-up at their guns but were allowed to go to sleep. My place of watchkeeping was on the bridge. I had to go from the deck beneath the quarterdeck, through the port 4.5-inch gun barbettes manned by Royal Marines, thence by ladders to the bridge. All the marines were sprawled naked, or nearly so, by their guns, just lying on the bare metal decks, fast asleep and, as far as my embarrassed sight could comprehend, they all had permanent erections. Sacks were kept at the guns in case of a hit during action. Bits and pieces of people were to be put in the bags and tossed overboard as soon as possible to avoid de-moralizing the live ones. Decks in the barbettes were painted red so that blood would not be too obvious.

One day the midshipmen were told to attend a court martial of a leading seaman who had an altercation with the paymaster commander. The president of the court asked the killick what he called the paybob. "I called him a fat belly-robbing bastard," he said. I don't remember the punishment, but he was not hanged or shot. It was a solemn and picturesque affair, very impressive, but the reply provoked barely concealed smiles.

I always thought that the food was very good, but midshipmen used to spend their own money for extras such as fruit. One of the snotties was often seasick and did not care for fruit or even lime juice, which is rather sour. When we arrived back in Freetown from a patrol, the poor chap looked very ill. In those waters one wonders about fever. He was taken to the hospital ship and returned in a day or so, perfectly fit. Seasickness is a dreadful burden and sufferers who carry on are greatly to be admired. Lord Nelson was such a person.

In the lonely stretches of the South Atlantic without radar, it was imperative that lookouts remained constantly on the alert. The captain decided that in daylight a midshipman should look out from the crow's nest far above the bridge and scan the horizon for a steady four hours until relieved by another snotty. The gunnery officer, Lieutenant Commander Holmes, was not helpful. He would ask, "What do you chaps do up there? Sit and think yourselves off?" I don't know whether he was right or wrong but there were embarrassed snickers.

On one patrol we encountered a merchant ship wearing the flag of the United States of America. This was unusual because the South Atlantic seemed to me to be so barren of other ships, I wondered how *Graf Spee* found them. Anyway, *Renown* asked this guy (communication by morse lamps was not easy) what his cargo was. The reply was "Goon skins and foo foo dust." (The Goon was a character in the popular comic strip "Popeye the Sailor.") The captain did not go out of his British mind at this outrageous display of American impertinence, but cooly and calmly told the commander to send over a boarding party to inspect him, and signalled the Yanks to heave to. We lowered a cutter, which is a very large rowboat, with a lieutenant and 25 or 30 seamen in full blue uniforms, armed with rifles and bayonets. At that time, men still wore their ship's name on the cap tally, a ribbon around the cap (later they just wore HMS or HMCS on the ribbon so that their ship was not advertised to possible enemy agents when it was in port). We did not wish to reveal which ship we were so the commander told the boarding party to remove their cap ribbons. A cutter is large, unwieldy, heavy and dangerous to lower and hoist as well as being sturdy work to row. The sea was running high and the cutter disappeared from time to time among the waves. The American, facing six 15-inch guns, wisely decided to heave to and in due course our boat arrived alongside. A rope ladder was lowered and our tars, in full dress and heavy boots, loaded with rifles and bayonets, clambered up the side and, limp with exhaustion, handed their rifles to the Yanks as they tumbled over the bulwark. "What ship is that?" asked the Yanks. *Re-nown* they replied and then realized their mistake. Lord Haw Haw still was asking every night, "British people, where is the *Ark Royal*?" implying that all of us were in Davy Jones's locker. The American was "clean" and our red-faced people returned.

Hoisting boats by crane or by boat's falls (huge pulleys) was exciting even in harbour because of the way the boats bounced around on the waves. There always was lots of shouting, cursing, bad tempers and sometimes bad accidents. One of our leading seamen had his hand torn off when it was caught in the hoisting block. As the war went on though, ships' companies became more efficient and accidents were rare.

On another cruise we came across a German cargo ship, ss *Uhenfells*. She had a prize crew aboard and was headed into Freetown. She was a lovely design and truly a beautiful ship. I imagine she was quite a valuable prize. A number of Italian cargo ships stopped in Freetown for fuel or cargo. When I went by one of these in my picket boat, the Italian crews seemed always to be leaning over the side, jeering, hooting and spitting at us. They were loyal Fascists, friends of the Germans. My crew never said a word but gave them looks that should have conveyed a hint of the fate that awaited them – often in person – and their unfortunate country: "One day we will get you, you bastards."

Now *Graf Spee* turned up in the South Indian Ocean so *Renown* and *Ark Royal* set off down the coast of Africa and south of the Cape of Good Hope. The Roaring Forties were our patrol area. The weather was cooler and more like that west of Britain. Often the skies were leaden and dra-

THE WANDERING ALBATROSS
WING SPAN 11 FEET

L.B.JENSON

THE WAR GETS UNDER WAY

matic with heavy cloud. Here was where the strong westerlies blew unchecked around the whole globe, piling up impressive seas. As we steamed along we were accompanied by the great albatross, most magnificent of birds. What impressive creatures they are, with noble features and a wingspread of greater than eight feet! No matter what the speed of the ship, one or more would be stationed by the bridge gliding along just a few feet away at eye level. For hours on end they would remain in the same relative position, I suppose adjusting their course, speed and height by imperceptibly altering their trim. We would watch them and they would watch us.

The dark skies, the howling wind, the great greybeards rolling along in endless procession, and in the forefront, the great albatross, gave me the feeling that I was looking upon the Eternal. I am sure that others were equally affected. Many years later I heard that the commander of the *Ark Royal* became interested in learning more about these wonderful birds and found that very little was known about them. None of the British libraries or museums had any information on their life and habits. When he left the service a few years later, he obtained financing to mount an expedition to Antarctica to study them. This was successful and provided most of the information we now possess on albatrosses.

When I look back on those days in the Roaring Forties, my most vivid image is of the great expanse of turbulent grey waters, stormy skies and howling winds. It reminded one of the magnificent engravings of the Crea-

tion by Doré. When darkness approached one might expect to see a ghostly ship, plunging along under tattered sails, condemned for an eternity of struggle to beat its way about the Cape of Good Hope, the Flying Dutchman. We did not encounter this ship or any others like it.

On this patrol, however, we did encounter another German merchant ship. This ship had been attacked already by the South African Air Force; she was abandoned and her crew taken to South Africa. Our captain decided that we would use her for target practice for our 15-inch guns. We opened fire at a range of five miles or so, gradually closing in. We fired about 10 or so salvos, about 60 rounds, but I couldn't see any hits or splashes, even though visibility was excellent. The shells must have been passing right through her and splashing in the ocean beyond, the splashes being obscured by the target. The poor ship eventually sank, but I never heard whether she sank from our shelling or from bomb damage. Later on our gunnery proved to be very accurate so probably we were hitting her.

We were getting low on oil fuel so we put in to Cape Town. The most striking thing about Cape Town is Table Mountain, which looms over the city. Cape Town was beautiful with buildings and shops equal in appearance to any in the world. While we were there, a bitter and dusty north wind blew down through the streets and reminded us of our northern homes. In this part of the world white men did not have much to do with black people, a change from West Africa where our sailors mingled freely with the local people.

The gentleman who provided *Renown* and *Ark Royal* with fuel oil invited a number of midshipmen out to his place several miles outside Cape Town. His house was in the country, overlooking cultivated fields surrounded by hills which led up to mountains. The climate was mild and his living room completely opened up to a garden, complete with large trees. It was a beautiful house. Other houses in the area were the large, traditional Dutch-style farm houses, whitewashed and sparkling in the sun. The scene was Eden-like in appearance, the white houses in the green fields lying among the foothills of imposing mountains. When we were driving around we saw a troop of 30 or so baboons running along. They were quite large creatures with formidable-looking teeth but our host said they were relatively harmless.

We saw the "Tin Can City" outside Cape Town, a dreadful slum inhabited by coloured people. The crude shelters were made of tin cans pounded flat, sheet metal and old boards. I believe the population was as large as that of Cape Town itself. It was obvious that this beautiful country was, and would continue, facing monumental problems of black and white. We stood on a point of land, the Cape of Good Hope. As we looked out to sea, the Indian Ocean spread out on our left, and the South Atlantic on our right. They looked remarkably similar to me, but it was interesting to contemplate five centuries of European navigation concentrated in this area. According to maritime lore, when one has rounded the Cape of Good Hope, one is entitled to put one foot on the table. If one also has done Cape Horn, two feet on the dining table is the reward.

Off to sea again but not back to those realms where we might meet the ghostly mariners of the Flying Dutchman. We were bound north once more, as *Graf Spee* had reappeared in the South Atlantic and sunk more ships. We found nothing, however, and made our way into Freetown. Now a report came from Brazil that *Graf Spee* was sinking ships just south of the mouth of the Amazon, so we got under way immediately, setting course for South America. I can't remember whether this was the time when some of the petty officers talked about (only in fun I think) having the boy seamen live in with them. There was considerable talk about some old customs of which I had never heard.

In early December we were midway between Africa and South America when we learned that *Graf Spee* was off the River Plate near Argentina and sinking ships. We headed for Rio de Janeiro to fuel up. As we moved southerly down the coast, the weather became cooler and we wore white trousers and shoes with our blue reefers, looking just like people in the movies. Soon we heard that our cruisers *Ajax*, *Achilles* and *Exeter* were engaging *Graf Spee*. She had 11-inch main armament with a much greater range and hitting power than our 6- and 8-inch-gunned cruisers. Theoretically *Graf Spee* should have been able to demolish our cruisers one by one. However, she was damaged quite badly herself by our cruisers and sought refuge in Uruguay.

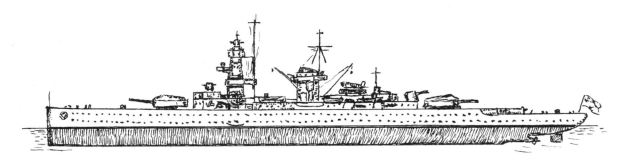

The *Admiral Graf Spee,* scuttled in the River Plate, Uruguay, 17 December 1939. HMS *Renown* was fuelling in Rio de Janeiro at the time.

We closed the land and soon could see the mountains of Brazil. Gradually the harbour of Rio with the magnificent Sugar Loaf Mountain came in sight. I don't think one could imagine a more beautiful land. We anchored and I was sent into Rio with my picket boat to land the postman. Perhaps it was because I had been so long at sea that Rio appeared as it did, wonderful buildings and spacious streets with fountains and trees. The sidewalks were lovely mosaics. Soon the ship was fuelling and we were invaded by hundreds of British ladies and gentlemen, living and doing business in Brazil. Drinks were being served on the quarterdeck when it was announced that *Graf Spee* was under way and leaving Uruguay. We completed our fuelling, landed our visitors and got under way for the River Plate and battle. Just as we moved away word came from Admiralty that *Graf Spee* had scuttled and burned herself in the River Plate on 17 December 1939. A few days later her captain, standing on a German flag in his hotel room, blew his brains out. Our delight was complete.

Soon we were back in Freetown, swimming at Lumley Beach and wondering what we would be doing next. Running my boat, I often chatted with the seagoing Kroomen in their dugout canoes. They told me that we were going to go to the Falkland Islands to pick up *Exeter* to bring her back to England. They also said the Germans were waiting with submarines to get us on the way home.

I would say, "Oh rubbish!" and they would say, "No, sir, you will see that we are right."

"How do you know?" I would say. "Drums?"

"Yeah Captain, drums. That's how we hear."

And so we sailed towards the Falklands to meet the gallant *Exeter*. Down through the South Atlantic we steamed. Ascension Island appeared to port; surely this volcanic dot must be one of the loneliest places in the world. I had hoped that we might pass close to St. Helena, where Napoleon had been kept after Waterloo until he died, but we were many miles to the westward. About this latitude, however, we met *Exeter*. She had a fresh coat of paint and looked fit in every respect, but appearances are deceiving.

The shell holes had been patched over and some of her 8-inch guns which had been destroyed were replaced with long wooden "gun barrels." A few days later we arrived back in Freetown and all our people had the opportunity to go aboard *Exeter* to see what had occurred. A lot had happened – the inside of the ship was a wreck from shell fire and the fires set by shellfire. Everyone was curious as to whether the Germans had used gas shells, but there was no sign of such a thing. Ordinary gunfire is bad enough. For anyone interested there was lots of blood splashed about. The officers we spoke to were more sombre than I would have expected after such a great victory. Although all one's training is devoted to the single subject of warfare at sea, the reality of dead enemies and fallen shipmates, combined with horrendous damage to one's house and home, is not easily accepted.

Back came our bum boat friends cheerfully telling us that the Germans were determined to get us by hook or by crook and that *Renown*, *Ark Royal* and *Exeter* never would make the English Channel. Lord Haw Haw's unpleasant sneering voice said the same thing, and finally we were told not to listen to the German radio. It became rather dull sitting in Freetown and it was with great relief that we got the news from the bum boatmen that we were about to leave for home. We sailed, just as they said we would, and we hoped the remainder of their information was not true. Fortunately, the voyage home was uneventful except for the shocking change in temperature from West Africa to the Channel. I felt as if my blood was as thin as water and I had spells of violent shivering.

Exeter went into Plymouth harbour to be met by Winston Churchill, the First Lord of the Admiralty, plus thousands of proud English. The country had needed that victory and made the most of it. *Renown* came alongside quietly, a few line handlers at our jetty and no one else to greet us. We all were given a bit of leave and I went to stay with an older couple near Whitchurch in Dorset, a beautiful county of rolling hills and picturesque villages. They were Drogo Montagues, ex-tea planters from Ceylon, descendants of the Earl of Sandwich. They had a midshipman's journal of an ancestor of the 1830s who had visited Pitcairn Island of HMS *Bounty* fame and had made an illustration of one of the descendants of Fletcher Christian. (By an odd coincidence, I later bought a very old naval officer's fighting sword from a Miss Christian, originally from Pitcairn, who had an antique shop in Vancouver.) The Drogo Montagues pointed out with good humour the nearby beach where Vikings had landed about a thousand years before and ravaged the countryside in one of their last great raids. Don't people forget anything? It was a delightful experience living in such a beautiful old house furnished with English antiques and items such as Japanese suits of armour, made of papier maché, hard like plastic.

The Royal Commonwealth Society, I think it was, had asked people in England if they would accept guests from the Empire and I am sure many Canadians, Australians, South Africans and so on were entertained quietly but in a most generous manner by affluent English families. The Drogo Montagues arranged for me to meet other young people in nearby villages. What a country!

I returned to *Renown* and shortly afterwards we sailed from Plymouth bound for Scapa Flow. The booms and gates to the Flow were much improved from the time we left and I was not unhappy to be in Scapa again. The treeless hills surrounding the Flow possessed the most marvellous shadows, lights and soft colours. The skies were constantly changing and with them of course the sea. My picket boat was allocated for use by Vice-Admiral W.J. Whitworth, who had joined us. He was, I think, president of the Royal Naval Bird Watching Society and from time to time we would go to some of the smaller islands in the Flow and he and his flag captain would clamber ashore, laden with binoculars, looking for birds. This was great for me because the admiral would tell me to close right in and generally handle my boat more daringly than I would on my own. On one such occasion, I got wedged in some large rocks so the admiral and flag captain were up to their waists in the water pushing me off, I might say with great good humour.

To deceive the Germans, a number of merchant ships now lay at anchor in the Flow disguised to look like warships with wooden superstructures, funnels, guns and turrets. Even close up they were amazingly real, but there were no people and this conveyed a weird sensation as one passed by.

One event attracted considerable attention. A marine from *Nelson* or *Rodney* had gone ashore and had found a sheep with whom he attempted a sexual act. The sheep had locked on or contracted on him so he had to carry the sheep in his arms down to the liberty jetty where the ship's boat would pick them up. At his court martial he claimed that he had mistaken the sheep for a Wren in a fur coat, but this was not believed for some reason and he was sent off to hard labour for five years. From then on whenever one of the boats from his ship went by, the companies of other ships would line the rails, making a chorus of "baa baa." The admiral ordered the practice of *baa-ing* to cease, which it did. This was a sad case because our Royal Marines were very highly respected.

By this time, the old professional crews of the destroyers were diluted by young "hostilities only" RNVR men, on average about 19 to 20 years old. It was believed that young crews would be considerably strengthened in morale in time of battle if they had a few older men among them. Some of our marines were thus drafted, and it turned out to be true when the one who had behaved so badly in Freetown was drafted and behaved so bravely in his destroyer in action that he won the Distinguished Service Medal. It was a quick path from disgrace to glory.

Many of my picket boat trips were made in rough weather. On one occasion, I went alongside *Warspite* to drop a man, and as I left, my starboard depth charge rack cut through the accommodation ladder purchase. The ladder dropped straight down. A sideboy on the ladder managed to cling on and then climb up vertically, thank God. There didn't seem to be much that I could do hanging around, so I returned to my ship and told the commander what had happened. He told me to return to *Warspite* and apologize to the captain for what I had done. It was even rougher this time, but I managed to get alongside, went aboard and conveyed my apologies to the captain. He thought it was funny, laughed and sent me on my way much relieved.

In those days some top secret documents were delivered by hand (in an attaché case chained to the wrist) by well dressed tough-looking civilian gentlemen known as "King's messengers." They wore a small, silver greyhound in the lapel of their coat. On one occasion, late on a windy, dark and rainy night, I was told to man my boat and come alongside the accommodation ladder. A King's messenger silently embarked and I took him to the jetty in Scapa Bay near Kirkwall. He disappeared into the darkness. Perhaps he was the original James Bond. I think his papers might have concerned the coming British invasion of Norway.

The Norwegian campaign

Midshipman Pitt, who bore a physical resemblance to portraits of Pitt the Younger, told me that when he was home on leave his mother told him the British were about to invade Norway and that this would happen shortly after we returned to the Orkneys. She said everyone in London was talking about it, although it was a secret.

As Mrs. Pitt had predicted, we sailed for Norwegian waters at the beginning of April 1940. *Renown* was covering a minelaying destroyer which was laying mines in Norwegian territorial waters. We never even saw her. As we sailed north off the coast, the weather steadily worsened and our destroyers started to suffer weather damage. Accordingly,

they were ordered to cease screening us and to fall in astern and keep up as best they could. The snow flurries increased, the seas became rougher, and as the night became blacker, visibility was very limited. A message was flashed to us up the line from the destroyers astern. It was from *Glowworm* and said that she was turning back to search for a man washed overboard. The following morning there was a wireless report from *Glowworm* that she had sighted a German battleship. Lieutenant Commander Roop, *Glowworm*'s captain, firing his 4.7-inch guns, had little effect on *Hipper*. German photographers were busy making movies of the little ship when she rammed and quite badly damaged *Hipper*. She then sank with heavy loss of life, and her captain was posthumously awarded the Victoria Cross.

Renown and her destroyers continued northerly that day and the following night. The weather stayed a mixture of snow flurries and strong northerly winds as we approached the Lofoten Islands. Before dawn on 9 April, I was on watch on the bridge at the torpedo sights. It was our practice to go to action stations every day as dawn broke. The Royal Marine boy bugler blew his bugle in the bridge microphone of the sound reproduction equipment, Surface Action Stations followed by the Action Stations bell. These sounds never failed to make my spine tingle. At the same time, the people who had been on the middle watch (midnight to four in the morning) had scarcely had time to get warmed up in their hammocks.

It was still pitch dark when all positions reported "closed up." Firing circuits were tested for all our guns and torpedoes, damage control parties were in position and all the other activities in the ship geared up in readiness for dealing with an enemy. We had done this every dawn at sea since the war started and it was very much a matter of routine. The only bad aspect was that one always felt so tired, day and night, and we midshipmen still had classes of instruction every weekday, at sea or in harbour. After our period in the tropics we were still unused to the cold. In addition, one often felt a bit sickly from too many cigarettes and mugs of cocoa or tea, also known as "ploo" or "char." ("Ploo" is the noise one makes when blowing on a hot mug of "char," an Indian word for tea.)

We had heard of *Glowworm* sighting and engaging a German battleship the morning before, but we had no idea of her fate. However, the sighting made us more alert, if possible. Gradually the sky lightened to reveal a turbulent slate coloured ocean, low scudding clouds and lighter patches of snow squalls. Everyone saw the two dark ships against the eastern sky at the same time. The captain, the navigator and the gunnery officer looked at them initially through their binoculars, discussing their silhouettes and whether they had any British characteristics in their masts, funnels, turrets, bridge; it would be a catastrophe if they were British and we engaged them. They decided that there were no other British ships in the area, and our destroyers were pounding along astern of us in line ahead.

Finally I heard our captain say, calmly and with a bit of his usual faint stutter, "They definitely look like *Gneisenau* and *Scharnhorst*, what range?"

"18,000 yards," said Guns.

"Well, Guns, l-l-l let them have it!"

"Shoot!" ordered Guns.

"Ting ting" went the fire bells, then the buzzer and *bang* and six 15-inch shells went off broad on the starboard bow. The signal bo'sun immediately hoisted our huge battle ensign on the starboard yard. Just seeing it stretched out in the wind made thoughts of Trafalgar and Jutland pass through my mind. The commander moved all the superfluous upper bridge people such as torpedo director crews down to the lower bridge by the upper conning tower behind 10 inches of armour, which was his station in the event the captain was killed or wounded. We distinctly saw a large flash and a column of black smoke about the bridge of the leading German. We had hit with our first salvo! Now we saw red winks coming from both German ships.

The commander was humming to himself and more cheerful than I had ever seen him. "They are firing now." Then, looking at his watch, "They should arrive in about twenty seconds," and so they did. They sounded like trains coming at us, "Woosh, woosh, woosh, woosh, woosh!" Then a 50-foot splash one side or another. More red winks, more howls, more splashes. More gunfire crashing off from us. I was thinking to myself, why don't we stop provoking these guys? Wouldn't it be nice to just go home? And so it went on until the Germans vanished in a cloud of snow. Then they appeared again and once more we exchanged greetings. We had increased to 30 or more knots and now we were ploughing through huge waves, crashing and lunging and causing great clouds of spray.

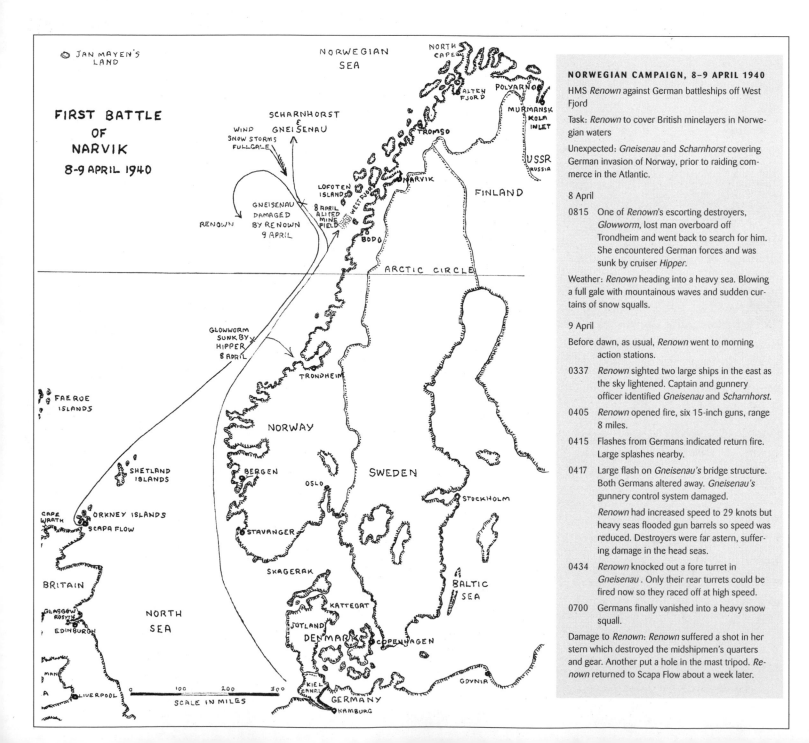

FIRST BATTLE
OF
NARVIK
8-9 APRIL 1940

JAN MAYEN'S LAND

NORWEGIAN SEA

SCHARNHORST & GNEISENAU

WIND
SNOW STORMS
FULL GALE

NORTH CAPE

ALTEN FJORD

POLYARNO

MURMANSK
KOLA INLET

TROMSO

USSR
RUSSIA

GNEISENAU
DAMAGED BY RENOWN
9 APRIL

RENOWN

LOFOTEN ISLANDS

WEST FJORD

NARVIK

FINLAND

8 APRIL
ALLIED MINE FIELD

BODO

ARCTIC CIRCLE

GLOWWORM SUNK BY HIPPER
8 APRIL

TRONDHEIM

FAEROE ISLANDS

NORWAY

BERGEN

OSLO

SWEDEN

STOCKHOLM

SHETLAND ISLANDS

CAPE WRATH

ORKNEY ISLANDS

SCAPA FLOW

STAVANGER

SKAGERAK

BALTIC SEA

BRITAIN

NORTH SEA

KATTEGAT

JUTLAND

DENMARK

COPENHAGEN

GLASGOW
ROSYTH

EDINBURGH

MAN

A

LIVERPOOL

0   100   200   300
SCALE IN MILES

KIEL CANAL

GERMANY

HAMBURG

GDYNIA

NORWEGIAN CAMPAIGN, 8–9 APRIL 1940

HMS *Renown* against German battleships off West Fjord

Task: *Renown* to cover British minelayers in Norwegian waters

Unexpected: *Gneisenau* and *Scharnhorst* covering German invasion of Norway, prior to raiding commerce in the Atlantic.

8 April

0815   One of *Renown*'s escorting destroyers, *Glowworm*, lost man overboard off Trondheim and went back to search for him. She encountered German forces and was sunk by cruiser *Hipper*.

Weather: *Renown* heading into a heavy sea. Blowing a full gale with mountainous waves and sudden curtains of snow squalls.

9 April

Before dawn, as usual, *Renown* went to morning action stations.

0337   *Renown* sighted two large ships in the east as the sky lightened. Captain and gunnery officer identified *Gneisenau* and *Scharnhorst*.

0405   *Renown* opened fire, six 15-inch guns, range 8 miles.

0415   Flashes from Germans indicated return fire. Large splashes nearby.

0417   Large flash on *Gneisenau*'s bridge structure. Both Germans altered away. *Gneisenau*'s gunnery control system damaged.

        Renown had increased speed to 29 knots but heavy seas flooded gun barrels so speed was reduced. Destroyers were far astern, suffering damage in the head seas.

0434   *Renown* knocked out a fore turret in *Gneisenau*. Only their rear turrets could be fired now so they raced off at high speed.

0700   Germans finally vanished into a heavy snow squall.

Damage to *Renown*: *Renown* suffered a shot in her stern which destroyed the midshipmen's quarters and gear. Another put a hole in the mast tripod. *Renown* returned to Scapa Flow about a week later.

The first engagement of capital ships since the Battle of Jutland, 1916. HMS *Renown* off the Lofoten Islands, Norway, engages the German battleships *Gneisenau* and *Scharnhorst*, first light, 9 April 1940 – view from starboard torpedo sight on the open bridge outside the upper armoured conning tower. This drawing is based on personal recollection; all my gear was destroyed by a shell passing through our chest flat.

"A" TURRET   "B" TURRET
SHELL SPLASH   SHELL SPLASH

"FLASHLESS" CORDITE, VERY LITTLE SMOKE

SNOWSTORM ON HORIZON INTO WHICH GERMANS DISAPPEAR

GNEISENAU HIT BY US IN BRIDGE STRUCTURE

SCHARNHORST FLASH OF HER GUNFIRE AT US INDICATED SHELLS WOULD ARRIVE IN 30-40 SECONDS   SHELL SPLASH

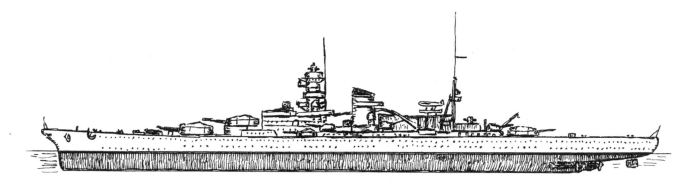

The twin battle cruisers *Scharnhorst* and *Gneisenau* were engaged by HMS *Renown* at the first Battle of Narvik, April 1940.

The Germans vanished again to the northeast and we pushed on in the hope of seeing them again. No luck. Now we became aware of something like a giant banging on the ship's side. I thought it was a blister or double bottom broken loose but it really was the bow pounding in the heavy seas. We did slow down and turned around to look for our poor old destroyers who couldn't keep up. We found them and secured from action stations so that we who were off watch could go down and eat. On the way down to the gunroom, we passed the admiral's cabin just ahead of "X" Turret. What a mess! All the lovely furniture was all over the place, upside down and smashed to bits. We passed by the wardroom, which looked much as usual. We were invited in for a drink. I thought it must be nearly lunch time but it was only about 7:00 a.m.! It seemed as though a whole day had gone by. I had a very tasty glass of gin and then went on down to the gunroom.

Here was a real astonishment! Daylight was shining in through holes on each side, everything was smashed to bits, my sea chest had vanished totally, a foot or so of water sloshed around what had been our living quarters. No clothes, no journals, no personal possessions – all we had was what we stood up in. Later when I went back to the bridge I had another shock. In the leg of the tripod mast, beside which I had been standing, and just above my head, was a neat 11-inch hole made by one of the Germans. Our only casualty was our navigator, whose first name was Herman, who was annoyed to have one of his new boots, which he had only worn four times, destroyed by a piece of shrapnel which also chopped off a toe. His foot was all bundled up to stop the blood. He had the piece of shrapnel mounted on a board with a brass plaque on which was engraved "To Herman from Adolf."

My worst loss was my midshipman's journal, which I treated as a special hobby. It was full of drawings of things in the ship as well as events of contemporary interest such as Molotov cocktails and other weapons being used in the Russian–Finnish War. I decided that I would work doubly hard and rewrite and re-illustrate it. Not only was it one of the subjects marked for promotion to sub-lieutenant but I thought it would be interesting in my old age. Alas!

We were relieved that the Germans had not used gas shells. Some people thought they had smelt mustard gas, but they were using armour piercing shells. If they had hit us with high explosive shells, we would have been a real mess. The shipwrights plugged up the holes in the gun-room and midshipmen's chest flat and things quickly got back to normal. Even the banging on the hull diminished. The only other damage was to Admiral Whitworth's attractive and well furnished day quarters just forward of our after 15-inch gun turret. The firing with the turret trained forward to starboard completely demolished every stick of his table, chairs, desk, cabinets, dishes and so on. It looked as if a madman with an axe had gone berserk in there.

I think it was that night that we transferred Admiral Whitworth to HMS *Warspite* to carry on the battle at Narvik. It was dark as pitch and fairly high seas were running and I couldn't even see *Warspite*. However, it was not my worry, thank God. I believe a really experienced petty officer handled the boat. *Renown* remained cruising the waters off northern Norway for several days. We were bombed by the Germans several times. The planes remained in formation at several thousand feet and dropped their bombs in unison. We called it "pattern bombing" and it must have been experimental. In any case, no bombs fell close to us.

It is not often that one is able to read reviews of one's own gunfire by those at the receiving end. An English translation of *Battleships of the Scharnhorst Class* (Lionel Leventhal Limited, 1999) stated the opinions of *Renown*'s gunnery found in the battle reports of gunnery officers of *Scharnhorst* and *Gneisenau*. They were quite complementary. I certainly had no complaints about *their* gunfire – it looked pretty good to me.

Scharnhorst stated that the astonishing high rate and continuity of *Renown*'s fire was not impaired by the movements of our ship. He stated that *Renown* was pounding so strongly in the heavy seas that our keel could be seen at the stern.

Gneisenau observed that *Renown* was shooting with both main and secondary armament. Her heavy guns were firing fast and regularly. He noted that *Renown*'s intense fire must have expended a large amount of ammunition. He observed that *Renown* was shipping seas very heavily over the forecastle, but this did not seem to hamper fire control and firing momentum. *Gneisenau* also mentioned that *Renown*'s intention seemed to be to damage the Germans at all costs. This certainly was correct!

As the days of April 1940 went by it became increasingly obvious that the British and French armies which had landed in Norway would have to withdraw, and this seemed to take place in a messy, unplanned sort of way, which has to be the way most retreats look. On reflection, it probably was just as well because I don't think that the British had the resources to occupy Norway and hold on to it.

We went back and forth to Norwegian waters covering the British and French evacuation and almost every time we were pattern-bombed by the Germans. We were not hit and we did not succeed in hitting any enemy aircraft. However, these German air attacks, which were not pressed home, were invaluable for our training and our people began to gain some confidence in high-angle fire. On a couple of occasions our close-range weapons, pom pom guns, were used and this was valuable experience for those crews.

Upon *Renown's* return to Scapa Flow we were visited by a Gieves representative and at the same time made out our claims for uniforms, plain clothes, etc. to be submitted to the Admiralty. Gieves replaced our gear very quickly, but I received precisely one half of what I had claimed from the Admiralty and I suppose that was the case for all of us.

Renown went down to Rosyth. We had to strike our topmast to pass under the Forth Bridge. This is a classic exercise in seamanship and very interesting professionally.

HMS *Matabele*, 1940

4

Small ship time

Finally the time came when some of our term of midshipmen were appointed to destroyers to do our "small ship time." I was appointed to HMS *Matabele*, a new Tribal Class destroyer, and she was at the opposite end of the British Isles, in Falmouth in Cornwall. On the way from Scapa via *St. Ninian* I visited the hotel in Wick where I had spent the night when I came up from England to join *Renown*. I had run out of money on that long trip and the hotel proprietor had heard that I would be unable to pay my bill and told me not to worry. Well, now I was able to visit him nearly a year later and pay my bill. This was an immense relief to me, and I felt tickled when he said that he had had no doubt that I would keep my word. He had never been let down, he said.

En route I visited my relatives in Sale, Manchester, and was introduced to the niceties of the flower and banana trade. Early each morning, transactions involving thousands of pounds were conducted in a coffee house, verbally with a handshake. Later on I suppose that forms would be written out but everything depended on men keeping their word. My uncle imported bananas from the Canary Islands, fruit from the Azores and flowers from the Scilly Islands. Bananas were stored under vaulted arches beneath Piccadilly Station in Manchester. Evidently, these maintained the right temperature for storage. Fruit and other items were stored in large brick warehouses. Uncle had lost a ship sunk during the Spanish Civil War.

All these people had a great zest for life and were greatly involved in cultural life, being among the supporters of the Hallé Orchestra, active in civic politics and the Methodist chapel. Relations with employees had the appearance of great informality. It was rather like a large family with everyone working equally. My cousin had been captured at Gallipoli with the regiment in which my father had been commissioned but had declined in order to remain with the Canadians. My female cousins, like thousands of other British women, had lost their loves, who were killed in Flanders.

Too soon I was on my way to Falmouth in Cornwall, a different world from Lancashire, with sunnier skies, milder temperatures and lovely pastoral scenery, rolling hills, lush fields and picturesque cliffs. HMS *Matabele* was lying in drydock in Sily Cox's Yard. Evidently, she had grounded on an uncharted rock near Bodö in the Norwegian campaign and had flooded the tiller flat and the spirit room, where the rum and officers' wines were stored. The hull had to be repaired but when I reflect on it, it seems to me that there was less urgency at this stage to get the ship back in action than there would have been later in the war when our situation had become increasingly serious.

Falmouth is an attractive small town. To my Alberta eyes, the vegetation seemed tropical with little palm trees and plants with large, spiky leaves. There was a friendly little tea room, the Seven Stars, run by two elderly ladies. There was no book store, but there was a picturesque pub-hotel on the outskirts of town which our officers seemed to enjoy. I really didn't like it much, too noisy and crowded. The tea room was more my style. The shipyard was overshadowed by a large hill. At anchor in the bay was something everyone took for granted, except me – the legendary sailing vessel *Cutty Sark,* unkempt and apparently abandoned. The first ship model I made was *Cutty Sark* and here she was in person.

Later on when walking along the coast with a friend, we saw the wrecks of, I believe, six U-boats surrendered after the Great War. They had been under a tow which parted and were cast up on this shore. One night our sailors went on a party and as a lark switched the hanging signs of the various businesses so that the hairdresser became a greengrocer, the ironmonger became something else, and so on. I don't think damage was done, but the police insisted that our people return the signs to their original positions and no charges were laid.

The first lieutenant was Lieutenant Commander P.K. Knowling, a short gentleman who had spent most of his service time in China. Each day he instructed me in gunnery as it applied to *Matabele*. Sometimes during his instruction there would be an air raid on Falmouth. The lessons carried on and I would do my best to act studiously. He was a kind, modest and brave man, admired by the crew.

The captain returned from leave and required me to report to him in his cabin. His name was Commander John Saint Vincent Sherbrooke, a thin, fine-featured gentleman with grey hair. He seemed pleased to have a Canadian because, as he said, he was a sort of Canadian himself. His direct ancestor was Sir John Sherbrooke, Lieutenant Governor of Nova Scotia in the 1800s, and Sherbrooke Village is named after him. Many years later I saw a portrait of Sir John in Government House in Halifax and was struck by the similarity of features. Our captain had won a DSO in a previous ship but I don't know what the circumstances were. His day cabin was very austere with delicate porcelains on the mantle and he was fastidious in his dress and deportment.

On 10 May 1940, the so-called phoney war ended when the Germans invaded Holland and Belgium on the way to France. Prior to this, while the navy had had lots to do, the British army in France had done nothing except sing about "hanging their washing on the Siegfried Line" and "Run Rabbit Run," catchy tunes scornful of the Germans. This was about to change, in a big way!

The German advance was rapid and we became aware that a catastrophe for the British and French was developing. Here we were in drydock and incapable of doing anything to help. By a miracle the British Expeditionary Force escaped from Dunkirk with few casualties or prisoners, but all their equipment was lost. Soon the French surrendered and the Germans consolidated themselves in France, establishing airfields and naval bases, in particular, submarine bases. Happily, if that is the word, the Royal Air Force managed to get out of France and re-established themselves in England.

Falmouth became a target for the German air force, who concentrated on the dockyard and harbour fittings. *Matabele* had a four-barrelled pom-pom aft of the after funnel. This was called the "Chicago Piano" and in the first raids it fired away with great gusto. Ships are designed to withstand the strains of gun firing, but the ship should be in the water. The effect of the Chicago Piano blasting away with the ship suspended in the air was memorable. It was as if a great hammer was pounding on her and everything was moving. It was hastily decided to lift the pom-pom to a secure base on the dockside. I was appointed officer of quarters for the pom-pom, which looked larger on the shore than it did on the ship. The crew were all permanent force sailors, professionals. The captain of the gun was a large Irish, red-headed, three-badge killick (leading seaman) who had been in a landing party near Manchester in the British General Strike in the 1920s. He told me how they had done their duty as required, but had made good friends with the strikers and had ended up playing football with them. We spent most of the day sitting at the gun, spinning yarns and keeping a special lookout at breakfast, dinner and supper times. It seemed to be the same German who came at meal times. He would shut off his engine, we thought, glide over the hill and drop his bombs. He seemed always to take us by surprise and we opened fire at him generally when he was rapidly getting out of range. One fine day though, a plane suddenly appeared over the hill, we were ready and opened fire. It was RAF and we slightly damaged a wing, much to the RAF's displeasure.

Most German bombs didn't do much damage, but a tanker undergoing repair nearby was hit, set on fire and sank. Her third officer was a friend of mine from the Seamark Club. He was in his bath and later claimed that when the bomb exploded he was blown out of the bath in a bathtub-shaped lump of water, landing unhurt. The oil which spilt in the water started burning and the fires were drifting under the jetties. We watched with interest to see if the jetties would burn but the fires flickered out. The crew of the ship being repaired next to us was Chinese. They moved into a large air raid shelter nearby and rarely came out. It made sense, not being their war. I have a vivid imagination and thought of a bomb landing by the drydock

TRIBAL CLASS DESTROYER

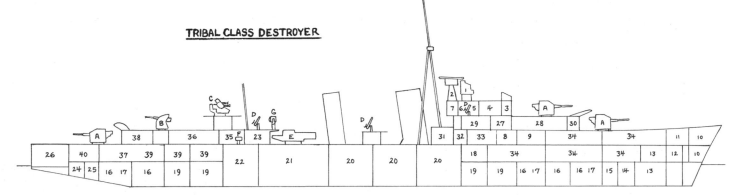

ARMAMENT

A 3 TWIN 4.7-INCH LOW-ANGLE GUNS (3×2)
B 1 TWIN 4-INCH HIGH-ANGLE GUN (1×2)
C 1 QUADRUPLE 2 POUNDER POM-POM (1×4)
D 6 SINGLE 20MM OERLIKONS
E 1 QUADRUPLE 21-INCH TORPEDO TUBES (1×4)
F 2 DEPTH CHARGE THROWERS
G 1 SEARCHLIGHT

BRIDGE STRUCTURE

1 DIRECTOR
2 RANGEFINDER
3 WHEELHOUSE
4 PLOT
5 CHART HOUSE
6 CAPTAIN'S SEA CABIN
7 RADAR OFFICE
8 RADIO OFFICE
9 TRANSMITTING STATION TO GUNS

HULL

10 FORE PEAK
11 LAMP & PAINT ROOM
12 CABLE LOCKER
13 CENTRAL STORE
14 PROVISION ROOM
15 COOL ROOM
16 MAGAZINE
17 SHELL ROOM
18 LOW POWER ROOM
19 OIL FUEL
20 BOILER ROOM
21 ENGINE ROOM
22 GEARING ROOM
23 ENGINEER'S WORKSHOP
24 SPIRIT ROOM
25 WARDROOM STORE
26 TILLER FLAT

PERSONNEL

27 CHIEF PETTY OFFICERS' MESS
28 PETTY OFFICERS' MESS
29 ENGINE ROOM ARTIFICERS' MESS
30 STORE
31 GALLEY
32 FOOD PREPARATION ROOM
33 WASHPLACE & HEADS
34 CREW SPACE
35 SICK BAY
36 CAPTAIN'S QUARTERS
37 WARD ROOM
38 OFFICER'S GALLEY
39 OFFICERS CABINS
40 STEWARDS' MESS

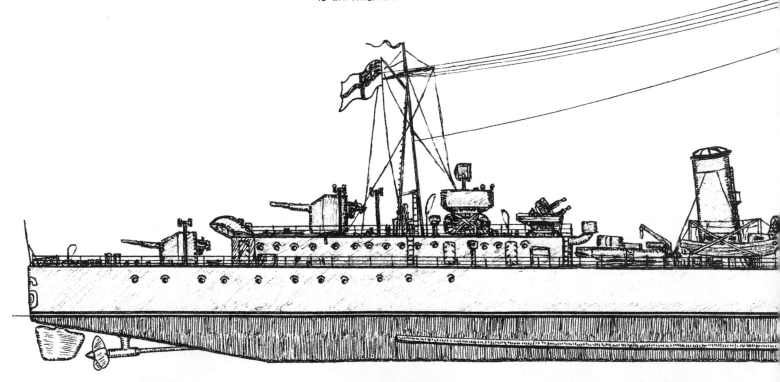

TRIBAL CLASS DESTROYER
HMS MATABELE

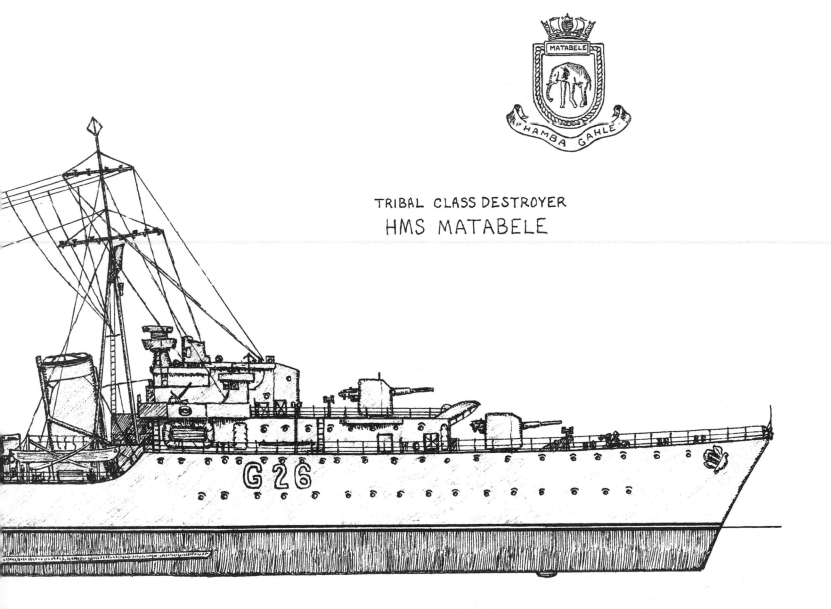

door, opening it and letting the harbour flood in through the holes in the ship.

My gun started getting daily visits from a shipyard electrician. He would tell the men we were bound to be defeated. Germany and Russia were allies and there was no hope for us. He praised the Russians and lauded German efficiency. The captain of the gun and the crew got the same looks on their faces that the picket boat's crew had in Freetown when the Italians laughed and jeered at us. All the time the news was getting worse, and we didn't need anyone telling us we would lose the war. Anyone could see that Britain was far from perfect, but even so we were better than Germany or Russia with their totalitarian governments. Later history has shown us that we could never have imagined just how much better we were.

I kept wondering if perhaps I felt too strongly about the electrician, but finally I went to the first lieutenant and told him about this man. Events moved swiftly. The police arrested him and he appeared in court a few days later. I had to testify to a group of magistrates and he was sentenced to five years in prison. As he was led away he pushed towards me and said in a clear voice, "I'll get you one of these days." Britain had suffered years of dreadful depression and people had been terribly hurt. Was he just letting off steam and had my reaction been too extreme? On several evenings we watched Plymouth being bombed. The gunfire, bombs and searchlights made quite a display and I tried not to think that what I was watching was a battle in which mostly innocent people, older folk, women and children were being killed.

France had collapsed and signs appeared all over Falmouth in French appealing for Frenchmen to follow the Cross of Lorraine and join the Free French under Colonel Charles de Gaulle. A party from *Matabele* had been ordered to take over a French navy escort, *Commandant Domine*, an Elan Class minesweeper, alongside in Falmouth. The gun's crew told me that the ship was filthy, discipline had broken down, most of the men had pointed knives (forbidden in the RN) in their lockers, and they had broken into their wine store and were totally drunk when they were escorted out of the dockyard, some of them in wheelbarrows.

Some days later a number of our officers were invited on board *Commandant Domine* for a little spin around the harbour. Free French officers and men had taken over. The ship now was reasonably clean and we were treated in a most friendly manner. The ship didn't have a wheel such as we had. They steered by a series of buttons which would put the rudder over to the desired degree. What a heartbreaking situation for those officers and men, to abandon their country for an unknown period of time, not to see their wives, children, mothers and fathers. I would not want to be so tested. One in every four young Frenchmen had been killed in World War One, the cream of the population. Their between-wars governments often were corrupt and confused.

Convoys were now going up and down the English Channel. They were escorted by whatever vessels could be provided, armed with machine guns and towed barrage balloons. One of these little ships came into Falmouth.

Aboard was a young sub-lieutenant RNR, an old Conway, a Canadian with a Distinguished Service Cross already, named Skinny Hayes. What fine company he was. He was just the same then as he is at the time of writing, an excellent officer and a fine seaman. We had a pleasant run ashore and then I suppose he sailed on another Channel run.

Matabele was short-handed and groups of new men arrived. They turned out to be H.O.s, Hostilities Only, and the permanent force hands were rude and bitter towards them, scornful of their supposed ignorance of the service. "Effing H.O.s! We don't need no H.O.'s on board 'ere. H.O.s ain't welcome!" What remarkable people we are! Here we had fine young men with no pretence of knowledge or skill in the arts of the seaman, but who had volunteered for the RN, many of them well educated and with the common ideal of wishing to serve their country. And then the permanent force chaps telling them they didn't want them in their mess and making fun of them! After a few days everyone settled down, tempers improved, bewilderment lessened and a ship's company began to take shape.

The wardroom officers were not madly happy with the new captain. The previous one had been a natural for the "boats," as destroyers were termed. He had no big ship nonsense about him and conducted affairs informally. Some officers recalled the time when *Matabele* was anchored off Lyness in Scapa Flow and the wardroom was invited to a party in another Tribal. When the party was over the captain said not to bother signalling for their boat to pick them up. Instead they all dived off the quarterdeck in their mess undress and swam back to *Matabele*. This was treated as the norm by the *Matabele* gangway staff, the quartermaster at the top of the accommodation ladder calling out to Mr. Kennedy, the Irish gunner, "Please lie off sir, the captain's coming alongside." It was hard to imagine Commander Sherbrooke countenancing such conduct.

Finally the repairs were completed, the drydock flooded and we got under way for Plymouth for storing up. On Sunday morning in Plymouth the captain asked me if I would like to attend church in the dockyard with him. I said I would very much like to so we went ashore in full dress with walking canes. His cane was taller than mine and had a large silver head on it. What a beautiful morning it was. The sky was blue with fluffy white clouds and a gentle breeze cooled us from the warm sun. In many apples there lurks a worm. A noise rather like a kettle drum made us look heavenwards to behold a busy little German plane shooting down barrage balloons. We stopped. Rat-a-tat-tat went the plane and down came the balloon, then on to the next balloon.

"My, how clever, isn't this interesting?" said the captain. "I imagine that when he finishes we will be treated to dive bombers." So we strolled back to our ship, where the guns were all manned, but the bombers didn't come that time.

The bombers came a few nights later when I went to a cinema. We were told to remain there until the raid was over, not an encouraging prospect as on some recent nights the customers had spent the whole night lying on the floor. On my way back to the ship, another raid began and a string of bombs fell nearby, causing everyone to run. I ran right into a deep hole, which, I was sure, indicated to everyone that I had lost my cool. To my relief no one laughed at me or at anything, each person being preoccupied with his or her own safety. My jacket and trousers were a bit dirty from the tumble but that was all.

It was lovely summer weather when we sailed for Scapa via the Minches – that is, up the Irish Sea and the west coast of Scotland. One afternoon when we were by the famous little Hebridean islands of Eigg, Rum and Muck, I was on the bridge and the captain told me to work out Zigzag Number whatever from the Zigzag Book. I awoke as from a dream, said, "Aye aye, sir," and having never worked out one before, I did it wrong. I was amazed that no one checked my work and horrified as I could see our mean line of advance would take us into the heart of the Highlands. I told the captain what I had done and what the right courses and times of turning should be. He did not appear upset, but it was a good lesson to me to check and double check my own work.

One of my duties was that of "tanky" to the navigator and that involved keeping all our charts up to date with the Admiralty Notices to Mariners. There were lots of notices involving marking where ships had been sunk, the location of swept channels, changes in navigation marks and signals and so on. I was assisted by an HO sailor, a young Anglo-Indian, Alderton, who had been a commercial artist in London. He was patient and helpful with me and gave me all sorts of pointers about sketching which I appreciated greatly.

I also acted as paymaster for the ship, collected the pay and making up the pay for the ship's company. I divided it all up into pounds, shillings and pence, counted it all again and paid everybody the correct change for whatever their pay was, say, six shillings, four pence a week, or four pence ha'penny. All this I sorted out in the small ship's office. The men lined up, came to my little table one by one, and put their hat, right side up, on the table. I then would put their pay on top of the hat. I have heard of men's pay being blown away by the wind. Thank God it never happened with me.

Another duty was reading Admiralty Fleet Orders and picking out the ones relevant to *Matabele*. One confidential order was to the effect that too many commanding officers were going down with their ships. It was not to be felt that to be sunk was a disgrace. Commanding officers took a long time to train and could not be as easily replaced as a ship; therefore, this practice was to cease. Later when HMCS *Ottawa* was sunk, I think our captain thought he had failed and made no effort to save himself. It was a point of honour which was wrong.

Soon we saw the Old Man of Hoy, a familiar landmark in the Orkneys, and we came to a buoy off Lyness. Although the Tribals were among the most modern of British destroyers, they were crowded and the midshipman had a chest in the officers' cabin flat and slung his hammock under the ladder and over the fuel tanks and magazines. For me the hammock was the most comfortable bed, especially in rough weather. Nothing could be more luxurious no matter what the weather or the state of the sea.

Speaking of hammocks, one night in Falmouth the wardroom had a party. Because of my age I was not invited, so I got in my hammock and had just drifted into sleep when, to my horror, a lot of the ladies came down my ladder somewhat tiddly to see the middy in his hammock. They were all whispering and being silly so I pretended to be sleeping. I am not as cute now as I used to be.

Before the war each Tribal had carried a number of marines. Probably a platoon was distributed to a flotilla. The first lieutenant said it was dreadful having these fellows on board, as they were so different from the sailors. For one thing, their heavy boots stomping about the steel decks didn't seem right, and whenever they came to the wardroom they left their caps or helmets on, stomped their feet and saluted the way they salute in the open air. Generally they were an upsetting element in the ship. Good sense prevailed and they were withdrawn and sent back to bigger ships. Marines were sworn men; that, is they had sworn an oath of allegiance.

The Royal Navy, officers and men, were not required to take the oath. If a marine mutinied it was mortally serious, whereas if naval people changed allegiance, as they once did, they were not necessarily hanged. As a punishment for changing allegiance once long ago, naval officers were not allowed to trice up their swords to the sword belts and they still must carry them or just drag them behind. All these different practices add to the interest of life and make one feel rather special in the service.

An interesting feature of our flotilla was that officers and men often received lovely gifts of candy bars, cigarettes, books, woollen mittens, scarves, sweaters, writing paper and so on from a lady in New York, the widow of a naval officer who had commanded an American destroyer in European waters during the First World War. I think we called her Auntie May. It certainly was an act of wonderful compassion and friendship and was greatly admired and appreciated by us all.

Lieutenant Commander Knowling, Number One, the first lieutenant, who had been so long in China, regaled us with stories of the barges laden with "night soil" from Shanghai drifting slowly by his ship as they breakfasted. A hideous cough was referred to as the "Chinese National Anthem." He liked the Chinese people but did not like the Japanese at all. An officer's wife surprised me one evening in the wardroom by showing me Chinese coins of different denominations with various forms of sexual intercourse moulded on them. I was embarrassed, not out of prudishness, but because I had no idea what reaction she would consider appropriate.

Knowling was appointed in command of a destroyer and Lieutenant Brittain took over as Number One. Brittain was not lighthearted; in fact he was very serious. One day he told me to supervise the rum issue. I went with the coxswain to the Spirit Room for the pump-up, the drawing of the rum. When we were setting up the rum for distribution to the cooks of the messes, the coxswain poured a tot in a copper measure and said, "Here is your tot, sir." I was an officer and under-age so I declined but he explained that this was the custom. So down the hatch went a 100 proof, two-ounce shot. How stupid can one be! Anyway the rum issue started and along came Number One to ask me how it was going. I replied, trying to inhale as I spoke. I did not fool him I am sure, but he made some pleasant comment and moved on. I felt I had let him down and my heart still aches when I think that when *Matabele* was sunk off North Cape a few months after I left, his body was one of the few recovered. He had frozen, doubled up in rigor mortis and had to be committed to the deep in that position.

The engineer officer was an older lieutenant commander. He was not a handsome man and had no wife, nor did he have any relations that we knew of. When he went on leave he went to London and stayed at his club, the Owls' Club. Every day, even in the most terrible weather, before lunch he would have a large gin which he insisted be brought to him on a silver salver. One awful noon the ship "hit a milestone" and the steward who was bringing Chief his gin was pitched to the deck and broke his wrist. The captain told Chief that the salver was to be dispensed with in heavy weather. Why would this shy, quiet, intelligent, thoughtful, kind gentleman have such a quirk?

The sub-lieutenant was interesting. He was ex-merchant service and was a grandson of the man who supervised the design and building of the Forth Bridge. Sub also was a bad-tempered autocrat. Breakfast in an RN wardroom is a sombre affair with people not speaking, just eating and reading the paper or whatever. Subby used breakfast to raise Cain with the quartermaster or some other rating who had incurred his displeasure. Finally, Brittain told him to smarten up and not do such things in the wardroom.

Another denizen was Father somebody, the chaplain, who had been a sort of Anglican Trappist Monk. They never, or rarely, spoke in his monastery. He never stopped talking in our ship and did rather inappropriate things, such as putting jam on the toilet seat in the officers' heads. Writing this, it is hard to believe that this happened. Often we were watch on watch, that is, four hours on, four hours off and trying to perform our ship's duties as well. He was a well meaning man and likeable, but he had made a habit of sitting very, very close to me on the fire stool or the settee. I mentioned this to Number One and the practice ceased.

The captain and the gunner were in their early forties. Most of the other officers were from 26 down to 19, me. Being endlessly at sea with not much happening makes for boredom and people do stupid things for the sake of variety. Bowel movements occupy one's thoughts from time to time, but being stuck on a cold, wet, windswept bridge for long hours concentrates one's mind on this subject. The gunnery officer invented a medal called the George Medal, before the real George Medal was invented. Our GM normally hung on a bulkhead in the wardroom. It was a saucer-sized piece of wood covered with silver paper and with a neck ribbon of Admiralty red tape. The idea was that when one had a particularly satisfying movement, or George, one would quietly show gratitude by wearing the George Medal.

The torpedo gunner was Mr. Kennedy, who originated in Southern Ireland and a more loyal or steadfast officer could not be found. I understand that the Irish Free State, which was neutral in the war, provided more people on a per capita basis for the armed forces of the Empire than any of the dominions.

The navigator lived a life of frustration because of the perpetual clouds, fog and poor visibility that prevented him from taking sights. For weeks on end it seemed that we depended on our ARL Plotting Table (Admiralty Research Laboratory) to plot our course and speed. Pilot then made adjustments for wind and currents which probably were only vaguely correct. Most of the time the errors must have cancelled each other because we often ended up where we aimed.

The navigator was an RNVR officer who, I think, was becoming a barrister in London and he had a serious nature. Often he would invite me to his cabin, where he would play various composers on his wind-up phonograph, particularly Beethoven, explaining various aspects of the symphony or composition. I used to say how I admired Wagner and this upset him. He explained that as I grew older I would find Beethoven much more satisfying. He, of course, was right, but somehow for me, under 20, the great drama of storms and battles that I was living was close to being Wagnerian. He used to get very annoyed over things that I would have thought funny. For example, he indicated that he was to be the first for a bath when we got into harbour. The gunnery officer decided to have a quick bath before Pilot got down from the bridge. Pilot was beside himself and would hardly speak to Guns for days. Being so tired and cold for so long in such close quarters does put people's nerves on edge, and we had to be extra careful in these conditions to avoid upsetting each other.

When we got to port, alongside, at a buoy or anchored, we felt we could relax. The men would go ashore to the wet canteen and drink beer, and the officers would let their hair down in the wardroom, generally with a good dinner with lots to drink. Then would follow singing bawdy and other songs. In *Matabele's* wardroom, Peter Dawson's songs, patriotic, Kiplingesque, Imperial, sentimental, historical, were very popular and I suppose jingoistic. By this time the British were alone against the might of Germany, almost totally unprepared against a well prepared and absolutely merciless enemy. It is amazing how songs can keep one's spirits up.

In case a midshipman seemed to lack humility, a captain might correct this. One fine bright day after breakfast I was on the upper deck and met my captain having a stroll. I saluted and cheerfully said, "Good morning, sir."

"What do you think you are, a weather prophet!?" said he. "It is up to your captain to decide whether it is a good morning or not!" Humbled, I snuck away, tail between my legs.

Many of our patrols took us out into the Atlantic west of Ireland and the Bay of Biscay. This is what was referred to in times past as the Western Ocean and it has its own special qualities. These set it apart from the North Atlantic, that is, the stretch from the Orkneys to the Faeroes to Iceland to Greenland to Newfoundland, which often is perfectly hellish. The Western Ocean, while often quite rough, is blessed by the better parts of the Gulf Stream and is not bitterly cold. If it was not so rough that spray was coming over the bridge, the dark nights when the clouds occasionally revealed the moonlight or bright stars could be quite heavenly. At that time I was steeped in Joseph Conrad's *Mirror of the Sea* and was able to experience myself many of his spellbinding descriptions of the sea and ships. That little book was almost like a bible to me.

Sometimes we were by ourselves but often we were part of the screen for battleships and battle cruisers. This would have been one of the last times in maritime history when one could see a line of five or six battleships and battle cruisers steaming along in readiness for battle. North of Iceland we were screening *Nelson* or *Rodney;* it was a beautiful day for once, the sky was clear and the sea was like a sheet of glass. I was looking at this huge ship through my binoculars when I saw a little figure going along the forecastle towards the bull ring in the bow. When he was level with the forward anchor on the starboard side, he jumped over the guard rail and landed in the water with a little splash. We were the closest destroyer and our officer of the watch altered course toward the spot where he jumped, increased speed and called the captain. Shortly we were over the spot. It was unmistakable because his cap was floating there. We slowed right down, looking into the clear water, but nothing was to be seen.

Several times we went over to the Norwegian coast. It was surprising to still see the Norwegian vessels, like small "dragon ships," unique with their peaked bow and stern, fishing as usual even though their country was occupied by the Germans. Most times we were pattern-bombed by the Germans and fired back. They didn't hit us nor we them. The captain gave me a movie camera to take pictures of action. I am ashamed to admit that I couldn't get the thing to work and no one knew enough about it to help me. I also found another thing that I didn't know how to operate – a portable rangefinder. The captain said, "Snotty, give me a range of that ship," a neutral Swede, so I got the portable rangefinder but couldn't see one thing through the eyepieces. Later I discovered that I had not removed the spray covers over the lenses. With such officers as I, who needs enemies?

Some places we went were interesting, but little known. Several times the captain asked me to make a drawing of a seascape from such and such a bearing and submitted them to the Admiralty.

Keeping station in destroyers is considered important. In those days without radar there was a little visual station keeper, a tiny rangefinder in which one set the mast height of the ship you were keeping station on and then lined up two images. On our bridge was fitted a large metal box with dials, handles and pushes, labelled "Mountbatten Station Keeper." I asked Commander Sherbrooke about it and was told that we were never to use it. It was an invention of Commander Lord Louis Mountbatten and I became aware that our captain was not a fan of Mountbatten or his father, Prince Louis of Battenburg.

On a couple of occasions we left Scapa with some of our flotilla, *Maori, Punjabi, Mashona* and *Ashanti,* and headed for the Shetland Islands at 25 knots. Off Lerwick we would increase speed to 30 knots or so and head for Norway. Here, at dusk, we intercepted German convoys of four or five ships with a small escort, sank them all by gunfire and roared back to the Shetlands. Apart from some wild machine gun fire and a few inaccurate salvoes from a small gun in the escorting armed trawler, there was little resistance. The five or six ships caught fire and sank as we rushed by. It all seemed too easy and I wondered if we might run into a big surprise. But we didn't. I am ashamed to say that in my humble opinion, this is war at its best, where the enemy is either unaware of his fate or unable to fire back. It was also the favourite form of war for the Germans at sea, in the air and on land.

We were one of the first RN ships to pop in to the Faeroe Islands. As we approached Thorshavn there was a crack and a whistle hum as someone with a rifle fired at us from a cliff top. The captain seemed to think this was quite normal and we pressed on unperturbed to deliver documents to a Royal Marine officer there.

German merchant men were still coming from Archangel so one of our forays was towards North Cape, Norway, via Iceland and Jan Mayen Land. The latter is east of northern Greenland and must be one of the most desolate places in the world. We never did see Jan Mayen, which was a disappointment to my Wagnerian mind, as surely it would be the resting place of the Valkyries or even the three dread spinners of fate of Viking lore. We did not see any German ships that time either. Sometimes German Focke-Wulf Condors would see us though, large planes of very long range used for reconnaissance. Once in daylight sparkling flares came down from the dark, overcast sky. "What do you think that was?" asked a fellow Tribal. "Angels' cigarette butts," replied our captain.

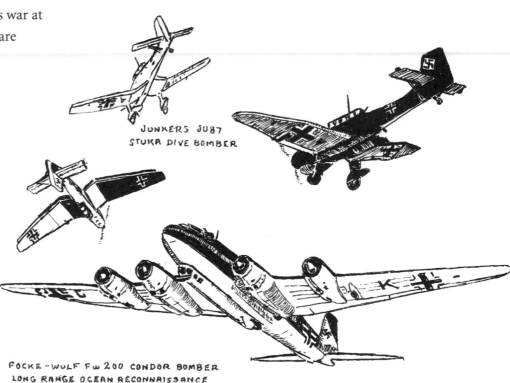

JUNKERS JU87
STUKA DIVE BOMBER

FOCKE-WULF FW 200 CONDOR BOMBER
LONG RANGE OCEAN RECONNAISSANCE

Focke-Wulf Condors were a good indication of trouble brewing, as they could home other aircraft, submarines or warships on us, and it was bad luck for the German navy that Mr. Goering did not use them more for naval reconnaissance than he did. Sometimes they would fly around us for hours, out of range of our guns. One captain is said to have told the signalman to flash at such a plane in Morse, "Please fly the other way round, you are making me dizzy." To everyone's astonishment he turned around just as asked.

There were two Tribal flotillas, ours and the one led by the famous *Cossack,* which had boarded the German merchantman *Altmark* in Norwegian waters and released all the British prisoners captured when *Graf Spee* sank our merchantmen. *Cossack's* captain was a red-faced, ferocious gentleman, Captain Vian. He came to inspect *Matabele* and first met all the officers.

"Where are you from?" he said to me.

"From Canada, sir," said I.

"I can tell that" he growled. "I mean what ship?"

"*Renown,*" I replied. That is my account of meeting this famous hero.

Most of the Tribals had recognition by their mother tribes. *Matabele* had a large, solid silver statue of the King of the Matabele for the centrepiece of the wardroom table when dining. On the bulkhead was a plate to which was secured a solid silver war club and a silver shield. *Maori* had Maori totem poles, one on either side of the after end of the after canopy. The ships' badges were appropriate to the tribe. Ours, for example, was an elephant.

I should mention the food in *Matabele.* The officers' cook had been chef to an Irish aristocrat and now and again we were treated to aristocratic culinary delights. Every night the captain, who usually ate his lunch and dinner in the wardroom, and sat at the head of the table, would appear in a sort of evening dress. This was a wing collar and bow tie with his ordinary jacket. He never suggested that we barbarians follow his example. The first lieutenant, navigator, gunnery officer and a few others pointedly wore turtleneck sweaters with their jackets. Nothing was ever said but there was a strong undercurrent of disapproval on both sides. One philosophy was that destroyers were the "boats" and because of the discomfort, a certain casualness in dress and discipline should be tolerated. The other philosophy was that the customs of the service should be strictly observed in all ships, large and small. I always wore an ordinary collar and tie with my jacket for dinner and hoped I upset no one.

Our provision ship to Scapa was sunk. For six weeks or so we had no fresh provisions. Officers and men lived on dry provisions, peas, and so on, with canned corned beef from Argentina. One of the cooks said that there were 365 different recipes to make corned beef interesting. Being a gannet I didn't mind our restricted diet. When everyone was closed up at action stations for a long time and over a meal hour, often with the weather cold, rough and wet, the cooks would win our hearts with mugs of soup and thick sandwiches of butter and corned beef. In *Matabele* we never had fresh milk, except in harbours in the mainland. It was always condensed milk. We were required to take a vitamin pill every day.

I had joined *Matabele* in July 1940, and in December 1940 my small ship time was complete. Commander Sherbrooke said in my report that I was diplomatic, bright, cheerful and a born seaman. He was a fine officer and a very cool customer, as he later proved by winning the Victoria Cross in HMS *Onslow* in December 1942 fighting the more powerful German warships *Lutzow* and *Admiral Hipper* in what became known as the Battle of the Barents Sea. He continued to command his flotilla in battle even when his eye was shot out, keeping the Germans at bay all afternoon. I was sorry indeed to leave this ship. I liked everyone and would not have minded staying there. My big ship, HMS *Renown*, was serving in the Mediterranean and I was in Scapa so it was only sensible that I go to another capital ship that had just arrived there, HMS *Hood*.

Matabele was sunk with all hands off North Cape a few months later. The British film *In Which We Serve* with Noel Coward seemed too upright to be true, but I can vouch for the authenticity of that ship and the experiences and the types and social mores of the officers and men, with their patience, decency, quiet courage, burning love of country and belief in the justice of their cause.

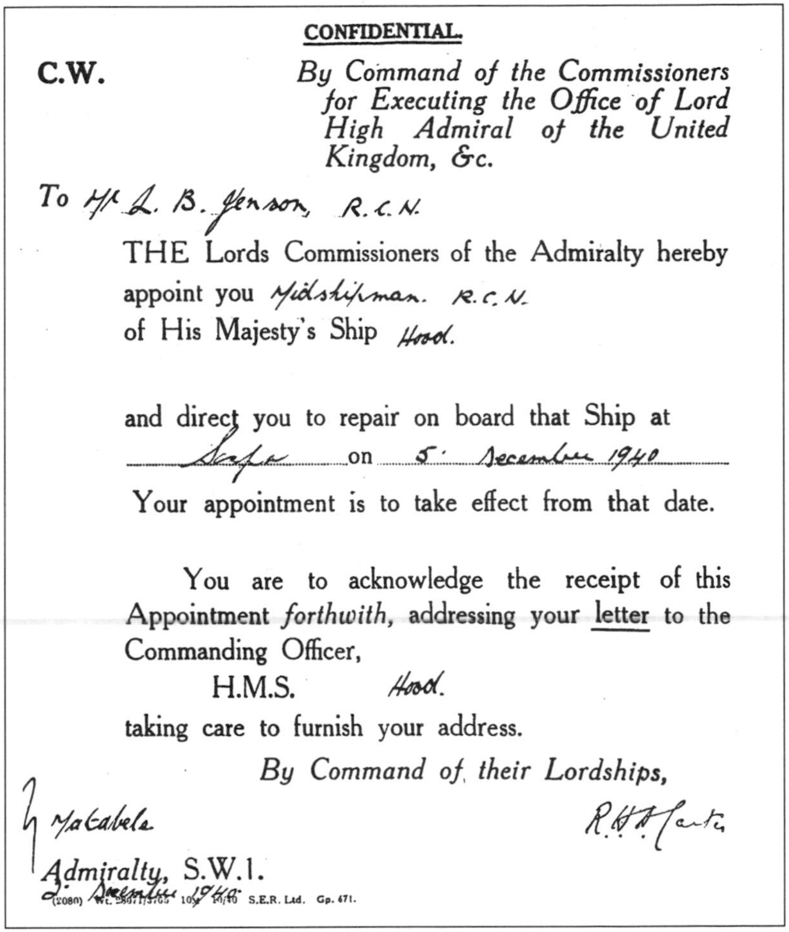

CONFIDENTIAL.

C.W.

By Command of the Commissioners for Executing the Office of Lord High Admiral of the United Kingdom, &c.

To *Mr L. B. Jenson, R.C.N.*

THE Lords Commissioners of the Admiralty hereby appoint you *Midshipman. R.C.N.* of His Majesty's Ship *Hood.*

and direct you to repair on board that Ship at *Scapa* on *5. December 1940*
Your appointment is to take effect from that date.

You are to acknowledge the receipt of this Appointment *forthwith*, addressing your <u>letter</u> to the Commanding Officer,
H.M.S. *Hood.*
taking care to furnish your address.
By Command of their Lordships,

R.H.A. Carter

Matabele

Admiralty, S.W.1.
2. December 1940
(2080) Wt. 360/5705 10 50/40 S.E.R. Ltd. Gp. 671.

HMS "Matabele" October, 1940, East of Iceland

Sub. Lt. Mackenzie RCNVR, Myself,

Lt. R. Britten R.N. (First Lieut.)

5

Big ship time

HMS *Hood*, although built during the First World War, still was the largest battle cruiser in the world. She had beautiful lines and was a happy ship, the pride of the Royal Navy and the British people. In the 1930s the Fleet mutinied over pay reductions. When *Hood* was ordered to sea, midshipmen lit the boilers and weighed anchor. The men, saying nothing, let go the anchors again and the ship had to stop. One of our officers, the snotties' nurse, who had been there, told us it was a dreadful experience. An officer would order a man to do something and the man, saying nothing, would turn his back and walk away. When the affair was settled, Commander Rory O'Connor, a huge Irishman, was appointed to *Hood* as executive officer. He concentrated on the Divisional System, the essence of which is that every man in a ship has a division and a divisional officer. It is the duty of this officer to know his men in detail, to be their friend (but not their pal). The result is that one generally has a contented and efficient ship.

When I joined, *Hood* had just arrived from the Mediterranean, where she had taken part in the destruction of the Vichy French naval ships at Mers el Kabir, Oran, Algeria. This was sad and no one wanted to talk about this terrible affair. Some of the midshipmen who were junior to me were envious of people who had seen action and said they hoped that soon we would see some real action. My view was and is that it isn't an experience any sane person should seek. Our "nurse" overheard the conversation and interjected, "My young friends. You have no idea of what you are talking about. Action means seeing your friends lying dead and wounded in pools of blood. Who would ever wish to see such a thing?" The worst of this exchange was that almost all of them, including the "nurse" himself, would suffer a fate far worse than he had described.

I was astonished at the treatment received by those of us who had just arrived from destroyers to complete our big ship time. We were excused watchkeeping, boat work or any other duties. Every consideration was given to perfecting us in our knowledge of seamanship, gunnery, torpedo, navigation, pilotage, engineering and ship construction. Our journals were of importance in our qualifying for sub-lieutenant and mine still was also my hobby. In addition, I had begun a set of elaborate seamanship notes covering the masting and rigging of capital ships and the organization of evolutions.

One of the first *Hood* stories I heard was rather similar to that of the *Matabele* officers swimming back to their ship. During the Spanish Civil War *Hood* was lying at anchor off Gibraltar. Anchored nearby was a German cruiser. After a football game with German officers, *Hood's* officers were entertained aboard the cruiser. When it was time to go, the senior *Hood* officer thanked everyone, and said, "Come on chaps," and one by one they dived off the quarterdeck to swim back to their ship. The last officer to go overheard a German scornfully say to another, "These British officers are just overgrown schoolboys."

The employment of capital ships must not have been easy for the Admiralty. Our sole object in being in Scapa Flow was to take on the German Fleet, such as it was. We were kept busy covering convoys which we never saw. Scapa was such a lonely and isolated spot, a wonderful harbour surrounded by hilly islands, large and small, which would have presented a bleak and melancholy appearance to most normal people. I was the exception in liking the place. For me, it was ideal for peace and reflection and I used to enjoy walking up and down the long quarterdeck, especially in the evenings. The facilities ashore for the men consisted of a wet canteen where some would drink too much. Sometimes there were concerts but generally these were in the nature of string quartets and were poorly attended.

Early in 1941, HMS *Hood* went to Rosyth, where extensive changes were made. Midshipmen were not privy to the details of the dockyard work done, but it seemed to us that RDF (radio direction finding) was being fitted high on our masts and bridge. I also thought that armour plate was being removed from the deck under the two after 15-inch turrets. When the turrets were trained fore and aft, the lightened armour would be covered by the turret if an armour piercing bomb were dropped on us. Reducing top weight was necessary to compensate for heavy new electronic sets and controls being fitted at a higher level, for example on the bridge.

I don't think there was a great effort to make watertight the various bulkheads at every level, which since 1920 had been penetrated for new electrical leads and so on and were full of holes. In fact, the whole ship was full of little faults that compromised safety and which had accumulated over many years. There were rust holes and patches of endless coats of paint, as well as great lengths of lead-covered electrical cable, much of which was redundant and extremely heavy. It would have been a waste of time and effort to correct all the things which were wrong and basically the ship was about as safe and as efficient as the most modern battleship or battle cruiser.

We midshipmen had the creeps when someone pointed out the cabin in which a lieutenant commander had been confined while awaiting court martial for a homosexual act. The officer sentry had quietly handed the accused his revolver and within a few minutes the poor man, seated in his deck chair, blew his brains out.

The advent of RDF, which became known as radar, was one of the most significant advances in the history of marine technology. Until this time, fog, rain, snow, smoke or darkness blinded a ship, particularly during war when ships were blacked out and navigation marks unlighted. Fog with icebergs in the northwest Atlantic was a major non-military danger. Ships in company in fog used to trail fog buoys, sound their sirens and post special lookouts. Ships at anchor rang their bells at regular intervals. Navigation in fog in narrow waters often depended on listening and timing the echoes of one's sirens from the cliffs. Hair-raising! On one occasion in *Hood* we had poked into a fjord in southeast Iceland. Dense fog settled on us and then we were assailed with loud bangs at a close range. It turned out to be a thunderstorm on top of the fog, but certainly sounded like heavy guns being fired. I believe the radar fitted in *Hood* was designed not for navigation but for gunnery purposes. In any case, it was top secret and we midshipmen were told nothing of it.

When *Hood* was in drydock we were obliged to use the heads or lavatories ashore. It was winter and these were unheated, primitive affairs with warnings to use paper only and not cotton wool or rags. They also had notices about promptly reporting venereal disease to medical authorities.

I managed to contract a very bad cold and fever and the doctor sent me off to the Gleneagles Hotel by the famous Scottish golf course. The hotel had been set up as a hospital for air raid victims from Edinburgh, but there were none there, only two Canadians, an army captain who later died of influenza and myself. A doctor saw me, I was treated with aspirin and fruit drinks and in two days I felt much improved. I became worried that *Hood* would sail without me and tried to get a doctor to release me. Finally a charming young nurse took the responsibility to let me go. Before I finally went I managed to have a good look at Dunfermline, the ancient seat of Scottish kings.

When I got back to *Hood*, she was out of drydock and taking stores and provisions on board. Finally, one nice bright sunny day we ammunitioned ship from lighters alongside. My position was on the quarterdeck looking over the loading of 15-inch shells in the after magazine. Seeing these huge shells being hoisted aboard and then lowered down the hatches into the shell room at the very bottom of the ship was impressive. They were about a yard long and weighed half a ton. With the correct amount of propellant which was packed in silk bags, our guns could fire these shells a good 20 miles. Shells were of various types: armour piercing (AP), semi-armour piercing (SAP), high explosive (HE) and shrapnel. A shell at deck level was about to be lowered when it slipped out of the jaws of the hoist and fell 40 or more feet, landing with hideous clangs on the steel deck. The first question was did it hit anybody?

BATTLE CRUISER
HMS HOOD

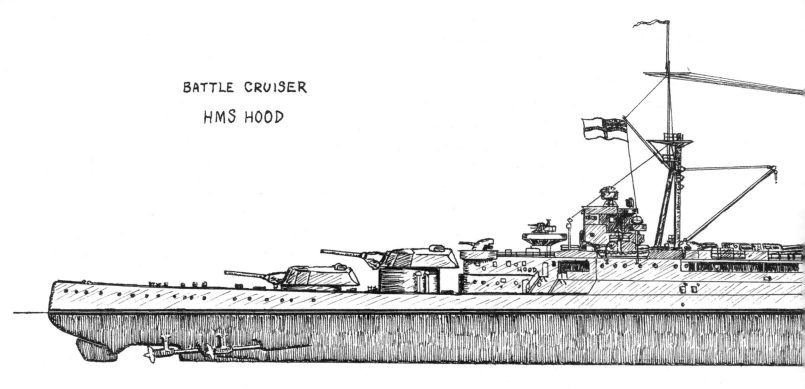

By some act of fate, no one was close. Second question, was the shell damaged? The answer was no and the deck was not even marked.

The silk bags of propellant were treated with the utmost respect. No matches or lighters were allowed in their vicinity and the men handling the charges wore special clothing and felt boots which could not cause sparks. The old saying was that ammunition is perfectly safe until you forget that it is dangerous. I think all this is a good illustration of the importance of every single person in a ship's company, regardless of rank. Even a careless boy seaman can damage or destroy a ship, and the efficiency of all hands is the business of everybody. When action is joined we are all in it together; there is no other place to go or to hide.

Soon we were back in Scapa Flow. Spring was coming and some days were heavenly. My group of midshipmen were studying night and day. I was busy with my journal and preparing my seamanship notes. These notes were not required but I had in mind that writing down all the seamanship matters that were unique to big ships would improve my own understanding and also be a record for the future. Seamanship is a wonderfully interesting subject. I

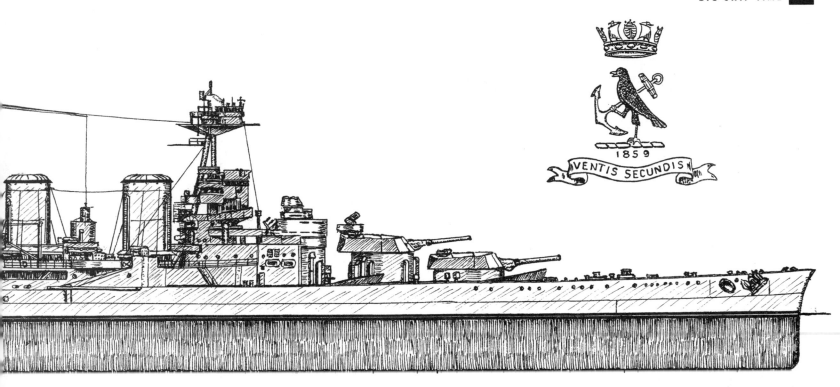

1859

VENTIS SECUNDIS

have seen seamanship and gunnery notes made by some chief and petty officers, fine practical men who also possessed remarkable descriptive and illustrative talents.

One thing about being based in Scapa Flow was that one's ship had to go south to Scotland, at the least, for repairs and for boiler cleaning. Generally we were in Rosyth from time to time for a couple of weeks and that was an opportunity for leave. We also often had leave when proceeding from one appointment to another. Thanks to the Royal Commonwealth Society I stayed with some wonderful people. One such was an elderly lady in Hove whose house was full of flags, ensigns, drums, bugles, swords,

scimitars, daggers, spears, Brown Bess muskets and many other relics of her father's lifetime of service in India. Midshipman Bill Kidd stayed with me and we had great fun in Brighton riding in dodgem cars, but we never succeeded in meeting girls there. Canadians did not have a very good reputation in Brighton at that time, perhaps for good reason. They had smashed up several pubs and restaurants fighting with each other.

On another leave I stayed as a guest of Miss Talbot, the last of the Talbots, at Laycock Abbey. This had been given to the Talbot family by Henry VIII at the dissolution of the monasteries. Miss Talbot possessed an original copy of the Magna Carta, which she treated in a surprisingly casual fashion. Later on, I understand, it was sent to the United States for safekeeping. In the long and dusty passages of the abbey could be seen piles of armour, helmets and weapons of the Civil War.

Miss Talbot did not believe in electricity so at night we moved about the draughty corridors with candles. The BBC news was at eight o'clock in the evening and the butler brought a large battery radio into the hall so that we were kept informed. There was supposed to be a resident ghost who had flung herself from the old hall balcony (which was for musicians) to the stone floor below. The stain from the pool of blood could not be erased, but it was so faint that I could not see it myself.

Most interesting was that Miss Talbot's ancestor, Fox Talbot, who had made the first photographs in England, had left all his boxes and gear lying about. It had never been picked up from where it was laid down 70 years before. It seemed amazing to me at the time that such a thing could happen, but all was not lost: there is now a museum of photography in the vicinity where everything has been preserved.

The bedroom in which I slept was supposed to have been used by Queen Elizabeth I. A toilet, a large bath and a basin had been installed in a nearby room in the late 1800s and these must have been among the first of their kind. The toilet had been designed by Mr. Thomas Crapper. The fittings were of white porcelain, decorated in blue in elabo-

rate detail. I suppose the abbey was heated only by open fireplaces, and there sometimes was a nice open fire in the great hall. Generally, however, it was cold and warm clothing was appreciated.

I spent most of my time there wandering through the halls gaping at the museum pieces lying around and looking at the venerable old books. Sometimes I wandered into the nearby village, but this was embarrassing because the villagers were unjustifiably respectful to people from the abbey. I would have found it hard to be that way myself.

Another time, my friend Charlie Allen invited me to spend my leave with him and his family in York, where his father taught biology in a high school. He had a charming sister who was training to be a nurse. I was treated just as I would have been at home in Calgary, perhaps even better. We walked the walls of old York and saw the remarkable Shambles. It is a beautiful city, the home of many of my ancestors.

Another memorable leave was with my term mate Dave Darling in Tunbridge Wells. His father had come to England with the Canadian army in 1915 and, of course, served in Flanders. On leave he met and married an English woman and was demobilized in England, where he settled and became successful. He loved Canada still and considered himself a Canadian. They seemed pleased to receive the Canadian papers and magazines which my mother sent to me.

A particularly fine messmate was Charlie Stuart, who must have made more people than myself think of Bonnie Prince Charlie. He played the bagpipes and had a dreamy

Gaelic air about him. His fine appearance, his strong character, his humour, his intelligence and judgement, his love of Scotland and all things Scottish, impressed me so much that I thought he truly was an aristocrat. When he kindly invited a number of us to meet his family, I was rather disappointed to find his home was rather like my own and his father, mother and brother similar to mine. He had been to Helsinki in Finland with his parents and was madly in love with a 13-year-old girl who had moved with her family to Buenos Aires.

Harry Hyndman was a midshipman in *Hood* with me, but one or two terms astern of me. Being from a most distinguished family, he had called on R.B. Bennett, the former prime minister of Canada, who had retired somewhat bitter to England and been made a viscount. Harry mentioned to him that I was serving with him and R.B. remembered my grandfather as a political opponent in Alberta. He asked Harry to invite me to call upon him when I was visiting London. This I did. We drove in his chauffeured car to his home at Juniper Hill, just south of London. The house was beautiful with a large conservatory containing a waterfall that tumbled down a wall of native rocks. What a delightful place in which to meditate, study or reflect, but I would be willing to bet that this never happened. My room was most pleasant, though sterile. What fascinated me was the bidet, next to the toilet; I had never seen such a thing before and would still appreciate a course of instruction in appropriate use of the contraption.

Meals were simple, without liquor, with plain but delicious food. His lady secretary shared the table but did not act as hostess or indeed even say anything. Viscount Bennett spoke of the great services he had done for Calgary, mostly the airport and the Currie Barracks. I had the impression that he was very proud of his accomplishments in Canada. He spoke of my being at the bottom of the ladder but with diligence and care it would be possible to rise to the top. In any case, it was gracious of him to entertain me and I am honoured to have dined with a former prime minister of our country.

I was sorry about the dreadful death of Viscount Bennett a short time later. I understand that his bath was heated by live steam and somehow the poor man was boiled alive in it, like a lobster. He was the ultimate conventional man and I suppose that is why he was elected. His opponent, Mr. King, certainly seemed also to be the ultimate in conventional conduct, except that he really was not. All this leads me to the conclusion that it is impossible for most of us to make valid judgements of history. Our judgements are shaped by our own experiences of the world around us. Events in history are shaped by the experiences of the people at their time. We can only comment, not judge.

Now *Hood* was back in Scapa secured to a buoy off Flotta. The buoy had a telephone connection to the Admiralty, a wonderful development when one considers that only a few years earlier communications at any distance at all were carried on by letter in a frigate or other small fast vessel. The sun was warm and in the evenings one could stroll the quarterdeck in comfort, even smoking a cigar and pretending to be grown up! We midshipmen were approaching our exams in gunnery, torpedo, astronomical navigation, ship construction, seamanship, engineering and last but not least, our journals.

Before the age of photography, it often was imperative to have as exact a description as possible of a place, weapon or whatever might be of importance in deciding upon a course of action. All officers were encouraged to acquire the capability of drawing, painting and writing intelligibly, and this ability was initially measured for the young officer writing and illustrating his journal. There were no rules; photographs, drawings, movie reviews, comments on places, events, history, science, nature, all were acceptable. Journals were reviewed once a month by the captain, giving him an idea of each young officer's views, attitudes and abilities. Young officers were expected to be particularly observant and this contributed to their efficiency as they advanced in rank and played their part in serving the great British Empire. Looking back on that Empire "upon which the sun never set," it was a remarkably peaceful and relatively prosperous Empire, generally fair and just, and advanced the well-being of most of the subjects of the Crown. Unfortunately, it is not that way now.

Each morning at 0900, the ship's companies fell in for Divisions and Prayers. All hands were accounted for, inspected for shaves, haircuts and general neatness and correct dress and then the captain or the commander would discuss what the ship's program would be or just make general announcements. Roman Catholics, generally few in number, were then instructed to fall out and gather at the forward end of the quarterdeck. The remainder of us were ordered to "off caps" and the Padre led us in a psalm, prayers and a hymn. The Royal Marine band played during the inspections and, of course, for the hymns. Divisions concluded with playing the national anthems of any ships of other countries anchored or moored in Scapa Flow. For a time, the national anthems of all the Allies fighting the Germans were played in full before "God Save the King." All officers stood and saluted for these renditions. The renditions became more nominal after a time, only a few bars played before another few bars and so on. Gradually, as our Allies diminished in numbers, the performance times shrank. Eventually, it was back to just "the King." The Royals then marched off to "A Life on the Ocean Wave," back to their ordinary duties in the wardroom and as sentries at keyboards and so on. On a bright sunny morning it would be hard to imagine a more cheerful way to start the day, purified in body and soul. It was nearly as good on any other kind of day. It also was a good time for reflection, if one did not have divisional duties, and those of us facing our examinations for acting sub-lieutenant those lovely Scapa days in April had lots to reflect upon, more than we knew. Failure, and consequently remaining on board for another run, in this case actually would mean death!

The exams were mostly oral and were conducted with the sympathy and understanding of older brothers for younger. The officers examining us wanted us to pass, but had to satisfy themselves that we were fit to pass. What could be more important to the future of our navy in time of peril than our professional ability and knowledge.

Two or three days after the exams concluded, the midshipmen concerned were mustered outside the captain's cabin. It was an exquisite jewel-like Scottish spring day with a gentle wind and the cry of gulls. Eventually, it came my turn to enter. Facing me were not just the captain but the commander and several other officers. The captain read out my marks and smiled. I had done well, and in a sort of dream I shook hands with all these smiling gentlemen. They mentioned in particular my journal with its many illustrations. For that I was awarded 100%, the only one in the fleet.

The last event in my memories of that lovely ship concerns gunnery. Even though my object in being aboard was to finalize my studies for promotion, I had an action station. I was the officer of quarters for the port 4-inch gun batteries. Our secondary armament, the 4-inch guns consisted of separate single mountings. Renown had a different arrangement: the twin 4.7-inch high angle/low angle guns were in barbettes, which were much more sheltered and efficient for the gun crews.

On one particular occasion, the object as I understood it was to fire all the guns, eight 15-inch and the six 4-inch (on the port or starboard side) at the same time, once on the starboard beam and once on the port beam. This took place in the evening when darkness was complete. I do not recollect whether there was a target. No one that I knew of bothered wearing ear plugs, perhaps because they seemed

unmanly, so I suppose many would be as deaf as I am now. The guns did all fire together, producing an immense smothering explosion which sent me sprawling. I was surprised that the flashes were very subdued and not blinding in any way. Our propellants were supposed to be "flashless." The ship did not lurch for either broadside, nor did she fly apart or break down.

One delightful morning the midshipmen who had passed the exams were taken by picket boat to embark in the St. Ninian in Kirkwall, thence to Portsmouth for our sub-lieutenant's courses at the various schools. As Hood receded in the distance we sort of saluted and someone took a photograph. Some midshipmen had not passed and remained on board. Two Canadians were junior midshipmen and, of course, they remained. They were Chris Norman, who was a nephew of Lord Birdwood, and Norman Tachereau Beard, the son of Captain Beard, RCN. Beard had requested to transfer to the Royal Navy, telling the captain of Hood his reason was "the brass in the RCN has their knife in my old man." Norm and Chris were charming young men and I am sure they would have developed into splendid officers.

My journal, and all the other journals, remained in Hood to be returned to Admiralty in due course and retained as secret documents until the conclusion of the war. I also left a good friend, Midshipman Dundas, who would become the sole surviving officer of the ship when she was lost. Dundas later went to Prince of Wales to be sunk again by the Japanese. He survived but I understand he suffered a nervous breakdown. I heard a story that a sailor survived the sinking of the *Hood* on a piece of wreckage and was picked up by a British trawler off Iceland a day or two later. He was an orphan and decided he would just stay fishing with his new friends. Some years later, his conscience got the better of him and he surrendered to the Admiralty, who released him from the service without penalty.

The Luftwaffe was bombing Britain regularly now. My people in Manchester were using family members and anyone else they could find to fire-watch on the roof of their warehouse, their object being to throw out or dump water or sand on incendiary bombs. This certainly was a barbaric form of warfare which the Germans instigated and it was hard to feel sympathy for them when they got it back, pressed down and brimming over.

The German bombings strengthened the will of the people. My Aunt Sarah now kept chickens in the yard and they always had eggs. My female cousins, who had lost their potential husbands in the previous slaughter on the Western Front and the Dardanelles, cheerfully did their best in the new war effort. All the people I met strongly supported all the measures of rationing and controls imposed by the government.

Who sank the *Hood?*

Shortly after I left *Hood,* she sailed with the new battleship *Prince of Wales* to search for *Bismarck,* which had broken out into the Atlantic. *Prince of Wales* had just arrived in Scapa and was a source of great interest to us midshipmen. She did not have her full crew, civilian workers still were aboard and some of her 14-inch turrets were not operable.

The cruisers *Norfolk* (an old friend) and *Suffolk* sighted *Bismarck* and *Prinz Eugen* entering the north end of the Denmark Strait between Greenland and Iceland. *Hood* and *Prince of Wales* sighted the Germans in the strait at 5:35, about dawn, the next morning, 24 May. There were intermittent snow flurries. *Hood* opened fire at 6:40 at the leading ship, believing it to be *Bismarck.* It actually was *Prinz Eugen,* which was similar in profile. *Hood* then shifted fire to *Bismarck.*

When *Hood* and *Prince of Wales* opened fire, the Germans responded at once. *Prinz Eugen* observed one of her 8-inch shells hit *Hood* on the boat deck just behind the after funnel. Immediately, a fire blazed high above the upper deck. This was followed almost at once, at 6:56, by a huge explosion hundreds of feet in the air. This could only have come from a cordite explosion in a 15-inch magazine. (Cordite was contained in large silk bags and was the propellant for the 15-inch shells.)

After *Hood* blew up, *Bismarck* and *Prinz Eugen* then concentrated on *Prince of Wales.* She was hit four times by *Bismarck* and three times by *Prinz Eugen* and broke off and

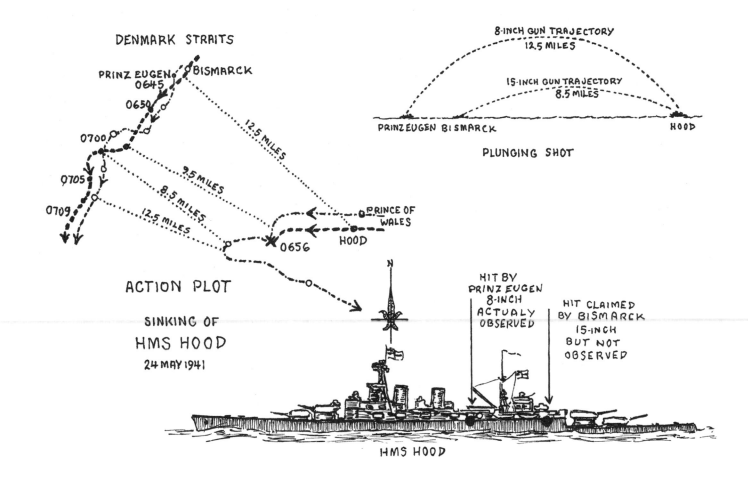

DENMARK STRAITS

PRINZ EUGEN 0645 — BISMARCK
0650
0700
0705
0709

12.5 MILES
9.5 MILES
8.5 MILES
12.5 MILES

PRINCE OF WALES
HOOD
0656

ACTION PLOT

SINKING OF
HMS HOOD
24 MAY 1941

N

8-INCH GUN TRAJECTORY
12.5 MILES

15-INCH GUN TRAJECTORY
8.5 MILES

PRINZ EUGEN   BISMARCK   HOOD

PLUNGING SHOT

HIT BY
PRINZ EUGEN
8-INCH
ACTUALY
OBSERVED

HIT CLAIMED
BY BISMARCK
15-INCH
BUT NOT
OBSERVED

HMS HOOD

retired. She had hit *Bismarck* three times. *Bismarck* headed for Brest in France and *Prinz Eugen* was detached for commerce raiding.

In 1957 I was a student at the NATO Defence College at L'École Militaire in Paris. One of my course mates was a German naval officer, Commander von Stolpnagel. He told me that he had spent the entire war in the cruiser *Prinz Eugen* and had been her gunnery officer. He would have witnessed the destruction of HMS *Hood* in May 1941. It seemed pointless to discuss this with him, but some years later I realized that his ship, *Prinz Eugen,* actually may have sunk *Hood,* and not *Bismarck* as is popularly supposed. This tall, pleasant, quiet gentleman may have been responsible for sinking my ship.

A young sub-lieutenant

Just after our group arrived in Portsmouth and were getting settled down, we heard the unbelievable news that *Hood* had been sunk by the first salvo from (we thought at the time) the great new German battleship *Bismarck*. The next two days we were transfixed as the whole Home Fleet gathered its forces to find the *Bismarck*. Terrible errors occurred when ships turned back and searched the reciprocal rather than the true bearing. Finally, luck was with our forces and the mighty *Bismarck* was sent to the bottom. The feelings of the ex-*Hoods* can be imagined – terrible shock, great sadness and deep thankfulness at having been spared. The dark thought that crossed my mind, as I am sure happened to others, was why was I spared when others, much finer than I, were taken. Perhaps it was merely a matter of time.

HMS *Vernon*, the torpedo school in Portsmouth, had been bombed on several nights before our arrival and I was shown what I thought was to be my cabin on the second deck of a wooden building which appeared quite normal from the front. We opened the cabin door to look at nothing, just open air – staff's little joke! Our classrooms had been destroyed as well. Happily, very nice quarters were available for us at the Marine Gate Hotel in Brighton while our classes were conducted at Roedean, a famous girls' school, not far away. The Marine Gate Hotel was near the waterfront, was quite new and built in the modern, plain and simplified style of the 1930s. Some of the locals said that when the air raids started in London, there was an influx of rich Jews to Brighton. In several places in the hotel, we were startled to see that someone had scrawled on the walls "Down With Jews" and similar sentiments. I don't suppose that it was until we and our Allies overran Germany that it was realized to what hideous extremes such primitive expressions can lead.

Perhaps there were other residents in the hotel who had rooms. Our group was settled in a large hall or space on the ground floor and we slept on camp cots with our suitcases and possessions laid out by the cots. The bathrooms and toilets always were spotless, the food in the restaurant was excellent and the staff were bright, cheerful and helpful. We were bused to Roedean early each morning, but if we were so inclined we could walk. It was a delightful exercise, strolling along the roadside, looking down over the chalk cliffs at the green ocean breaking on the shore. To me, different parts of the ocean have their own special characteristics, or so I imagine. Perhaps the distinctive grey green colour of the water here results from the chalky bottom.

There were no girls remaining at Roedean, unfortunately. We took turns sleeping there in an uncomfortable cubicle on fire prevention duty. Here was the unforgettable notice on the wall, "If you require a mistress during the night, please ring the bell." One can imagine the snickering stupidity of us young, sex-starved idiots. Alas, no mistresses came when we pressed the bell.

At this school we learned all the intricacies of the torpedo and also learned about electricity and how it was produced, distributed and used in ships of various types. One of the gunners (torpedo) fascinated us. We called him the Worm Bo'sun because he was responsible for the grounds. The poor gentleman had bad corns so with his uniform he wore running shoes, painted black. Over each corn he had cut a cross so that the corn stuck out. The Torpedo Branch was famous for taking a relaxed view of life, as opposed to the Gunnery Branch of ranters and roarers. I am a Jekyll and Hyde, being a lover of "gunnery funnery" with a torpedo disposition.

The seashore of Brighton and Hove was sealed off with barbed wire and mines to discourage invasion, and no lights were allowed anywhere after dark. Blackout curtains shielded the windows and doors, and gas and everything else was rationed. The ordinary road signs were removed and some roads were blocked with large cubes of concrete. For young persons almost everything was a new experience, but for older people all the beauty, order and convenience had gone out of their lives.

The gunnery course at Whale Island in Portsmouth was splendid. We were accommodated in blocks of cabins on the island. We each had a retired Royal Marine servant to look after us, making sure our appearance reflected credit on themselves. Our working uniform was a blue uniform jacket with a white flannel shirt and scarf, white flannel trousers, gaiters and boots, presenting an exceedingly smart appearance. All those white things had to be sparkling clean and pressed; the servant didn't let one get away with anything.

The first lieutenant of *Matabele* had stated that he would resign from the navy if women ever came into the service. Sadly he was killed by the Germans. Anyway his worst fears were realized and we now had these nice women called Wrens, Women's Royal Naval Service, looking after our cabins and serving at table. The lady who looked after my cabin was the wife of a petty officer on the China Station, and what a kind and thoughtful person she was. She was the first Wren I ever met. Soon these lovely ladies took the place ashore of officers and men of all branches required at sea. In fact, later in the war they even served in training duties at sea.

Whale island itself was beautifully cared for, still with the zoo of ships' mascots, lovely lawns and huge trees. Figureheads from ships of the line of the days of Nelson were sited here and there, and the whole impression was of everything being shipshape, coiled down and in Bristol fashion. Perhaps because the island was so beautiful from the air with its green lawns and discreet buildings, the Germans thought the activities of the ants down there were innocent and beneath their Teutonic dignity. In any case, they didn't bother us much there.

The guns we studied were in various buildings about the grounds and we learned the details of rifles, revolvers, machine guns, 3-inch, 4-inch, 6-inch, 8-inch and 15-inch guns. Whenever our group moved from one place to another, we did not simply march. We went everywhere at the double. We also did a good deal of parade ground drill, battalion manoeuvres, all the rifle movements there ever were and ceremonial drill with swords.

The worst experience for me was giving commands to large bodies of men. If you made a mistake or forgot an order, your failure could not be more public. A stentorian voice would announce to Portsmouth that the entire movement was spoiled by Sub-Lieutenant Jenson who failed to do anything correctly. You could not even slink off. The most enjoyable part was instruction in the intricacies of fire control, the workings of the Admiralty Fire Control Tables, fire control clocks, firing circuits, rangefinders and so on. Gun drill also was exciting. The details of life in a 15-inch gun turret were awesome with the heavy machinery bringing up the huge shells and the heavy silk bags of propellant, ramming all this into the great breach of the gun, the breach swinging shut and turning to lock itself in the gun. It did not need much imagination to envisage what could go wrong and what the dire consequences would be.

The course was shortened somewhat from that of peacetime and I worried at the time that we would not be as well qualified as we should be. However, on reflection as I write, most of the young officers under training already had seen more gun actions than peacetime officers would see in a lifetime.

We were allowed ashore on Wednesday, Friday, Saturday and Sunday afternoons. Most of us would go to tea dances in Southsea. These were lovely, with music in Palm Court style. Ladies were taking tea, we would take tea, eat cakes covered with icing, chat with each other and dance with the ladies. I never heard of any romances developing but I'm sure it was possible.

With the end of the gunnery course we had a huge mess dinner. Each group did something that they thought was spectacular to mark the occasion. A previous group had rolled some old cannons in their wooden carriages down a hill. Another group released a platoon of chickens dressed in little naval officer jackets (which the Wrens had made) and with gaiters on their little feet. They ran back and forth among the glasses and port decanters on the dining tables, making little messes here and there. Our group got hold of a deflated barrage balloon, put it in the large drill shed and inflated it so that the whole drill shed was full of barrage balloon. I went ashore with a couple of friends and when we got back we found a piano had been hoisted to the rafters of the wardroom anteroom. Someone was lying on the strings and as he stirred in his sleep it made a twanging sound, a sort of contemporary music.

Our navigation course at HMS *Dryad* was the most gentlemanly course of all. HMS *Dryad*, HMS *Excellent*, HMS *Vernon*, HMS *Mercury* and so on – all these schools were on land. In order to qualify as HM Ships they had small tenders which actually were HMS *Dryad, Excellent*, etc. and on whose books the officers and men were borne. At one time, of course, *Vernon* and the others were hulks lying alongside sans masts and rigging, but HM Ships nevertheless. At *Dryad* we walked around just like ordinary human beings and people did not scream and yell at us. We only ran if the mood took us. This was and is a way of life which has much appeal for me.

As the Germans had demolished our living quarters at *Dryad* we were sent to live in Southwick House, about 10 miles away, to and from which we travelled in a blue RN bus. It was a lovely and large old house where the owner still lived with his Gainsboroughs hanging on the walls. The sub-lieutenants had little cots in a sort of dusty, draughty and unheated attic. Wrens brought us small pots of hot tea early each morning; never was tea so welcome.

German night air attacks were frequent and Southwick House apparently was a target, so the subs stood watches as fire spotters on the roof. Most nights the bombs were dropped well clear of us and did not cause much anxiety. One night we heard a plane or planes but no bombs. Off

we went early in the morning for our studies. When we returned in the evening we learned that just after we had left, a huge land mine had been found caught by its parachute in a tree right beside the house. The place had been evacuated and a disposal squad with their usual superb courage had removed the mine. As far as I know, Southwick House was never hit and later it gained fame by being the headquarters from which General Eisenhower oversaw the Invasion of Normandy.

This was my last course. I had done well in all of them and was a confirmed sub-lieutenant. After a period of sea time, during which I would obtain my watchkeeping certificate, I could be promoted to lieutenant. Now I was free to return to Canada, visit my parents and join a ship in the Royal Canadian Navy.

After courses were completed in September 1941, I sailed for Canada in a troopship, the ss *Pasteur*, departing from Liverpool. She was a fine, modern passenger ship which had been seized by the British from the French after that country surrendered. The passengers included Wrens and other personnel going to serve with the British Embassy in Washington as well as Canadian army and air force personnel returning to Canada. There were one or two hundred British merchant seamen who were being sent to pick up newly built merchant ships in the United States.

I was told by a Canadian wing commander or group captain who was senior officer that I was to take charge of these merchant seamen. I found them still waiting to board, or else had been on board and had returned ashore. In any case, when I appeared they were gathered in a bunch by the gangway calling out and milling around. I called for silence and to my surprise there was. I asked the ones in front what the trouble was. One spokesman said that the messdeck where they were to be billeted was dirty and they were not going to accept that. They were refusing to board unless it was cleaned up. I said they were required to board and that when they did we would clean the place up ourselves. To my relief they reluctantly and angrily conformed. Merchant seamen were brave men and suffered heavy casualties. However, if they did not like a ship, they would not serve in it. Often they were paid danger money, in addition to excellent wages.

When we got in the messdeck, I divided them into four watches which would take turns to maintain cleanliness. I was much younger than these grizzled seadogs and was surprised that they let themselves be organized and put to work, as I don't think I had any legal authority over them and had no means of enforcing my will. In short order the mess decks were swept and scrubbed and all the dishes, cups, tea pots and fannies given a good wash. Soon we had a pleasant relationship with good humour in clean and neat surroundings. As the days went by at sea their messdeck showed up all the others. They were seamen and knew how to look after themselves. The food which had been embarked in Canada was delicious and varied in comparison with the drabness we had become used to in wartime Britain. As far as I was concerned, my responsibilities with the merchant seamen made the trip more interesting and rewarding.

The weather was fine all the way to Halifax. We travelled at high speed, perhaps 25 knots, and did not have an escort of any kind. No escort of the time could have kept up with us on a steady basis. If they had had to take time to investigate something, they might never have caught up with us. The first land we saw was Chebucto Head on our port bow and before long we were secured alongside Pier 21 in Halifax.

I had met a very neat little Wren, a Miss St. John, bound for Washington. She and I took a taxi to Spring Garden Road, thinking we might find a place to have a quiet drink before she went on her way and I on mine. To our amazement, having just come from the British Isles where pubs were part of every community, we learned that it was not possible to buy an alcoholic drink of any kind in any public place in Nova Scotia. We found ourselves at the Public Gardens opposite the Lord Nelson Hotel, so we decided to walk in there. It was one of the most beautiful places I had ever seen and we walked through the lovely trees by a stream, and then by a lake with ducks and a large floating model of the *Titanic*. As it grew darker we heard a loud whistle and were told politely by an attendant that the gardens were closed.

Miss St. John returned to *Pasteur* and I took a taxi to Admiralty House, or "Admirality" House as the driver called it. This was the Command Wardroom and certainly liquor was much in evidence here. I had never before seen such devoted attention to the subject. I shared a room with

Admiralty House — 1814

Sub-Lieutenant Chadwick in a large house which later became a nurses' residence. Admiralty House, which was the Wardroom Mess, had a few cabins for more senior officers. It had been built at the conclusion of the War of 1812 between Britain and the United States and had been the residence of the commander in chief of the America and West Indies Station. The stately building surrounded by gardens and lawns was used as a hospital in the First World War and became the Wardroom in the 1930s.

I had a chance to explore Halifax during this period. My experience of Canadian cities was limited to Calgary, Vancouver and, for two days, Ottawa, and I thought that generally they compared favourably with the cities and towns I had seen in the British Isles. Parts of Manchester and London were not very pleasant, but nothing had prepared me for Halifax. The buildings for the most part were run down, and the streets were dirty with newspapers and garbage blowing about. Houses were unpainted and some of the streets were still not paved. There were houses on

Market Street, just below Citadel Hill, that were worse than the houses in Freetown, West Africa. Even in the South End the large Victorian homes needed painting. It was believed that painting a house increased the taxes.

The streetcars were smaller than those I had seen elsewhere; the sailors called them "yellow ditty boxes." Everywhere was crowded by the huge influx of sailors, soldiers and airmen stationed in ships, barracks, schools, coastal defence and so on. Many had brought their wives to live in the city and every apartment and house was occupied. The few restaurants were crowded and most theatres had long queues outside every evening. Liquor could be purchased at government liquor stores but was rationed and one had to have a permit. There were no public places where one could drink one's liquor legally. Consequently, there was considerable illegal drinking and public drunkenness. At-

tempts had been made to set up a club for sailors where they could drink beer, but this was closed by public demand.

At the time of Confederation in 1867, Halifax was one of the richest cities in the British Empire. Gradually her manufacturing diminished and so did her wealth. By 1900 Halifax was approaching depression and the situation continued to worsen. In 1917 the Halifax Explosion, the most powerful explosion in history until the atomic bomb, was especially devastating in the north end and killed thousands of people. The city had been restored by aid in large measure from Boston. In no way did Halifax have the infrastructure to support the hordes of service people that filled the unfortunate city. Walking along Barrington or Gottingen streets was not an agreeable experience.

Admiralty House was something different. Liquor enjoyed great popularity and the bar in the Anteroom was full at noon and in the evenings. The Royal Canadian Navy, the permanent force, was small and, therefore, not well represented. The RCN Volunteer Reserve and RCN Reserve from the merchant service were the main denizens. The saying was that the RCNR were seamen pretending to be gentlemen, the RCNVR were gentlemen pretending to be seamen and the RCN were neither. Before the war many Nova Scotia sailors had been involved in rum-running, and the main occupation of the Marine Division of the RCMP had been attempting to catch them. Now both sides were represented in the Canadian navy and I heard a few conversations between ex-hunters and hunted.

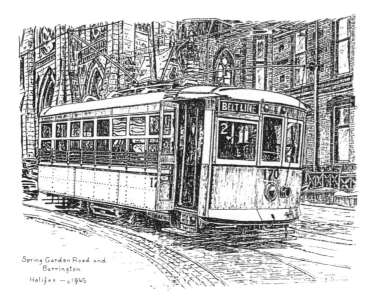

Spring Garden Road and
Barrington
Halifax — c.1945

All things being in order, I was permitted to go home on leave to Calgary to see my family and my old dog Sport. It would be just over three years since I had left home. As I write, it is no longer possible to travel as I did in late 1941. Even though the trains were crowded, they were comfortable, the food was excellent and one met all sorts of people. On one trip I made sometime later, Tommy Douglas, the CCF leader, shared my carriage and I was entertained with the fascinating ideas and charming personality of this gentleman. It would be hard to imagine a man more sincerely devoted to the wellbeing of his fellow humans.

At almost every station the train stopped for half an hour or so, and people rushed off to the nearest liquor store to buy what they could. Each car had a smoking room which was for men only, and it was well patronized as a rule, the air blue with tobacco smoke. As the trains used coal as fuel, there was much smoke and cinders drifting around and it was not easy to keep clean. The lavatories were situated with Ladies at one end of the car and Gentlemen at the other. The one notice that everyone knew and most people even could sing was "Passengers will please refrain from flushing toilets while the train is standing in the station, I love you." (Humoresque!)

My parents knew that I was due home at any time, but I did not give them a particular date because I was not sure. Consequently, I arrived in Calgary, got a taxi and arrived unannounced. I don't know if I expected my mother to collapse with surprise, or what, but she disappointed me by simply opening the front door and giving me a nice hug. It didn't seem that I had been away long. My father was busy in the army; he had started off lecturing on trench warfare and now was in the rail transportation office for Military District 13. He was in his element and having a very nice war. I took several drives with him and his colonel through southern Alberta and renewed friendship with school mates, but this was not particularly interesting as they didn't have a clue what I was talking about. My brother was studying for his naval exams for cadet. It later turned out that he didn't make it so he joined the RCNVR as a seaman, specializing in the gunnery branch.

My father had belonged to the Alberta Military Institute for many years and I was asked if I would give a talk on my experiences with the Royal Navy. Despite my nervousness, I seemed to capture the attention of my audience, many of whom were veterans of the First World War. Thank God I did not have the horrifying experiences of war that most of them had suffered. Now that I reflect on the matter, it seems that time, in their case 24 years, had lessened the awfulness of their memories, leaving mostly good recollections of the warmth, support, fellowship and deep friendship they shared with old comrades. I now feel exactly that way about my dear old shipmates of past years.

My godfather, Colonel Jull, now commanded the Calgary Tanks. He became a brigadier and lost an eye to a tree branch when driving through a forest in a tank. Mrs. Jull was in her element, entertaining and giving advice to the wives of the young officers. Old Mr. Jull, the colonel's father, who had served in the Indian Army in the Bengal

Halifax – seen here in a
view from the 1960s but
little changed since the
war

Lancers and had been a champion pig sticker, was also very much a part of the scene. It was rather like the Noel Coward film *Cavalcade*.

Everybody in Alberta knew there was a war on and most people enthusiastically supported the Canadian war effort, but the war for them really meant all the wrong things. The war put an end to the Depression, and as if by divine providence, the dust storms stopped. Rain now fell from time to time, grain was growing and prosperity had returned. The problem of thousands of young men being unable to find work vanished. The fit were welcomed into the armed forces and those who were not completely fit had no difficulty in finding employment. It was a sort of dream world.

People were prosperous after a decade of hopelessness. They were also bellicose, but perfectly safe in a war being fought thousands of miles away. They really could have no way of knowing the fears, the concerns and the privations of the people of Britain and occupied Europe. It was psychologically disturbing to me and I had a feeling of disorientation in what I perceived to be a happy, boastful, prosperous, ignorant, self-indulgent society. In reality, they were a perfectly normal group of people getting used to a strange state of affairs. I was pleased when my leave was about to conclude and I had to return to "an East Coast port," as Halifax was termed in the news, and join my ship.

Once again I said goodbye to Mother, Dad, brother and sister. As Tom Wolfe said, "You Can't Go Home Again." It is a shock to leave home as a boy and to return years later a man. The old home is not exactly as pictured in one's memories. If you are the eldest, your mother and father might find it difficult to discover that they now own a large, gross young adult instead of the dear, pimply-faced boy of yesteryear. This particular young man also had a phoney English accent and thought he knew everything. For all these reasons, dumb though they may be, I was happy to board the train for another wondrous trip across our lovely country back to old Halifax.

The Sail Loft Clock — 1772
HMC Dockyard

LB JENSON

7

On convoy escort duty

After the month with my family in Calgary, I reported back to Halifax and was appointed to HMCS *Ottawa,* a River Class destroyer, as a sub-lieutenant. The *Ottawa,* I was told, was in St. John's, Newfoundland, and I was given rail and ferry tickets to get there. The train ran to the Gut of Canso (there was not a causeway), from where it was ferried to Cape Breton Island and continued to the ferry terminal at Sydney. It was a leisurely and comfortable trip through the lovely Nova Scotia countryside. A Cape Breton lady with her young daughter sat by me. They were returning home from Halifax, where the daughter had had dental treatment. The child, blond hair in tight braids, dressed in tartans, had such a bright and shining smile, I hope the happy promise of her life has been fulfilled.

In Sydney I boarded the SS *Caribou* for the overnight voyage to Port aux Basques on the southwestern tip of the old colony of Newfoundland. *Caribou* was a fine ferry. Built in Rotterdam in 1925, she was 265 feet long and spe-cially designed for the Cabot Strait and strengthened for ice. She could carry 50 freight cars and 400 passengers, covering the 95-mile trip in eight hours. Less than a year later, *Caribou* was torpedoed at night, without warning, by a German U-boat and 137 men, women and children were lost. 101 were rescued.

Now, however, I was happily aboard the Newfoundland "Bullet" express trundling the length of this great island, rocking and rolling along the narrow-gauge rail line. It was of rather old-fashioned elegance and surprisingly comfort-able. At almost every stop, children swarmed aboard asking for pennies in what sounded to me like broad Irish accents, even using "sure and begorrah, mister." Considering the place had been known to Europeans for 400 years, the scenery was wilder and more spectacular than I had anticipated.

A few weeks before, President Roosevelt had made available to the Royal Navy 50 escort destroyers from the First World War. In exchange the United States gained bases in some British colonies. One such was to be

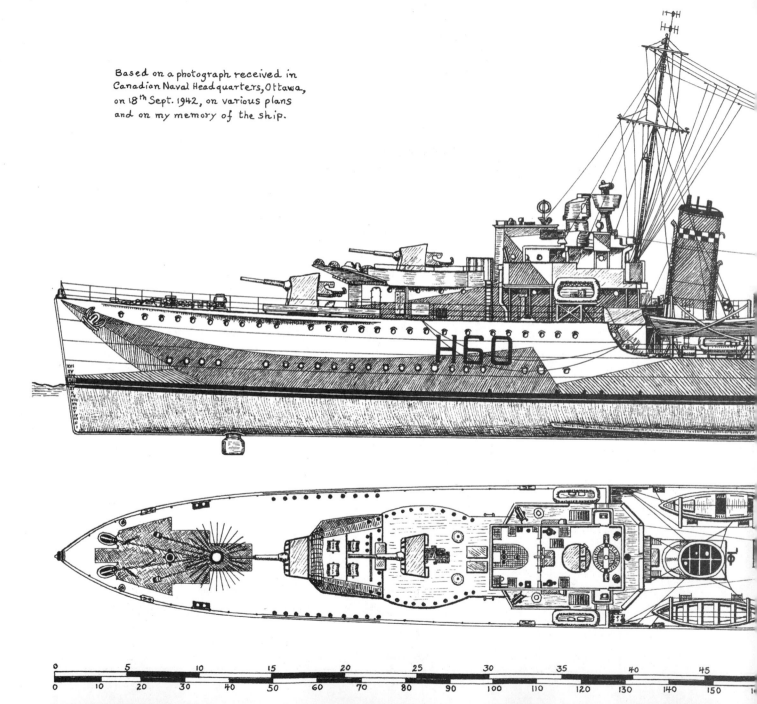

Based on a photograph received in
Canadian Naval Headquarters, Ottawa,
on 18th Sept. 1942, on various plans
and on my memory of the ship.

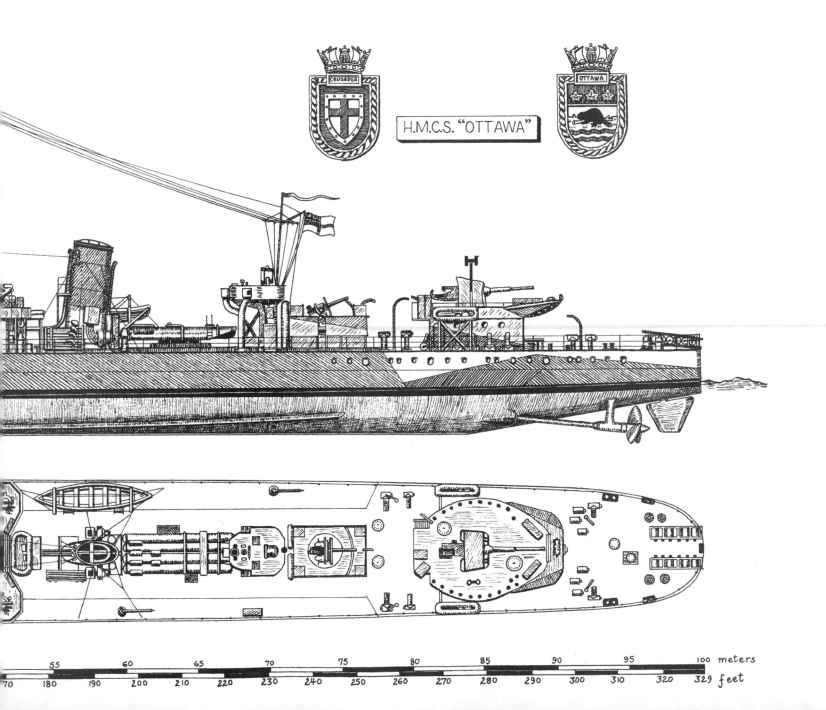

H.M.C.S. "OTTAWA"

Argentia in Placentia Bay on the southeast corner of New-foundland.

On the train there were a number of older Americans who, I assume, were on their way to start setting up the base. One of these gentlemen was sitting across the aisle, and I think he had been drinking hard for a few days. When I could figure out what he was saying, he seemed pleasant and sensible, but he surprised me by suddenly grabbing my hand and putting it over his heart, the object being to make sure it kept on beating! His grip was like iron and as I was in uniform I was particularly embar-rassed. After an eternity he passed out and I escaped to the next carriage.

Not many seats were available in this carriage so I was forced to sit near two attractive young women. It turned out that they were the wives of engine room artificers in the *Ottawa* whom they were joining in St. John's. This gave me a fine excuse to invite them to have dinner with me in the dining car. Little could I know what an effect this little incident was to have upon my life about a year later.

HMCS *Ottawa* was in drydock not far from the rail-way station and soon I was in my cabin with all my gear. *Ottawa* was a typical British destroyer of the time. About 330 feet in length, 1,400 tons displacement, top speed of 32 knots (37 miles per hour), with a crew of 13 officers and around 170 men, she was armed with three 4.7-inch guns, one 3-inch high-angle gun (anti-aircraft), two Oerlikon anti-aircraft guns and four 21-inch torpedoes. As well, she had depth charge throwers and many depth

charges. She had been launched in Portsmouth in 1931 as HMS *Crusader* and served in the Home Fleet until 1938 when she was sold to Canada, became HMCS *Ottawa* and was stationed in Esquimalt near Victoria.

When war broke out with Germany, *Ottawa* was sent to the East Coast and then to the United Kingdom for convoy escort duties. When I joined she was a member of the Mid Ocean Escort Force. My first impression was that the ship was neat and scrupulously clean and those men that I had seen so far were well turned out, bright and cheerful.

Sometime before lunch a messenger informed me that the captain would see me in his cabin. The captain's day cabin was situated just astern of the engine room. The chintz-covered sofa, armchairs, desk, mahogany table and chairs, fireplace, paintings and so on, made it rather like a pleasant living room ashore. Instead of windows, however, there were round scuttles and the deckhead (ceiling) was a mass of pipes, electric cables and ventilator trunks. Com-mander H.F. Pullen, short, stocky and seamanlike, greeted me affably and invited me to sit down and have a glass of sherry, delivered immediately on a silver tray by Hockley, his steward. My duties were explained. I was to be gunnery officer, signals officer and confidential books officer. I also was to be forecastle officer, looking after the anchors and cables and securing the bow of the ship when we came alongside. I was to be responsible for the men in the Sig-nals Division and the fo'c's'lemen (forecastlemen). It was a great introduction to the Royal Canadian Navy and I felt that I had come to a fine ship with a fine skipper. It also

A Sunny Saturday Morning Long Ago
Messdeck Ready for Captain's Rounds

was the start of an interesting and pleasant relationship with the captain which lasted off and on for over 40 years.

Soon our repairs were completed and *Ottawa* left St. John's, covering a convoy eastward-bound for the United Kingdom. As I recollect, the first place we dropped anchor was off Greenock at the mouth of the River Clyde in Scotland. After a wardroom party some of us climbed into the motor cutter to visit the Bay Hotel, where a pleasant lady named Jeanie held sway. This evidently was a place *Ottawa* had frequented in the past, especially when Commander Rollo Mainguy was in command. We were welcomed royally but after a while, being tired out, I was thinking about my nice bunk. It was too far to swim so I carried on roistering, so to speak. Suddenly, to my horror, I noticed a large, ruddy-faced Royal Navy captain quietly dining with his wife and young son and ignoring the noisy, uncouth Canadians. It was Uncle Cedric, Aunt Sarah and my cousin, none of whom had I seen since 1938, before the war! For the next hour I drank ginger ale and tried to be invisible so that their wild, colonial relation would not embarrass them. What a relief it was to get back to my floating home.

The first lieutenant of a destroyer was the second in command or executive officer. He was also known as Number One, Jimmy the One or plain Jimmy. Hence the old song,

> You take the paint brush and I'll take the paint pot
> And we will paint the ship's side together,
> And when Jimmy comes along, we will sing our little
>   song,
> Thank God we didn't join forever!

Another one was:

> Don't give us a make and mend, Sir
> We might come over faint.
> There's not many Jimmys like you, Sir.
> It's a bloody good job there ain't!"

A "make and mend" was a half-day holiday.

When I joined, our Number One was Gus Bolton, who was succeeded by Frank Caldwell. Other officers were Jack Blakelot and Jim Mills, but they left after a couple of Atlantic crossings and joined other ships. Caldwell was replaced by Lieutenant Tom Pullen, the captain's young brother. This was extremely unusual in the navy. One of the things most officers do when relaxing in the wardroom is to make remarks about the captain. Often the remarks are in the Old Man's favour, but sometimes they are not. At first, we were shy in expressing our feelings, particularly if Number One was there, but this slowly changed and there were few inhibitions. Most of us felt that the captain was too hard on the first lieutenant because he was his brother. In any case, this would be what one might expect and my impression was that all in all *Ottawa* was a happy ship.

Escorting convoys during the Second World War was, for just a little under 100 per cent of the time, extraordinarily dull work. Most Canadian ships were stuck in the North Atlantic, famous for storms, fog, icebergs and anything else unpleasant. Echoes picked up by the Asdic, as the Sonar then was called, mostly turned out to be fish or

Scene in the Fore Lower Messdeck
The Torpedomen's Mess

wrecks. If the echoes behaved in a submarine-like manner and even if you dropped depth charges, the net result could almost be guaranteed to be a disappointment; nothing would surface. Most of us hoped that escorting convoys was a temporary affair for our noble destroyers and that soon we would be engaging more worthy enemies – German warships – with gunfire and torpedoes the way that nature intended. Such are the idiotic thoughts of young men.

The captain and the first lieutenant of *Ottawa* were both highly qualified gunnery officers, graduates of HMS *Excellent*, the Royal Naval Gunnery School, Whale Island. *Ottawa* was to have a practice shoot off Northern Ireland, but unfortunately a target was not available to be towed by the tug – there was just the tug itself. No problem! We would "throw off" on the tug. This means altering the guns so that they point 10 degrees to the right or left of the tug, while your telescopes, dials and pointers are lined up on the tug. Now when you fire your guns, the observers on the quarterdeck of the tug can safely observe the fall of your shot and signal back whether you are "short" or "over". The gunner's mate, Petty Officer Sam Short, and I checked each gun to ensure it was "thrown off" properly. All was correct, so I thought, action guns' crews were closed up (manning their guns) and I reported all this to the captain. Then followed the sequence:

Me: "Ready to open fire, sir."
Captain: "Very well, open fire."
Me, to the director: "Shoot!"

Director fire bell: "Ting, ting."
And all the guns go off.
Sometimes the sequence went as follows:
Me: "Ready to open fire, sir."
Captain: "Very well, open fire."
Me, to the director: "Shoot!"
Director fire bell: "Ting, ting."
Silence…
Captain: "What is the delay? There are two kinds of people in this world, the quick and the dead. If you are not quick you will be dead!"
Me to the director: "What is the delay?"
Silence…
The captain's kindly face becomes more red and upset.
Silence…
All hands now think nothing's going to happen. Suddenly, just the closest gun goes off with a terrible bang.

Weapons practice was complicated enough with relatively simple weapons like the guns of the time. Think how mixed-up things could be with computers, rockets and nuclear warheads!

In this case, all the guns went off as planned and for a wild moment I had a feeling of contentment. How unwise! All hands now were looking astern of the tug to see the shots splashing down. Nothing! What can have happened? I trained my glasses on the tug as it vanished in clouds of spray. Well, we were pretty good for range even if we threw off the wrong way and nearly sank the tug! Commander Pullen was known to some as "Von Pullen" and I was wondering if I would just be shot or whether being hanged from the yardarm was still on the books. Happily no one was hurt and the captain merely hoped we would do better next time, and, of course, we did.

The entry requirements for the navy, followed by the sorting-out process in basic training, helped ensure that by the time a man was drafted to a ship he probably would fit in and carry out his duties satisfactorily. This was not guaranteed, however, and there were exceptions. Such a case was in our ship, a seaman, slightly older than the others, a Nova Scotian. Shy and soft-spoken from a small farm in a remote part of the province, he had worked in the woods in the winter and fished from a schooner in the summer. He was used to a life of hard work with small reward and had little in common with his more urban messmates.

For the purposes of cleaning ship and other routine requirements, warships are greatly overmanned, but these relatively huge complements of officers and men are required if the ship goes into battle. As a consequence a good deal of naval shipboard routine and fussiness of dress is designed simply to keep the hands occupied. Having to shave every day, wear a clean uniform, have one's hair cut and to scrub and polish decks, paintwork and woodwork struck our friend as nonsense. To top it off, a destroyer was much more uncomfortable than a schooner, which was powered by the wind and remained fairly steady on a tack. A destroyer banged about regardless of the wind and sea and seemed never to stop rolling, plunging and crashing about. He had made a mistake in joining the navy and he wanted out.

Finally he found a reason to get out: he had hurt his knee, or said he had. This made him limp, or so he said. The surgeon could find nothing wrong. This did not discourage our friend. He limped about everywhere in a most un-naval manner, wearing a doleful expression of pain. These habits did not win him any friends among the officers or his messmates. Nowadays, I imagine it has to be accepted that the last thing one wishes aboard one's ship is a malcontent. His attitude might spread to others or he might damage machinery or instruments. Even a tiny pin stuck in an electronic cable could cause great damage to a ship or its fighting ability.

In those times, however, every attempt was made to hold men to the terms of their engagement and there was no understanding attitude on the part of the officers or petty officers. In this case, it seemed likely to some officers that this man was just pretending that his knee was injured. When he was spotted on a run ashore there was great speculation as to whether he limped only when he suspected that he was being watched. No final verdict was reached before another event solved the problem.

Shortly after I joined *Ottawa* our government held a referendum on whether Canada should conscript men for our armed forces. This was opposed by most French Canadians, although we already had many on active service. In *Ottawa* a substantial number of our men were French-speaking as well as two officers. Both the captain and the first lieutenant ardently believed that conscription was the right thing to do, but the French Canadians aboard did not agree. One day the captain and X.O.'s father visited us in Halifax and I found myself in the wardroom with just the father and a French-Canadian officer. The impending referendum came under discussion. Father was deaf and thought that Lieutenant S. was agreeing with him; quite a shouting match ensued. I fled the wardroom to get on with my duties. It was a sad and doubtful referendum.

One day at Captain's Defaulters an older able seaman was charged with creating a disturbance ashore in St. John's. The police had complained to the shore patrol that this man had been trying to kick in the door of a private house. The captain's moral principles were very high and he expected the highest standard of conduct from everyone. The poor man before him was still hung over and his uniform was a mess.

"Is this true?" asked the captain.

"Yes sir" he replied.

"Why were you trying to get in?" was the next question.

"I wanted into my lady friend's house and she locked me out," mumbled the unfortunate man.

All of us expected the captain to explode but he said quietly, "Are you married?"

"Yes sir."

"What would your wife think of you?"

"I don't know."

"Do you have children?"

"Yes sir. Two little ones."

"What would your children think of you?"

"I don't know," said the criminal and began to bawl, tears streaming down his beard, and he carried on bawling loudly while the torpedo coxswain, in charge of defaulters, was saying, "Control yourself, man."

"Take him away," said the captain, and I think that was the end of the case. Lots of bark, but a bite was not needed.

At church, which the captain conducted, gale or calm, he always concluded with a sermon which brought the Old Testament to life. He would describe how one day we would paint the funnels with German blood, nail German ears to the main mast and do other things which would make the fiercest old prophet proud of us. Well, we never caught any Germans but if we had I would bet my life that this ferocious gentleman would have treated them with honour, decency, kindness and compassion, just as he did all of us who served him. However, whenever we were at sea, Commander Pullen was on the bridge day and night always hoping to sight the enemy and hit first, hit hard and keep on hitting. Before Christmas 1941 he was relieved by Commander Donald Farmer Donald (that was his name) and went to another appointment on his way to becoming one of our best known and most respected admirals.

Commander Donald was of impressive athletic build and had been one of the navy's champion sportsmen. He was quite different from Commander Pullen, being more casual in his manner, but it was not wise to cross his bows. I believe that we made just one convoy with him to Londonderry when the "incident" occurred.

L.B.JENSON

The Bridge of H.M.C.S.Ottawa
1941

It was a fine morning during the winter of 1941/42 when our ship, in preparation for another westbound convoy, was fuelling alongside a tanker anchored off Moville near the mouth of Loch Foyle. In the distance rose the green and lovely hills of Donegal in Eire, the Irish Free State. Somewhat closer lay the shores of Ulster, equally beautiful. When we were up the river alongside at Londonderry, we often went ashore on short leave to cross the border in plain clothes and delight ourselves for a few hours in the Free State. This haven of peace, although it never declared war on Germany, provided many men for the British forces. On a pleasant Sunday afternoon one could visit Moville and find young and old dancing in the open air to the music of an accordion. It was not hard to understand why the Emerald Isle inspired so many sentimental songs. The border officials always treated us with great kindness and courtesy, and it stretches the mind to reflect on the frightful disturbances that have stricken this area in more recent years.

But I must return to that morning, the fuel oil from the tanker gurgling into the tanks, the sunlight dancing on the water and streaming down the hatch into the captain's cabin flat. Here I was in my confidential books officer's hat getting "one time" cypher pads for the coders. Four hundred and seventy tons of fuel oil were pouring into the tanks, some of which were directly under the captain's cabin. Others were forward of the boiler room and also under the fore lower messdeck. Next to the fuel tanks were the magazines with all our ammunition, perfectly safe un-

less one forgot it was extremely dangerous. The "one time" pads were stored in a heavy steel chest just outside the door of the captain's cabin.

The door curtain was drawn back and Hockley, the captain's steward, was bustling about dusting and tidying up. The captain was not to be seen as he was in his bath. I got my pads, locked up the chest and was about to hop up the ladder and go to the coding office when I glanced in the cabin again. Hockley evidently was in the sleeping cabin getting towels and laying out the captain's uniform. The green carpet looked like a field of prairie wheat in the wind, as gentle waves rolled to and fro upon it. I tried to focus my eyes. Hockley emerged from the inner sanctum and his feet squished deep in the carpet. Oil now was oozing out everywhere, and it started bubbling as the steel deck itself began to bulge. Hockley yelled and the captain himself, large, hairy and pink, rushed out, pulling on his dressing gown. I vanished up the ladder to the upper deck. By the time the oil flow was turned off, the mess was beyond description and all my beloved confidential books, codes and cyphers were saturated in fuel oil and mostly unreadable and beyond restoration.

So it was that instead of returning homeward, we spent the coming weeks in Belfast at Harland & Wolff's yard for repairs. I loaded up heavy canvas bags with my oil-soaked books and teetered over to a World War One cruiser, HMS *Caroline*, the depot ship for Belfast. Here I had to sit with a trim, brisk and rather fetching young third officer Wren and make a page by page accounting of every secret piece of paper before destroying them by fire in the small furnace. Some of the books were quite old. Two of them constituted Canada's war plans in case of invasion by the United States. At a quick glance, it appeared that what was anticipated was the War of 1812 updated.

It would have been a pleasure to have become better acquainted with this third officer, but I could not escape the feeling that she didn't like her desk covered with filthy oil-soaked top-secret books and papers, all of which had to be minutely examined and accounted for with absolutely no allowance for error or omission. The smell of oil fuel seemed to get more sickening as the days wore on and I truly felt unwanted. On top of everything, it was not top drawer in the middle of a terrible war to come from a ship which had carelessly burst her oil tanks when fuelling.

Belfast, like Glasgow and other large British industrial centres, was full to the brim with busy people, most of whom were in war production. I often think of the crowded public houses of that time. My impression is that there were many heavy drinkers but few drunks. Canadians came from a land which allowed few pubs and practised what appeared to many to be close to prohibition. As a consequence, Canadians often publicly demonstrated their lack of experience with alcohol.

Maps of the city were given to us with certain areas coloured over with, as I recollect, red, green or yellow. Red meant "Keep out of this area." Yellow meant that servicemen should be in groups of three or more. Green indicated a safe area where one could shop or drink in safety. A few months later, my brother, serving in a corvette and in Bel-

fast for repairs, inadvertently wandered into a red or yellow zone in his uniform and attracted the attention of a group of young men. He took off and for safety's sake darted into a church where sanctuary was afforded. After a time he was guided into a green sector by a policeman. I cannot help but feel that strong passions such as are felt by the IRA or the Ulster Volunteers are nourished to the busting point by liberal splashes of Irish whiskey.

Belfast is nearly as far north as Churchill, Manitoba, and winters are long and dark. It has a fair share of fog and rain and these factors, combined with a practically complete blackout, might be thought to have greatly limited the nightlife, but this was not the case. Crowds seethed along the major streets no matter how dark or foggy it was. How we found our way around has vanished from my mind but I seem to remember moving through the night with a tide of humanity and somehow finding the dance hall or whatever we were looking for.

Dance halls were the place to establish a pleasant relationship with a "female of the opposite sex" or "long-haired chum" as it used to be said. Such chances were rare in our usual female-deprived wartime anchorages. It was my fortune to meet a charming Irish lady who was extremely keen on dancing. Night after night I made my way through the blackout to the dance hall. She would dance all evening and into the morning hours with inexhaustible enthusiasm. I then would try to take her home but she would allow me only so far as a certain corner. After some time I learned that this dancing fanatic then met her husband and they went home together. I think of him as not being keen on dancing and, therefore, happy for someone else to take the strain. I did not hear of any shipmates who were more fortunate than I. If I were to be asked, it would not be my recommendation to go to Belfast in search of romance.

While *Ottawa* was being repaired, I was flown over to Campbeltown to do an anti-submarine course. Anti-submarine warfare had not become an art and, looking back, I suppose our instructors were just learning too. The most I remember is how foggy and damp the whole place was, with the exception of the bright and cheerful bar.

In a relatively short time our damage was repaired and the ship was cleaned up. A great stack of crisp, clean confidential books arrived in lead-weighted sacks, all for me, to enter in my registers and guard with my life. We happily sailed out of the Irish Sea into the Western Ocean once again and headed for Londonderry, going up Loch Foyle, with a pilot, all the way to the city. There had been many improvements and Derry was starting to become a major naval base. In December 1941, the Japanese had attacked Pearl Harbor. Before that American destroyers had been acting as convoy escorts and patrolling as far east in the Atlantic as Iceland. Now that the Americans were in the war their destroyers came all the way to Derry, some of them announcing to everyone that they had sunk submarines all the way across from the States. Needless to say, we didn't believe them.

Another major base was St. John's in Newfoundland. St. John's is a relatively small harbour, but it is sheltered, easy to defend and is able to depend on the local infrastructure for support. When we were there, we often found ourselves berthed near or next to HMCS *Niagara*, a four-stacker, ex-USN destroyer. Her captain was the infamous "Two Gun" Ryan. The favourite hang-out was the old Colony Club (which later burned down with terrible loss of life).

My captain, "Do" Donald, found a kindred spirit in Two Gun and ordered me, as his sub-lieutenant, to go ashore with the pair of them, I suppose to bring them home. They conversed in what sounded like grunts, not that it interfered with their consumption. On one occasion when we went to a club, Donald said that he was interested to find a glove in the urinal. As he was urinating, he was able to move the glove back and forth. Ryan, who was rather intoxicated, grunted from time to time in response to Donald's story. Then when we left the club, Donald discovered he only had one glove.

On New Year's Day 1941-'42 some Niagaras wanted to get into a Chinese restaurant in St. John's. The restaurant would not open up so the Niagaras broke in and during the melee, killed two Chinese. The culprits could not be determined. As a consequence, Canadian naval ships' companies were not given leave in St. John's for several months. When we arrived there after a stormy crossing with a westbound convoy, instead of leave we went on a route march around the town. We marched for hours in the mist along a rocky, muddy road through a landscape such as God gave to Cain, no other living souls in sight. It was like being in a penal battalion. I think this must have been ordered by the admiral, who had strange ideas, in my opinion, about how to treat eager young Canadian volunteers.

Captain (Destroyers) Mainguy's last command had been *Ottawa,* where he was extremely popular. He felt that naval officers from the ships which escorted the convoys should have a pleasant place ashore where they could relax over a drink, spin yarns and share experiences. He must have believed that this would be a sign of respect for the difficult task we had, a boost to our morale and a way of getting officers from various ships together where they could discuss informally any subjects they wished. Out of this would come the spread of knowledge and perhaps ideas for improving our tactics. Accordingly, he set aside a pleasant room on the ground floor of the Newfoundland Hotel where we could attend a weekly cocktail party if we happened to be in port. Later on, a room on the third floor of an old building close to the waterfront was made available as a club for all seagoing officers. It was approached by a precarious outside wooden staircase, 33 or so steps, down which many were expected to tumble and break their necks. As God takes care of drunks and sailors, such never happened. The club was named the Crowsnest and it was an immediate success, fulfilling all Mainguy's expectations. In fact, the Crowsnest Club still exists in St. John's in the same spot, a historic treasure.

Newfoundland for many years was in a disastrous state. They didn't even have their own government. Instead, the government was appointed by the British Colonial Office.

The majority of Newfoundlanders were poverty stricken. Many had never even seen coinage and money bills. About 40 families of rich merchants ruled the roost. Known as the Forty Thieves, they lived in luxury and sent their children to expensive private schools in Canada and the United Kingdom. The situation drastically changed under Lend/Lease when the United States was granted bases in Newfoundland and the British West Indies. American civilians and armed forces people started arriving in large numbers, spending money and hiring local labour for an unheard of level of pay. The initial consequence was startling. When we came ashore in the evening, we encountered the usual blackout and, of course, could not see well. Feeling our way along the street, we became aware of bodies lying here and there on the sidewalk and road. These were passed-out men who had drunk too much. A favourite liquor was Screech, which was practically pure alcohol. It must have been very dangerous to drink. In any case, such blatant drunkenness soon ceased to be seen. The redeeming feature of Newfoundland was the nature of the inhabitants. Kind, friendly, generous and decent, rich and poor alike, they could not have been more supportive of all these strangers who had descended upon them.

The escorts generally berthed near the oil tanks on the other side of the harbour from the city. It was a long walk on a rocky road to St. John's and most people took a bum boat over for a few cents. In the harbour were several merchant ships that had been damaged by the weather or the enemy and were awaiting repair. One ship had a large hole blown through her stern and the bum boat man often took his boat and passengers right through the hole. The one lung engine really echoed while we were in the great hole.

Sailing from St. John's was a wrenching experience. We threaded our way through the boom gate, a very short distance. Then we passed the opening in the cliffs in no time flat. Suddenly, here we were in the open Atlantic, bobbing and plunging about, soaring aloft and below. It was like being on a crazy elevator and the fo'c's'le officer (me) and his men had to be very nippy securing and lashing the anchors and cables.

Iceland's claims to fame, apart from the frigid inhabitants who regarded us as an army (or navy) of occupation, included the dreadful "williwaws," winds roaring down the fjord. Several times *Ottawa* secured alongside the depot ship, HMS *Hecla*. It always seemed that it was nearly dark when the wind struck and soon all our lines were bar taut. The only thing to be done was to get out the hurricane hawser, seldom used because this combination of heavy rope and heavy wire was a real devil to handle, particularly in the dark and with a screaming wind and the ship bouncing about. Anchors had to be made ready to let go and the engineers were asked to raise steam. Failure to do these things could be fatal, as it was for *Skeena* near the end of the war when she was blown ashore, a total loss, and a number of crewmen drowned. Years later, in peacetime, I had the sad honour of laying wreaths on their graves. A hideous combination, particularly in the days before radar, was a williwaw combined with a blizzard of snow.

The routine now was that we sailed from Londonderry, picked up a convoy coming from English and Scottish ports and escorted it to the vicinity of Newfoundland, where another escort took over and we went in to St. John's for fuel, provisions and minor repairs. The so-called Western Ocean often can be lovely to sail upon and it was delightful to arrive off Ulster, pick up a pilot and sail up the Foyle to Derry. The river was beautiful, its banks covered with trees, everything the most luscious shade of Irish green – from the abundant rain. We made several crossings, back and forth, peacefully and in favourable weather, seeing no sign of the enemy.

In early summer of 1942 we were heading back to St. John's when the weather changed dramatically. We ran into a heavy westerly gale and soon were heading into towering seas, with huge waves approaching 60 feet in height. The troughs were deep and seemed sheltered from the wind. The ship would then climb the next monster wave. Finally, at the top, the sea looked like the dawn of creation, an awesome view of great mounds of water all striped with greybeards, long lines of foam. Then down into the trough again, and so it went on and on. From time to time waves would sweep down the upper deck forcing anyone on deck to grab the lifeline and hang on for dear life. Now and again the ship's bow would lift high out of the water and crash down with a terrible bang, "hitting milestones" as they say.

For almost five days the ship steamed ahead at 12 knots, but actually went astern about 200 miles over the ground. Eventually, the wind and waves abated. As gunnery officer I thought I should check the magazines, starting in the after lower messdeck. Considering the battering we had received, the messdeck was quite neat and tidy, except for a couple of bent stanchions. This was better than the wardroom, which, being near the stern, had been flipped about considerably and was a shambles. However, the after magazines were in the usual perfect order. Then we went to the forward lower messdeck. The messdecks appeared not too bad, but the stanchions between the upper and lower decks were very bent. The gunner's mate and I opened the magazine hatch, which was flush with the deck. I couldn't believe my eyes. I looked at my own reflection in water, which was right up to the lower deck level. We rapidly closed the hatch and I doubled off to tell the first lieutenant. The magazine was pumped out and we proceeded to Halifax for an inspection in the drydock. We were condemned for mid-ocean work and could only work in the Western Local Force, escorting convoys in and out of Halifax. In fact, this wouldn't make much difference because ordinary weather in coastal waters off Nova Scotia and Newfoundland greatly resembled the open ocean.

While we were in Halifax, we entertained a number of the local set and I learned what a nice place it really is. One Saturday the captain, Commander Donald, asked me to meet his guest for lunch at the Dockyard North Gate. He turned out to be Major James Boyle Uniacke, who was a great-grandson of Richard John Uniacke, the builder of Uniacke House in the early 1800s. The major had been born in 1880 at St. George's Rectory, the famous Round Church built by the Duke of Kent when he was the commander-in-chief. After Royal Military College, the major served in India and later in France in the Great War. He was merry and one of the best natured of men. I mention this gentleman because he was a real representative of his times, so very far away from the time of this writing.

Repairs were made to *Ottawa* and soon we were again escorting convoys back and forth over the North Atlantic.

L.B. JENSON

On the way to the Centre Gate of the Dockyard. The corner of Barrington and North, Halifax

St. George's — the "Round Church," 1800

LB Jensen

We were using Londonderry regularly now, and one morning were due to sail down the River Foyle to Moville to fuel. As we sat at breakfast, I remarked to my messmates that I had a dream that I was on the fo'c's'le with my hands when the captain called from the bridge, "Let go the starboard anchor." I ordered the fo'c's'le petty officer to let go and then looked over the side to see the shank of the anchor sticking up out of the water. The ship had stopped. My friends all laughed heartily. We sailed, the Irish pilot was too enthusiastic and everything happened as in my

dream. Even the dark green water was correct. Happily, we went astern a wee bit, I weighed anchor and soon we were safely at anchor in deep water, waiting to fuel. Every time I mentioned a dream from then on I got a lot of attention.

It was a happy summer for me except that I seemed to have too many different duties. Our captain was relieved and went on to command the new repair base west of Halifax, at Shelburne. Our new commanding officer was Lieutenant Commander C.A. Rutherford, a graduate of the Royal Military College, Kingston, before going to the Royal Navy for training. He told us that his motto was "Work hard and play hard" and he certainly was a fine example of the clever, experienced and tough young destroyer commanders in our navy. He was a good ship handler and very much in charge.

I was still gunnery officer, signals officer, correspondence officer, RDF (radar) officer, confidential books officer and fo'c's'le officer. I had so much to do I scarcely had time to breathe. Also I was watchkeeping, and so I had an arrangement whereby I stood two standing watches. I thought then, and still think, that standing watches are a good thing. If one is on watch at the same times, month after month, one has a fixed routine, which the body gets used to. In *Matabele,* for instance, we stood four hours on and four off and it was like a living death, because we would work also in the so-called four hours off. When I went to *Ottawa,* I made an arrangement with the first lieutenant that I could keep a standing middle and a standing afternoon. Then I could adjust my day, my meals and my bowels around this schedule. Staggering the watch is physiologically unsound. In *Ottawa* I would sleep in in the morning, have lunch at eleven-thirty, go on watch at twelve o'clock, come off watch at four and start my day's work. I would go to bed at nine o'clock (2100), then get up at eleven-thirty (2330) for my other watch.

Our new captain said, "This has to stop," as though I was doing something indecent. So I went back into my previous routine with the watches changing all the time and with all these things to do. There was rest camp in Newfoundland that people were supposed to go to, but I could never get to that rest camp because I had too much to do – and I really did need a rest.

Physical fitness was an absolute requirement for entry in the navy, and I can recollect only one man who seemed to have an inherent physical defect of a significant nature. He was a fair-haired, good-looking, well-spoken young man. I do not believe that he had an exceptional level of education, but nevertheless as an able seaman he had been given a brief course in RDF, as radar then was known. We had a very primitive set, a 286, which had to be trained by hand, and it was sometimes difficult to determine whether an echo came from one direction or the reciprocal, the absolute opposite.

In civilian life many years ago the absence of schemes for medical care meant that many diseases or physical defects were left untreated. In the navy, if one was at sea, one became accustomed to being surrounded by physically sound young men in excellent health. One day I was astonished to learn that the RDF operator, who was in my divi-

The Dartmouth Ferry

sion, quite often would have fits in his messdeck. He would foam at the mouth and convulse so violently that it would require as many as six of his messmates to hold him down. I tried to disregard this because it was unlikely we could obtain a replacement. "I am prepared to chance it," I stupidly announced. As certain as sunrise at dawn, the next day I was present for a spectacular fit. Happily the doctor was close at hand and arrived just as the last man piled on top of the heap. The doctor got down on his hands and knees on the deck, said something to the struggling, convulsive patient, and within four or five seconds the boy was quiet and his messmates climbed off him.

Afterward in the wardroom the doctor explained that all he had done was to hypnotise our poor friend out of his fit. He said that because his fits were so dangerous to himself, to others and to the ship, he would have to be sent ashore. I was prepared to have the man with us even if he had continued to have the odd fit; he would have only one task, to keep the RDF operating. But we were not allowed to keep him, and his replacement was hospitalized with influenza the day before he was supposed to join us. So we crossed the Atlantic without a maintenance man and came back to Newfoundland. If the RDF went on the blink I was the one who had to attend to it. One pleasant day at sea I was on the bridge as was the captain. We received a

Officers of HMCS Ottawa. 1942

Surgeon Lt Hendry Lt Lantier Lt MacLeod   Sub-Lt Buchanan Lt(E)?   Mr. Jones
RCNVR   RCNVR   RCNVR   RCNVR   RCNVR Gunner(T) RCN

Sub-Lt Savard   Lt(G)Pullen Cdr.Donald   Lt(E) Clarke   Sub-Lt Jenson
RCN   RCN   RCN   RCN   RCN

(G) Gunnery (E) Engineer (T) Torpedo

report that the RDF was not working; everything was a complete nothing on the set.

"Go and have a look at it, Sub" said the captain. So I went down one deck to where the set was. It was a total mystery. The dials were not in any familiar form, there were no handbooks, and there was no one to turn to. What to do? All the plugs were in that I could see, and no water was dripping on the set. Finally in exasperation I gave the wretched thing a good thump or two with the palm of my hand. Lights came on and the operator somewhere below reported that the set was operating again. I strolled up to the bridge. The captain was delighted. "Well done, Sub," he said, and from then on seemed to think I knew what I was doing with the radar. Even when working perfectly, it could not be depended on to pick up targets.

One day when I was on watch, the captain said, "Don't lose sight of the convoy."

I said, "No, sir."

We were somewhere between Iceland and Newfoundland and suddenly, not long after he had left the bridge, a thick fog suddenly descended. I called up the captain on the voice pipe and said, "Sir, it's dense fog. The convoy is not in sight."

He came roaring up to the bridge and said, "I told you not to lose sight of the convoy."

I said, "Sir, the convoy is right there (gesturing with my hands) just beyond that fog."

He said, "Close in until you see the convoy."

I said, "Sir, if we do we are in danger."

"Don't argue with me," he replied.

So I gave the order "Starboard fifteen." And I'd just said that when the starboard lookout shouted, and towering above us was this huge ship, its port light gleaming down on us, and so I said, "Midships hard a'port."

The captain stormed off the bridge as if it was all my fault. That was hard to forget, but the ship was nearly lost.

In Londonderry just before our last trip a lovely new 271 radar set appeared on the jetty next to *Ottawa*. The captain had not been informed of this major change to his ship, and when I told him what was planned, he was furious. He had been given no authority to accept this and I was to tell them they were not to install it. I am sure a 271 would have given us an excellent picture of the submarines gathering to attack our convoy and its escorts. Sadly, this was not to be.

We were off again on the Derry–Newfie run, expecting it to be uneventful as usual. Other convoys were attacked but not ours. Northern Ireland is beautiful and we were allowed to visit the south as much as we wished in plain clothes. I explored historic ruins along Loch Foyle and with the help of a vivacious Wren from 'Derry toured the old city walls. Just before we left, Sub-Lieutenant Ray Phillips, who had used my sword during his gunnery course, popped on board. He returned my good old sword. I wish he had waited a little longer.

The Anti-Submarine Boom and Nets Halifax Harbour 1939–1945

L.B. JENSON — ©1986

H.M.C.S. Ottawa sailing from Ireland on her last voyage
September, 1942.

8

The Valley of the Shadow of Death

In Derry we painted ship in the new Western Approaches camouflage scheme. When we finished, we came down Loch Foyle to anchor off Moville. Tom Pullen and I went off in one of the ship's boats to inspect the paint job. We were well pleased; Tom took several photographs of the ship, mailing the film to Canada with the last post. At that time, I was steeped in Joseph Conrad's wonderful classic *The Mirror of the Sea,* and as we sailed to pick up our convoy ON127, I looked at the blue hills of western Ireland under a cloudless sky and thought of Conrad's remarks on departures, the last sight of land. Also I thought of that charming Wren.

We were part of Convoy Escort Group C4. Our senior officer was *St. Croix,* an ex-American four-stacker. The other escorts were Canadian corvettes *Amherst, Sherbrooke, Arvida* and an RN corvette, *Celandine.* We sailed to join our convoy of 31 ships off Rathlan Island on Saturday, 5 September 1942. Under the convoy commodore they formed into nine columns and we were away, our course westerly to North America.

The next day, Sunday, one of our sailors was found to have acute appendicitis, and it was decided that we could not weaken the escort to return the unfortunate man to harbour. The surgeon lieutenant would have to perform the operation in the captain's day cabin. The operation was performed on Monday afternoon in a moderate sea which gave the ship considerable motion. It took three hours. One of the operating room "staff" was the shipwright, "possibly because he was handy with tools," said Tom Pullen, who also assisted.

German wartime records indicate that while this was going on, a wolf pack of 13 U-boats was being assembled to the westward in a long line across our path. This area was the German happy hunting ground, out of range of our land-based aircraft. On Wednesday U-584 sighted us and the wolf pack was moved southerly. Of course we were happily unaware of this immediate threat.

H.M.C.S. ST.CROIX
Based on a photograph in June 1942.
The three after funnels have been lowered
by 5 feet; only one set of torpedo tubes is
left, now sited amidships; an AA gun is aft.

Thursday was a lovely day, a sparkling blue ocean under a cloudless sky. I had the afternoon watch and was thinking what a fine sight the convoy presented. Suddenly the second ship in the first column was obscured by a huge white spout of water and started to sink. A tanker in the next column then was torpedoed but didn't sink. Now a ship in the third column became a victim and started to sink. *St. Croix, Ottawa* and *Celandine* swept through the convoy on the possibility that the attacker was hiding in the wakes. We had no luck.

Just at suppertime another ship, a tanker, was torpedoed, not once but twice. The survivors were picked up by *St. Croix*, 26, and ourselves, 24. One of the men we rescued was badly wounded, a rivet buried deep in his abdomen.

Stopping for survivors was nerveracking. The ship presented a sitting target and the Germans showed no compassion. It was a relief to be under way again. Some of the survivors had been torpedoed twice. One man was very small: he told me he was the smallest man in the British merchant service. He said there had been one smaller than he, so he had to kill him – gallows humour. It always seems so strange when it is a beautiful day and one sees dreadful things happening. It is like a nightmare. Ships should only be sunk and people killed on dark, gloomy days.

U-boat attacks continued during the night. Two Norwegian tankers were hit and damaged, and two British tankers were sunk. Records indicate that four torpedoes were fired at *Ottawa* but missed. In those days just before efficient radar was fitted, submarine tactics at night were to speed about on the surface, firing when they could. Because of their low silhouette they were practically invisible, and when they were illuminated by starshell or searchlight they dived.

One can imagine the frustration and confusion of the escorts. A flash and a noise would indicate another torpedoing, but from where? The action taken was to fire starshell and turn in various standard directions according to the particular search pattern ordered by the senior officer. In most cases, all this was an exercise in futility and would accomplish nothing except the rescue of survivors. Aboard *Ottawa* on Friday our surgeon, assisted by the sick berth attendant and the first lieutenant, spent four hours patching together the poor wounded survivor.

Saturday provided no successful attacks for the Germans, but on Sunday an American straggler was torpedoed and sunk. The score now was six ships sunk and two damaged. An aircraft from Newfoundland arrived to support us, at last a light at the end of a very dark tunnel.

During the forenoon on Sunday our badly wounded survivor died of peritonitis and at sunset all hands not on watch and all our survivors gathered on the quarterdeck. The burial service was conducted by the first lieutenant and with prayers and a volley of rifle fire as a last salute, his body was consigned to the deep. I went on watch at 8:00 p.m. (2000) with Mr. Lloyd Jones, our torpedo gunner. It was a dark, clear evening, becoming overcast. The sea was fairly calm but a westerly breeze was getting up. Most of the time we couldn't discern the ships in the convoy, but as

we patrolled back and forth on our station two and a half miles ahead of the lead ship of the starboard column, we could check that all was well. *St. Croix* and *Ottawa* were getting low on fuel and we were supposed to be relieved by HMS *Witch* and HMCS *Annapolis* out of St. John's.

The Asdic was pinging away as it always did at sea, searching steadily either side of our bow, but we had no echoes. Our radar, one of the first and not reliable, swept complete circles around the ship, but could not be depended upon even to show the convoy. The lookouts either side of the bridge, constantly searching through their binoculars, saw nothing but the blackness of the night. Jones and I drank cocoa and gave the helm orders zigzagging on our random patrol. It was a typical night watch.

Sometime before 11 p.m. (2300) the radar operator reported an object at Green 30 degrees. With our radar it might well have been Red 150 degrees, the reciprocal bearing. I called the captain, the signalman made AA (What ship?) on Green 30 and a tiny flash back said, *"Witch."* I turned *Ottawa* towards the signal light and by the time the captain arrived on the bridge we were closing well. I told the captain what we were doing and added that perhaps we should alter away. The radar then reported a small echo on the port bow but he wasn't sure about it. The captain agreed with the alteration so I said port 15 to the quartermaster, who repeated the order, the ship started swinging to port, about 20 degrees.

An amazing geranium-coloured flash forward was followed by a great pillar of water which went straight up! All of us took shelter under the overhang at the front of the bridge as the water and all sorts of solid objects tumbled down from the sky. When the downpour stopped, I went back to the compass and we stopped engines. The ship lay still in the water, rocking gently. The forecastle with anchors and cables together with A Gun had vanished, and the forward canopy with B Gun drooped down towards the water. This was visible because the interior lights were all on and shining out over the ocean. We obviously were a lovely target so the engines were ordered slow astern. A number of British destroyers had suffered similar damage and some had made port going astern much of the way. Mr. Jones left the bridge and hurried at once to the quarterdeck, where he set all the depth charges to "safe" so that if the ship sank survivors would not be blown up by our own charges.

I asked the captain if I could do a quick inspection of the damage and report back. He agreed and I went down the ladders to the starboard passage into the messdecks. The forward messdecks, upper and lower, were gone, and the ocean splashed outside the great open hole, illuminated by the messdeck lights and a calcium flare from a lifebuoy burning in the tossing waters. In the after upper messdeck a group of about 20 men were clustered by a hammock netting. A number were terribly wounded. Men with grotesquely twisted limbs were lying there; it was like a scene from hell. I started aft along the upper deck, encountering first the surgeon rushing forward, next the first lieutenant, to whom I quickly told what little I knew.

Finally I encountered Sub-Lieutenant Wilson, recently joined from his courses in the RN. He had just taken over the Confidential Books from me, that is, codes and cyphers plus intelligence and other secret documents. He understood that it was his duty to take all these from their steel chests, put them in weighted bags and drop them overboard. I tried to convince him not to go below again as I feared another "fish" and told him that the rule applied only to loose books on the bridge which might float away and be found. He would not be convinced and despite my pleadings went below decks to do as he intended.

Back up on the bridge I found the captain and the first lieutenant engaged in firing a rocket, a signal that we had been torpedoed. At almost that very moment a second torpedo hit us, this time in number 2 boiler room, a huge flash then water deluging downwards on us. It was obvious that the ship was doomed. She started to settle in the water and the captain called out to abandon ship. Men were trapped in the Asdic compartment in the bottom of the ship and called and called up the voice pipe. I cannot bear to think of it. Others were trapped in the seamen's wash place, where a steel sliding door had jammed shut. If one thinks of war as a policy, also think for a moment of what I heard that night and cannot bring myself to describe. These are the sounds of a terrible century! Strong men become like little children calling for their mothers, not like John Wayne the motion picture hero.

The ship was sinking. I left the bridge and went to the port side of the forecastle. Acting Petty Officer Hard was standing there.

TORPEDOED & SINKING —
VOICES FROM MEN TRAPPED BELOW
CALLING UP THE BRIDGE VOICEPIPES

I said, "Well Petty Officer Hard, I'm going."

So am I," said Hard, and off he went. Later he found the captain in the water without a lifebelt and tried to take him to a Carley float, but the captain swam away. Hard grabbed him by the hair, but the hair came out in his hand and the captain vanished. When I jumped in I noticed a Dan buoy, a wooden spar with a watertight drum in the centre, floating off the port bow. A man was clinging to it, a Jewish man from Montreal I think, who may have lost a foot. After a few minutes he dropped off and I was alone.

My lifebelt was what was termed a Mae West, a simple rubber tube which I inflated and secured around my chest. The water was about 59 degrees Fahrenheit as we were still in the Gulf Stream, a few miles from the western edge. I kicked off my shoes and with my spar floated fairly comfortably. I was glad I had a heavy sweater and shirt on, with battledress trousers and wool socks. Clothes keep one warm in water just as in the open air, and men with less on died more rapidly.

The ship started to go down before my eyes. I could only see the stern part, tipping out of the water as the forward part sank. Soon the rudder and propellers were right out of the water and the after 4.7-inch gun slipped out of its mounting and plunged downwards. The stern now vanished beneath the waves. It was like a dream. Would all of us nearby be sucked down as our ship sank? No. There was no such effect. Would our depth charges explode, crushing our chests and killing us? Thank God and Mr. Jones, nothing happened. Oil started spreading out from where the ship had been. It was all over my face, my head and hands.

The smell filled the air and the taste was in my mouth. Gradually it lessened and the waves now were fresh and clean. Three or four Carley floats bobbed around hundreds of yards away. They were crowded with men, some of whom were sitting inside the floats, and the floats kept turning over. Each time there would be fewer men on the float.

I decided my Dan buoy was better than a float. I started to pray that my life would be spared, but I reasoned that would never do. I then prayed that I be given strength to cope with my fate, whatever it might be, and recited the Lord's Prayer. In the distance, I could hear, and feel, depth charges exploding. Perhaps someone had a contact – suppose the contact was under us? Should he attack it? I thought yes, it would be more important to kill the U-boat, which would only take more lives. Mercifully, the explosions became more distant and then ceased.

Now to my astonishment the ships of the convoy passed through us – the huge ships' sides (how could they be so big?) and small people at the top calling down to us. One voice told us they dare not stop and I hoped they wouldn't because we would still be in the water when they were fished (torpedoed). Ship after ship passed us and then they were gone and we were alone on the face of the deep. The night was getting darker, the waves were steeper, the breeze stronger and it seemed to be raining. The men on one of the rafts were singing. I recognized the cheerfully commanding voice of the gunner's mate, Petty Officer George Grivel, a splendid man. The songs were "Pack up Your Troubles," "It's a Long Way to Tipperary" and "There's a Long Long Trail Awinding to the Land of My Dreams."

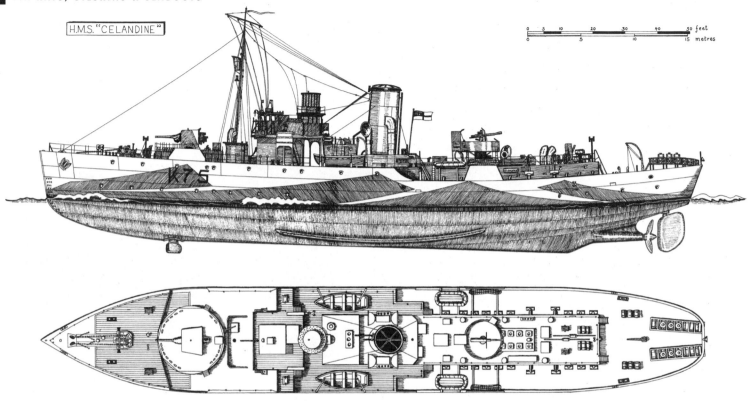

H.M.S. "CELANDINE"

These were hit songs of the First World War, sung by our fathers and uncles as they had faced death in the hideous mud and trenches of the Western Front.

The hours went by, the cold became colder and now jellyfish brushed against my hands and arms like touches of cold fire. My spar was gradually drifting in towards one of the floats. It had lost most of the original crowd, the centre part was empty and the sides were crammed with men hanging on. When my spar drifted closer in, one of the men, a petty officer named Locke, grabbed me

and held me between him and float. He could hardly have had much more strength than I at this stage. Years later I asked this gentleman, who by then was a lieutenant, why he was so kind and good to me. When I was on the Newfie Bullet travelling to join *Ottawa*, his wife and a shipmate's wife had been on the train going to St. John's to be closer to their husbands. I had taken them to dinner and been pleasant and helpful to them. I had no recollection of this other than just meeting two nice ladies, but my reward was great.

Out of the darkness loomed a ship, a corvette, and she was picking up survivors. Would she be fished? Would she rush off? Would she not see us and just leave? Would her turning propeller kill some of us? Now she was practically alongside and stopped, rolling gently. Some men climbed up the scramble net and were hauled aboard. Now it was my turn. I started to climb and then fell back in the water. I did not care now what happened. If I were to drown I was resigned. It was God's will. Strong hands from the float pushed me in towards the ship again. I feebly reached up the net and a great muscular arm reached down like the arm of God and hauled me out of the water like a fish. It was about five o'clock in the morning.

FROM THE VALLEY OF
THE SHADOW OF DEATH

I staggered clear and climbed a ladder to the upper deck. It was right over the engine room and I still can feel the warmth of the deck. Dripping wet and oil covered, totally exhausted and half frozen, yet wonderfully contented, I had to urinate and decided to just do it, like a baby in diapers. After half an hour or so, I felt able to move and went below to the messdeck. Someone asked if I was an officer and directed me to the wardroom.

Immediately I entered, Barriault, our leading steward, came over and said, as if nothing unusual had happened, "Good evening, sir. Would you like a cup of tea?"

So I replied, "Good evening, Barriault. That would be very nice, thank you," and had a cup of delicious, wonderful, hot tea. He had been picked up earlier – a Newfoundlander, he probably was more used to catastrophes than I.

The ship was a Royal Navy corvette from our escort group, HMS *Celandine*. On the way to St. John's she went to action stations several times, which all the survivors found interesting, but nothing happened and we arrived in port three days later.

At about 2300 on 13 September, Lieutenant Commander Heinz Walkering, the commanding officer of *U-91*, sitting on the surface, had discovered to his pleasure that a whole convoy was approaching. An escort destroyer, our *Ottawa*, was about a mile away when he fired torpedoes at us. One hit and blew off our bow. The tubes were reloaded and he fired again, this time hitting us amidships. While we were sinking he passed down through the columns of ships. This was the final successful attack by the submarine wolf pack on our convoy.

Altogether 137 officers, men and all the survivors we had picked up lost their lives; 5 officers and 71 men survived. This was *U-91*'s first operation; she sank *Ottawa* and later damaged a merchant ship in another convoy. The next year, Walkering sank four more merchant ships, leaving *U-91* in March 1943. He was one of the lucky German submariners to survive the war and when last heard of about 1970 was a bank manager in West Germany. *U-91* was sunk by depth charges in early 1944.

When we arrived at St. John's we were housed in the service quarters at Buckmasters Field and given civilian clothing by the Red Cross. I had an ill-fitting brown tweed jacket and flannel trousers and felt like an old tramp. We appeared individually before a board of inquiry. Commander "Scarface" Holmes (who was not officially part of the enquiry) asked me when the first torpedo hit. I replied at 11:03 or so and received quite a blast for not saying 2303. I am not complaining, happy as I was and am to be alive. The jellyfish stings had made my hands itchy, red and swollen, and for weeks I smelled and tasted oil fuel. It seemed to have got into all the pores of my skin. I submitted a claim for the loss of all my possessions and carefully made it double what it actually was, it being my previous experience that I would receive exactly half of what I claimed. In due course, exactly half my claim was approved.

Warm bunk, uniforms and plain clothes, letters, books, sword, telescope, certainly some good friends, the ship which had been my happy home for the past year, all gone forever, sunk to the bottom of the North Atlantic. Still today I can imagine myself, as in a dream, clinging to a wood and metal buoy on a black, windy, rainy night on the ocean with the closest shore an icy Greenland, hundreds of miles away. This truly was the Valley of the Shadow of Death.

Translation from *Chronik des Seekrieges 1939-45*
by J. Rohwer and G. Hummelchen, Oldenburg,
G. Stalling, c1968.

31.8.42–14.9.42, North Atlantic

From the "Stier" [*i.e.* "Bull"] Group, consisting of boats that had been outward bound during the operation against SC-97, and from boats that had been engaged with SC-97, a new Group "Vorwarts" ["Forwards"] was formed consisting of *U-96, U-594, U-608, U-380, U-404, U-584, U-211, U-218, U-407, U-91, U-411, U-92,* and *U-659.* On the evening of 9.9, *U-584* (Kapitanleutnant Deecke) reported Convoy ON-127 – 32 ships, Escort Group C-4 with the Canadian destroyers *St. Croix* (LCdr. Dobson) and *Ottawa,* corvettes *Amherst, Arvida* and *Sherbrooke,* and HMS *Celandine.* Contact was lost during the night and not regained until the afternoon of the 10th. *U-96* (Oberleutnant zur See Hellriegel) sank two ships totalling 10,554 tons and damaged another of 12,190 tons, attacking on the surface. On the night of 10.11.9 a series of attacks were made: *U-659* (Kptlt. Stock) damaged a ship of 8,029 tons that was later sunk by *U-584*; *U-404* (Kptlt. V. Bulow) damaged a ship of 7,417 tons; *U-608* (Oblt. Z.S. Struckmeier) missed; *U-218* (Kptlt. Becker) damaged a ship of 7,361 tons; *U-92* (Oblt. Z.S. Oelrich), missed; and *U-594* (Oblt. Z.S. Mumm) missed. The escort was severely handicapped by the breakdown of all radar sets. In daylight on the 11th *U-96* sank a trawler of 415 tons by gunfire near the convoy. On the night of 11-12.9 attacks were made in succession by: *U-584* – 1 ship, 4,885 tons, sunk; *U-380* (Kptlt. Rother) – missed; *U-211* (Kptlt. Hauser) – 2 ships (20,646 tons) damaged (both later finished off by *U-608*; *U-92* – missed *Ottawa* and *U-404* – 1 ship of 9,272 tons damaged. The escort which had damaged *U-659* on the 11th, managed to drive the submarines away during the day, but they returned with the darkness.

The attacks of *U-594* and *U-407* (Oblt. Z.S. Bruller) on the night of 12-13.9 came to nothing. Next day a straggler of 6,131 tons fell victim to *U-594.* Air escort arriving from Newfoundland drove off some of the submarines. In the night of 13-14.9, *U-91* sank the destroyer *Ottawa* (LCdr. Rutherford) in two attacks. *U-92* lost the convoy, *U-411* missed a corvette. Because of the proximity of the air bases in Newfoundland, the operation had to be broken off on 14.9. This was the only occasion in 1942 when all the submarines operating against a convoy managed to make attacks.

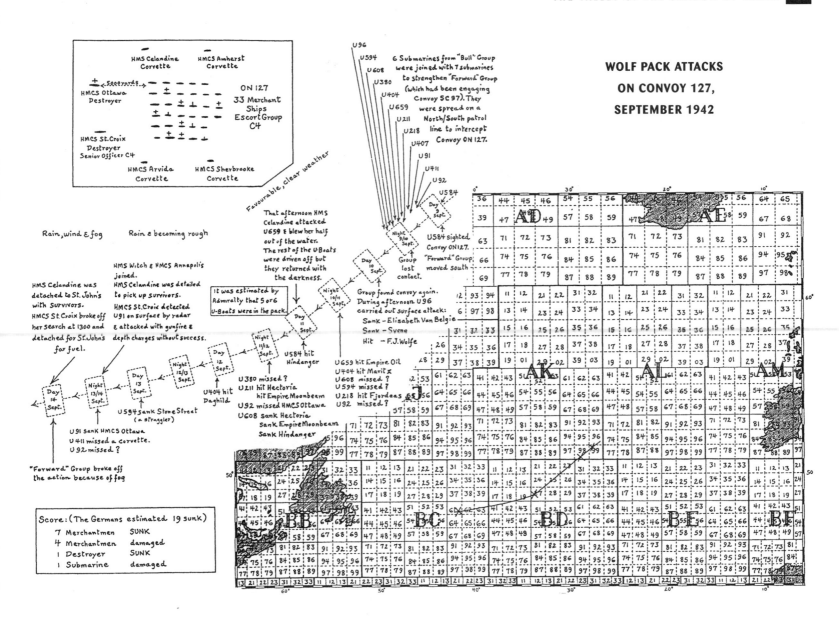

**WOLF PACK ATTACKS
ON CONVOY 127,
SEPTEMBER 1942**

HMS Celandine
Corvette   HMCS Amherst
Corvette

5000 yards

HMCS Ottawa
Destroyer

ON 127

33 Merchant
Ships
Escort Group
C4

HMCS St. Croix
Destroyer
Senior Officer C4

HMCS Arvida
Corvette   HMCS Sherbrooke
Corvette

Favourable, clear weather

U96
U594
U608
U380
U404
U659
U211
U218
U407
U91
U411
U92
U584

6 Submarines from "Bull" Group
were joined with 7 submarines
to strengthen "Forward" Group
(which had been engaging
Convoy SC 97). They
were spread on a
North/South patrol
line to intercept
Convoy ON 127.

Rain, wind & fog

Rain & becoming rough

That afternoon HMS
Celandine attacked
U659 & blew her half
out of the water.
The rest of the U-Boats
were driven off but
they returned with
the darkness.

Day 9 Sept.

Night 9/10 Sept.

U584 sighted
Convoy ON 127.
"Forward" Group
moved south

Group
lost
contact.

HMS Witch & HMCS Annapolis
joined.
HMCS Celandine was detailed
to pick up survivors.
HMCS St. Croix detected
U91 on surface by radar
& attacked with gunfire &
depth charges without success.

HMS Celandine was
detached to St. John's
with survivors.
HMCS St Croix broke off
her search at 1300 and
detached for St. John's
for fuel.

Day 10 Sept.

Night 10/11 Sept.

Group found convoy again.
During afternoon U96
carried out surface attack:
Sank – Elisabeth Van Belgie
Sank – Svene
Hit – F. J. Wolfe

It was estimated by
Admiralty that 5 or 6
U-Boats were in the pack.

Day 11 Sept.

Night 11/12 Sept.

U584 hit
Hindanger

U659 hit Empire Oil
U404 hit Marit x
U608 missed ?
U594 missed ?
U218 hit Fjordaas
U92 missed ?

Day 12 Sept.

U404 hit
Daghild

U380 missed ?
U211 hit Hectoria
hit Empire Moonbeam
U92 missed HMCS Ottawa
U608 sank Hectoria
Sank Empire Moonbeam
Sank Hindanger

Night 12/13 Sept.

Day 13 Sept.

U594 Sank Stone Street
(a straggler)

Night 13/14 Sept.

Day 14 Sept.

U91 Sank HMCS Ottawa
U411 missed a corvette.
U92 missed ?

"Forward" Group broke off
the action because of fog

Score: (The Germans estimated 19 sunk)

7 Merchantmen   SUNK
4 Merchantmen   damaged
1 Destroyer   SUNK
1 Submarine   damaged

AD
AE
AK
AL
AM
J
BB
BC
BD
BE
BF

Confidential

Office of Captain (D), Newfoundland,
Old Knights of Columbus Building,
St. John's, Newfoundland.
20 September 1942.

FINDINGS OF BOARD OF ENQUIRY INTO THE CIRCUMSTANCES ATTENDING THE LOSS OF H.M.C.S. OTTAWA ON SUNDAY, 13 SEPTEMBER 1942

Sir,

We have the honour to report that we have held a full and careful investigation into the circumstances attending the loss of H.M.C.S. OTTAWA on Sunday, 13th September, 1942. The Board is of the opinion that:–

H.M.C.S. OTTAWA was lost at about 2330 on 13th September, 1942 due to enemy action being hit by two torpedoes at 2305 and 2320. The first torpedo striking the ship between 28 station and the stem port side. 28 bulkhead held. The second torpedo struck in No. 2 boiler room, starboard side. The ship then listed to starboard, broke in half and sank bow and stern up. Weather – moderate sea, wind force 3, very dark, no moon.

Reconstruction of the Action.

H.M.C.S. OTTAWA stationed 5000 yards ahead of convoy between 1 and 2 columns obtained two RDF contacts about green 20, 8000 yards and 6000 yards turned towards and increased to 12 and then 15 knots and set a shallow pattern. H.M.S. WITCH, H.M.C.S. ANNAPOLIS in company were expected to join convoy. WITCH had made a signal to OTTAWA "am joining and taking station 8000 yards ahead of convoy". This was intercepted by ST. CROIX but there is no evidence that OTTAWA received it. When RDF range had closed to about 2000 yards an object was sighted fine on the starboard bow and challenged, no reply was received. Commanding Officer appears to have been satisfied that this object was H.M.S. WITCH as he did not order the challenge to be made again. WITCH then called up with shaded light using A's. OTTAWA replied "OT-

TAWA" and received "WITCH" back. The range at this time was approximately 1000 yards closing fast and OTTAWA altered to port using 20 of rudder. A/S cabinet who had reported H.E. on WITCH's bearing, was ordered to disregard and carry out an all round sweep for H.E. After the ship had swung some 20 the first torpedo struck. Commanding Officer stopped engines, gave orders for examination and report of damage, prepare for abandon ship, prepare for destruction of Confidential Books and for signal "Have been torpedoed no immediate danger of sinking" to be passed by R/T to ST. CROIX. It is not clear if this signal was made but it was not received by ST. CROIX. Depth charges were set to safe and primers withdrawn by order of the first Lieutenant. It is considered that the ship continued to swing to port and lost way after turning about 180 when the U-Boat without changing position apparently fired the second torpedo. When this torpedo had struck the ship started to list to starboard and break up. The order to abandon ship was given.

Contributing Factors

The Commanding Officer had in mind the possibility of getting stern way on his ship but was waiting reports on damage. He appears to have expected a second torpedo. It is considered that under these circumstances it would have been better to risk going astern in order to present a more difficult target.

Had action been sounded when RDF contacts were reported the loss of life would have been considerably less. It is estimated that approximately half the casualties were due to the explosion of the first torpedo, many of the ships' company being turned in on the mess decks at the time. The Board does not attach blame to the Commanding Officer for not sounding off action under the circumstances. The RDF contacts were obviously not a U-Boat. Two destroyers were expected from ahead and the ships' company had had little rest for some days.

Had H.M.C.S. OTTAWA been fitted with Type 271 RDF the U-Boat would probably have been picked up in the sweep as well as the two destroyers.

The fact that a dark object was sighted to starboard and that an exchange of signals took place diverted most of the lookout to starboard.

Signals made by WITCH were probably seen by the U-Boat and assisted her in her attack.

General Remarks

The ship was efficient and well organized as is shown by the evidence that everybody knew and carried out their duties in the emergency.

The morale of the ship's company throughout was magnificent.

The Board wishes to draw special attention to the commendable devotion to duty (shown in evidence) of the following officers and men:

The Commanding Officer, Acting Lieutenant Commander Clark A. Rutherford, RCN and the Medical Officer, Surgeon Lieutenant George A. Hendry, RCNVR. These officers lost their lives largely through exhaustion caused by little or no rest for some days previous. Also to Sub-Lieutenant L. B. Jenson, RCN who for a young officer displayed considerable initiative and powers of command.

> Acting Gunner (T) L. E. Jones
> Petty Officer Gridel
> Leading Stoker McLeod
> and Sub-Lieutenant Arnold of H.M.S. CELANDINE

It is not clear why H.M.S. WITCH was not aware that OTTAWA had been torpedoed.

H.M.S. WITCH was not available at the time of the investigation.

Lessons learned and suggestion:

1. That the fitting of type 271 RDF to all convoy escorts and HFD/F FH3 to destroyers be pressed on with to the maximum.

2. That more lifesaving appliances of the float and raft types are fitted to ships and that special attention be paid to releasing and launching of them. Boats in escort vessels, if not already rendered unserviceable by stress of weather seldom get launched when the vessel is torpedoed.

3. That some secondary exit is provided in asdic cabinets type 124. There have been so many cases of the operators being trapped through the door becoming jammed. Ships where no deck or deckhead escape can be fitted mount the door on double acting hinges fitted with large and easily removable hinge pins on the inner side so that the door can be pulled inwards if prevented by debris from opening outwards.

4. That all non-essential doors such as heads bathroom, etc. be replaced by screens or curtains.

5. That rescue nets be made long enough to reach well below the water line so that an exhausted man can get his feet on to something as well as his hands.

6. That the merchant service type of lifesaving jacket fitted with watertight torch be supplied to H.M. ships and that these jackets are fitted with a becket and toggle with which an exhausted man can secure himself to the life saving lanyard of a float or raft.

7. That the old type of emergency rations in boats and rafts which take up a lot of space and add weight, be replaced by condensed rations.

8. That better communication to boiler rooms is fitted.

9. That in new construction the possibility of leading pipes in living spaces along the deck instead of under the deckhead be investigated, thereby minimizing the likelihood of pinning men down when the pipes fracture and fall.

10. The merit of the old order that a sailor should always carry a knife was undoubtedly proved.

> We have the honour to be,
> Sir,
> Your obedient servants,

[signed] H. Frewer, LIEUTENANT, RCN, Member
[signed] R. Jackson, LIEUTENANT COMMANDER, RCNVR, Member
[signed] G. A. Harrison, COMMANDER, RN, President

TYPE VIIC

Most combat action was accomplished by some 670 U-boats of Type VIIC.

Displacement: 769 to 871 tons
Dimensions: 220¼' long, 20¼' beam, 15¾' draft
Machinery: 2 shaft diesel/electric motors, 2,800–3,200 bhp, twin rudders
Bunkers: 114 tons diesel oil
Speeds / range: Max. 17.7 knots (on surface)
Surface: 10 knots / 8,500 nautical miles. 17 knots / 3,250 nautical miles
Underwater: 4 knots / 80 nautical miles. 2 knots / 130 nautical miles
Guns: One 88 mm, 250 rounds
One 37 mm anti-aircraft, 1,195 rounds. Two 20 mm anti-aircraft, 4,380 rounds
Torpedoes: Four 533 mm tubes for'd and one aft
18 torpedoes or 39 mines
Crew: 4 officers and 40–56 men
Radar search set on conning tower

The Ensign worn by U-Boats with honour and fought under with great bravery & fortitude.

U-BOAT 91

Built by Flenderwerft in Lubeck on the Baltic Sea, launched 30 October 1941. Kapitänleutnant Walkerling commanded her from her commissioning until April 1943. She carried out the following missions:

Aug./Sept. 1942 Vorwärts Group – engaged convoys SC97, ON127, RB1.
November 1942 Westwall Group – operation Torch
Feb./Mar. 1943 Knappen Group – engaged convoys ON166 with Burggraf Group; SC121 with Raubgraf Group; SC122 and HX229.

In these actions she sank HMCS *Ottawa* (destroyer) and 5 convoy vessels (35,577 gross registered tons). *U-91* was destroyed by depth charges in the North Atlantic on 25 February 1944 by Royal Navy frigates HMS *Affleck*, HMS *Gore* and HMS *Gould*.

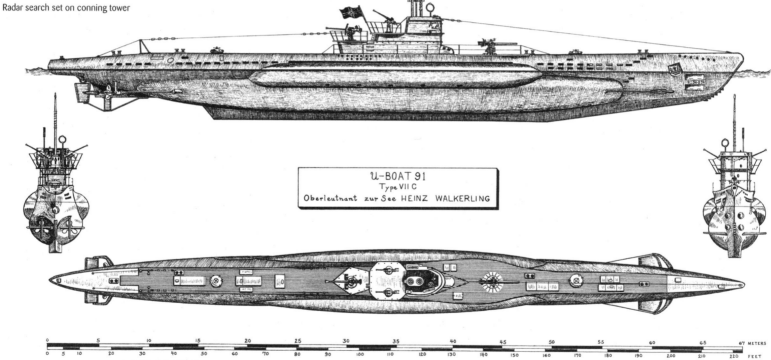

U-BOAT 91
Type VII C
Oberleutnant zur See HEINZ WALKERLING

Submarines of Type VIIC were numbered as follows: U-69 to U-72, U-77 to U-82, U-88 to U-98, U-132 to U-136, U-201 to U-212, U-221 to U-232, U-235 to U-458, U-465 to U-486, U-551 to U-790, U-821 to U-840, U-901 to U-1058, U-1063 to U-1080.

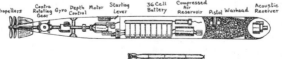

Propellers, Contra Rotating Gear, Gyro, Depth Control, Motor, Starting Lever, 36 Cell Battery, Compressed Air Reservoir, Pistol Warhead, Acoustic Receiver

Type V Acoustic Torpedo

Torpedo
(to scale of the submarine)

Guardian Angel

As told by AB C.R. Skillen for the book Fading Memories: Canadian Sailors and the Battle of the Atlantic, *edited by Thomas G. Lynch. Reproduced with the kind permission of C.R. Skillen of Nipigon, Ontario, and the Atlantic Chief and Petty Officers Association.*

In late December, 1941 HMCS *Ottawa* was senior escorting the westbound convoy from Derry to NewfyJohn. The North Atlantic was in the midst of one of her notorious gales. The crew did not think they would make NewfyJohn for Xmas but their relief arrived a day early so they were able to arrive in St. John's Christmas Eve.

Skillen writes that everyone had gone ashore except for the duty watch. Christmas Eve had meant a lot to him as he grew up. He knew what he wanted to do on this most solemn of nights was to attend midnight Mass. His next priority was to see some of St. John's night life.

On his way up the dock he noticed a sailor looking lonesome and glum. He stopped to chat and found out that the sailor was off HMS *Celandine*, a Royal Navy corvette that was part of their recent convoy escort and now tied up astern of the *Ottawa*. His name was Pat Riches and he was returning to his ship – it was no fun for a sailor ashore with no funds. Skillen asked him to tag along as he had a few dollars; when that was gone they would then return to their ships. He also mentioned that he wanted to attend midnight Mass. Pat was of the same faith and welcomed the chance to go as it had been seven years since he last attended church. They did what they set out to do and returned early in the morning to their ships, broke but satisfied with their evening. At the gangway they wished each other a Merry Christmas and good luck. Pat shook hands and thanked him for making it a brighter Christmas Eve and said the next time they met he would like to return the favour.

The routine of excorting convoys that winter and during the summer of 1942 was without incidents. September saw the *Ottawa* with its escorts gathering a large convoy from Britain to shepherd it west back to North America. Suddenly on the 10th September the convoy was under attack. This continued for three long days as the U-boats picked merchant ships one by one. Then just before midnight of the 13th September the *Ottawa* received her first torpedo hit directly under the seamen's mess. Everyone was at action stations when the order came to help with the removal of the dead and wounded from the forward part of the ship. The *Ottawa* lay dead in the water. At first they thought they could proceed slowly and perhaps make it into port, but that was not to be. Skillen was climbing a ladder when the second torpedo smashed into midships, exploded and split the *Ottawa* in two. When Skillen came to he was lying on the upper deck, his legs pinned by the guard rail. He desperately tried to free himself but to no avail. The bow of the ship had already sunk and he knew it was only a matter of time before the stern would sink too. It crossed his mind that he too could lose his life. However, he was not going to give up that easily.

He offered his Maker a little prayer asking him to forgive him and gave another try – his legs came free and he was able to roll off the deck into the cold waters of the North Atlantic. When he surfaced he heard his shipmates yelling and moaning. He made for the noise just as the stern disappeared beneath the surface. The Carley float held many of his shipmates and what was to become his lifeline for the next five hours. The cold and rough seas began to take their toll; more and more of his shipmates silently slipped away. He wanted to sleep, but he knew one false move would spell the end and he too would suffer the same fate. So he hung on with grim determination.

Where a ship loomed out of the dark, there were only six left out of 22 still clinging to the Carley float. It was HMS *Celandine* – she had a scrambling net hung over the side – like a welcoming mat. A pair of arms reached down and helped Skillen aboard. As he rolled over on the deck he looked up into the eyes of Pat Riches, the English sailor he befriended that Christmas eve so long ago. Pat was surprised to see him.

By now Skillen had lost the feeling in his legs so they carried him below and from then on Pat was his nurse and held him like a guardian angel. Arriving in port, they took Skillen off on a stretcher. At the gangway they said their goodbyes. Like ships that pass in the night, they would not see each other again. Skillen would lose his right leg and suffer the wounds of his left leg. He thanked his God for listening that night in 1942 and putting Pat in the right place so that he could return the favour.

A letter to Captain Thomas Pullen from Vice Admiral Sir Peter Gretton, who was one of the most distinguished escort commanders in the Battle of the Atlantic:

14th April, 1981

Dear Tom,

Many thanks for your most helpful and interesting letter. It provided me with just what I wanted. And it solved one or two problems.

I have only one query. You say that you were warned of being shadowed on 9th September. But the Admiralty were not getting Ultra at that time and I can find no trace of any signal telling you that shadowers were about. Were you relying on memory or evidence? Did you know that the German B service was reading all our signals at that time and knew where you were quite accurately, which accounts for the fact that ten U boats got to you so quickly.

Collins lives near here and I have seen him several times. He cherishes your cigarette case. He is a good chap who has done well in business after leaving the sea at the end of the war.

One or two points of interest about ON127. I found a signal from Mainguy in St. Johns saying that you and *St. Croix* should fuel from tankers in the convoy when *St. C.* asked for relief as he was short of fuel. There were no tankers in the convoy fitted to fuel at sea as far as I can find out so it was not a very helpful signal.

The *Witch* and *Annapolis* arrived to strengthen the escort from St. J. just before you were fished. I did not realise that you had got so close to the *Witch*. It probably took your eye off the U boat.

It is disappointing to find from German records that from the 25 or so attacks made by the escorts of ON127, one U boat was damaged a little and had to return to base.

You might be interested in the statistics. As you said, seven ships plus *Ottawa* were sunk. Five were torpedoed but got back to harbour – three with the convoy, two on their own.

Two others broke out of convoy and reached harbour safely.

I think that this accounts for the exaggerated stories about losses.

You will be interested in the times of your sinking as logged by *Celandine* and *St. C.* Hit first at 2305, second at 2330.

A tanker, No. 23 the *Clausina*, stopped to try to pick up survivors at once, but I don't think got any. But she helped the *Celandine* to find you at 0110 when the *C.* first started to pick up survivors. At 0200, as a result of a request by *Celandine*, the *St. C.* told the *Arvida* to help with survivors. The *Celandine* reports that the last survivor – it must have been you – was picked up at 0535. It was lucky that you were so close to the Gulf Stream, otherwise you would have frozen to death!

Collins hinted that the escort thought that *Ottawa* should have been made SO Escort. But Rutherford was very young, I suppose, and *St. Croix* experienced.

It was fascinating to read the German accounts alongside the Canadian! They tallied fairly well but both sides thought that they had done better than they actually did. Eight of your U boat Captains were on their first patrol and though every one made an attack, some did not do as well as more experienced chaps would have done.

Donitz was pleased but noted that air cover was not there!

You may be interested to learn that Mainguy relieved *Arvida* on the spot after arrival in harbour, and that the *Sherbrooke* was given plotting exercises specially.

St. Croix is criticised for spending too much time in sinking torpedoed ships.

Remembrances of the *Ottawa*

The heavy blue curtain drifts back and forth across the doorway of the darkened cabin. Occasionally, a rifle shifts its position with a rattle in the cabin flat arms rack and a wheel spanner clanks in its bed. Water drips through the hatch cover each time a green one gushes over the deck above. Above these and a host of other ship sounds is the steady rumble – a rumble felt rather than heard – of the main engines, mingled with the ghostly rushing and lapping of the water outside. The mottled reflection of the dim red police light wanders in the restless films of oil and water on the deck. The air here is close but damp and cold and only causes the scene to be more desolate and dreary. So it remains as the small powerful ship ploughs on through the wind, waves and darkness. The hatch opens and two leather seaboots followed by a body encased in a glinting oilskin coat laboriously descend the ladder. Clutching the rifle racks and advancing as the rolling permits, the figure reaches the cabin door, pushes aside the curtain and switches on the light.

"Twenty to four, sir, and you've got the morning watch. It's raining hard and the spray is coming over the bridge. The officer of the watch suggests oilskins."

Having said his piece, the messenger waits until the shapeless lump on the bunk mumbles, "Thanks, I heard."

The messenger starts up the ladder and in a few moments announces his departure from the flat by closing down the hatch cover. The victim mutters, "Roll on my leave," sits up, rubs his hands over his face and reaches for a cigarette beside the bunk. An extra heavy lurch almost sends him flying to the deck. Casting off the blanket, he appears practically dressed with his once-navy-blue trousers, stiff and shiny with brine, heavy woollen socks, a woollen sweater and inflatable lifebelt. Out of the bunk then and, setting a chair on its four legs again, he sits down and completes his rig with seaboots, scarf, monkey jacket and then, standing up, dons an oilskin coat, big leather mitts and sou'wester. Out cigarette, which tastes rotten anyway and gets into one's eyes, off light and up the ladder.

Onto the upper deck, he finds himself in a deafening shambles of sea and wind which hit him with a slapping, buffeting hand. The occasional white fleck of a breaking wave roaring past is all that can be seen in the darkness. He gropes his way along a lifeline on the leeward side towards the bridge, alert to warn anyone coming in the opposite direction. As he advances he turns his head to leeward to protect his face from the sharp, cold rain and spray driven between the funnels from the windward side of the ship.

A figure bumps gently into him, murmurs, "Sorry chum," and passes on. At last the bridge structure – now up and up, ladder to ladder. "Hey, is this the blasted bridge?" he says, knowing full well it is but thinking it as good a greeting as any other. Besides one couldn't really call this a good morning.

"You're late!" a voice says, "as usual."

He retorts, "I suppose you wolves gobbled up all the kye and sandwiches. I don't know what the devil you guys do up here – picnic all your watch? Where's the convoy anyway – lost it?"

"Look, when you shut up, I'll turn over this glorious watch to you. Hedy Lamarr is in my cabin at this very moment cooking some ham and eggs for me. Besides there are other important reasons why I must get below. Four hours is a long time on a cold bridge. Now the course is 075 degrees, we have 112 revolutions on. We are in Position B for Beer. The old man wants a shake at dawn. Anti-Submarine …" and so on. In the meantime, the second officer of the watch arrives complaining that he wasn't shaken properly.

As soon as our officer of the morning watch is sure that all the relieving lookouts and gun crews have their eyes adjusted to the black night, he orders the bosun's mate to pipe the middle watch men below. Now we are settled down for the watch when another figure stumbles up from below and reports something to the signalman.

"No," we hear, "the officer of the watch is over there by the binnacle."

"Watch correct," reports this figure.

"All the boats all right?" the OOW asks.

"Everything fine, sir. Nothing carried away."

"Very good, thank you," replies the OOW.

Our eyes gradually become accustomed to the dark and we can detect one figure braced between the gyro compass binnacle and the magnetic binnacle. This is the second OOW; the first OOW is wedged between the magnetic compass and the chart table. Our signalman is clutching on to some voice pipes at the forepart of the bridge, his face pressed behind the glass windscreen so that he can see if there is anything to see.

Officers and men are indistinguishable as they are dressed completely alike. From time to time, they raise heavy binoculars to their eyes and sweep the darkness around them, put them down and relapse into a watchful quiescence.

The communication number to the depth charge crew crouches in the rear of the bridge. Occasionally the ship shudders heavily as it crashes into a big wave and then all crouch lower to dodge the bitter spray that whips through the air.

The tempestuous wind howling and blustering in the shrouds and rigging barely is felt on the well designed bridge. Once in a while a sharp puff hurls the rain under sou'wester brims in a cold and bitter shower. Occasionally, the ship shudders heavily as the bows bury into an unusually large wave and then all crouch lower again to dodge the curtain of spray that whips through the air.

Because of the heavy weather it is impractical to zigzag. Consequently, there is little to do except think, watch and try to ward off the advances of Morpheus. An officer is supposed to busy himself by speculating what he will do with the ship in various circumstances. "What will I do if a submarine suddenly appears on my starboard quarter? What will I do if the steering engines break down" and so on. By constantly thinking of all the accidents and events that can possibly occur, and the action that should be taken, an officer prepares himself for what might happen while he is in charge.

Hey, is that a rocket? No, that's the trouble with looking too hard. One begins to see things that aren't there. I wish this bloody rain would pack up, wish I had my head down – funny, doesn't seem to matter how cold or wet it is, it still doesn't keep you wide awake.

And so we leave our friend on the Atlantic in 1942.

9

The Atlantic Lifeline

By 1942 the convoy system was well established and could be expanded on a worldwide basis according to the threat of attack and the availability of escorts. On the North Atlantic routes to and from the United Kingdom, merchant ship movements and cargoes were integrated by naval and civilian coordinators. Trainloads of trucks, locomotives, tanks, ammunition, guns, chemicals, grain, flour, meat, sugar, and all the other materials to wage war and to take care of the civilian populations and those under arms were planned weeks, even months, ahead to meet the ships as they arrived in various ports and assembled for convoy.

Bedford Basin in Halifax (the famous "East Coast Port") was the main assembly point for the HX convoys, ships capable of 9 to 15 knots, while Sydney in Cape Breton was used for the SC convoys, slower ships of 6 to 9 knots. Ships capable of 15 knots or more were routed independently. Most merchantmen were fitted with guns and given DEMS (Defensively Equipped Merchant Ships) gun crews.

Before sailing, a convoy conference was held at which naval authorities explained to the masters the arrangement of ships in the convoy according to cargo and destination, the signals which the convoy commodore (a retired senior naval officer) would use, details of the route, the necessity for good station-keeping, plans in the event of enemy action; masters were warned not to make smoke, not to show lights at night, not to drop garbage or pump out oily bilges other than at sunset – all to avoid detection.

The merchantmen represented men of many nations. Some were well paid compared to naval personnel (which made for interesting comments at times) but all faced the possibility of sudden or hideous death.

The major advantage of convoys was that large numbers of ships on ocean passage were concentrated in, say, 30 square miles in an area of tens of thousands of square miles, making the convoy hard to find. The disadvantage was that ships and cargoes were delayed by assembly times and the speed of the convoy being that of the slowest ship.

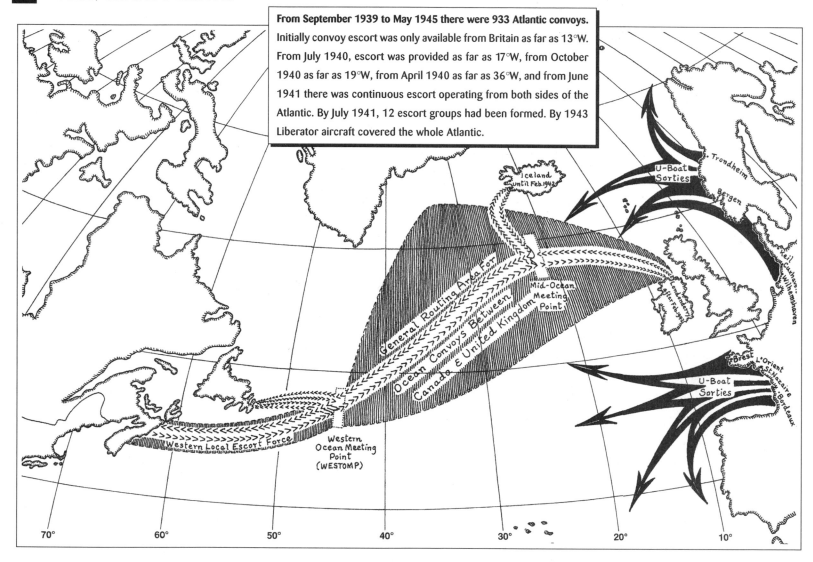

From September 1939 to May 1945 there were 933 Atlantic convoys. Initially convoy escort was only available from Britain as far as 13°W. From July 1940, escort was provided as far as 17°W, from October 1940 as far as 19°W, from April 1940 as far as 36°W, and from June 1941 there was continuous escort operating from both sides of the Atlantic. By July 1941, 12 escort groups had been formed. By 1943 Liberator aircraft covered the whole Atlantic.

Atlantic convoys and attacking U-boats

The Battle of the Atlantic mainly involved the convoys and independent ships carrying food, fuel and weapons from Canada and the United States to the United Kingdom (Britain). Convoys were made up of five to fifty merchant ships escorted by three or four (or more) escorting warships, most of which were corvettes, often manned by Canadians. The opponents were German submarines dedicated to sinking merchant ships and escorts. The trans-Atlantic convoys were a lifeline to Britain and the battle would decide the fate of the world! The major departure point from North America was Halifax, Nova Scotia.

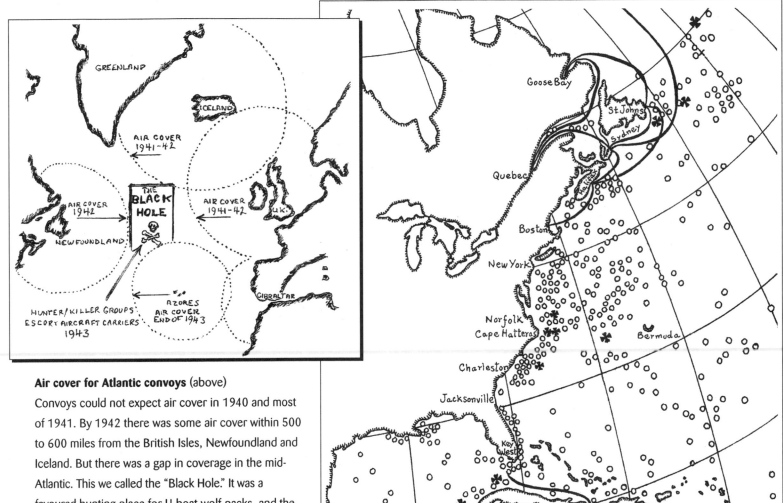

Air cover for Atlantic convoys (above)

Convoys could not expect air cover in 1940 and most of 1941. By 1942 there was some air cover within 500 to 600 miles from the British Isles, Newfoundland and Iceland. But there was a gap in coverage in the mid-Atlantic. This we called the "Black Hole." It was a favoured hunting place for U-boat wolf packs, and the area where Convoy ON 127 was attacked and HMCS *Ottawa* was sunk. By mid-1943, radar, HF/DF and hunter-killer groups brought the end of the wolf packs.

"Happy time" for U-boats, January to July 1942

After Pearl Harbor, 7 December 1941, there were few escorts for the North American eastern seaboard. The terrible slaughter and destruction of shipping are illustrated in the map at right.

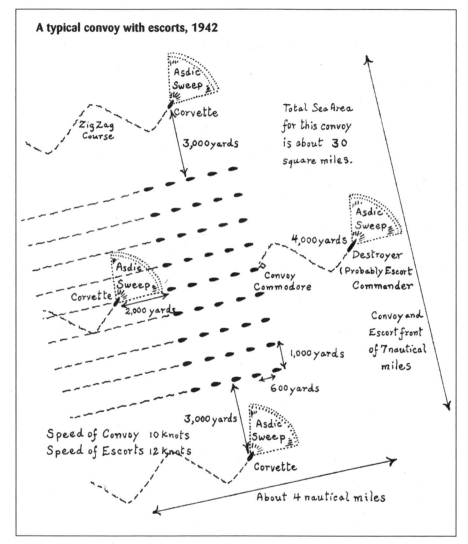

A typical convoy with escorts, 1942

Asdic Sweep

Corvette

ZigZag Course

3,000 yards

Total Sea Area for this convoy is about 30 square miles.

Asdic Sweep

4,000 yards

Destroyer (Probably Escort Commander)

Asdic Sweep

Corvette

2,000 yards

Convoy Commodore

Convoy and Escort front of 7 nautical miles

1,000 yards

600 yards

3,000 yards

Asdic Sweep

Speed of Convoy 10 knots
Speed of Escorts 12 knots

Corvette

About 4 nautical miles

The escorts

In 1942 there was a perilous shortage of escort vessels – destroyers, corvettes and sloops. As there was no way of knowing when, where and how many submarines would be deployed, escorts were spread very thinly. In addition, ship breakdowns were not uncommon. In the Royal Navy, and in the Royal Canadian Navy especially, there was a serious shortage of experienced officers and men.

In the stormy North Atlantic, where sun, moon and stars were clouded over for weeks on end, much of our navigation was by dead reckoning. Snowstorms, fog, icebergs, minefields, lack of lights and buoys and other navigational aids – all combined to complicate the navigational problems.

Radio Direction Finding (RDF) was the primitive ancestor of radar. It was awkward and unreliable, particularly for surface echoes. Asdic (see overleaf) was a narrow beam of sound ranging out about a mile, and could be confused by wakes of other ships and even by schools of fish.

Zigzag patterns were selected from tables to present a varying course and were carried out precisely. In later years escorts simply patrolled about their station in an unpredictable manner.

Signals were by flag hoist, shaded lamp, sirens or rocket.

Flower Class corvette (facing page)

Rugged, dirty, rusty, salt-stained, sea-battered warriors in the merciless Battle of the Atlantic, these uncomfortable little warships fought the battle without respite from 1940 to 1945. By the end of the war most of them were completely worn out. 145 were built in the United Kingdom, and 124 were built in Canada. Corvettes killed more than 50 German and Italian submarines. 19 RN and 9 RCN corvettes were lost in action.

Convoy numbers

Each convoy had an identifying code. Eastbound convoys to the UK were prefixed HX –Halifax to UK, or SC – Sydney to UK. Westbound convoys were prefixed ON – UK to Halifax, or ONS – UK to Halifax Slow. Other prefixes were JW – UK to Russia, RA – Russia to UK.

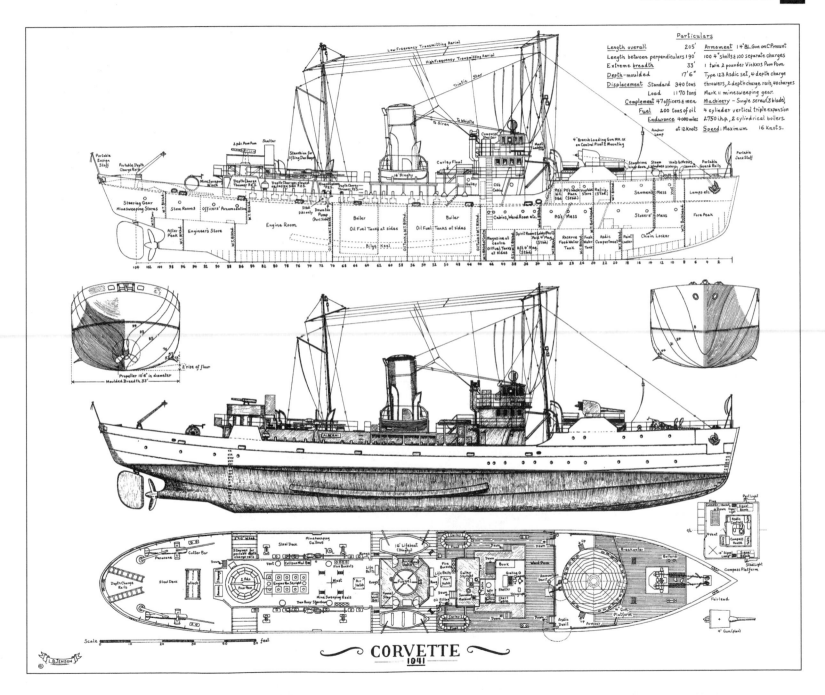

Particulars

Length overall   205'
Length between perpendiculars 190'
Extreme breadth   33'
Depth-moulded   17'6"
Displacement   Standard   940 tons
               Load   1170 tons
Complement   47 officers & men
Fuel   200 tons of oil
Endurance   4000 miles   at 12 knots

Armament 1 4"BL Gun on CP mount
100 4" shells & 100 separate charges
1 twin 2 pounder Vickers Pom Pom
Type 123 Asdic set, 4 depth charge
throwers, 2 depth charge rails, 40 charges
Mark II minesweeping gear.
Machinery — Single screw (3 blade),
4 cylinder vertical triple expansion
2750 i.h.p., 2 cylindrical boilers.
Speed: Maximum   16 Knots.

CORVETTE
1941

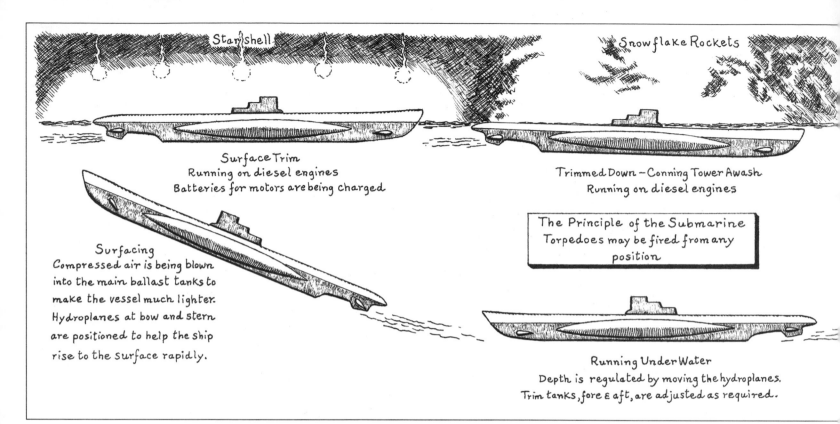

Star shell

Snowflake Rockets

Surface Trim
Running on diesel engines
Batteries for motors are being charged

Trimmed Down — Conning Tower Awash
Running on diesel engines

The Principle of the Submarine
Torpedoes may be fired from any
position

Surfacing
Compressed air is being blown
into the main ballast tanks to
make the vessel much lighter.
Hydroplanes at bow and stern
are positioned to help the ship
rise to the surface rapidly.

Running Under Water
Depth is regulated by moving the hydroplanes.
Trim tanks, fore & aft, are adjusted as required.

The enemy

The U-boat was the weapon that nearly defeated the British in the Second World War. This dreadful situation had also arisen in the First World War, and it was surprising that there had not been greater emphasis on anti-submarine work and convoy protection between the wars.

U-boats could remain at sea for up to 3 months, and each could carry 21 torpedoes. Torpedoes had a speed of 40 knots and range up to 8 miles; they could be fired from the surface or from a depth as great as 200 feet. The U-boats in use for most of the war had a maximum surface speed of 16 knots, 9 knots submerged. They could crash dive in 30 seconds and were fantastically tough – a depth charge had to explode within 21 feet to be lethal.

As an example of their use, in June 1941 25 U-boats were in the northwest Atlantic, mostly south and east of Newfoundland. They were strung across the convoy routes at intervals of 30 miles. Their movements were controlled by the command post at L'Orient on the Bay of Biscay.

"Wolf pack" attacks could take place day or night. In the daylight, attacks were made at periscope depth; in darkness, the attacks were made on the surface, the U-boats trimmed down and moving at top speed. A wolf pack attack presented a scene of ships blowing up, on fire and sinking, escorts moving in every direction, rockets going up, depth charges exploding, torpedo tracks, possible glimpses of submarines, general confusion, and then the remaining convoy sedately steaming on.

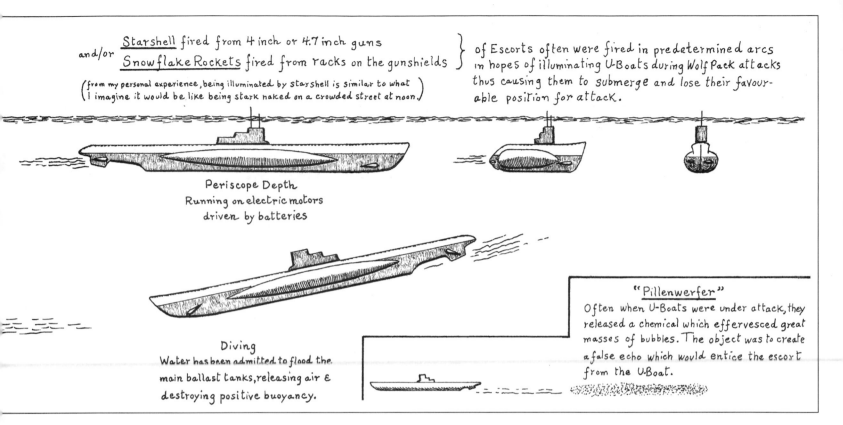

and/or <u>Starshell</u> fired from 4 inch or 4.7 inch guns
<u>Snowflake Rockets</u> fired from racks on the gunshields } of Escorts often were fired in predetermined arcs in hopes of illuminating U-Boats during Wolf Pack attacks thus causing them to submerge and lose their favourable position for attack.

(from my personal experience, being illuminated by starshell is similar to what I imagine it would be like being stark naked on a crowded street at noon.)

Periscope Depth
Running on electric motors
driven by batteries

Diving
Water has been admitted to flood the main ballast tanks, releasing air & destroying positive buoyancy.

"Pillenwerfer"
Often when U-Boats were under attack, they released a chemical which effervesced great masses of bubbles. The object was to create a false echo which would entice the escort from the U-Boat.

German U-boat torpedoes

At the start of the war, U-boats were supplied with compressed-air-driven torpedoes much like those of the British. Warheads were fitted with magnetic detonation to explode under or near the target. These "fish" were unreliable in every way, including depth-keeping, and were soon replaced by reliable torpedoes, electrically driven and thus trackless, so that they gave away neither their position nor the direction from which they were launched. They were fitted with a contact warhead.

German torpedoes had an important feature that British ones lacked. From British vessels, torpedoes were aimed by the ship firing her salvo one by one as the ship "swung" and the target passed the sights. For the Germans, the director angle, i.e. the angle of aim ahead of the target, was set on the torpedo. After the fish was launched it would automatically turn to the course desired. The submarine did not even have to aim at the target. A "fan" of four torpedoes, each set with its own director angle, would be fired if the target appeared worthwhile.

GNATS (German Naval Acoustic Torpedo) appeared in 1943 to deal with attacking escorts. No matter what evasive course was steered, the acoustic homing device steered this 25-knot torpedo towards the selected propeller noise. Submarines had to take care not to torpedo themselves with these horrors.

LUTS torpedoes were designed for large convoy targets and were based on the same principle as the British "W"-ing torpedoes. They could be fired at long range with an initial straight run; then they steered a predetermined irregular course inside the convoy.

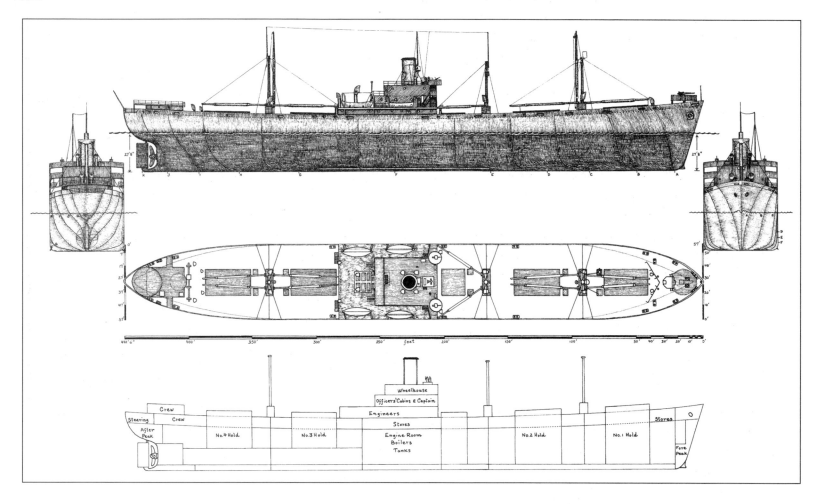

The Liberty ship

The Allied object in the Battle of the Atlantic was the safe and timely arrival of shipping, usually in the form of convoys made up of merchant ships. The enemy's object was to sink these vessels.

The Liberty ship was simple in design, and easily and quickly built. Overall length was 441 feet 6 inches, beam 57 feet, draft 27 feet 8 inches, displacement 14,100 tons. Reciprocating engine of 2,500 shaft horsepower, speed 11 knots, crew 40. Gross tonnage 7,170. Net tonnage 4,380. Armament one or two 3-inch guns, four 20mm anti-aircraft guns (varied from ship to ship).

More than 2,600 of these ships were built in 1941–1943. Many were used as special types and naval auxiliaries.

Wolf pack attacks

These attacks were conducted in darkness using all submarines in the area, running on the surface, trimmed down with conning towers awash and very difficult to see. The submarines thus kept their flexibility, speed and vision, which were lost when they dived. Dashing in between the escorts, they fired their torpedoes at will, leaving a wake of sinking and burning ships.

Admiralty tracking of submarines

Shore-based intercept stations enabled the British Admiralty to obtain "fixes" on U-boats which transmitted position reports and other communications on high-frequency radio. Thus there was often warning to escort commanders and convoy commanders that U-boats were forming up for an attack. This was nerve-racking news for the commodore and the escort skippers because little could be done other than warn lookouts and perhaps carry out an emergency turn of the convoy at dusk in the hope of evading the attackers. Submarines could hear convoy propellers at up to 20 miles, and this often nullified any evasive action by the convoy.

Zigzagging

Zigzagging was an important defence against U-boats. To avoid collision while in convoy, zigzags were done in accordance with tables of times and courses (say Zig Zag No.15) laid down by the Admiralty.

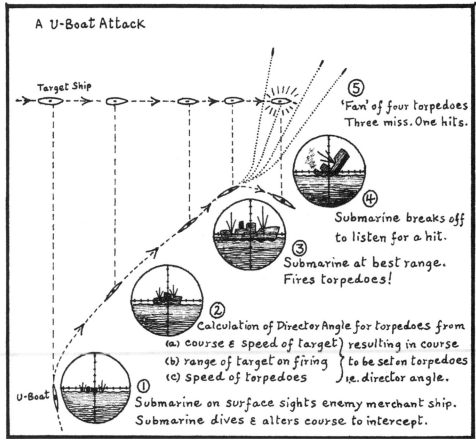

A U-Boat Attack

Target Ship

⑤ 'Fan' of four torpedoes Three miss. One hits.

④ Submarine breaks off to listen for a hit.

③ Submarine at best range. Fires torpedoes!

② Calculation of Director Angle for torpedoes from
(a) course & speed of target
(b) range of target on firing
(c) speed of torpedoes
} resulting in course to be set on torpedoes i.e. director angle.

U-Boat

① Submarine on surface sights enemy merchant ship. Submarine dives & alters course to intercept.

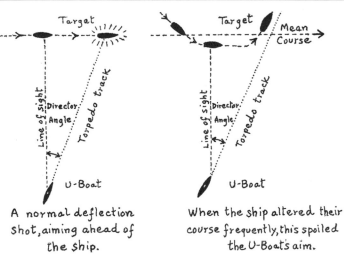

Target

Line of sight — Director Angle — Torpedo track

U-Boat

A normal deflection shot, aiming ahead of the ship.

Target — Mean Course

Line of sight — Director Angle — Torpedo track

U-Boat

When the ship altered their course frequently, this spoiled the U-Boat's aim.

ASDIC (Allied Submarine Detection Investigation Committee)

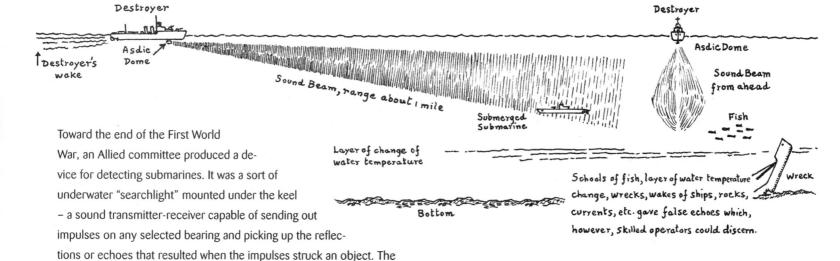

Toward the end of the First World War, an Allied committee produced a device for detecting submarines. It was a sort of underwater "searchlight" mounted under the keel – a sound transmitter-receiver capable of sending out impulses on any selected bearing and picking up the reflections or echoes that resulted when the impulses struck an object. The transmissions were made audible through earphones and loudspeakers, producing a "pinging" noise. The direction of the transmission and therefore the echo could be read on a compass repeater. The difference in time between the initial transmitted "ping" and receipt of the echo indicated the range of the object detected.

Between the wars a small band of dedicated scientists and Royal Navy officers, without official encouragement, continued to work on the anti-submarine problem. By 1939 Asdic had been fitted in most destroyers and small vessels of the Royal Navy. The "ping" of the Asdic could be heard like a "searching finger" in the submarine, as well as the sound of the propellers of the hunting escort. The effect on submarine crews must have been ghastly. It was a bloody and horrible business on both sides!

The main limitation of Asdic was the speed of the ship. Above 20 knots in calm weather, less in heavy weather, the streamlining effect of the dome was lost and water noise overwhelmed the Asdic sound impulses. Furthermore, heavy wave pounding could damage or destroy

the dome. Because the dome protruded downwards from the keel, it had to be withdrawn flush with the keel on entering harbour or it could be torn off by the bottom or the anchor cable.

Wreck charts were prepared by the Admiralty for areas such as the English Channel to assist captains and anti-submarine operators in classifying echoes.

"Foxer," a Canadian invention

From mid-1943, escorts began to have their sterns blown off by torpedoes fired from the submarine under attack – it was the German Naval Acoustic Torpedo (GNAT) which homed on the propeller noise, at 25 knots. Counter-action consisted of throwing-off by 60° to avoid "getting it down the throat," or to increase speed to more than 25 knots and then slow down to silent speed, less than 7 knots. "Foxer" could be streamed. It consisted of two steel bars towed astern which "chattered" together at speeds above 10 knots and decoyed the GNAT. "Foxer" made a hideous underwater noise that drowned out the Asdic.

The A.R.L. Plotting Table (Admiralty Research Laboratory)

The "plot" was situated in the bridge structure, generally in the chart house (abaft the wheelhouse in destroyers). It could be seen by the officer of the watch, captain, etc. from the upper bridge through an aperture – the "view plot." The plotting table consisted of a glass-topped table on which a dot of light shone upwards on the underside of the glass. The light moved forwards and sideways as governed by the course and speed of the ship. A piece of translucent paper was pinned to the wooden frame and this was marked at regular time intervals in pencil to record the ship's track. When an echo was detected, its ranges and bearings were plotted from the spot of light on the paper (one's position at that moment) and its true track also was thus recorded. In the first years of the war, the navigator or a midshipman, etc. did the plotting but later the Radar Plot Branch was established and very sophisticated apparatus developed.

Plot of an Anti-Submarine Attack. A "real-life" plot usually was much more obscure & untidy.

Creeping attacks

Later in the war, when escorts were more numerous with greater experience and there was less urgency, an escort gaining contact often called in a second escort. She then would stand off maintaining the contact and, by plotting with radar, direct the second escort over the ASDIC contact, telling her when to fire charges. This technique ensured that contact was never lost and resulted in many kills.

Huff Duff

When the British gave up permitting ships to sail independently and enforced the convoy system, it became more difficult for submarines to find targets. The German answer was to station lines of U-boats across likely convoy routes, patrolling on the surface, there being no threat from aircraft at that time. When a U-boat sighted a convoy, she made a high-frequency radio report to headquarters at L'Orient in France. The other U-boats then would be ordered to close in, diving only when necessary to avoid detection. The entire operation was coordinated from L'Orient.

It seems incredible that the Germans had no inhibitions about using high-frequency (short-wave) radio! The British almost always maintained radio silence at sea until action was joined. The Germans evidently did not learn that the British had developed an efficient ship-borne high-frequency direction finder (H/F D/F). By 1943 at least two ships in each escort group were equipped with "Huff Duff."

High frequency radio signals radiate to the ionosphere and are reflected back to earth and thus received at great distances. But there is also a "ground wave" with a range of 15–20 miles which showed on H/F D/F. A "B-Bar" German signal indicated that a U-boat was making an urgent report. "Huff Duff" picked this up, got a bearing and possibly a fix, and an escort would be sent to attack.

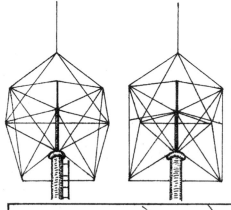

An H/F D/F Aerial

Two views of a major A/S weapon. The aerial did not revolve but it achieved its directional sensitivity by measuring the signal strength received by each of the several loops. A skilled operator could distinguish a "sky wave" from a "ground wave" & even estimate the range of a ground wave!

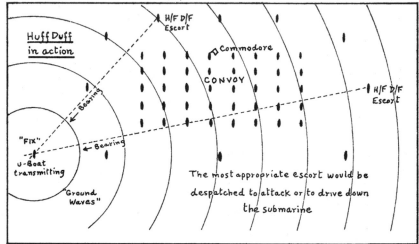

Huff Duff in action

H/F D/F Escort

Commodore

CONVOY

H/F D/F Escort

Bearing

"FIX"

U-Boat transmitting

← Bearing

"Ground Waves"

The most appropriate escort would be despatched to attack or to drive down the submarine

Submarine Detector Badge

Radar

RDF (Radio Direction Finding) was invented in the 1930s, primarily as a warning device against bombing attacks. At the end of 1940 high priority was given to the development of a set for escort vessels. By early 1941 a type was fitted which looked like a large wire mattress at the masthead. It could not be rotated but gave an echo which helped in keeping station at night and in fog. By July 1942, the "10 centimetre" set was fitted in many escorts – this was the ancestor of modern radar.

Type 286P RDF Warning Combined was primarily an air warning set, but it had a surface capability. At first the aerial was turned by hand; within a few months power for rotation was provided. Echoes were displayed on an "A Scan."

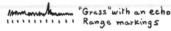

"Grass" with an echo
Range markings

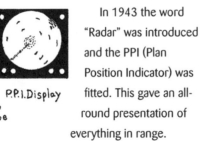

Type 286P
RDF

I.F.F.
Identification
Friend from Foe

P.P.I. Display

In 1943 the word "Radar" was introduced and the PPI (Plan Position Indicator) was fitted. This gave an all-round presentation of everything in range.

In photographs of ships during the war aerials usually did not appear, for security reasons.

Radar took on great importance in achieving accuracy in surface and anti-aircraft gunfire and in the navigation of ships.

Type 271 radar

Type 271 SW (Surface Warning) Radar consisted of two dipole aerials with half-cheese reflectors – a transmitter and a receiver – mounted on one on top of the other. Part of the circuitry was in the aerials and it was protected from the weather by a perspex "lantern." This set could detect a very small target (e.g. a conning tower awash) at $2^1/_2$ miles. It was so valuable and important that in order to fit it, the director control tower (for the control of the guns) was removed when it was fitted.

German submarines were fitted with radar but it never came up to British standards.

Type 271
Radar

The 271 Perspex "Lantern."

Radar – in my opinion the major weapon

The first set I served with was in *Ottawa*. It was called the 286M air and surface warning. Clumsy and fragile, it had to be trained by hand. It was hard to differentiate the bearing of an echo, which could be in one direction or the exact opposite. The next set I encountered was in *Niagara*, the 271 air and surface warning, which rotated automatically and presented a visual display of echoes of ships, aircraft and land within several miles. It could even show an echo of the periscope of a submerged submarine. This radar made attacks at night by surfaced submarines very risky and ended German wolf pack attacks.

A large variety of radar sets for special purposes were developed. In *Algonquin* our main sets were:

276 surface and air warning display on the plan position indicator (PPI)

242 identification of friend or foe (IFF)

285 gunnery main armament control

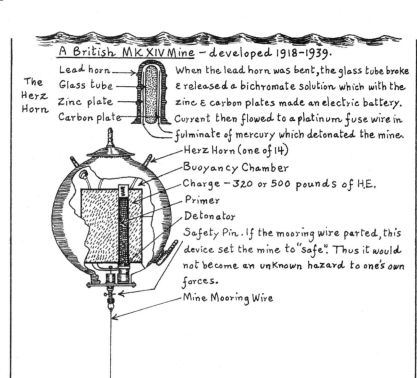

A British MK XIV Mine – developed 1918-1939.

The Herz Horn

Lead horn
Glass tube
Zinc plate
Carbon plate

When the lead horn was bent, the glass tube broke & released a bichromate solution which with the zinc & carbon plates made an electric battery. Current then flowed to a platinum fuse wire in fulminate of mercury which detonated the mine.

Herz Horn (one of 14)
Buoyancy Chamber
Charge – 320 or 500 pounds of H.E.
Primer
Detonator
Safety Pin. If the mooring wire parted, this device set the mine to "safe". Thus it would not become an unknown hazard to one's own forces.
Mine Mooring Wire

The minelaying carriage (note wheels) for dropping over the stern of the minelayer. Depth was set on a hydrostatic valve. When the mine & carriage struck bottom, the mine released itself & floated upwards. At the preset depth the ratchet engaged & held the mine mooring wire, thus anchoring it.

Moored mines

Minefields of the moored type could be seen on Sonar. It was a horrifying experience to find one's ship passing through such a field – whether friendly or enemy – because of a navigation error or lack of information. A personal experience off the Isle of Wight came about when we were involved in rescuing a small warship whose engine had broken down and was drifting in a minefield.

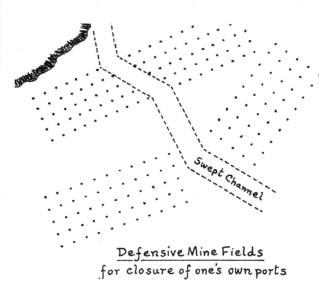

Swept Channel

Defensive Mine Fields
for closure of one's own ports

Minefields

Fields of moored mines were laid in depths up to 1,000 fathoms as well as in shallow waters. Mines were laid with greatest navigational accuracy by minelayers. The distance apart of mines was determined by the countermining distance

Magnetic mines

Magnetic mines operated on the principle that the magnetic field surrounding a metal ship could deflect a needle and set off a detonator and explode the mine. These mines caused heavy losses when first used. They were countered by a heavy, charged coil of wire wound around each ship at deck level. This cancelled the magnetic field of the ship and was called "degaussing."

A German Magnetic Mine 1940
(about 2 feet in diameter)

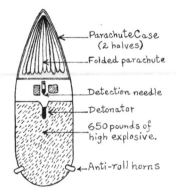

Parachute Case (2 halves)

Folded parachute

Detection needle

Detonator

650 pounds of high explosive.

Anti-roll horns

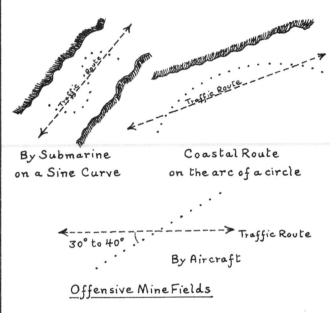

By Submarine on a Sine Curve

Coastal Route on the arc of a circle

Traffic Route

30° to 40°

By Aircraft

Offensive Mine Fields

A later version was the **Acoustic Mine** which was **detonated** by the sound of ships' propellers.

Mine dropped by plane or laid by surface ship or submarine.
1.

Parachute releases & drifts free.
2.

Mine at rest on sea bed.
3.

Magnetic field of ship detonates the mine.
4.

Offensive minefields

Ground mines (pressure, acoustic and magnetic) were laid at focal points in depths of less than 30 fathoms. These carried two or three times the amount of explosive of moored mines.

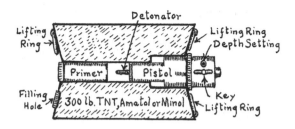

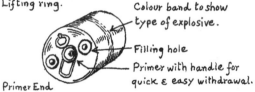

Depth charges

The pistol was a hydrostatic device. Explosion depth was set by hand. At the desired depth, the pistol fired the detonator, and this small explosion caused the primer to explode, in turn setting off the TNT, Amatol or Minol. If the ship itself was sinking and there was sufficient time, someone pulled out all the primers so that the charges could not explode as the ship went down and kill the crew in the water or lifeboats. The "key" was a further safety device.

Pistol End

Rubber cap covering the pistol – it was removed before firing.

Lifting ring.

Colour band to show type of explosive.

Filling hole

Primer with handle for quick & easy withdrawal.

Primer End

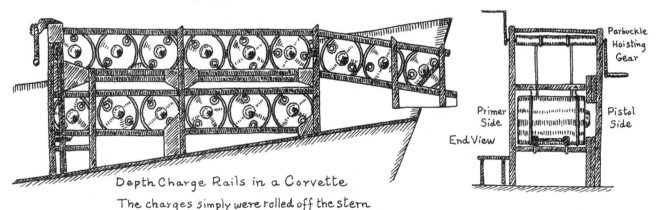

Depth Charge Rails in a Corvette

The charges simply were rolled off the stern

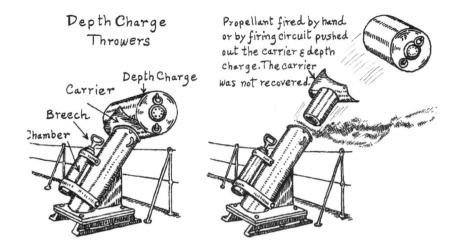

Depth Charge Throwers

Carrier

Depth Charge

Breech

Chamber

Propellant fired by hand or by firing circuit pushed out the carrier & depth charge. The carrier was not recovered.

Depth charge throwers

In later models of depth charge throwers the carrier became an integral part of the thrower, saving weight as well as steel. A convenient, large depth-charge storage rack was fitted ~~was fitted~~ beside each thrower. Depth charges were "heavy," in which case a ballast weight was bolted to one end and the charge sank at 16 feet per second, or they were "light" and sank at 10 feet per second. Maximum depth settings were 500 feet for light charges and 900 feet for "heavies."

A Mark 10 depth charge sometimes was carried in one of the torpedo tubes. It consisted of a ton of Minol and was regarded by the ships' officers and men with a mixture of respect and horror.

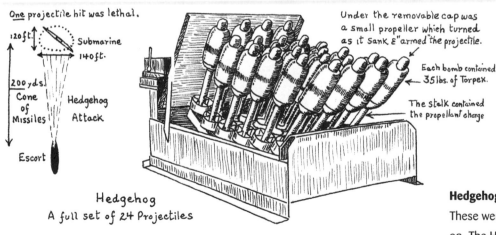

One projectile hit was lethal.

120 ft.
Submarine
140 ft.

200 yds.
Cone of Missiles

Hedgehog Attack

Escort

Hedgehog
A full set of 24 Projectiles

Under the removable cap was a small propeller which turned as it sank & "armed" the projectile.

Each bomb contained 35 lbs. of Torpex.

The stalk contained the propellant charge

Hedgehog

These were fitted forward in most escorts from 1943 on. The Hedgehog fired ahead of the ship at a predetermined range. Contact on the submarine was not lost at the last critical moment of the attack. The projectiles only exploded upon actually hitting the submarine.

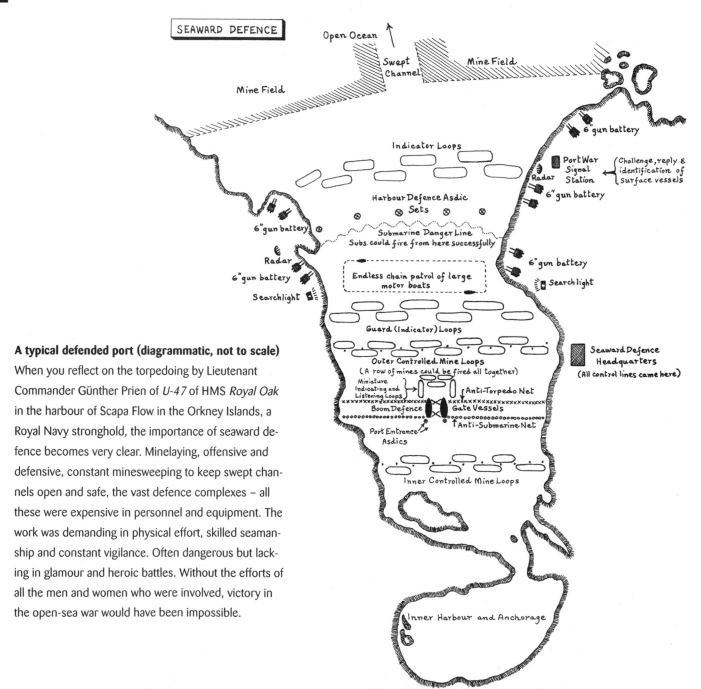

SEAWARD DEFENCE

Open Ocean

Swept Channel

Mine Field

Mine Field

Indicator Loops

Harbour Defence Asdic Sets

6" gun battery

Port War Signal Station

Radar

6" gun battery

Challenge, reply & identification of surface vessels

6" gun battery

Radar

6" gun battery

Searchlight

6" gun battery

Submarine Danger Line
Subs. could fire from here successfully

Endless chain patrol of large motor boats

Searchlight

Guard (Indicator) Loops

Outer Controlled Mine Loops
(A row of mines could be fired all together)

Seaward Defence Headquarters
(All control lines came here)

Miniature Indicating and Listening Loops

Anti-Torpedo Net

Boom Defence

Gate Vessels

Port Entrance Asdics

Anti-Submarine Net

Inner Controlled Mine Loops

Inner Harbour and Anchorage

A typical defended port (diagrammatic, not to scale)

When you reflect on the torpedoing by Lieutenant Commander Günther Prien of *U-47* of HMS *Royal Oak* in the harbour of Scapa Flow in the Orkney Islands, a Royal Navy stronghold, the importance of seaward defence becomes very clear. Minelaying, offensive and defensive, constant minesweeping to keep swept channels open and safe, the vast defence complexes – all these were expensive in personnel and equipment. The work was demanding in physical effort, skilled seamanship and constant vigilance. Often dangerous but lacking in glamour and heroic battles. Without the efforts of all the men and women who were involved, victory in the open-sea war would have been impossible.

10

Of Canadians and convoys

In time of war, most ships sailing independently are easy and safe targets for enemy submarines lurking around shipping lanes. Ships in convoy occupy a very small space on the ocean and are hard to find. Furthermore, submarines that do find convoys are in danger of counterattack by the convoy's escorts. The defenders have chosen their own battlefield.

In 1942, in the mid-Atlantic on a dark night, four small escorts were screening a 30-ship convoy from Canada to the United Kingdom. There were six columns of five ships, distance apart of columns 200 yards. Each side of the rectangle of ships was covered by an escort, top speed of 15 knots, patrolling back and forth. The escorts were fitted with an Asdic (sonar) with a possible underwater detection range of about a mile. A type of radar had been fitted in some escorts, but it was unreliable, hard to read and maintain. The human eye provided the most accurate information. However, on a night such as this the convoy was barely visible.

Suddenly, somewhere in the middle of the convoy there was a dull red glow and the sound of an explosion. A ship had been torpedoed. The escort commander ordered Operation RASPBERRY: the escorts turned outwards and began a prearranged search pattern. No luck. Escorts were recalled to their stations and one was detached to pick up survivors.

A U-boat had been sitting on the surface waiting to get a shot at the approaching ships. At the right time, he fired a salvo of torpedoes and heard an explosion. At the same time, he discerned an escort headed in his direction and left the scene on the surface, unobserved, at 18 knots.

If an escort had been lucky, it would have detected the U-boat by sonar or even seen it. Sometimes, a submarine was rammed and sunk. Usually, the U-boat dived. Its speed was 4 knots under water, but it could do a short burst of 7 knots. The escort dropped depth charges, but the explosions had to be within a yard or so of the U-boat's hull to be effective. The explosions caused the escort to lose sonar contact, and if it could not be regained quickly, the escort had to return to its station. She did not have the luxury of hunting the submarine to exhaustion.

This was the state of affairs for both Canadian and British escorts until mid-1942 or so. Up to then neither sank many U-boats. About this time a greatly improved radar, the Type 271, started being installed in British escorts. This provided a visual display of echoes, large and small, at ranges up to 10 miles or more. It was one of the most important inventions of the war.

I believe Canadians wanted to develop their own radar sets. In any case, HMCS *Ottawa* was offered a type 271 in Londonderry and the captain ordered it to be taken away. That was just before we were sunk. About that time, some of our ships were offered and accepted another wonderful invention by the British. This was a very sensitive radio transmission detection device for determining the direction of radio signals from U-boats, the HF/DF (Huff Duff).

Canadians continued to escort convoys until the end of the war, but did not destroy many U-boats. The British established hunter/killer groups which were very successful at hunting submarines to exhaustion, and the Americans established task forces of small aircraft carriers with screens of escorts, which also were successful. By the later stages of the war, shore-based aircraft patrols extended right across the North Atlantic. Because of the hunter/killer groups and shore-based and carrier aircraft, the convoys were attacked less often, and the Canadians, in their escort role, had fewer opportunities to engage U-boats than did the British and Americans.

Most of the permanent officers of the Royal Canadian Navy had spent years of training in ships of the Royal Navy. The training was excellent and I enjoyed everything about the RN. It was a wonderful system. British, Canadians, Australians, New Zealanders, Indians, South Africans and other members of our Empire were trained and treated with complete equality in every way. Our national navies were part of a huge navy, based all over the world, with a common doctrine and practically the same dress, rules and regulations.

Of course, the British had a very different social structure from Canadians and this was reflected in the attitudes of officers and men in the RN. To begin with, RN officers spoke with quite a different accent from their men. Officers had a common manner of speaking, almost without accent, and after the manner of King George V. The men spoke in all the regional accents of the British Isles.

Some RN officers, however, brought to mind the voice, manner and style of the actor Charles Laughton in his role as Captain Bligh in *Mutiny on the Bounty*, and there were some Canadian officers who brought these unfamiliar notes to Canada. In the Royal Navy this dictatorial approach was thought by some to be the way to keep order among what were perceived as a naturally turbulent and ignorant group of men. Instant, unquestioning obedience was demanded at all times with no possibility of discussion. When some Canadians got command, I think they pictured themselves as the hard, strict, unyielding captain that everybody loved. They might have been hard, strict and unyielding, but everybody did not love or, perhaps,

HMCS *St Croix* returning to Halifax, after nearly foundering in a terrible winter storm. This was typical of the sad appearance of many a destroyer returning to port from its arduous duties.

respect them as much as they thought. Taking command of a body of men is a very delicate thing.

Some of our captains were without a great deal of experience. They thought they had experience, but they lacked experience in handling Canadians. Some ex-merchant service officers had 15 or 20 years of experience in handling Hindu or Chinese crews and often handled young Canadians very badly indeed and alienated their ships' companies.

When I became a member of the RCN in 1938, I understand that there were 1,365 of us altogether, officers and men. When the war broke out, Canadians volunteered in great numbers to join their navy. The farther away from the ocean they lived, the more eager the young men were to go to sea. Born and raised on the great wide prairies, I was a typical case. Whether you came from Alberta, Nova Scotia or anywhere else in Canada, some factors were much the same. Most of us, officers and men, spoke with about the same accent and, for the most part, came from similar social backgrounds and basic schooling. Our navy had expanded to nearly 100,000 by the time the war ended and most of us were equally inexperienced on entry.

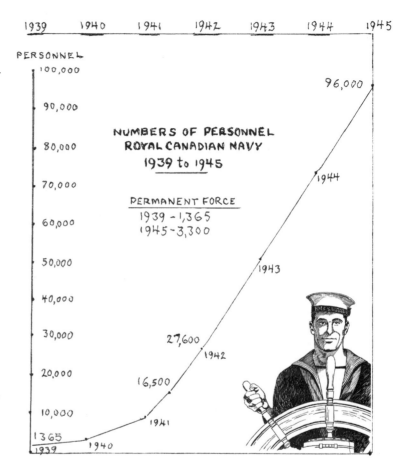

NUMBERS OF PERSONNEL
ROYAL CANADIAN NAVY
1939 to 1945

PERMANENT FORCE
1939 – 1,365
1945 – 3,300

Our war went on for years in small, crowded and uncomfortable ships on one of the roughest, coldest and most soul-destroying stretches of ocean in the world, the North Atlantic. I have often wondered if some of us should have been a bit more "Canadian" instead of trying to be so "pusser" and British. On the other hand, for many of us there was a desire to be like the Royal Navy in every way, and I remember how fed up some of us professed to be when in 1941 we were ordered to have "Canada" flashes on our shoulders.

In those days there was another factor that was unique to the Canadian navy. This was that some of our sailors were French Canadians. Being from Alberta, I had not met even one French Canadian before I joined the *Ottawa*. There certainly had been no French serving in the Royal Navy, where they had been hereditary enemies. Nelson once said, "The first duty of an officer is to hate the French." In Canada if someone mentioned French, the English Canadians thought of the Plains of Abraham and how the French had been defeated. Be that as it may, all sorts of French Canadian boys joined the navy and many of them could speak scarcely a word of English.

Looking back, I am filled with admiration for their courage and strength of character. To begin with, this war and the First World War were not perceived by many French Canadians to be any of their business. Nevertheless, these young men joined up, against the popular feeling in their community, and found themselves in uncomfortable messdecks crowded in with a majority of guys speaking a language they barely understood and with customs and mores different from their own. They were not always treated well by their English-speaking messmates.

Our Prime Minister, Mackenzie King, found himself in 1942 faced with the possibility that Canada would be unable to meet the military manpower commitments it had agreed to provide the British. Conscription had caused such awful difficulties in French Canada during the First World War that King was reluctant to see it tried again. He had little choice, however, and decided to hold a referendum on the subject. Every Canadian over 18 years of age would vote for or against conscription, whether he or she was in Canada, Europe or on the ocean. It was popularly supposed among the English speakers that all the French Canadians would vote no when they should be voting yes like all red-blooded patriotic English-Canadians.

My view was that the question should not have been asked. I suspected that our French-Canadian shipmates would indeed vote no because they would not want a repeat of the First World War riots in Quebec. Some of our anglophone officers were quite vehement in their views and I imagine that the feeling in the messdecks was similar. The referendum took place and the overall vote was for conscription, but the vote in French Canada, of course, was against. Most of us would have preferred that the government take a position of leadership and not risk stirring up trouble among those of us, Anglo and French, who already had freely volunteered and, if required, were prepared to give our lives.

Considering that all our men were volunteers and that the navy continued to sign on only volunteers for the entire war, I often have wondered why many of our regulations were so harsh. Men were selected for the navy with great care; I believe that on average out of every 10 men who applied only one was accepted. Age, height, weight, eyesight, physical and mental fitness of the highest level were requirements that eliminated many candidates. Education, character references, police record and general appearance further sorted out the applicants. They then had to survive basic and advanced training. The result was that we had the finest material in the world for the manning of our ships. Yet our preoccupation with the Articles of War, the Naval Discipline Act and punishments of various kinds was unnecessary and perhaps resulted sometimes in men being treated as children.

One of the interesting points about our ship's company in the *Ottawa* was that nearly every part of the country was represented. The list given to the press of those who lost their lives after we were torpedoed showed the following numbers:

British Columbia	18	Alberta	2
Saskatchewan	8	Manitoba	10
Ontario	29	Quebec	16
New Brunswick	3	Nova Scotia	19
P.E.I.	3	Newfoundland	1
United States	1	United Kingdom	1

The necessity of going to war is the ultimate challenge for any nation, but it is an ill wind that blows nobody any good, and this even applies to some wars. In Canada's case, both the two world wars had the effect of drawing the country together, the second largest nation in area in the world. Young men and women from every part of Canada travelled all over the country at the very least, and most served overseas together. They mixed at close quarters and learned things about themselves, their fellow Canadians and their country which otherwise they probably never would have known.

Rum and Coca-Cola

On a lighter note is the subject of rum. Whenever the navy is mentioned, in the minds of many people there is a word association: rum. Rum was carried in all ships under the White Ensign in small wooden casks in the spirit room. This was situated in the vicinity of the tiller flat. Wardroom liquor also was stowed there, as was the communion wine. The total daily issue of rum was pumped up by the victualling department with the utmost care as every last drop (except "spillage") had to be accounted for.

At the pipe "up spirits," cooks of messes would gather with their fannies (containers) at the place of issue. They were given grog, tots of rum mixed with two parts of water, according to the number entitled in their mess. All men age 21 or over were entitled to rum. Men could decide to be Grog or Temperance (G or T on their papers). If Temperance, they were entitled to an extra shilling or 25 cents a day with their pay. The reason for grog, as opposed to neat rum, was that grog would not keep and had to be consumed the same day. There was a custom called "sippers" (quite illegal) which meant that someone having a birthday or other event of importance might have a sip from each of his messmates' tots. The result often was drunkenness and into the "rattle," the first lieutenant's or captain's report for appropriate punishment. In the early 1950s, a pair of popular twins in one RN ship came of age and were given "sippers" by their messmates. They perished from alcoholic poisoning. This sad event shocked everyone and certainly curtailed the old custom.

In the 1700s, a really heroic slug of spirits (brandy) was issued each day to each man. As a consequence, as can be imagined, men kept falling out of the rigging to their death. Several graves in the old Royal Naval Burying Ground, now part of HMCS *Stadacona* in Halifax, are of seamen and marines who suffered this misfortune. Admiral Vernon, a commander in chief of the time, wore a coat made of grogram, a green cloth now used as a cover for billiard tables. He was known to his men as Old Groggy. He decided to stop this waste of manpower and ordered a much reduced ration and this was to be diluted with two parts of water. This was the origin of the word grog for the rum issue.

The "kippers," "limeys" or "juicers," as we affectionately called the RN, called the RCN the "Coca-Cola navy" – with good reason. Coca-Cola bottles could be found all over our floating homes. In the ships where I was the "Jimmy," the welfare committee, of which I was chairman, said that they would sooner have rum and Coke than grog. That was all right with me, but they would have to drink it in front of the officer of the

day. That worked well most of the time. One of the most popular songs in Canadian ships in 1943 was "Rum and Coca-Cola," just ahead of "Lay That Pistol Down, Babe." After a while, some men said they did not like rum and Coke. Could they have "neaters," a straight shot of rum down the hatch? I said I would ask the captain.

The Old Man said, "OK Number One, but watch out. I don't want any nonsense, or else…"

It went well, though I know the odd man cheated and poured the tot into a container tucked inside his jersey. Neaters, two ounces of over-proof neat rum, went straight down to your boots and, I suppose, was a test of manhood. The rum issue was the height of the day for most men and was a major factor in maintaining morale.

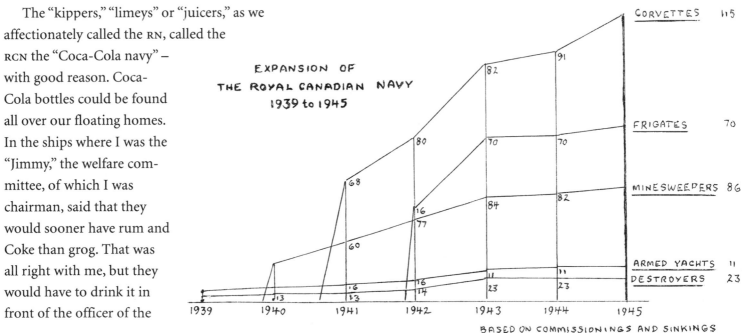

EXPANSION OF THE ROYAL CANADIAN NAVY 1939 to 1945

CORVETTES 115
FRIGATES 70
MINESWEEPERS 86
ARMED YACHTS 11
DESTROYERS 23

BASED ON COMMISSIONINGS AND SINKINGS

I do not know if this is an appropriate place to bring in a ghost story. It was said in HMS *Hood* that on a wild and stormy night the forecastle officer went with his fo'c's'le-men to secure the anchors. One hand was not wearing his oilskin and the officer ordered him below to get it. He never returned and it was said that he fell overboard and was drowned. Afterwards the poor officer claimed that on dark nights on deck he was followed by a creature in wet oilskins dripping with seaweed. This eventually drove him mad. Was this a ghost? Or what? Alcohol?

The Messman

Painting Ship

Gambling was not allowed in ships and officers were cautioned to keep their eyes open for money lying on mess tables. Tombola (Bingo) was played in RN ships and profits went into the ship's fund. It was with considerable surprise that I recently learned from an old shipmate (a leading seaman) that "on a good night I could make at least $250 Canadian and the best was around $800 Canadian. When I got discharged from the navy, I had $5,000 in my father's bank account and I never earned more than $72 a month from the navy." I guess I didn't know half of what went on in that ship.

11

Gem of the Ocean

Niagara's the Gem of the Ocean it's true,
A damned good ship and a damned fine crew.
So charge up your glasses and up on your feet
And drink to Niagara, The Queen of the Fleet.

When *Ottawa* was sunk I was entitled to 30 days survivor's leave in addition to 30 days annual leave so I went home to Calgary. I was quite nerved up, and although it was pleasant to see my family, the atmosphere so far from the war seemed quite unreal and very different from the environment to which I had become accustomed over the last three years or so. An interview with a newspaper made me feel rather foolish, and most of my school friends were overseas, so I decided after three weeks or so to return to Halifax. I had a new uniform of a sort. The gold lace for my sleeves was the thin Volunteer Reserve braid instead of the broader permanent force braid, and while it certainly looked peculiar to me, I must

have been about the only person to notice it, so little did most people know about such refinements. Someone in Calgary had a naval officer son who was killed in North Africa. His kit was sent to them and I purchased his great coat. It never fitted comfortably but we wore these so rarely that it did not matter. I had been promoted to lieutenant, this being the ordinary course of my seniority.

In Halifax I reported to Captain Mitchell, the manning captain. He had graduated from the old Royal Naval College of Canada, Halifax, just after the First World War and was a kind and gracious gentleman. He asked if I would like to be appointed first lieutenant of the destroyer *Niagara*. I said I would be honoured indeed. I had never heard of a brand new lieutenant being executive officer of a destroyer; to me this was a great distinction.

HMCS *Niagara* was an ex-American four-stacker (ex-USS *Thatcher, DD162)* and quite famous in our navy for a couple of reasons. Her most recent captain had been Lieutenant Commander "Two Gun" Ryan, RCNR, whom we have

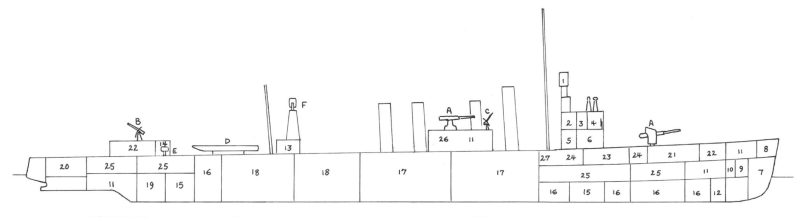

ARMAMENT

- 3 SINGLE 4 INCH LOW ANGLE GUNS
- 1 12 POUNDER HIGH ANGLE GUN
- 2 SINGLE 20MM OERLIKONS
- 1 TRIPLE 21 INCH TORPEDO TUBES
- 2 DEPTH CHARGE THROWERS
- 1 SEARCHLIGHT

BRIDGE STRUCTURE

1	RADAR	7	FORE PEAK
2	CHART HOUSE	8	LAMP ROOM
3	PLOT	9	PAINT STORE
4	WHEEL HOUSE	10	CABLE LOCKER
5	RADIO OFFICE	11	CENTRAL STORE
6	CAPTAIN'S QUARTERS	12	SONAR ROOM
		13	SHIPWRIGHT'S SHOP

HULL

14	TORPEDO SHOP	21	CHIEF & PETTY OFFICERS' MESS
15	MAGAZINE	22	WASH PLACE & HEADS
16	OIL FUEL	23	WARD ROOM
17	BOILER ROOM	24	OFFICERS' CABINS
18	ENGINE ROOM	25	CREW SPACE
19	PROVISION ROOM	26	GALLEY
20	TILLER FLAT	27	SICK BAY

PERSONNEL

TOWN CLASS DESTROYER

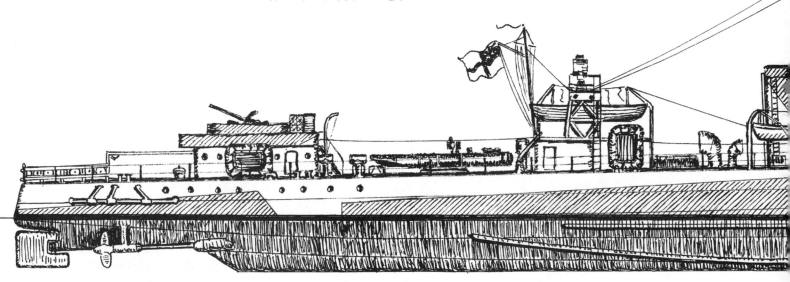

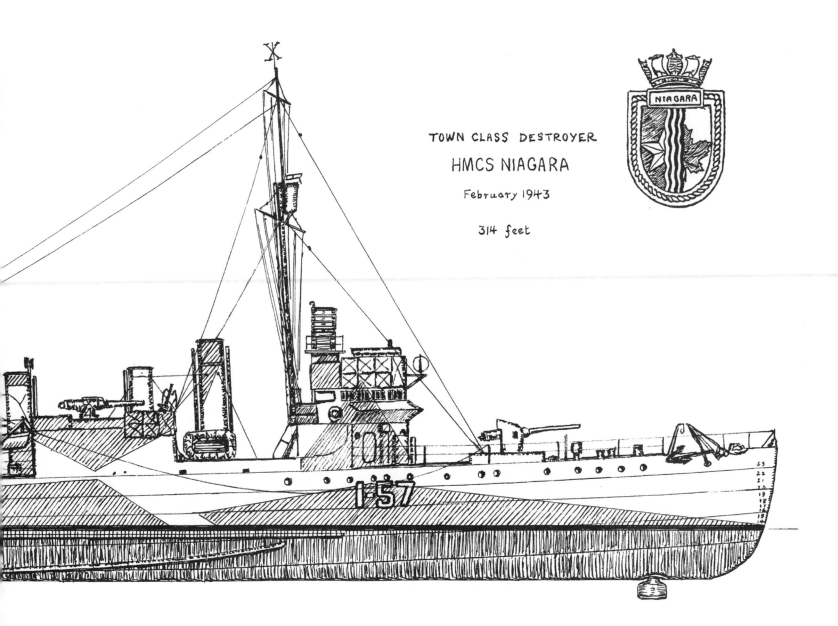

TOWN CLASS DESTROYER

HMCS NIAGARA

February 1943

314 feet

already met as the drinking companion of my captain in *Ottawa*. He had served in the Imperial Army in the First World War, I think, and when that war ended he served as an officer in the infamous Black and Tans against the Irish nationalists. When he had to leave Ireland, never to return, I believe he served in various capacities in Latin American republics and in the Middle East, ending up in China on the staff of a war lord. It was there that he became known as "Two Gun" Ryan. He joined the RCN in Hong Kong along with a number of British "China Coasters" employed in hydrography, the Chinese customs and so on. One evening when I was still in HMCS *Ottawa* and we were alongside *Niagara*, Ryan showed me all his credentials, well worn citations in various languages, bits of grubby, torn, official-looking paper, kept in a large, black, old wallet. The ones I could read were impressive. "Two Gun" was a character and a heavy drinker. He had brought a newly built minesweeper from Esquimalt to Halifax via San Pedro, Los Angeles and Panama. In San Pedro he had been lionized by Hollywood and stayed much longer than had been allowed. Because he had been unable to get even primitive radar for his ship, he painted large eyes on his bow as per Chinese custom. After his arrival in Halifax, he was appointed in command of *Niagara*. As I discussed earlier, on New Year's day 1942 two of his crew were reputed to have murdered two men in St. John's for not opening their Chinese restaurant.

In Iceland *Niagara* was secured alongside the RN Depot Ship, HMS *Hecla*, in Hvalfjord. "Two Gun" noticed the commander of *Hecla,* immaculate in every way, strolling his quarterdeck with his telescope tucked under his left arm. He decided to emulate the Commander by walking *Niagara's* pitiful little quarterdeck with his telescope under his arm. It was no ordinary telescope but a huge thing which his yeoman of signals used. This roused comment, to say the least.

Later when escorting off Iceland, *Niagara* had picked up the crew of a sinking U-boat in a rather confused air/sea action. As a consequence when I joined the ship a number of the crew were wearing odd items of German uniform in addition to hockey sweaters, toques and so on, all unauthorized dress. Lieutenant Commander Ryan had been relieved of his command in Halifax that summer and, I understand, had to be carried off his ship struggling, kicking and screaming. It must have been embarrassing for everyone. His relief was Lieutenant Commander Roland Fraser Harris, RCNR, a native of Pictou, Nova Scotia, and a former officer with Canada Steamship Lines.

This was the ship to which I had been appointed as executive officer, first lieutenant or Jimmy the One. I reported on board *Niagara*, lying alongside a jetty in the dockyard, looking not too bad for an ex-American boat. When the Americans turned them over to the RN and RCN in Halifax, the Canadians and the Brits were intrigued. The Americans had stocked them with all sorts of good food, offices had typewriters and the men all had bunks instead of hammocks. Each officer's cabin even had a little safe. They really had behaved very decently and done their best for us all. However, these American destroyers seemed almost top heavy; boats and main guns seemed to be very high above the waterline. Bridges were enclosed and we preferred to have visibility all round and to be in the open air where aircraft and distant ships could be better seen. The bunks were in tiers of three, 18 inches or so apart. RN hammocks, even though they had to be first slung close to the deckhead when in use and when not in use lashed up and stowed in hammock nettings, did not take the space required for bunks. Also they were very comfortable in rough weather. *Niagara's* messdecks seemed crowded with mess tables, benches, lockers and bunks whereas British messdecks were more open and airy. All this was relative, and no destroyer, RN, RCN or USN, was comfortable in any way. In rough weather with water sloshing around the deck, wet clothes, air thick with tobacco smoke and so on, messdecks were not pleasant.

Niagara had developed rust problems over the years. There were a few small places where the decks had rusted right through, but these did not endanger the ship significantly. The wardroom and officers' cabins were snug and comfortable. They were beneath the bridge, a more efficient layout than in British ships, where the officers' quarters were in the stern (as in the old sailing warships) and far from the bridge. There was not much woodwork anywhere and the spartan painted steel plates did not make for the home atmosphere of the *Ottawa*.

The men's heads (toilets) were situated in the after canopy, a good distance from the messdecks. The plumbing consisted of a long metal trough through which a con-stant stream of cold sea water flowed. A row of partitions and toilet seats sat atop the trough, so most men did not waste time reading there. A lunatic idea for clearing the place of idlers, if necessary, was to set afire a crumpled piece of newspaper and drop it at the headwater to rush downstream.

The officers' heads were more private and *Niagara's* actually had their own little library, a civilized idea that was carried on to *Algonquin*. The officers did not have a bath. At the forward end of the "officers country" (USN term) there was a small shower. The cold water was heated by a jet of live steam and the odd officer (including the poor captain) was slightly scalded from time to time.

In any case, I had to report to the captain before learning all about my new ship. The quartermaster, at my request, showed me to the captain's cabin, a small dark place on the main deck beneath the bridge. By a dim light, I discerned a stocky figure at a desk, back towards me.

"Yes?" said the back.

"I am Lieutenant Jenson and I have been appointed to this ship as first lieutenant," I replied.

"Did you know the last first lieutenant?" asked the back.

"Yes sir," I replied.

"Do you know why I'm getting rid of him?"

"No sir," said I.

"Because he is no goddam good! And if you're no goddam good I'll get rid of you too."

"I'll do my best, sir," I replied.

"Carry on," said the back.

From then on we never had a cross word. Roland Fraser Harris was a fine seaman. I was the only permanent force officer aboard; all the others were Reserves and several years older than I, but I was accepted with courtesy and understanding by all these gentlemen. I never encountered meanness of any kind, and, if I may say so, we became like brothers, each with our capabilities and weaknesses.

The captain told me he wanted me to smarten up the ship. He said that my predecessor did not even know how to blacken down rigging. I said, "Good heavens, imagine that!" and rushed off to look in Nicholls Seamanship, the merchantman's seamanship manual, to see what such a sin was about. I had noticed that the officers did not get up for Hands Fall In at eight in the morning, so I told them I expected to see them on deck with their divisions. A few days later I missed this myself, having had rather a large night ashore. No one bothered to point the finger at me, which was decent of them, but I was ashamed of myself and I don't think I did such a thing again. I just did, or left undone, other things that still cause me to wince.

The people at the Drafting Depot told me that I was to feel free to change my chiefs, petty officers or men as I wished. The torpedo coxswain, Lou Gould, the senior chief in the ship, a short, tough man from Toronto, was my right hand in this exercise and all the time I served in *Niagara*. We sat down in the ship's office with the nominal list which showed every man on board. He described each one's strengths and weaknesses and suggested who should remain and who should be sent to another ship. In the end

we drafted about 25 or so "birds" as they were termed and got a new collection in return. My experience is that 70 per cent or so of a crew are well behaved and easy to get along with, 15 per cent are easily led into mischief and the remaining 15 per cent commit almost 100 per cent of the offences. If one is able to get rid of that latter 15 per cent, an entirely different 15 per cent, previously innocent, will arise phoenix-like from the ashes to take their place. As executive officer I gradually learned that it was my feeble brain pitted against 150 or so very active brains, thinking how not to do what I wanted them to do.

It is a weakness of mine that most of the time when I hear an excuse it seems reasonable to me. I hate arguments and have a fear of being unfair. In the North Atlantic winters are cold and a toque is sensible headgear. The rules were that men should wear the service cap, but the winter service cap with ear flaps hadn't been issued yet and anyway a Maple Leafs toque was more appealing. Similarly, hockey sweaters were warmer and nicer than the blue service sweater. The German articles of clothing worn by some men were comfortable and warm. Being attached to the RCN, it was necessary that we at least look like naval people and we finally accomplished that most of the time.

In those days, popular reading was "pulps." These were westerns or crime stories, cheap paper magazines with dramatic colourful covers showing murders, skeletons in a desert, that sort of thing. Almost every sailor carried a "pulp" in his back pocket and I turned a blind eye on that one. Almost all the men had tattoos, some very good. One

L.B.JENSON

SOUTH OF ICELAND

of our officers' stewards had "stinky" tattooed on a middle finger. This made one thoughtful at meal times. One didn't like to ask him if he had been ashore the night before. Another had an entire fox hunt taking place on his back: horses, riders and hounds galloping over the countryside. As for the fox, only his disappearing tail could be seen as he went to ground.

A couple of weeks after I joined the ship we sailed off on a convoy run. As usual the weather was rough, but not bad enough to damage the ship. I had a standing morning watch as executive officer. Dawn was a dangerous time. As the light increased one might suddenly discern or be discerned by an enemy ship. For the first two years of war, at least in the ships in which I served, we sounded Action Stations before daylight so that all positions were manned and ready for action at first light. The practice was discontinued because people were not getting sufficient sleep to enable them to remain alert when they were on ordinary watches. The original watch on/watch off port and starboard watch system was replaced, except for very dangerous, prolonged periods, by a three-watch system, red, white and blue. In any case, the second-in-command, that is, the executive officer, always was on watch at dawn, and the captain would be spared from tiring himself unnecessarily.

The RN and RCN had constructed an open bridge above the old enclosed bridge and I was up there pitching and rolling about as daylight gradually revealed a wilderness of large, bitterly cold waves with streaming greybeards under a gloomy, heavy sky. I was at the rear of the bridge looking at the weather and the ship, wondering how I would employ the hands after breakfast. The odd man was moving along the upper deck now, and I saw the ordnance artificer coming along the starboard side of the after canopy. As I watched a large wave came up over the deck beside him and lifted him overboard to vanish instantly. He was a young man of cheerful and gentle nature, devoted to his work. We searched for two hours, but it was a hopeless task. I cannot remember that we even had a memorial service, which saddens me. From then on I made it a disciplinary offence not to have one's personal lifebelt with one at all times. The deflated Mae West could be rolled and bound into a fruit can size and slung over one shoulder or even worn with little inconvenience. I also forbade anyone, officer or man, to undress at sea except to wash. It made all of us even more smelly.

From time to time, we went to New York. Someone had told me to watch out for our heaving lines. These are the light lines which are thrown from the ship to the jetty. The dockside staff then would haul in the heaving line to which our berthing line had been secured and put the eye over a bollard. The crew then could help haul the ship alongside. The heaving line ended in a "monkey's fist," a round ball of rope to aid the distance and accuracy of the throw. By putting a lump of lead or an iron nut inside the monkey fist, greater distance and accuracy could be achieved, but if a loaded monkey fist ever hit the man on the jetty, that man could be knocked out or even killed. Consequently, if the dockside staff found a loaded fist, they cut it right off and this would upset the captain, busy waging a fight with wind and tide in a crowded harbour. All our fists were loaded so they were replaced, and we were not in danger of wearing out our welcome even before we arrived.

New York was hospitable beyond description. Everywhere we went we were treated with the kindness and generosity which ennobled the Americans of those terrible times. It is wonderful how common troubles, fears and suffering bring us together. The contempt developed for Hitler, Mussolini and Hirohito was total. I don't think that trio had one ally left in the USA. These madmen had provoked a seemingly indifferent giant of industry, intelligence and energy into action. A popular show in New York was Olson and Johnson's "Hell's Apoppin," a hilarious event best typified by the urinals in the theatre's washroom, each of which had the cartoon head of Hitler, Mussolini or Hirohito with a great wide open mouth.

We wandered the fabulous city without fear of assault or robbery, visiting the famous restaurants, clubs and shops. Too soon it would be time to be back at sea, picking up another convoy bound for the United Kingdom with urgent supplies. I sent a letter to my sister with a drawing of a person on a destroyer bridge thinking of a girl and another person on the bridge of a U-boat also thinking of a girl.

One night, quite dark, off Nova Scotia, we had some excitement. Our convoy, steaming northeast, met another convoy steaming northwest, evidently unaware of us. Their columns threaded through our ships and there were many sound signals for emergency alterations of course. Although *Niagara* was the escort commander, we could do little to bring order out of chaos; in fact we were busy saving our own skin. The other convoy did not have any escorts that we could discern. Our poor captain, having been in the merchant service for many years, and therefore particularly concerned, could only watch helplessly. We kept thinking we could hear collisions in the darkness but could only vaguely see the huge ship shapes lumbering around in all directions. Miraculously, there were no collisions.

Once we received a message that a U-boat had surfaced off Cape Race at the southern tip of Newfoundland and had spent several pleasant hours firing a machine gun at the light house. The next day we found ourselves off Cape Race and completely alone. It was a lovely day of unlimited visibility, a sea like glass, and we were bound for St. John's. One of the engines had been acting up and suddenly it stopped. The engineers believed that there was a good possibility of fixing it if we stopped the other engine. Almost everything else stopped as well. It was uncanny as a destroyer usually is a noisy place with fans and a variety of engines. Loud noises travel long distances under water and could be detected by hydrophones, especially German submarine hydrophones. It was bad enough just sitting there in the lovely sun in unlimited visibility. Now the pounding started as the engineers began taking things apart. Bang! Bang! Bang! as the sound waves raced over the horizon in every direction for 30 or 40 miles. This went on for hours and I prayed that the U-boat was on its way home to the

"Niagara" broken down off Cape Race, 1943.

Fatherland. Eventually, thank God, the noble stokers put everything together again and we carried on to St. John's.

The North Atlantic is well known for its frightful weather, and this gave us bad moments in *Niagara*. We picked up a convoy, or parts of a convoy, off the Cabot Strait and escorted it in the general direction of Iceland to the Western Ocean Meeting Point where other escorts took over. We started to turn the ship around to go back to St. John's, but each time we did so, the poor ship nearly rolled over on its side. It was like being on a fun ride at a fair except it wasn't much fun. We hit a few milestones and stove in scuttles in the forecastle. Water came pouring in and the lower messdeck soon was sloshing around with a foot or so of the North Atlantic. Petty Officer Whittier, our shipwright (and now a neighbour with his own woodworking business), braced the smashed scuttles and stopped the little *Niagara* taking in more salt water. Next, a huge wave sloshed over the upper deck and flooded our generators. This ended electricity, so we lit our candle lamps, already in place as power cuts were not uncommon. They swung wildly about leaving great patches of candle wax on the

deck, lockers and tables. By now gear and food were sloshing about. Our oil fuel was low and would run out in a few days. The gale was right out of Wagner.

The captain and I were on the bridge, the wind howling, sleet blinding us, fumes from the funnel blowing in our noses and eyes, a bleaker scene hard to imagine. We thought we might roll over if we tried to turn around. On the other hand, if we didn't turn our fuel would run so low that we couldn't get back to Newfoundland or anywhere. I suggested we might let ourselves be blown to Africa, eat what food we had raw and so on. This decided our next move. The captain would give me the wheel orders, I would pass them to the helmsman and together we would judge second by second how we were doing. "Port 15," said the captain and 15 of port wheel went on. The ship started swinging, steady as one would wish, so port 20 was ordered and we raced around to a reciprocal course into the eye of the wind. The terrible danger had been of broaching, that is, having the stern pushed sideways by a huge wave so that the ship would lie beam-on to the sea and then be pushed over and under. The other horror was that as the ship was turning, she might stop "beam on," unable to go farther, start rolling violently and capsize. We were prepared to use our engines full ahead and full astern to turn, if necessary, but *Niagara* showed her good side by remaining as steady as can be.

That was easy as pie we agreed, we had just hit it right! Now the wind and sleet were in our faces and the ship was pounding and the screws were racing out of the water from time to time. However, all other things being equal, we were reasonably safe. With head seas, no matter how big, one can generally manage by adjusting course and speed. Finally, we arrived at St. John's with a cup or two of oil fuel left. We were lucky. One of our type of destroyer, belonging to the RN and steaming in the same area, had the bottom of the bridge crushed by a heavy sea, killing the captain in his bunk.

Perhaps our experience gained a few converts to Christianity, at least for a while. St. John's harbour was crowded with shipping. Our captain asked for a day or two to collect our wits and have the dockyard assist with repairs. No such luck! They couldn't cope with what they had already, let alone take on something like us. We were to fuel and proceed to Halifax for repairs. So we took off for Halifax, a modern version of the Flying Dutchman, our candle lamps burning and dripping away. At least we had oil fuel, which made us more stable. We sailed down the coast and crossed the Cabot Strait. The weather was very cold and a strong northwest wind was blowing off the coast, but the ship was riding along in a reasonably com-

Passage through ice
from the Crowsnest, looking ahead

Passage through ice
from the Crowsnest, looking aft

fortable manner. Night fell, I did my rounds, reported all correct to the captain and toddled off to my bunk. The bo'sun's mate called me at 0330 for the morning watch, 4 to 8. I put on more clothes and climbed up to the bridge.

The chart indicated that we were in the lee of the wind off Cape Breton. I had some cocoa from a wooden bucket often used for onions. Our cocoa, thick and lumpy with a *petit soupçon* of onion put hair on your chest and was not for the faint or fastidious. As the brew warmed the cockles of my heart, I thought that the wind was quite brisk for offshore. The ship was pretty steady, but was leaning into the wind on the starboard side. It was quite a lean, about 20 degrees, and poor *Niagara* wasn't rolling – she was lolling, which is dangerous. I started looking at the ship through more open eyes and saw we had an accumulation of ice everywhere. The wind was picking up spray, and the spray was landing on us and freezing.

The trouble with freezing spray is that it compounds itself exponentially. The more iced-up the ship is, the greater the area on which more spray freezes and the greater the top weight. Eventually, the weight increases so much that there is a real possibility of rolling over. An ordinary wire rope, say one inch in circumference, starts with a thin film of ice and rapidly grows. Our guard rails had became an icy bulwark. It was a dangerous situation.

There was nothing to be done but to call all hands and get them on deck with whatever they could find to pound off the ice. Soon the pitch darkness was filled with bundled-up people with hammers, baseball bats, shovels, axes, rolling pins and who knows what else, all pounding and

Clearing away "A" Gun

Back in harbour - the front of the Bridge

banging, seeming to make little progress. By eight o'clock it was getting light and the ship was still covered with ice. The chief boatswain's mate said to me that the hands were going to quit and have some breakfast. I replied in rather a loud voice, "Fine, you tell them to enjoy it because it probably will be the last meal they will have." Everyone kept

Back in harbour — looking aft on the port side, our Carley Floats (Life Rafts) sheathed in ice.

right on pounding and within an hour or two the ice was diminished and the ship felt much better. By that evening, we were alongside in Halifax.

There must have been some moaning, but I never heard a word of complaint about that trip. My feeling is that we all recognized that we had come through a demanding experience together, were still in one piece and that it could have been different. Everyone had pulled together, we were closer to one another and the ship was better for it.

While we were being fixed up in Halifax, we cleaned the ship thoroughly, painted her as best we could in the wintry weather and went to the various teaching facilities in the dockyard. Here we practised anti-submarine and gunnery drills on the new trainers. These were getting better and better; rolling bridges were simulated so that crews could practice in darkness and fairly realistic conditions. The instructors were officers and petty officers with lots of successful sea experience, and the training and drills were in deadly earnest with each ship and individual observed. Results were discussed in painful detail at wash-ups and any incompetence, by officers or men, was obvious to all hands.

Sometime after we got ourselves in shape again, we were inspected by Commander "Chummy" Prentice, RCN. He had been a passed-over two and a half (lieutenant commander) in the RN who immigrated to British Columbia and became a rancher. He came into the RCN when the war broke out and commanded a corvette, HMCS *Chambly*. She was a spectacularly messy ship every time I saw her, but she was supposed to be efficient. Prentice was a man of apparently supreme self-confidence, his cap was tipped over like Admiral Beatty's and he wore a monocle. This fascinated all the Canadians, including me, peasants of a lower order. He swept through my ship finding all sorts of fault and blaming it all on me. With him was Lieutenant Commander Puxley, RN, captain of a four-stacker like ours, HMS *Buxton*. After the inspection, feeling thoroughly chastened, I remarked to Puxley about our recent experience. He replied sympathetically that he thought we were not too bad and this restored my morale.

I heard that on one occasion when Prentice went aboard a ship, six or seven of the crew fell in for inspection wearing monocles. I would never countenance making fun of a guy like Prentice; it could prove dangerous. Anyway, so the story went, Commander Prentice appeared not to notice as he inspected the men. He then stood in front of them and flipped his head, his monocle popped up in the air and he neatly caught it again in his eye. Without a word, he turned and set out on his inspection of the ship, winning everyone's respect in a different, uncomprehending way. Of course I realize that this story might have been a fable.

Often when sailing northeasterly out of St. John's we ran into ice fields. Most of the time, the ice was only an inch or two thick and it often had long leads, passages, which we could follow. It did present a most desolate sight and for us it was a serious hazard. Our hull was three sixteenths of an inch thick and was considerably weakened because of rust. Rust holes in decks were a disease; behind one of the wardroom easy chairs was a large rust hole in the deck through which, if one was interested, one could observe the men living in the seamen's mess below.

In St. John's I bought a pair of mukluks, high Eskimo sealskin boots. I wore them over two pairs of thick woollen socks and found them very comfortable unless I trod on a bolt or ring in the deck. They were warm and waterproof, a great blessing under our circumstances. They had one disadvantage, however, which was the smell. It was revolting, sickening, unforgettable, everlasting and stunk up my cabin and all my other clothes. The mukluks were so comfortable though that I kept them the whole time I was in the ship, finally burying them at sea.

In addition to people living in the ship, we had considerable livestock beyond the odd ship's cat which, in our case, used to desert after one voyage. The most obvious creatures were the cockroaches, which lived in great concentrations wherever there was food. They were a little under an inch in length, clean-looking creatures in a shiny, hard, brown body. Mrs. Cockroach often had a segment of half a dozen or so eggs attached to her stern. I do not know of many insects which have such small families, but evidently cockroaches are among the most ancient of insects so they have been extremely successful. When one went into the darkened pantry at night and switched on the light, there would be a rustling as thousands of roaches scuttled from the bulkheads and countertops to vanish.

Now and then the ship would be fumigated, the crew moving out for a few hours and returning to the faint stink of the insecticide. Within a week or two, pioneer roaches would appear and in no time everything would be back to normal, roach-wise. As far as I know cockroaches did not spread disease and they were clever enough to escape being caught in food about to be eaten. They were untroubled by stormy weather; they just kept soldiering on, so to speak, in the worst gales.

During the entire Second World War, there was a constant fear that the Germans might use gas – one reason for not feeling badly about bombing them. A gas mask container was part of the uniform for a long time, although later in the war the khaki bag often contained not a gas mask but snacks and other small items. I often wondered how many people's homes had a little cockroach visitor that came in someone's gas mask bag.

Rats shared our ships with us but usually were not as visible as cockroaches. When we came alongside, we put large metal shields around our lines, either to prevent rats coming aboard or our rats proceeding ashore on leave. Rats lived in our ventilation trunks and every now and again were sighted looking out the punka louvres in the trunk. Often we would simply hear their little feet pattering along. Most of the ship's company, coming from decent homes in large Canadian cities only a year or two before joining *Niagara*, were not accustomed to rats as shipmates. One day I decided to unreel an eight-inch coir rope, made of coconut fibres, stowed vertically on the upper deck. The rope had been untouched for a number of years, and since it was large and difficult to handle, the chief bo'sun's mate had gathered some hands to flake it down on the deck so we could have a look at it. As it was unreeled, a rat or two hopped out much to most people's astonishment. As we continued unreeling, large numbers of rats were running in every direction, as were sailors, who, it seemed, feared a rat might run up their pant leg. Braver crewmen ran after the poor creatures, swatting at them, but without much luck. Most of the rats escaped onto the jetty and disappeared. *The New Yorker* had a long article about rats in which it was claimed that once rats reached a certain population level in a ship, the rat complement stabilized. Such sensible controls don't seem to apply to humans.

Sailors were supposed to wear caps at all times on deck. People might look at photographs of merry matelots and not realize that many caps contained more than the head of the owner. Very often the cap held one or more cigarette butts or a package of cigarettes. Hats at times also contained letters and photographs. Once when crossing the upper deck of an RN four-stacker to get to my own ship, my passage was blocked by an absorbed group clustered about some photographs. I couldn't help but notice they were of a lady in her birthday suit. The owner suddenly noticed me, snatched them back, popped them in his cap and put it on his head. "Disgustin', ain't they?" was his righteous comment.

When I first sailed in RN destroyers, some officers off watch played bridge to pass the time and then discussed their hands endlessly. Gunrooms played a lot of poker, as did a lot of wardrooms. In *Niagara* the favourite wardroom game at sea was Chinese checkers. The basic idea is to move a number of marbles from one side of a board to another. Night and day we had a group of idiots, including me, huddled around the board. I have seen us in the middle of a game when the officer of the watch rang Action Stations, standing up, puffing up our inflatable life belts, pulling on heavy coats, rushing out and then suddenly rushing back to make another move. The captain was the worst offender. I suppose it was the perfect trust he had that officers and men could be relied on to fight the enemy whether he was there or not. Depth charges exploding nearby, the ship shaking, and the captain would stand there pondering. A sailor told me confidentially when we were drinking at a "smoker" that some officers were so stupid that even the other officers noticed it. Chinese checkers sort of proved this.

Having left home at the age of 17 with junior matriculation, my continuing education was confined to current events and naval subjects. Normally in peacetime one's "arts" education would be part of the sub-lieutenants courses at Greenwich, with excellent lectures and encouragement to explore culture in nearby London. Because of the war and the shortage of time this course was cancelled, a serious loss for us. The good news was that the majority of the Volunteer Reserve officers who were called up for active duty at sea were professionals from every ordinary activity of society: lawyers, architects, journalists, scientists, business executives and so on. The more junior reservists often had been in university courses when they were called up.

When I joined HMS *Renown* in 1939, most of her officers were career naval people who had spent most of their adult lives in ships. In HMS *Matabele* I saw many of the permanent force officers and men sent to new ships, to be replaced by volunteers. For me, it was a wonderful experience to be in close quarters with many of these reservists. On quiet watches or off watch in the wardroom, they would discuss the things that interested them and I would have the good fortune to listen to some expert artist or musician or journalist chatting in a learned way on subjects I would rarely hear even mentioned by permanent officers.

Similarly, when I returned to the Canadian navy, I was blessed with messmates who only a year or two before had been in university studying the ancient classics, modern poetry, philosophy, biology, pre-medicine and so on. They often stayed up late at night with a glass or more, smoking and talking about whatever it was they had been studying. It was an unhealthy atmosphere of cigarettes and liquor, but the conversation was delightful. Often I managed to find and read the books they discussed: Steinbeck, Plato, modern poets, Durant's *Story of the Philosophers,* Tolstoy, Dostoevsky and so on. The instruction in classical music appreciation I received in *Matabele* while we listened to gramophone records has been a continuing contribution to my enjoyment of life. Politics, religion and women were not supposed to be discussed in wardrooms because they could cause such deep emotions, even duels. We did refrain from discussing politics and women but we certainly explored religion. However, on reflection I believe all our religious discussion was between moderate Protestants and never became heated.

Most of us smoked cigarettes. In the wardroom and the messdecks there was a constant haze of cigarette smoke. In the prewar navy smoking was allowed only when the hands were not working, that is, before 0800, at stand-easy for 10 minutes at 1030, and after secure at 1155. In the Royal Navy at stand-easy in cruisers and above, spitkids were placed on the wooden decks. These were like large spittoons, diameter three feet, for pipe ashes, cigarette butts,

matches, packages and so on. In destroyers, old 4.7-inch shell cases were often belled out and partially filled with water. Sometimes there could be heard the loud cry, "Fire in the spitkid!" as the wrappings caught fire. Men working in offices and stores, not usually observed, smoked as they wished. Sailors on the upper deck smoked at the laid-down times, or were supposed to.

Much work in a little ship, with the many hands required for action, was of a "make work" nature. Sailors went off to the heads (lavatories) to smoke in great numbers, and I used to try to flush them out. Finally I asked the

CONVOY 1943

captain if I could let the men smoke as they worked, providing we were not alongside another ship with different rules. Of course, ordinary rules of safety were to be observed. This worked well for my people and ended up being pretty general in the fleet. Cigarettes were 10 cents a pack of 25 and often people would give us gifts of free cigarettes together with books and wool clothing. How nice it was to have a steaming cup of cocoa and a cigarette when we were wet and frozen. What a consolation these stupid things were. If only we had known what we were doing to ourselves. Would we have avoided them? I think

about 80 or 90 per cent of people smoked and 100 per cent were exposed to levels of smoke which equalled the act of smoking a couple of packs a day.

Most of our officers and men were so young that they had little experience of alcohol. In the RN, as I recall, beer, port and sherry were the only drinks allowed in the gunroom and wine bills were examined with great care. I think there was a very low limit. Men were not allowed to draw their tot of rum until they were 21 years old and had

declared whether they were "Grog" or "Temperance." When an officer was a lieutenant, he lived in the wardroom and had access to any sort of alcohol that he wished, but the wine books were examined weekly by the captain. As I remember, before the war it was unacceptable most of the time for an officer to become intoxicated. It was in order, however, for people to get a little "high" at a mess dinner. As the war progressed, formal mess dinners ceased to be a routine once-a-week sort of thing, but casual drinking greatly increased and many of us commonly drank more than we should.

Canadians were not as disciplined drinkers as the British. We practically had a sort of prohibition in Canada, but our liquor customs in the navy were borrowed from the British and some of us went a bit overboard. Our American navy friends had total prohibition for officers and men in their ships, but it was my understanding that they evaded the rules in a variety of ways – some of these ways being unhealthy. Most Canadian officers did not drink at sea, but when they got to port, they made up for lost time. After a hard voyage it was an immense relief to drink and let our hair down. It was something to look forward to, even if the port or anchorage was in some wild, barren spot such as Hvalfjord in Iceland or Scapa Flow. It would be interesting to compare numbers of nervous breakdowns in Canadian ships with, say, American ships, if it were possible to level differences of weather, temperature, food, mail and so on. I suspect Canadians would come out pretty well in every way.

The officers in *Niagara* were a diverse group. Two sub-lieutenants RCNVR were millionaires in automobile manufacturing and towel manufacturing. The latter was a friend of the famous skater Barbara Ann Scott. A lieutenant RCNVR was also of a millionaire family, in the grain business in Manitoba. Another very likeable sub-lieutenant RCNVR was studying philosophy and literature and was appropriately dishevelled and disorganized. The gunnery officer had run a radio station, and the first navigator was a salmon biologist from British Columbia. His successor from the British merchant service had been in a hydrographic survey ship in China and related how his servant always shaved him before he woke up. Another lieutenant RCNVR had completed pre-med at McGill University and in his last ship, HMCS *Sackville*, had assisted in the destruction of a German submarine, and another was a practising psychologist – I had the impression that he was overwhelmed by the wealth of psychological material in *Niagara*. All in all, one could not wish to serve with more pleasant companions who could be depended upon to do their duty in every way.

The captain was deaf in his starboard ear (from gunnery practice) and this caused some misunderstandings. When people addressed him, he might turn away without replying. "What a snob!" some of them said. Now I am a bit deaf and probably create the same impression.

A mate RCNR, Mr. Fitz Clark, a short and stout ex-Brit, had gone to sea with the Royal Navy in the First World War, and he often said, "Admirals used to fight over me you know." He was in Odessa in the Crimea for the Russian

Old St. John's —
a memory

Revolution. He described how he and the peasants got off the sidewalk when an Imperial officer hove in sight. A poor old dog had the effrontery to bark at the heels of one, whereupon the officer drew his sabre and with one stroke beheaded the creature and walked on.

The everyday uniform of many merchant service cadets of Fitz Clark's days included a "bum freezer," a short jacket with many buttons down the front. Fitz related how, one evening in Japan, he and fellow cadets visited a place of entertainment. On departing, a fellow cadet, probably conscience-stricken, was bent over and unable to straighten up. He believed, for a moment, that he was the victim of some terrible disease. Later to his relief the lad realized that somehow his trousers were buttoned to his jacket.

Another of Fitz's yarns involved one of his many merchant ships with Oriental crews. The bo'sun, a bad actor, was discovered stabbed to death. The first mate conducted burial service, and when the body was consigned to the

The "Narrows"
Old St. Johns

deep, the new bo'sun said to him, "By 'n by him come back cow."

"In that case," replied the mate, "I'll never drink milk again!"

And he never did, said Mr. Fitz Clark. After many years in the British merchant service, Fitz Clark worked on B.C. ferries.

Happily for *Niagara*, she did not encounter any enemies and have to prove herself. I think she would have acquitted herself well, but her anti-aircraft capability was severely limited. She was very fast, 32-plus knots, but was otherwise an antique in destroyer design. For example, on one horrifying occasion when we were leaving St. John's harbour, we found the steering gear jammed. Passing through the seaward defence gates required two or three radical alterations of course with no room for turning about, so our captain steered the ship by main engines, doing remarkably well. The other side of the gate was the open ocean with a perpetual huge swell, which made securing our antique Admiralty-pattern anchors an adventure. We found that heavy stores embarked just before we sailed had been placed on the steering chains, which went from the wheelhouse along the upper deck to the steering engine over the rudder and were exposed in several places.

Other adventures included fuelling at sea. The standard practice was for the destroyer to go alongside the tanker, remaining about 20 or 30 feet clear. A crane from the tanker lifted the hose over and it was connected at the upper deck. In ordinary weather it was not difficult, but in rough weather the destroyer would roll and plunge, and might even close right in to the tanker causing serious damage. We tried an experimental method of picking up a trailing line from the tanker followed by a fuel line for an oil connection on our forecastle. The weather was not great and the experiment didn't work well. I heard of one ship which parted the fuel line and sprayed the whole ship and lots of hands with Bunker C, a messy business.

In the Bay of Fundy one dark night just past Yarmouth heading for Saint John, we were well clear of any hazards. Suddenly we hit something that felt very large. Later we ascertained that the ship was undamaged and concluded we had run into a whale.

I had a personal adventure of a minor sort. I embarked in a Canso aircraft on an anti-submarine patrol. It was a large plane, with a boat-like hull, based at Naval Air Station *Shearwater*. The plane was moored near a large hangar at the waterside that had been built in World War One under Commander Byrd, later Admiral Byrd, USN, who won fame at the South Pole. The flight was a good lesson to me. Each time we saw one of these aircraft from a pitching, rolling destroyer, we would jealously reflect that soon he would be home, with a girl perhaps. In fact the plane was very uncomfortable and cold, the food was appalling and 10 hours up there was noisy and dull in the extreme. We didn't see a thing. If we had, it might not have been dull at all. I was happy to get down to earth again.

In Boston the pilot boat was a sailing schooner that patrolled back and forth. What a beautiful vessel she was and how precisely her captain sailed her! She must have been one of the last professional schooners in the world. She probably had an engine, but each time I saw her I marvelled at her manoeuvrability under sail, in high winds and low. I reflected that ship handling in the Age of Sail would have been a revelation to us who were used to steam power.

On one occasion when we were alongside in Halifax, the captain had been notified that he had been awarded the Distinguished Service Cross. At the same time, a flotilla of Russian submarines had arrived, having come from Vladivostok via the Panama Canal, bound for the White Sea near Murmansk. *Niagara* invited the Russian officers over for a drink and soon we had a real party going. It turned out that we didn't have to know each other's language. The only trouble was that our captain would only take a little sip of alcohol when the Russian captain used his only English, which was "bottoms up." Finally the

ABJ   Iceberg

Russian said something to his translator, which turned out to be, "When my captain says bottoms up he means bottoms up!" It was a memorable little party.

From time to time, when there was no space to come alongside, *Niagara* was told to moor at a buoy in the middle of Halifax Harbour. What a treat to have a steady ship, not rolling and pitching, not going anywhere. I could settle down in my cabin with a pile of books. I think the sailors didn't mind being out there either; they got on with sewing, writing letters, reading and so on.

Niagara was fitted with a Radar Type 271, the aerial of which was in a sort of plexiglass lighthouse on the bridge. This was the radar type which the RN wanted to fit *Ottawa* with in Londonderry. What a blessing our 271 was. Now we could see at night and in the fog, and in fact it was the beginning of the end of the submarine danger in World War Two. There were limitations but it was the equivalent of emerging from the dark ages of navigation. The desperate means of bouncing whistle blasts off a coast and listening for echoes was no longer the only solution to navigating close to land in dense fog, and this was just the beginning of the wonders of radar.

There was one awful occasion that winter when we were steaming out of Halifax Harbour. The hands were fallen in looking their best. Suddenly the starboard anchor, one of those terrible Admiralty-pattern anchors that the Town Class destroyers had, let go right in front of the flag officer's building. The worst of it was we had only painted the starboard side of the ship because I didn't have time to get the port side done. Of course, the damned anchor went down, caught on the bottom, the ship spun around and our unpainted port side, covered with rust and crap, was revealed. The starboard side would look like this too in a couple of weeks in the North Atlantic and the difference wouldn't be noticeable. But why would the anchor suddenly let go? Why God would see fit to have this happen to me in front of the flag's building is beyond me. Hal Lawrence (an old friend), who had experience in such matters, explained to me that it is called "the malignancy of inanimate matter."

As summer began, the wear and tear of ice and gales had left *Niagara* in dire need of repair. The waterline was so rusted and thin that a hammer blow could make a hole and there were rust holes in most of the decks. We went to Ferguson Brothers in Pictou for our refit. A number of other ships were there, mostly corvettes and minesweepers in various stages of repair. It is a lovely harbour and the surrounding countryside is beautiful. The town was founded from Philadelphia in the mid-1700s before the American Revolution. Later a number of Scottish settlers, displaced by the Highland Clearances, arrived in an old Dutch sailing vessel, the *Hector*. It was the home town for many Bluenose skippers, including our captain, a graduate of the famous Pictou Academy. The workers were skilled, enthusiastic and eager to please. When the ship became temporarily uninhabitable we lived ashore. I had a room in a pleasant old house. On Sundays the Salvation Army band played right outside the house, divine support perhaps for my honour after so long at sea.

The Cabot Tower
St. John's

LBJ

In 1901 Marconi, the Italian inventor, transmitted the first radio signal from Europe to North America. The signal was received at this tower.

On the corvettes ordinary naval discipline was seldom evident, particularly in dress. The hockey sweaters, baseball caps, turned-down seaboots and blue jean trousers made me think of pirates. I think it was HMCS *Camrose* which had the most remarkable commanding officer, Lieutenant Pavillard, RCNR. As far as I know this gentleman was not a Canadian but a Spanish national. He was known generally as the "Mad Spaniard" and appeared to have an unlimited capacity for hard liquor. He always seemed a little bit tight but never drunk and was full of theories of man management. I never did find out what his officers and men thought of him. For his parties he had a uniform jacket with rank stripes going up past his elbows and a chestful of medal ribbons made of old pyjama cuttings. One morning about nine, when Pav had been partying all night, he was sent for by a visiting senior officer, a captain RCN. Pav didn't remove his jacket; he simply put on his burberry, a rankless raincoat – the "old equalizer" some called it. The meeting was lengthy and the room was hot, but he dared not remove his burberry.

One evening I was walking along the road by the golf club overlooking the harbour. I heard machine-gun fire somewhere in the port but could see nothing unusual. I later learned that a sad incident had occurred. A young French Canadian coxswain was driving a "skimming dish," a small fast motorboat. He passed an RN four-stacker destroyer from which he was challenged by a sentry in the standard naval manner, "Boat ahoy." He was supposed to respond in the standard manner, "Passing," or whatever. Like 99 per cent of all RCN personnel, he had never heard of such a thing. Indeed he could barely speak English. The sentry opened fire with his Sten gun. The skimmer came to rest by the destroyer's accommodation ladder but the poor coxswain was dead. His fingers had to be forced from the wheel.

I was appointed to a board of inquiry to investigate this sad and dreadful incident. It transpired that the first lieutenant of the destroyer had just been appointed. His last ship had been in Alexandria in Egypt, where it was attacked by small high-speed motor boats from the Italian navy, and he had resolved that it would not happen again. Accordingly, when his ship anchored in Pictou Harbour, which was open without a boom defence, he posted a sentry on the forecastle and a sentry on the quarterdeck, each armed with a sten gun. The inevitable occurred and a man died. Our little board, sitting in a sun-soaked room of the golf club, did not find the first lieutenant guilty of anything. It was an example of the foolish and sad deeds that make up war and no further action was taken.

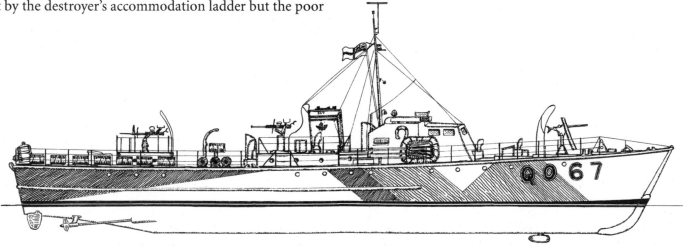

Fairmile Motor Launch Type "B"
Late 1944

While we were refitting, a flotilla of MLs (motor launches) came through the Gut of Canso bound for the Northumberland Strait. The senior officer decided to follow a merchant ship in what he thought was the right direction. Unfortunately, this was a bad decision and the whole flotilla went aground. The little vessels were not damaged, but the matter had to be reported. The Flag Officer Atlantic Coast decided that a board of inquiry was to investigate the circumstances leading to the grounding, and I sat on this board as well. Evidently, the MLs were navigating mostly by eye and did not even have a chart on the bridge. As a destroyer person, I believed there should have been a chart on the bridge and the course should have been plotted constantly to avoid hazards. The poor ML senior officer did not offer any defence; he seemed quite defeated. We did not recommend any disciplinary action and none was taken.

A week or two later *Niagara's* officers were asked if they would like a trip to Charlottetown in the MLs, a day's outing. It occurred to me that this was an opportunity to see first-hand how navigation was done in these small craft. I happily accepted and we all embarked. Within minutes we were zipping out to sea, spray was deluging the bridge and we were soaking wet. The clouds of spray limited visibility and the slapping up and down in the short, steep seas of the Northumberland Strait didn't do much to settle our breakfasts. I don't know how others felt, but for me it was heavenly when the noise and spray subsided and we were snug alongside in Charlottetown. I'm not sure how we found the place.

Our gunnery officer's father-in-law owned the radio station there and he invited us to the station to meet Don Messer and the Islanders, a jolly and amusing group of Maritimers who performed there. We played with the equipment, recording and playing back our voices, a new experience. Back to our motor launches and another soaking in the cold waters. I didn't bother looking to see if the captain was keeping his chart up-to-date, or whether the chart was even there. I am so glad our board did not make harsh recommendations.

We had vague ideas of organizing a deer hunt for our officers, but it never came to fruition. The "Mad Spaniard" and a group of fellow lunatics from the corvettes actually went on a deer hunt but only managed to shoot a cow and get lost. We did arrange a landing exercise with the army. The navy were supposed to be the enemy and landed near Pictou Lodge at midnight. They never got close to Pictou, but had a battle with each other while the army in Pictou had a spirited engagement with themselves as they defended the town.

Gradually the ship was put together again. Lieutenant Commander Harris was appointed to an aircraft carrier and an acting lieutenant commander replaced him. This officer joined the RCN three or four years before me and we had not met until then. He had commanded another four-stacker for a while. He had a rather English way of speaking, had taken on the style of some RN officers and did not appreciate opinions different from his own. He was a distinct contrast to the previous captain. The first event I had with him began before he joined the ship. His chair arrived. I had never heard of somebody having his own personal chair, but he did. I didn't know that the large crate on the jetty contained a chair, and it sat there in the sun and rain. His first question to me was what had happened to his chair. "Chair?" And why wasn't it in his cabin. "Cabin?" I was supposed to have known that the crate contained a chair and that it should have been treated with great care and respect. I incurred his displeasure over that. In his previous ship he had had a bicycle, probably a good idea if you are captain of a ship. It wouldn't do for every officer and man to have his own bicycle on board, but the captain can. If you like exercise and getting about, a bicycle would be handy. I understand that, unfortunately, his bicycle disappeared overboard.

When we were anchored in Pictou Roads, he told me to shorten cable about an hour before sailing. I suggested that we should wait before heaving in cable until we had raised steam; the wind was very strong and we would drag on to the shore. He cut me off and ordered me to do as I was told. I had the cable party shorten in, and sure enough we started to drag at a great rate. I rushed off to tell the captain what was happening and we got our engines started just in time to avoid grounding.

This was a lesson to me for the future. A captain should encourage his officers and men to speak up if they think the safety of the ship is at risk. Inexperience and the pressures of wartime were hard to handle. I have to say that this gentleman stayed about four months, then went on to earn a well deserved DSC while commanding another destroyer in action.

We sailed from Pictou to Shelburne on the Nova Scotian South Shore, where a new floating dock had been established. We were the first to use this dock and it was a pleasure to see how neat *Niagara* looked after her refit. While she was on the floating dock I fooled around Shelburne Harbour in our skimming dish. It is almost too embarrassing to admit that I took a sten gun with me and fired at rocks in an imbecilic fashion. However, I experienced how this cheap and efficient little machine gun works. By the way, it is not a good idea to put your hand on the barrel just after firing.

The commanding officer of the base was my old captain in *Ottawa*, Commander Donald Farmer Donald, but we only got a glimpse of him. We carried on to Halifax and St. Margarets Bay to work ourselves up. The training commander, Lieutenant Commander D.W. Piers, lectured our officers on *noblesse oblige*, the duty of everyone in a privileged position towards his fellow men and, in particular, his subordinates. He also spoke of honour, duty and truth. It was a very inspiring talk. Often the difficulties that come with being a human being make it hard for us to conduct ourselves as we should at all times, but we should never be discouraged from trying to do our best. We have a particular responsibility to do so if, by good fortune, birth or position, we have authority over others.

The contrast between the ship and her people when I joined *Niagara* and the way she was when we finished working up was a tribute to the professional standards developing in our navy after nearly four years of war. People like "Two Gun" Ryan had the ability to take a ship to sea and bring her back safely and enabled the RCN at least to get ships to sea, even if they were not efficient fighting ships. Our new sailors, better trained at new shore facilities and with constant exercises at sea, developed an all round capability. *Niagara* and our other ships got better and better in 1943. It was the story of the Canadian navy, really, in a nutshell. The sailors were getting better and more experienced and officers were getting better as well.

We passed Lieutenant Commander Piers's final work-up inspection with flying colours. There used to be a saying in the RN, "Chatty but happy," for a ship that was not very clean or strictly disciplined. A "chat" was Cockney for louse. My experience was that easygoing ships often were happy but also came near the last in fleet competitions. The bottom line had to be that "fleet" might equal "enemy," and even being second might mean being dead. *Niagara* had fulfilled every requirement in the terrible winter of '42–'43, battered and banged about as she was. As far as I know, no other destroyer had more sea time than we did that winter. Ferguson Brothers

Officers HMCS Niagara

Sub Lt Fairley RCNVR — Lt Bird RCNVR — Lt Cdr Harris RCNR — Surgeon Lt Hoegstraten RCNVR — Mate Fitzclark RCNR

Lt Wickett RCNVR — Lt Jenson RCN — Lt (E) Creighton RCNR — Lt Hatch RCNVR

Sub Lt McLaghlin RCNVR — Sub Lt McColl RCNVR

in Pictou had done their best to satisfy us in every way; I never observed even one employee slacking. All of us, officers and men, were proud of our ship and proud of the way we had come along.

Niagara continued to serve, now as a torpedo training ship, until the end of the war. But I went elsewhere.

The "Sparker"

12

Fairest of my loves

"Great Britain, sprawling across the North Sea, covering the mouth of the Baltic, had complete control of the sea except for coastal traffic and U-boats. Destroyers (mainly Tribals) working from Plymouth and Portsmouth harassed enemy shipping of all kinds from Bayonne south in the Bay of Biscay past La Rochelle, Lorient, Brest, Le Havre and Dieppe in the English Channel while our motor torpedo and motor gun boats ranged from Ushant to the Frisians. Hunt Class destroyers had by then the dull job of covering the East Coast Convoys while striking groups of corvettes and frigates operating from Northern Ireland and Irish Sea ports rushed out to investigate U-boat sightings from the Canaries to the Faeroes. This left the coast of Norway from the Naze to North Cape as the spinal property of the main body of the Home Fleet. This was a pretty big order and only the bare minimum of cruisers, carriers and destroyers could be spared from the navy, which was heavily committed in the Indian Ocean. So Rear Admiral Destroyers had a hard job and the boats were kept busy the whole time."

I found the above note in my handwriting among my papers. It is unusually perceptive for me and probably was copied from somewhere. If so, I apologize. In any case, it is a very accurate description of the "big picture" in January 1944.

The part played by HMCS *Algonquin* as a member of the Royal Navy's Home Fleet may sound like a specialized case, but actually our experiences were almost identical to those of 30 or more other destroyers on the same sort of work. I suppose it is every keen sea-officer's ambition to serve with a fleet whose activities are almost entirely aggressive. The results of the fight can be seen, whether it be sinking an enemy vessel or shooting down an aircraft. Serving with a task force screening a slow convoy or doing dreary and monotonous patrols is less rewarding. However, with the privilege of being a striking force member come many not-so-pleasant features, such as being at two hours notice for steam for long periods, lack of leave, poor but strategic harbours with no recreational facilities, bad food and sleepless days and nights. In short it's hard and unpleasant work.

It was with considerable surprise that I received an appointment as executive officer of HMCS *Algonquin*, building at John Brown's Yard on the River Clyde in Scotland. Our captain was to be Lieutenant Commander D.W. Piers, DSC, whom I had already met. Neil Chapman, torpedo officer in *Niagara,* was coming as well. The officers and men forming *Algonquin's* company mustered in the drill hall in HMCS *Peregrine*, the shore base in Halifax, where our new captain spoke to us. *Algonquin* was a new Fleet destroyer, top of the line, a successor to the famous Tribals.

We took passage from Halifax in *Mauretania,* one of the most illustrious liners of all time. She held the prized "Blue Riband" for speedy crossing of the Atlantic for 22 years, longer than any other liner, and was now a troopship. We sailed independently at high speed, without escort, and landed at Liverpool in seven days or so. It was fortunate that the German High Command did not give much aircraft support to their navy. If they had used long-range bombers to attack our troopships crossing the Atlantic independently at high speed, they could have created terrible difficulties for us.

We reported to HMCS *Niobe*, near Glasgow, our shore base in Scotland, housed in an old insane asylum, and were told to go to John Brown's Yard on the Clyde. We found our HMCS *Algonquin* was still HMS *Valentine* and a rather

startled Tom Troubridge was already standing by as *Valentine's* first lieutenant designate, but he was reappointed at once to another ship. It was November 1943 and Glasgow seemed perpetually in rain or fog. Days were short, nights were long, and not helped by blackouts and air raids. *Valentine* was a mess of wires, pipes, machinery waiting to be installed, thick asbestos insulation being plastered all over the inside of the hull and so on.

Having had a look at our future home, we repaired to the Grand Central Hotel, where the manager was reputed to be the brother of our old friend "Two Gun" Ryan. The beautiful British actress Vivien Leigh was staying there, as was Laurence Olivier, or so we believed. Those of us standing by were the navigator, Dick Steele, the torpedo officer, Neil Chapman, and I.

We got into a routine of going to the ship every day by tramcar. Our fellow passengers were shipyard workers in their working clothes, most smoking pipes or cigarettes. Many of the workmen seemed to be very dirty in their person and several times I had the impression that I had one or two fleas. My father had talked about lice in the First World War and how they burned them by candle flame. Fortunately, in my experience, the navy never was so afflicted. Cockroaches and rats were our *bêtes noires*.

At noon the officers designate for *Algonquin* lunched with the officers of John Brown's. This was the yard that built the mighty *Hood* and great passenger liners such as the *Queen Elizabeth*. All these civilian gentlemen shipbuilders dressed quite formally, in heavy dark suits with vests and gold watch chains, starched collars and cuffs and, when they were outdoors, always a bowler hat. The first item for lunch was a large glass of whisky, then soup, fish, meat, sweet, cheese, coffee, cigars perhaps and another whisky. These gentlemen were the picture of health, ruddy, with weather-beaten complexions, stocky and strongly built. Shipbuilding entails a lot of climbing and walking around and these men did not appear to spare themselves. The lunches were more substantial than I required for energy; in fact I would have been happy to have an hour's sleep after lunch.

HMCS *Long Branch*

I was spared from becoming too used to large luncheons by a surprise appointment to a corvette. The whole of Clydebank was lined with shipyards large and small, all building ships of various kinds, war and merchant. An experiment had been tried with an improved Flower Class corvette which had been designated for Canada. I think the arrangement was that her hull was completed by White's Yard and she was turned over to John Brown's for completion. This had been delayed by a strike of steamfitters because another union team had cut holes in the bulkheads, which was contrary to the way the unions had divided the jobs. I was amazed to learn that strikes took place among shipbuilders when our needs for shipping were so great. Someone pointed out to me that the strikers had been out of work for most of the 1930-39 depression. The dole was small and they and their families suffered great privations

and humiliations. They believed they didn't owe Britain a thing and were quite prepared to take advantage, even during a war. Centuries ago, after the Black Death, there was such a shortage of labour that, when the plague ceased, workers could get what they wanted. Indeed it was the end of feudalism. It's an ill wind that blows no one any good.

This particular corvette had a further problem. None of her Canadian officers had turned up in *Niobe*. Someone suggested they had been torpedoed and lost *en route* to Scotland. The chief and petty officers and crew were all present. So I was appointed to HMCS *Long Branch* in command, Dick Steele became first lieutenant and three or four other officers from *Algonquin* joined us.

We reported to the ship, which was just down the street, so to speak, from *Algonquin*. I took command 23 December 1943 and a few days later we began her sea trials in the Irish Sea. This was entirely coastal navigation, with all the rocks, tides, currents and local oddities one could wish for. As was required, a trials pilot handled the ship at this stage. *Long Branch*, named after a suburb of Toronto, was an attractive vessel, but having spent a number of years in destroyers, I found that I had been spoiled. *Long Branch* did not have a gyro compass, only a magnetic compass, and this takes some getting used to. A gyro doesn't swing back and forth and it doesn't require corrections for variation and deviation. After a while these become as familiar as breathing, but gyro guys don't have to become accustomed to such things. *Long Branch* had only one propeller. Even my picket boat, when I was a midshipman, had three pro-

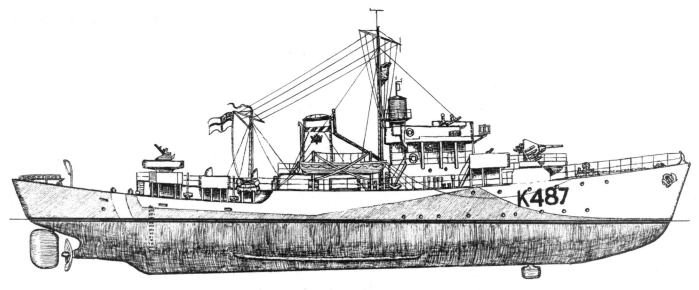

INCREASED ENDURANCE CORVETTE
H.M.C.S. LONG BRANCH
5 JANUARY 1944

LB JENSON

pellers. Destroyers have two as a rule. With one propeller one has to be very thoughtful when coming alongside or manoeuvring. Another little point was that *Long Branch* had no writer (or secretary) to take care of incoming or outgoing correspondence. There was not even a typewriter. I would have to write all my letters myself. Spelling, writing, copies – Xerox had not been invented.

Then there was the coxswain. I had never before met an RCNR coxswain. He was old, perhaps fortyish, and had a rum smell about him all the time. He was not too fussy about shaving every day. I had been used to coxswains keeping me on my toes. Within a day or two he told me that a keg of rum had vanished from stores. I fancied I could see where the contents of the keg had gone in a

number of the ship's company. I told the coxswain to investigate this, but I could not escape the feeling that I did not have his full attention.

The dress of the crew started to bother me. Within a few days we were starting to look like a pirate ship. I was the only permanent force person for miles and I had the impression that these volunteers and reserves considered this the normal lifestyle in our navy. As I was going to be there only a short time, I didn't make any particular effort to change their style.

The trials went well for the ship and her armament. The amiable pilot shocked me by peeing in a corner of the bridge, where it swished around. It was a source of satisfaction later to find a nice little urinal installed on *Algonquin's* bridge. In time a new commanding officer and five or six officers arrived from Canada. I would not have been happy remaining in command of that vessel with no gyro compass, no typewriter and no secretary writer. These deficiencies didn't bother Commander Edgar Skinner, DSC, RCNR, one bit. He had never sailed with a gyro in his life, so he didn't know what he was missing. Typewriter? Well, who ever bothered writing reports? He had been a rumrunner in his day, but he got out of that trade when highjacking, a sort of piracy, developed and he had a couple of perilous experiences off New York. He had been a private soldier in the Royal Newfoundland Regiment in the First World War and had the misfortune to have taken part in the terrible battle on the first day at the Somme that left most of his regiment dead. He had been wounded 40 times, as I understood him. As he lay unconscious on the battlefield, the advancing German soldiers had poked him with their bayonets to see if he was alive.

The night before I left we had a party in the wardroom. Commander Skinner asked who would like to see his scars and undressed completely. His white body, accentuated by reddened hands, neck and face, was covered with whiter, shiny scars – back, stomach, buttocks, thighs, all over. He was the toughest of the tough, used to difficulties and with many years of experience fishing under sail and steam. He also had nearly four years of experience in escort duty under his belt. I had no concerns that he would have any problems with the coxswain or crew or anybody.

Return to *Algonquin*

Back to the Grand Central Hotel in Glasgow. Back to the fog, rain and blackout, more aware than ever of the long nights and short days. Back to the trolley rides, with fleas and lice, to the shipyard. The officers had pleasant experiences with the kind people of Glasgow. One older lady entertained three or four of us on New Year's Day. We were the first to enter her house that year and each had to bring in a piece of coal, this being the custom. It was the experience of every Canadian I met to be treated by strangers with kindness and generosity in this great industrial city. Of all the places in the United Kingdom, no other reminded Canadians so much of home. Almost every Scottish family, it seems, has close relations living in Canada so the ties are strong.

As mentioned earlier, *Algonquin's* name had been *Valentine* before she was turned over to the Canadians, and *Valentine's* ship's badge would be easy to visualize. *Algonquin* was not as simple. I went to the Glasgow Public Library to learn about the tribe for whom we were named. Algonquins lived in Ontario and Quebec, and the name in their tongue indicated "the place of spearing fish and eels." I made a drawing of an arm holding a spear over heraldic waves. Impaled on the spear writhed an eel which was meant to represent an evil German submarine. I showed my drawing to the captain. His reaction was to show the arm coming up out of the water bent exactly like the arm on the Royal Military College of Canada's badge. I adjusted my drawing and we passed the design on to John Brown's, our builder, and they turned out badges for our boats and

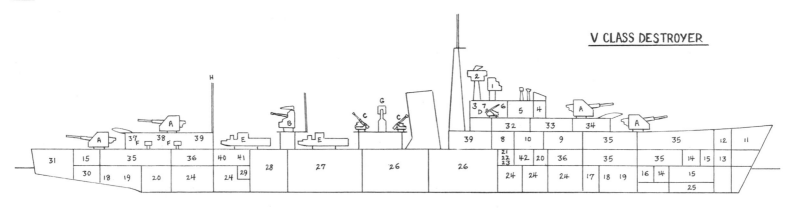

V CLASS DESTROYER

ARMAMENT		BRIDGE STRUCTURE		HULL				PERSONNEL	
A	4 SINGLE 4.7 INCH HIGH/LOW ANGLE GUNS	1	DIRECTOR	11	FORE PEAK	18	MAGAZINE	25	FRESH WATER TANK
B	1 TWIN 40 MM BOFORS	2	RANGEFINDER	12	LAMP & PAINT ROOM	19	SHELL ROOM	26	BOILER ROOM
C	2 SINGLE 40 MM BOFORS	3	HF/DF OFFICE	13	CABLE LOCKER	20	GUNNER'S STORE	27	ENGINE ROOM
D	2 TWIN 20 MM OERLIKONS	4	WHEELHOUSE	14	SONAR ROOM	21	LOW POWER ROOM	28	GEARING ROOM
E	2 QUADRUPLE 21 INCH TORPEDO TUBES	5	OPERATIONS ROOM	15	CENTRAL STORE	22	ENGINEER'S STORE	29	DIESEL OIL
F	4 DEPTH CHARGE THROWERS	6	CHART HOUSE	16	PROVISION ROOM	23	GYRO ROOM	30	SPIRIT ROOM
G	1 SEARCHLIGHT	7	CAPTAIN'S SEA CABIN	17	COOL ROOM	24	OIL FUEL	31	TILLER FLAT
H	HF/DF DIRECTION FINDER	8	RADAR OFFICE						
		9	TRANSMITTING STATION TO GUNS						
		10	RADIO OFFICE						

PERSONNEL	
32	CAPTAIN'S QUARTERS
33	WARD ROOM
34	PETTY OFFICERS' MESS
35	CREW SPACE
36	OFFICERS' CABINS
37	WASH PLACE & HEADS
38	SICK BAY
39	GALLEY
40	ENGINE ROOM ARTIFICERS' MESS
41	STOKER PETTY OFFICERS' MESS
42	STEWARDS' MESS

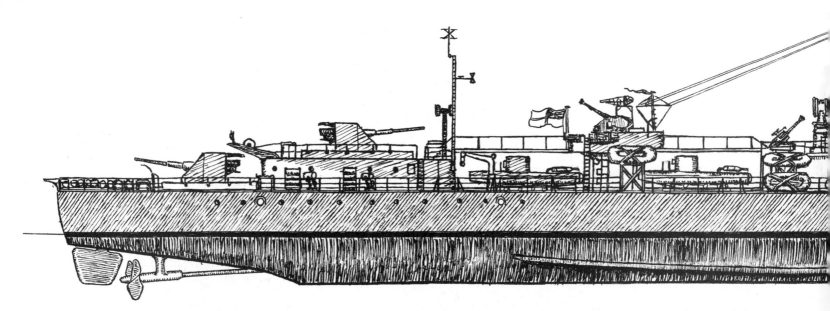

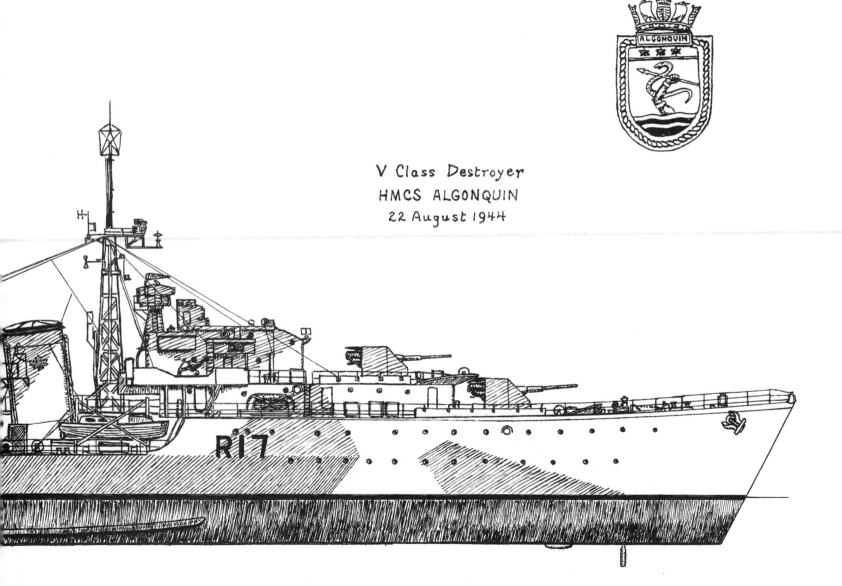

V Class Destroyer
HMCS ALGONQUIN
22 August 1944

gun tampions, the plugs that keep water out of the gun barrels.

Soon we were ready for our acceptance inspection by a captain RN representing the Admiralty. My job as first lieutenant was to make sure every compartment in the ship was unlocked so that the inspecting officer could look in to make sure that all looked completed. It was also a way of making sure the first lieutenant had himself checked the whole ship from stem to stern. On conclusion, he handed me a halfpenny as a reward for having satisfied him. It seems a small thing, but it gave me a good feeling about the ship in which, for the next year or more, I would fight and live, or even die. I still have the halfpenny. I like to think it brought us luck.

HMCS *Algonquin* was commissioned on 17 February 1944. Vice Admiral Percy Nelles, who had been Chief of the Canadian Naval Staff for a number of years, attended the ceremony and spoke to us. Sir Stephen Pigott, the chairman of John Brown's, was there. He was American-born and had come to work in Britain, rising to head one of the largest and most important shipbuilding firms in the United Kingdom.

Two days later we raised steam and proceeded down the Clyde to anchor off Greenock. Here we started steaming, steering, fire fighting and bilge pump trials. These being satisfactory, we took on board our full allowance of ammunition and went through the process of de-perming for protection against magnetic mines. For the next week we carried out vital full-power, gunnery, depth charge thrower and other trials. All these went smoothly and the builder's

staff disembarked. On the last day of the month we fuelled at an oiler. A few days later we sailed for Scapa Flow up through the Minches, past Rum, Eigg and Muck, the unforgettably named islands. We came to a buoy in Gutter Sound, our home for the next year.

I had already spent two years of my life based in Scapa Flow, and the place suited me. Ward Hill, under which we lay at rest, had looked down on Viking longboats, probably some ships of the Spanish Armada, countless British warships and the defeated German fleet of World War One. There was even a link with Canada because it was here that the Hudson's Bay Company recruited Orkney men for their isolated posts in northern Canada. In fact, our chief bo'sun's mate's father came from here to work for "the Bay." The colours of Scapa Flow and the surrounding islands were always changing, reflecting every possible mood known to nature and to man.

Under the direction of Vice Admiral, Destroyers, I.G. Glennie, we began an intensive five-week working-up period. I had met Glennie when I was serving in the Royal Navy. Some captains and admirals have strong personalities and odd, or not odd, characteristics which make them unforgettable to their juniors, and some even are a source of inspiration. I never was close to Glennie and never felt influenced by him. We gave him passage from Scapa to Thurso at the northern tip of Scotland, a voyage happily uneventful.

We exercised with a submarine in the Flow and fired torpedoes and guns. We did high-angle anti-aircraft shoots, many Bofors and Oerlikon shoots and practised fuelling at sea. Most of our equipment was new to us and very advanced. While the ship was building, all our gunnery types had been at Whale Island in Portsmouth training on the new guns and control systems. Torpedomen were brought up to date at HMS *Vernon*. All hands paid close attention because they knew that in this ship we were likely to be playing for keeps with skilled and determined German sailors fighting for their lives. For the work-ups we embarked teams of RN experts in all the specialties concerned. I never did find out if our officers and men had been hand-picked for *Algonquin*. I do know that we had no "birds" to begin with and that all the officers and men were happy to be serving in such a fine ship. By the end of March, we were considered sufficiently capable to take part in Operation TUNGSTEN.

I was fortunate indeed to serve under Lieutenant Commander D.W. "Debby" Piers. He was a graduate of the Royal Military College and had considerable wartime experience. He had been present at the debacle of the French collapse in 1940 and was escort commander of a convoy in a terrible attack by a U-boat wolf pack. After *Algonquin* commissioned, all of us, officers and men, were impressed by his qualities of leadership. He was bright and cheerful and a fine messmate, thoughtful and considerate of us all. Debby had very high standards and expected everyone to do his best. He was a superb ship handler and in action he was always cool and collected. We had complete confidence in his judgements and ability. In short, Lieutenant Commander Piers was an ideal destroyer captain, admired by his officers and men. In my opinion, there was no destroyer in our navy that was as contented and efficient as *Algonquin*.

My particular roles were the maintenance and cleanliness of the ship, inside and out, the clean and seamanlike appearance as well as the physical fitness of the ship's company, and all the drills and exercises involving pure seamanship. Such things were boat work, life saving, masts, booms and rigging, accommodation ladders, anchor work, towing, fire fighting, damage control, weighing anchor by hand and the general organization of the ship including action stations, port and starboard watches, red, white and blue watches, routines, divisions and the daily employment of the men. In addition, I had to be sure that all the officers were doing their divisional work and arranging for courses, studies and promotion for their men. This sounds like a great deal of work and it was.

My right-hand man was the coxswain, who is the senior rating aboard and who steers the ship in action, during manoeuvres and entering and leaving harbour. He kept the watch and quarter bill up to date, supervised the rum issue, and prepared disciplinary charges for defaulters, requests and all the formal paper work for personnel. My other right-hand man was the chief boatswain's mate. Most of our petty officers were permanent force and one or two I had served with before in the *Ottawa*. Most of them, like myself, had been sent for qualifying training in the RN gunnery, torpedo and other specialty schools.

Our introduction to fleet work came when we sailed with our flotilla on Operation TUNGSTEN at the end of

March. After fuelling from a tanker in the Faeroe Islands, we joined a destroyer screen for four escort carriers whose planes were going to attack the German battleship *Tirpitz* in Alten Fjord at the northern tip of Norway. En route we attacked a submarine contact but without seeing any results. Our duty was to act as rescue ship for any aircraft that crashed in the sea after the attack on *Tirpitz*.

The air attack was a huge success. The Barracuda bombers, covered by Seafire and Corsair fighters, got many hits and put *Tirpitz* out of action for several months. A number of Canadian pilots with the Fleet Air Arm distinguished themselves in this action. One of the fighters had his arrester gear shot away so he ditched close to us and we picked him up by whaler in record time. He was a VR sub-lieutenant from New Zealand.

When we returned to Scapa Flow we went alongside depot ship HMS *Tyne* for a boiler clean. Captain Blunt, Royal Artillery, joined us as bombardment liaison officer mid-month and we carried out a bombardment shoot a few days later. Our first salvoes landed everywhere except where they should and we had a nasty message from the range staff, who fortunately had survived. After that, all went well and we didn't succeed in killing any Englishmen.

Shortly afterwards we escorted the new battleship HMS *Anson* from Cape Wrath to Scapa, and this completed our working-up program. We now joined the 26th Destroyer Flotilla and within a few days sailed with fleet carriers for another attack on *Tirpitz*. Unfortunately, we had rough weather and had to abandon the attack, returning to Scapa Flow.

At the beginning of May, we formed part of the destroyer screen for the fleet carrier *Furious* and the cruiser *Berwick* on Operation CROQUET, an attack on shipping in the Norwegian leads, the area off the coast where vessels had to leave the shelter of the islands for a stretch in the open sea. It was impressive to see the squadrons of aircraft taking off and forming up for attack. It was particularly satisfying to think of the Germans getting some of their own medicine after what we had endured from their air attacks in the Norwegian campaign three years before.

I think our aircraft sank 10 or 11 German ships without suffering any damage. We returned to the Flow to paint ship. This was an interesting exercise because each time we painted ship it was a different camouflage scheme which had to be worked out in different colours and patterns. This time, it was a Western Approaches scheme, a mixture of patches of blue, white and green. His Majesty King George VI inspected parties of about 50 men from each destroyer in our flotilla. I was struck by the makeup worn by the King; it was rather grotesque but necessary for the newsreel cameras. The King then went aboard HMCS *Sioux*, where the captain, Lieutenant Commander Boak, asked him to sign the guest book. The pen wouldn't write so Boak took it from the King and shook it. The King was standing behind Boak, who noticed that he had shaken ink all over the King's uniform. His Majesty did not say anything but it can be imagined that four centuries earlier Boak might have been beheaded.

It was about this time that our young sub-lieutenant became extremely withdrawn and irrational. It was concluded that he had a nervous breakdown and was released to hospital. I never encountered another such a case in an officer, before or after. This young man of fine appearance and high intelligence had been sunk in a cruiser off Algeria. He and others had made it to the shore, where they were taken prisoner by the Vichy French. They were marched 500 miles over the desert and imprisoned in an old French Foreign Legion fort. Here they were not treated with humanity as required by the Geneva Convention for prisoners of war. They were released when Rommel was driven out of Africa. Sub's experience had been too much for him and I was sad to see him go ashore.

In May we began an intensive training program, 15 hours a day, with every type of gunnery firing, including bombardment. All forms of action organization were tested and tested again in readiness for the opening of a second front, the invasion of northern Europe by the Allied Forces. The main conflict on land in Europe had been the attempted conquest of Russia by Germany, their friend and ally of 1939. The first days of the German invasion apparently had been welcomed by the Ukrainians in particular, but German behaviour quickly degenerated into unspeakable atrocities and cruelty, which rallied the Russian people, and, like Napoleon and his Grand Army, the Germans bogged down in that vast country.

The Russians now were driving the Germans back, inch by inch. The British and Americans finally had the weapons and training to undertake an invasion of northern Europe, which would force the Germans to defend two fronts. The Russians and the American and British forces would come together, crush the Germans and bring an end to this terrible war.

Engine Room
Artificer

A Ward Room Scene

Bob Swan   ?   Harry Toller
Peter Cock   Neil Chapman   Corky Knight

13

The invasion of Normandy

On 25 May, *Algonquin* sailed from Scapa Flow in company with the rest of the 26th Flotilla. Some of these were *Sioux, Venus, Verulam, Sword, Swift* and *Zest*. In the Irish Sea the weather became balmy, quite different from our recent experience. Our navigator was quite overcome, changed into tropical shorts and shirt and exposed his hockey-scarred legs. When we arrived in the Channel we ran into low-lying fog. From the bridge I could see the mastheads of some of our flotilla poking above the white carpet. To my surprise, I saw two masts close to one another and then heard a loud prolonged crunch. I went into the operations room and looked at the Plan Position Indicator (PPI) for a radar picture. Sure enough, there were two echoes very close together. I mentioned what I had seen to several people but there were no reports of collision. On 27 May, we arrived at Spithead, the anchorage off Portsmouth, where we topped up with fuel and water.

After we fuelled we anchored off Seaview, near Ryde, on the Isle of Wight. The next day a flotilla regatta of whaler races was held. HMCS *Sioux* won and *Algonquin* was second. Visiting ashore at Seaview was rather like wandering in the Garden of Eden after our usual rambles in the mist and heather of the Orkneys. Discovered almost immediately was a public house called the Starboard Light. Algonquins found Siouxs there and it was pleasant to meet each other. After as many visits as possible to the Starboard Light in the limited time ashore, one of *Sioux's* observant officers noticed a lady of attractive form, but dissipated and somewhat sloshed, who was always present. "Why," said our hero to the proprietor, "do you allow such a woman in this place?" "Because she is my wife" was the reply. It was nice for our friend to sail for the invasion the next day and look for new fields to conquer.

Ships of every sort were gathering in preparation for one of the largest combined-operations offensive in history. Destroyers, landing craft, battleships, cruisers, minesweepers, all were there. *Algonquin* was ordered to weigh anchor and proceed on an outer patrol for the defence of

SUPREME HEADQUARTERS
ALLIED EXPEDITIONARY FORCE

Soldiers, Sailors and Airmen of the Allied Expeditionary Force!

You are about to embark upon the Great Crusade, toward which we have striven these many months. The eyes of the world are upon you. The hopes and prayers of liberty-loving people everywhere march with you. In company with our brave Allies and brothers-in-arms on other Fronts, you will bring about the destruction of the German war machine, the elimination of Nazi tyranny over the oppressed peoples of Europe, and security for ourselves in a free world.

Your task will not be an easy one. Your enemy is well trained, well equipped and battle-hardened. He will fight savagely.

But this is the year 1944! Much has happened since the Nazi triumphs of 1940-41. The United Nations have inflicted upon the Germans great defeats, in open battle, man-to-man. Our air offensive has seriously reduced their strength in the air and their capacity to wage war on the ground. Our Home Fronts have given us an overwhelming superiority in weapons and munitions of war, and placed at our disposal great reserves of trained fighting men. The tide has turned! The free men of the world are marching together to Victory!

I have full confidence in your courage, devotion to duty and skill in battle. We will accept nothing less than full Victory!

Good Luck! And let us all beseech the blessing of Almighty God upon this great and noble undertaking.

Dwight D Eisenhower

---

the area, there being a danger from submarines and E-boats. No enemy was discovered, but we had an unparalleled view of the whole great assembly.

Looking back over half a century, it seems surprising that our men could live as contentedly as they did, always in crowded conditions with the added discomfort of the ship rolling and pitching. The men got along with one another by respect, consideration, decency in their personal habits, keeping as clean as possible, sharing, and exercising a sense of humour. We had divine service every Sunday when possible, with singing of hymns and brief but meaningful prayers, a number having been used at sea for many centuries. We had a sound reproduction unit for the whole ship. Orders were passed on the SRE but generally only from Calling the Hands to Pipe Down. Favourite records were played by a hand learning to be a disc jockey. Near England we were able to get Music While You Work from the BBC.

On three or four occasions we had grudge fights on the forecastle deck. A square was formed by the messmates of the pair who were spoiling to get at one another. They punched each other about with no rounds, until one or both were exhausted. Almost invariably the two would end up somewhat battered, but laughing, joking and friends. We had a supply of up-to-date movies provided, many of them excellent. Bingo games were organized, and a certain amount of poker was played, even though gambling was forbidden. I turned a blind eye as long as I thought no one was being hurt. The officers were another matter. Some gambled too much, but developed self discipline after losing more money than they intended or could afford.

There were various competitions. A popular one was growing a beard. After a couple of months, there would be a beard beauty contest with a token award. One competition nearly resulted in a civil war – I can't remember anything which caused as much rancour and bitterness as the weekly cleanest mess/worst mess competition. The prize for the worst mess was a bottle, a "bottle" being the synonym for a rebuke. The mess selected had to hang the prize – an old beer bottle mounted in a wooden rack – in a prominent place in their mess for the week. It was twice awarded and caused destructive bitterness and despondency which I never would have believed. That was a competition I wish we had never started.

Our radar officer was an interesting person. He was a writer whose stories appeared in prestigious magazines such as *Esquire*. He had written a movie script for a Hollywood film about the fighting Canadian navy. It was called

NOTHING is to be written on this side except the date and signature of the sender. Sentences not required may be erased. if anything else is added, the postcard cannot be forwarded.

THIS CARD MUST BE POSTED IN THE SHIP'S MAIL.

I am quite well.

I have been admitted into hospital
{ sick } and am going on well.
{ wounded } and hope to be out again soon.

I have received your { letter(s) dated _____
{ telegram ,, _____
{ parcel ,, _____

I will send you a letter as soon as possible.

I have received no letter from you
{ lately
{ for a long time.

SIGNATURE }
ONLY }

Date _____
($849) Wt. 58185/D880] 250m 3/44 O.& Co. 745(8)

We were all issued these, but they were not needed.

Corvette K225 and starred Andy Devine, a plump, genial character with a squeaky voice who played a seaman. John Rhodes Sturdy cannot be said to have been a typical naval officer and some strange things went on in his radar section. However, he was a convivial person, and perhaps it was hoped that he would write a movie about us. He never did, as far as I know.

Sturdy was supported by Leading Seaman Garrett, a skilled specialist. It may be remembered that when I was in *Ottawa* I had required a radar specialist to take the place of the one who suffered from fits. A leading seaman named Garrett was drafted to us as his replacement but caught influenza and was hospitalized the day before we sailed. Garrett finally caught up with me in *Algonquin,* where he was the mainstay of our radar department. We have corresponded for years. Here are his remarks to me about D-day.

I knew you were busy being in charge of the welfare of the ship, I bet there were times you would have liked to change places with me.

Time 1500 hrs June 5th 1944, the bo'sun's mate Albert Revie blew the whistle that all hands are to fall in aft of the after torpedo tubes for a message from the Captain.

I recall the speech Debbie (Lieutenant Commander Piers) made. He stood on the after torpedo tubes with a message in his hand. He said, "I have just been informed that tomorrow June the 6th is D-day and we have been chosen to be in the spearhead of the invasion."

I could feel a sickening feeling in my stomach that tied me up in knots. He continued, "There will be no leave tonight as this information is so secret that we couldn't take a chance on someone releasing this information to the enemy carelessly by telling a girlfriend or wife." Everyone there gave a low moan about being in the spearhead of the invasion, but Debbie had more to say, which stunned everyone there. He mentioned that also we had been chosen to be the point on the end of the spear. I said to my fellow shipmates, "A spear sometimes gets blunted." Then the Captain had more to say. He said, "If our ship gets hit near the shore, we will run the ship right up on the shore and keep firing our guns, until the last shell is gone."

I was scared no longer. With a spirit like this, we couldn't lose. I felt right then and there, "We will succeed." It would have made a great movie scene!

I guess we all have a picture of this that was in the *Toronto Star* and other papers copied. You can easily see Jack Meisener, who was just below the Captain. When Meisener came to my place three years ago, he asked me who that fellow was in front of the Captain, and I replied, "It was you Jack." No one could forget the tailor, who never left the mess deck. He hardly ever went ashore. Jack sewed on some of my badges and shortened my pants for me, so they wouldn't drag in the mud ashore. He hardly ever charged more than two bob, unless it was an officer....

One thing I liked about my job, I could go anywhere I liked on board the ship. I used to like to talk to the officers when they weren't busy. Lt. Steel was a lot of fun, he always took time to answer a question, if it was in his powers to do so without violating secrecy. I often talked to you on the bridge when I had to get a gyro check for the 276 (Radar Plan Position Indicator). I always got good co-operation from the officers, who must have got tired of me checking my equipment on the bridge, or calling them on the voice pipe. I discovered this was very important, as the equipment was not 100% all the time.

One night before the invasion of Normandy, we were lying at anchor. The captain and I were walking up and down the quarterdeck when we saw five or six rats run out from somewhere in the after canopy and jump into the water. It happened so suddenly and unexpectedly that I scarcely could grasp what I had seen. The land was clearly visible, but not close, and I can't imagine they could make the shore. "Rats leaving a sinking ship" went through my mind; I don't remember discussing this incident with the captain. Would that be because it looked to be such a terrible omen?

WE ARE ALL OFF TO NORMANDY

We sailed shortly after supper on June 5 for Normandy. A number of descriptions that I have heard of the crossing implied that the weather was not good, but for me the weather was fine after our usual runs out of Scapa Flow. What worried me was that we had two or three war correspondents who were busy getting plastered in the wardroom. When they woke up the following morning with the crash of guns, they must have wondered if they had been wise. However, war correspondents have to be pretty cool.

When I went on watch at 0400, the coast of France was visible as it was lit up by bombs falling. It reminded me of watching, from Falmouth, a night bombing of Plymouth by the Germans in 1940. Overhead we heard aircraft towing gliders filled with soldiers for the airborne assault. As dawn broke, the whole invasion fleet behind us became visible. What a stupendous sight it was! Thousands of fighting ships and transports all on the same course bound for the Continent. If we were successful, it would be a magnificent victory in itself, the largest invasion ever by sea in the history of the world, comparable in importance to 1066 and the Spanish Armada. My readings in history had made me aware of terrible examples of failure in the past and the sometimes awful consequences of ships trying to engage land fortifications. If the enemy could concentrate on our landing areas, we could be part of a major catastrophe. Would the Germans unleash a terrible new secret weapon or a poison gas against us?

Algonquin closed in towards the shore as the day brightened. It had every appearance of the start of a lovely early summer day. The water was almost calm as we slowed to a stop in a predetermined position to lay a Dan buoy with a large metal reflector that was to be our reference

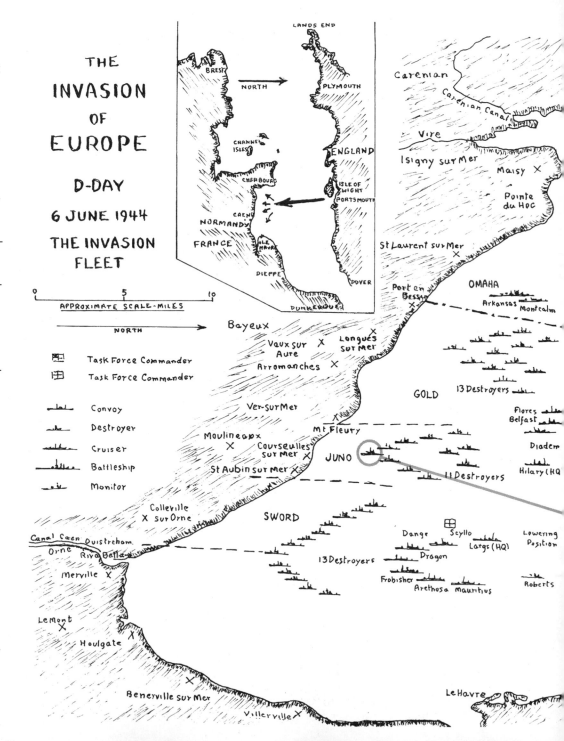

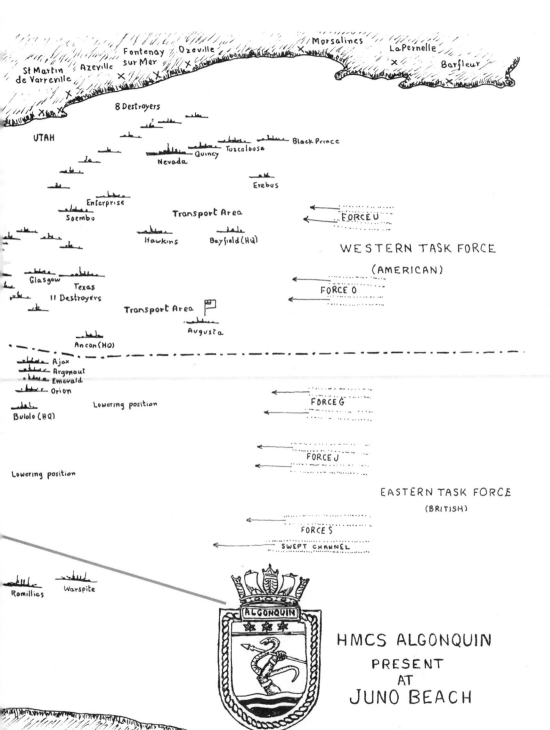

8 Destroyers

UTAH

Black Prince

Tuscaloosa

Quincy

Nevada

Erebus

Enterprise

Soembo

Transport Area

Hawkins   Bayfield (HQ)

WESTERN TASK FORCE

(AMERICAN)

FORCE U

FORCE O

Glasgow   Texas

11 Destroyers

Transport Area

Augusta

Ancon (HQ)

Ajax
Argonaut
Emerald
Orion

Lowering position

Bulolo (HQ)

FORCE G

Lowering position

FORCE J

EASTERN TASK FORCE

(BRITISH)

FORCE S

SWEPT CHANNEL

Romillies   Warspite

HMCS ALGONQUIN
PRESENT
AT
JUNO BEACH

mark as we moved up and down our line of bombardment. So far nothing was happening on the shore that we could see. A small town and a number of substantial houses were very clear. Any minute now, I thought, we will be surrounded by white columns of water, but all stayed quiet.

Our task, in a nutshell, had been to escort HMS *Hilary*, the headquarters ship of Force "J," to the assault area, JUNO Beach, and to carry out a direct bombardment on enemy batteries and strong points before "H" Hour. We then were to carry out indirect bombardment as required after the assault on the beaches.

At 0700, we hoisted our huge battle ensign to the masthead and opened fire at two 75mm gun positions on the shore at St. Aubin-sur-Mer and fired pretty steadily until "H" Hour at 0745.

The sea was getting a little choppy and the hundreds of landing craft going in looked rather uncomfortable. Soon the first units of the army were on the beach, where obstacles and defences were being overcome before our very eyes. So far no shells or bombs had come our way and we had the privilege of a grandstand view of British and Canadian forces in this incomparable assault. Fires were burning on shore and some landing craft also appeared to be on fire, while soldiers were clambering out of other landing craft and moving ashore without noticeable opposition. Royal Air Force planes appeared still to be bombing a short distance inland, and a haze of smoke, as on the battlefields of old, was slowly spreading over the beach.

For the time being, *Algonquin* had no further task except to stand by. About 0830 or so, a landing craft came alongside and we took on board one dead and five seriously wounded Royal Marine commandos. A mortar had landed in their craft just as it hit the beach. As we hoisted the dead and wounded from the landing craft, the American photographer aboard thrust me out of his way, saying in a loud voice as he took photographs, "Stand back! Jesus to God, the American people have got to see this!" Their terrible wounds were indeed a gruesome sight, some appearing like slabs of raw beef. They were hurriedly carried to the wardroom, where our surgeon lieutenant did his best. The landing craft headed back to the shore, the officers and men stricken with distress, but they carried on to death or victory. In their case, I like to think that they were able to land successfully this time and fight on.

Two of the most terribly wounded died during the night. The following morning the chief boatswain's mate sewed them up in canvas, the last stitch through their nose between the nostrils (a naval practice, to make sure they were really dead), with a 50-pound shell between their legs so that they would sink to the bottom and not pop up. I read the service for burial at sea, and their poor bodies were slid off a plank tipped over the side by the torpedo tubes. Individual courage or heroism generally counts for nothing in modern war. You are usually killed or wounded from a distance, suddenly, by a team that never even sees you or knows what they have done. Cowards and heroes all get the same treatment.

We had no idea whether we killed anyone at all. With direct bombardment, which we began with on D-day, you see explosions and buildings flying apart or burning, but as a rule you do not see people. Indirect bombardment does not give even the satisfaction of seeing the explosion. Someone tells you over the radio what you have or have not done. I understand that many of the enemy soldiers in Normandy that day were not even Germans. They were Ukrainians or Russians who had joined the German army after the invasion of Russia. I believe these were replaced by German nationals within a few days.

After our initial bombardment, we waited for a call from our forward observation bombardment officer. About 1100 he asked us to bombard a battery of three 88mm guns two miles inland. We complied and were informed that we had completely demolished the battery. We were told we were very accurate.

On the beach, masses of equipment poured in and a large artificial harbour took shape. The weather settled down and as the day went on the western sky filled with

AT REST BESIDE
THE TORPEDO TUBES

BURIAL AT SEA FOR A ROYAL MARINE COMMANDO

hundreds of planes – tow planes with gliders astern of them. The sky filled with parachutes and the gliders slipped their tows to land. Watching from the sea, we noticed German anti-aircraft fire and to our horror saw four huge four-engined planes shot down. Another one, badly damaged, managed a successful landing. It was hard to accept that these planes were filled with fellow human beings.

During the night German bombers attacked the great fleet lying off the shore but hit only one ship. The display of anti-aircraft fires was most impressive, but I don't believe we damaged any Germans. At dawn RAF fighters drove off the bombers and the fleet managed to shoot down two RAF planes, an unpopular success!

A truly awesome sight was our rocket craft firing huge salvoes at shore positions. There was so much smoke you could not see the results. We learned that evening that our Canadian troops, including two French-Canadian regiments, had advanced six miles ahead of the other Allied forces.

" WE THEREFORE COMMIT HIS BODY TO THE DEEP"
DIVINE SERVICE BOOK FOR THE ARMED FORCES

Unfortunately, they had to withdraw some miles in order to straighten the line of advance.

The next day, D plus 1, we lay at anchor all the fore-noon. After the burial service for the commandos, the men had the opportunity to stow empty shell cases and clean up the ship, inside and out. The wardroom was a hospital with our dining table serving as an operating table, and our lamp with the shade on which were pasted paintings of lovely girls, with some clothes on, had been replaced with a circular stainless steel operating room lamp. The officers were using the captain's day cabin as a temporary but convenient wardroom.

About noon we had a call to demolish a row of houses between JUNO and SWORD beaches. Delay-action fuses ensured that our shells burst inside the houses with flame and smoke providing total destruction and the end of the snipers concealed there. We completed the work in 20 minutes, then did an anti-submarine patrol around the anchorage.

We saw the British and American battleships and cruisers banging away at distant inland targets. Among them was my first ship, HMS *Erebus*. After dark we continued our patrol. German E-boats attacked the flanks of our force but did no damage. German bombers carried out pattern bombings on the anchorage but sank only one patrol craft.

On D plus 2, German air activity ceased as the sun rose. We went on with our perimeter patrol, attacking a possible submarine contact with two patterns of depth charges. An oil slick appeared but it was our guess that the contact was simply an old wreck. A carrier pigeon landed on our yard-arm. Men went up the mast to try to capture it but had no success, and it flew off to another destroyer.

After we anchored, we were able to watch the Mulberry harbour being put together, an amazing sight. Big transports were disembarking thousands of troops every hour. A large landing craft nearby was embarking German officer prisoners for transport to the United Kingdom. They did not impress me as looking very defeated. The ones I observed appeared well dressed, shaven and with caps on. It was a sight which gave me considerable satisfaction, some of the so-called master race who had been lording it over all of Europe. Our motor cutter took our three wounded commandos over to a hospital ship and our officers were able to occupy the wardroom once more. On patrolling to the westward side of the invasion area, we passed close to OMAHA Beach and in every direction saw countless dead Americans floating face down in the water, evidently washed away from the shore by the tide and wind.

We ferried Leonard Brockington, a Canadian well known in those days as a fine orator and splendid intellect, from *Sioux* to a landing ship. This gentleman, who possessed a unique appearance, a humpback like a philosopher of fable, had lived in Calgary two blocks from my home and his son went to the same school as I. Brockington described the great invasion in a talk on the CBC entitled "'D' Day on a Canadian Destroyer."

On D plus 3 we rested at anchor waiting for a target for bombardment. Our forces now were inland beyond the range of our guns and nothing else came up. German fighters, Messerschmitts, swarmed over the beaches, strafing with their machine guns, but did little damage. In *Algonquin* we watched a film, *Random Harvest*.

The next day we topped up *Sioux* with our remaining ammunition and fresh provisions and sailed for Portsmouth, where we topped up with ammunition, water, oil and provisions and at 2130 embarked Admiral Nelles, for many years our Chief of Naval Staff. We had rather a large party ending at 0400, sailed for Spithead at 0800, anchored, had Divisions and an inspection by the admiral, and sailed for Normandy that evening. Admiral Nelles had noticed the red maple leaf on our funnel and some weeks later wrote us that a maple leaf on the funnel would be official for all RCN ships.

On D plus 6, we were back in Normandy and Admiral Nelles left us to join the Admiral Commanding the Eastern Task Force. Later in the morning, we saw Winston Churchill and Anthony Eden in an RN destroyer speeding by. Lieutenant Commander Tony Law, the Canadian artist, came alongside with his MTB squadron. We gave them cake and fresh bread and they had baths. Two of Tony's men had flesh wounds from gunfire and I offered them passage to England. They declined, saying they preferred to stay with Law – a good indication of their high morale. They returned our admiral to England.

We sailed again for England that evening as escort for a small convoy. Starshells burst all around for our entire passage, but the chief menace was not the E-boat but other convoys bound for France, and not necessarily on the right side of the swept channel. Evidently there were several collisions among the merchant ships but no sinkings.

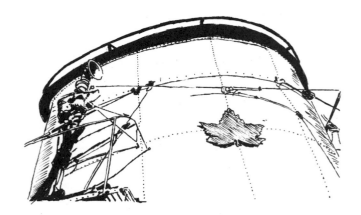

D plus 7 found us fuelling at a tanker off Portsmouth, then anchoring. It was a nasty day with rain and high wind. The British radio, after D-day, started to broadcast a special Allied Expeditionary Forces program. This was patterned after the best American and British radio with news every hour. The music was an eclectic mixture – popular and classical, vocal and instrumental, and certainly gave everyone a good feeling. By suppertime we were under way again with three other destroyers on a defensive patrol of the Portsmouth area. We soon had a sonar contact and we and our three friends dropped charges on it all night. Again, our conclusion was that our contact actually was a wreck. There were many of these in the English Channel from 1939 on, but we could not take a chance.

On D plus 8 we continued our patrol, stopping to attack with two salvoes of depth charges a contact by a U.S.

L.B. JENSON

H.M.C.S. "Sioux"

THE INVASION OF NORMANDY 231

frigate that had expended all her depth charges; it was judged to be another wreck. Our next contact, another wreck, yielded a fine harvest of haddock which were fished out with buckets on lines.

D plus 9 was a continuation of our patrol but was quiet, and we were able to clean up the ship, get our books up to date, and see men who had requests for promotion, badges and so on. In the afternoon all the hands not on watch piped down and relaxed.

D plus 10 found us in the early morning darkness off the Isle of Wight, trying to take a broken-down landing craft in tow. It was raining and blowing hard and the landing craft was drifting into one of our minefields. The navigator could see the moored mines on the sonar display, or so he said. The harder we tried, the more the wretched landing craft drifted in among the mines. Finally we got a line secured to her, dragged her clear into the swept channel and towed her to Portsmouth. Looking at the stormy seas about us when we started the tow, it was not hard to picture the mines swaying beneath the surface ready to deal us or our tow a mortal blow. However, nothing happened and we were able to go to the oiler and top up our tanks. Soon we were off the Needles, escorting an ex-armed merchant cruiser, *Cheshire*, to Plymouth, were we anchored for the night. *Huron*, a Canadian Tribal, was nearby and a group of us went over for a social visit.

We were up early on D plus 11, picking up a dock-ship off Portland and escorting her to Portsmouth, where we anchored off Seaview. Some went ashore for another run at the Starboard Club.

On D plus 12, we embarked the commander of the First Canadian Army, Lieutenant General H.D.G. Crerar, and his staff. This was the first time a Canadian army commander had proceeded to enemy territory in a Canadian warship. We escorted the battleship HMS *Rodney* to the assault area. It was a beautiful Sunday and we had divine service with General Crerar reading the lesson. Some of his staff had not experienced a trip in a destroyer before and their concern was noticeable.

Having delivered our distinguished guests to a landing craft, we were ordered to the eastern boundary of SWORD area, the mouth of the River Orne. The Germans still occupied the other side of the river and were bombarding SWORD Beach and the anchorage. Night fell but we were not bombarded by guns, only by a German plane flying around us. At four in the morning, we received a request for fire support from our commandos so we carried out blind fire on three targets. The commandos made a successful attack and later thanked us for our accurate gunfire.

This was D plus 13. The wind got up during the forenoon, becoming Force 7 from the northeast, the worst direction possible for the beaches. Our capstan broke down and temporary repairs were carried out. At 1930 we weighed anchor to go on patrol, and a battery of 155mm high explosive shells started firing into the anchorage. Fortunately for us, these landed about 400 yards short. The weather was too rough for efficient patrol so we and three other destroyers anchored well to seaward.

D plus 14 found a full gale still blowing. We anchored off SWORD again while the nearby cruisers bombarded continuously, but there were no targets for us. The gale howled all night, the third day in succession.

D plus 15 saw damage to the artificial harbours and to landing craft. Few supplies were getting ashore and this could have had serious consequences for our armies. Cruisers, with their longer-range guns, still had lots of targets but there were none for the destroyers. German aircraft had busied themselves at night dropping mines all over the anchorage area, and now the things were blowing up at random to make life interesting for us.

The night of D plus 16 gave us weather like the mid-Atlantic. At dawn the anchorage presented a scene like an 18th-century painting, ships in great numbers rolling and tumbling about in a world of grey-green surf with trails of old men's beards, all this under a dark and menacing cover of racing clouds, the coast of Normandy barely discernible in the haze. As the day went on, the weather improved and gradually the heavy rollers flattened out. Now was revealed flotsam of all kinds from that disastrous weather. Landing craft had foundered and the occasional dead body floated by. At the artificial harbours and on the beaches, superhuman efforts were being made to continue the flow of supplies needed to sustain the campaign.

D plus 17 found us continuing our patrol of the centre of the anchorage which we had started at sunset. The sea was flat calm and it was pitch dark except for starshell on our flanks where outer patrols were engaging German E-boats. The few German planes overhead were drawing ships' anti-aircraft fire, but not in our immediate vicinity. Suddenly four brilliant flares burst over the bridge and there was the roar of a diving aircraft, then the high-pitched whine of falling bombs. There was a loud *whoomph* as one burst a hundred feet to port of the bridge. Another splashed nearby but failed to explode. It may have been an armour piercing bomb. We lurched to starboard and increased to full speed, our decks wet from the spray of the explosion. A few minutes later we saw our patrol mate, another destroyer, illuminated as we had been and near-missed but with some equipment damage. Back came the aircraft over us and once more we were illuminated, but this time no bombs fell. At daylight we returned to our anchorage, well aware that many mines had been dropped by German aircraft during the night.

The morale of our people seemed unaffected by the near-bombing we had suffered. If anything it was improved, if that was possible, because we all felt so thankful to still be alive. We had good news that although the four-day gale had caused damage and delays in landing personnel and stores, there had been no overall delay as unloading had been well ahead of schedule before the bad weather.

Our captain went ashore for a few hours to have a look around. He looked in one apparently abandoned concrete emplacement and to his surprise was told in loud Cockney to "eff off" and find his own "effing" hole, so he returned to the "effing" ship. The captain said that the famed Atlantic Wall and other installations had been well smashed up by naval gunfire and bombing, and that damage caused by the gale was not heavy at all and had been cleaned up. He added that the French civilians, old people, women and children, to whom he had spoken seemed glad of the Allied arrival, despite the accompanying destruction of their property. I imagine they were still dazed and bewildered by the bombing and gunfire. It is ironic that our landings took place near Caen, from where William the Conqueror sallied forth for his successful invasion of England.

Four "doodlebugs," the infamous V1 flying bombs, puttered by overhead, on an inland course, presumably malfunctioning as they were supposed to be headed for southern England.

At dusk we were off on patrol again for the night of D plus 18. All night long enemy aircraft droned overhead and parachute mines splashed in the water near us. I went on watch at 0400 just as it was getting light. As we approached our anchor billet, we were in line ahead with HMS *Swift* astern of us. I sighted a floating mine on our port bow, called the captain on the voice pipe and was granted permission to sink it with gunfire. I decided to do it personally, using my Sten gun. Looking back, we were a bit too close and this was an unusually stupid thing to do. I did not stop to reflect that mines can blow up and shower you with shrapnel. God was with me. The mine with all its horns still intact quietly sank.

Swift snootily signalled us, "While you play around, may I anchor in your billet and you anchor in mine?" I signalled, "Yes please," and she steamed ahead to what had been our spot. I watched in my binoculars as she let go her anchor and immediately was enveloped in a cloud of white spray. There was a second explosion, her back was broken and she started to sink. Our captain had arrived on the bridge a few minutes before so I asked him if I could send the motor cutter to get *Swift's* whaler to replace ours, which, when we were anchored off Portsmouth, had been secured to our after boom one night and was stolen. I also wanted breech blocks for our 4.7-inch guns as ours were wearing out. Boats from various places were taking off *Swift's* people; as far as I knew none had been killed.

Dick Steele, our navigator, went off with the cutter. He later said that some Swifts had indicated that our conduct was inappropriate, we were barbarians, or words to that effect. It was difficult to insult the Algonquins, who had something in their minds which hadn't crossed mine. Their first stop on the sinking *Swift* was to pop into the petty officers' mess and take all the rum that those guys had been saving. Then they got a couple of breech blocks, binoculars, a sextant, name boards, large fenders and other odds and ends as the ship went to Davy Jones. They didn't get the whaler, which, being amidships when the ship folded and the bow and stern went up, was already 10 feet under the water. Little did I know about the rum. For months afterwards the odd chap would get rather drunk out of the blue, so to speak, and I would overlook it thinking perhaps his tot had gone the wrong way. If I had not seen the floating mine and decided to sink it, we could have been in *Swift's* place, on the bottom.

Only *Swift's* mainmast protruded from the water. Our notice boards were shielded with glass and in rough weather someone always fell against the glass, smashing it and messing up my notices. There was a 293 radar aerial on top of Swift's mast and it was shielded in plexiglass. I began to lust for this plexiglass to cover my notice boards.

We were anchored right on the eastern flank of the invasion area and for the first time since D-Day visibility was excellent. German gun batteries on the crest of the hill on the other side of the River Orne were firing into the anchorage, and some of the shells landed rather close to us. One particular heavy battery had been active since D-Day and today the flash and smoke of its firing was easy to see. It was out of range of *Algonquin's* guns but the larger ships had engaged it without success. It must have been well protected. We fired at a casino in line with the battery but short. That night enemy air attacks were heavy and a number of bombs landed uncomfortably close to us.

HMS SWIFT SINKING AFTER ANCHORING OVER A GERMAN MINE
NORMANDY JUNE 1944

IN THE BACKGROUND SMOKE IS FROM ONE OF OUR TROOP & SUPPLY SHIPS SHELLED & SINKING

A SHELL SPLASH & EXPLOSION
A RANGING SHOT ON US
PLUNDERING THE MAST OF H.M.S. SWIFT

D plus 19 was an anniversary of sorts. On 25 June 1940 HMCSS *Fraser* and *Restigouche* had left France filled with refugees for England. At last the situation seemed about to be reversed. It was a beautiful day, blue sky and flat calm. I asked the captain if I could take the motor cutter and remove the radar and plexiglass from the mast of the wreck of *Swift*. Off I went with a leading seaman and cutter crew. The leading seaman climbed up the mast eight feet or so and got to work on the radar. Within five or ten minutes there was a loud bang and a fountain of water beside us, then the howl of the shell and a patter of shrapnel. For anyone who hasn't been near a bursting shell, they make a lot of smoke and they stink. Again and again shells landed beside us. The hero up the mast continued to work at freeing the plexiglass as if this were just an ordinary routine. I didn't feel that way at all. The cutter crew sat there apparently calm, but not joking either. Eventually the radar aerial and plexiglass were in the boat as shells continued to land.

Our cutter got under way, and now the shells were landing astern of our ship. To our dismay *Algonquin* hastily weighed anchor. As she got going, shells landed in her wake and we followed along at our top speed, hoping we wouldn't lose sight of our floating home. Finally *Algonquin* got out of range of the German guns and we were able to

NORMANDY 1944   D+19
A SURPRISE GLIDER BOMB
"LOOK-OUT! THE DAMN THING IS COMING
OUR WAY"

LBJ
(VIEW ON OUR
BRIDGE)

come alongside to be hoisted aboard. My notice boards now could be protected with plexiglass. I was amused to learn later that one of our leading seamen was innocently doing his dhobi in a bucket on the quarterdeck. He became aware of water splashing all over him and thought it was a joker on the deck above. The water splashes were from German shells! Winston Churchill once remarked that being under fire is an exhilarating experience, especially when it misses.

During a quiet period in the afternoon we noted a German plane at a great height. A little speck left the plane and started flying in our direction. It was a bomb guided by the aircraft, and it was coming at us. All of us on the bridge took shelter under one another – no time for manners. The bomb turned around and went in another direction, hitting the water close to us and exploding. Occasionally mines went off for no reason. For all the enemy activities there was little damage to ships or artificial harbours.

D plus 20 was our last full day. Ashore the flash of our forces' guns still could be seen and overhead our air forces commanded the air. The invasion, though far from secure, appeared to be progressing favourably. The Americans had captured Cherbourg, and we were to return to England the next day. We went alongside HMS *Venus* to transfer our remaining ammunition to her. She was lying at anchor and we gave her a good bang in the process. There had not been one person visible on deck as we went alongside. The ship appeared deserted. With our bang, which caused her to tip a bit, a loud joyous cry arose from within the wounded body, "Refit! Refit! Refit!" Little damage had been done so we gave them our ammunition. They did not appear grateful.

The following day we escorted HMS *Bulolo* to Portsmouth. We sent a message to the dockyard that we had lost our whaler, and it seemed that within minutes we had a lovely brand new one. We embarked over one thousand rounds of ammunition, took on oil fuel and provisions and lay at anchor off Spithead for two days until the end of the month.

I t was a great honour to have taken part in the invasion of Europe and it was the beginning of the end for the Germans. Algonquins behaved splendidly – they could not have performed their duties more efficiently or with higher morale. Each officer and man understood that he was playing a part in one of the most significant events in history. It had not been as difficult as we had anticipated. We expected many more sinkings and much more of our blood

to be spilled. We now know that we have Corporal Hitler to thank. He did not give his generals a free hand. If he had done so, it might have been a terrible battle. For myself, I felt a great numbness as if it were a dream. I had buried men and supervised the everyday activities of the ship, keeping it clean and liveable, trying to maintain everything at a level of normality under conditions quite the opposite. Everyone, from gunner to cook to stoker, had a job to do, and all of us working together and supporting one another reinforced our brotherhood.

Our navigator remembers

I thought it would be interesting to record our navigator's recollections of the invasion of Normandy. I was busy doing all the housework while Dick Steele knew what was going on in the outside world, where we were going and what we were supposed to do when we got there. In June 1995, I asked him about our part in Operation OVERLORD. The following is a transcript of the recollections of Captain R.M. Steele, DSC, RCN (Rtd), navigation officer of HMCS *Algonquin* during the invasion of Normandy:

We got orders for the Invasion, Operation OVERLORD, about three months before the event. An enormous pile of orders about two feet high plus charts arrived. I read them carefully and went back and read them over again probably twice, at least. Then we got a message to land all our secret orders, much more than just OVERLORD. Perhaps this was in case the ship was sunk, as we were liable to be going in-

238 TIN HATS, OILSKINS & SEABOOTS

side shallow waters somewhere. It might have been that we would be going to Russia.

Then we got all the orders back and were sailed down to the Isle of Wight. I read all the orders again. We were allowed ashore and you and I and some of the others went along to the Starboard Club and had a big evening there. Neil Chapman was officer of the day and our whaler was secured at the stern boom. Somebody came during the night and stole it. It was hard to be mad at Neil because he was such a nice guy and so conscientious. It was an unlikely theft. Anyway, we embarked on the Invasion without a whaler. No leave was allowed 48 hours before sailing for the Invasion.

We set out the first day and turned around and came back in when it was cancelled. We finally set out the next day. I remember that after we got going the 43rd and 45th Royal Marine Commandos came right in behind us; the 33rd might have been there too and that was Lord Lovat's crowd. I remember looking astern and watching them through the glasses and all these poor chaps were heaving along on the short choppy sea, all lying down on the decks of their landing ships. I've forgotten where the Marines left us, but I've an idea that it was just before daylight when the minesweepers opened us up from the swept channel and let us go through into the clear areas in French coastal waters.

We went out into the unswept waters which we knew were pretty safe because it was an old, old minefield. Very few mines had been swept in the last stretch. We closed the coast and it got light enough that we could see our targets clearly. We could see the streets in Courseulles; I knew the street and the number of houses I had to count over to our first target and I could identify them clearly long before we opened fire.

When the minesweepers opened up the channel, we were followed by *Virago, Verulam* and *Venus*. We also had *Faulkner* and *Fury* with us. We kept steaming in and nobody opened fire on us. Everything was quiet and nothing was happening. I've forgotten exactly at what range we opened fire. It was 8000 yds or so. We opened fire and got our targets and got them quite soon.

After that the landing craft were going in. A small landing craft came over to us and we picked up all those wounded men. The strange thing about that was that out of all the ones we had, there were two Canadians and they were the ones that survived. The rest were all British Royal Marine Commandos. It seemed odd. It was supposed to be a whole Canadian outfit and these were Royal Marine Commandos who were strengthening the Canadian forces.

We went in and turned and took our targets out without any trouble but, as I remember, just as we were getting into position, the RAF came and bombed the beaches. I said something standing by the voice pipe and Irwin, who was the navigator's yeoman, was copying down everything that was said. Later somebody took that and transcribed it and put it in the log saying, "God damn RAF are buggering up." I noticed that came out in Joseph Schull's book *Far Distant Ships,* but that's a quotation out of *Algonquin's* log. We went in and got our batteries out and no problems involved.

We didn't anchor, but we just lay there and watched the invasion. There was very little opposition to it on the Courseulles beach. Then they started getting return fire. We started to just pick off targets here and there before bombarding in blind control.

In OVERLORD, the navigator did the blind bombardment, not the gunnery officer. The gunnery officer did all the visual targets, but when we came to firing in support of the troops in line of fire, the navigator did the shooting. For blind bombardment, we laid a Dan buoy with a large reflector on it so that we would know precisely where we were. With the strong tidal current and the wind blowing, we could drift off very much, and if we drifted off a cable (200 yds), we could not be sure enough to open fire on targets within 200 yds of our own troops. After we were there for a while, we got calls for fire on targets within 100 yds of our own troops. Later on, we anchored, fixed our position and actually made allowances for the swing of the ship. I remember where we were anchored. A big battleship, *Rodney*, was outside us. When we were firing at targets at fairly close range later in the afternoon, they were firing towards Caen or a target close to Caen. HMS *Erebus* also was firing, but they didn't fire very much. They only fired when they had a really good target to go after. I certainly remember when we were just inside *Rodney*, when she fired, her bricks went right over the top of us. I was fascinated that I could see the projectiles going up and up and up, very high!

We fired at targets where the Germans were opposing our troops going inland. Wherever we saw machine gun fire coming down, we opened fire on them. Captain Blunt, Royal Artillery, was our Bombardment Liaison Officer (BLO). We also had a FOB (Forward Bombardment Observation Officer). Blunt had been with us in Scapa and stayed with us. The other fellow went ashore before the invasion and went over to whatever regiment he was going in with and they, and a lot of others as well, were in contact with us.

In the afternoon, our engineering officer came up on the bridge and said he had missed all the shooting. Would we show him what had gone on. Debby said, "Sure Johnny," and he said to Corky Knight, the gunnery officer, "See that building over there, can you hit that?" Corky said, "Yes." With that he just peeled the roof right off. After Lieutenant Dennis James Patrick O'Hagen, George Medal, came to relieve the radar officer, we decided that was the building that O'Hagen, then Beach Master for JUNO Beach, had picked out for his Command Headquarters. Later he complained bitterly about such wanton destruction.

That afternoon, I remember we shot for the North Shore Regiment and the Chaudières. I noted the North Shore Regiment did better than anyone else and they got way in six miles ahead of the others and got up to their objectives and further on. They had to come back to straighten out the line. Later in the afternoon, there was a German tank attack and we got a call for fire on them. We started in and, if you remember, *Liddesdale* and *Glaisdale,* Hunt Class destroyers, were painted blue to attract attention. They were little things and they were supposed to go in and draw the fire – whether they knew it or not! They were supposed to draw

ALGONQUIN — NIGHT ACTION — VIEW FROM THE BRIDGE, LOOKING FORWARD — STARBOARD SIDE

the fire in the opening when we did the shoot on the invasion, but they got outside us. Again in the afternoon, they got outside us and whoever the German battery or tanks were who opened up on us, they fired over us at the Hunts.

We went in to get those tanks. The tanks punched their way right into a stone farm building near the beach defences at Petit Enfer. We brought that building down on the tanks one after the other and broke up the attack. I've seen no record of that in the history.

I remember, particularly, I think it was the first night when all those gliders came in towed by Stirlings. They came over the anchorage and I saw one of the Stirlings hit. He kept right on going, dropped his gliders and turned. He was turning and coming down and I noticed that the pilot took his plane right into the ocean to avoid our own ships. I thought that was terrific.

On the first or second day, *Faulkner* went to pick up General Montgomery and take him in. I was told that when they came in Montgomery kept saying, "Go closer!" He spoke to the captain and the captain said to the navigator, "How much further can we go before we would ground? The navigator said whatever it was and Montgomery said, "Go!" She went and she grounded.

Later on we went back to England and picked up the Canadian army staff and took them over to Normandy. We were going back in, we knew the area and had been there five or six days. It seemed the bloody war was about over, with General Crerar and his staff gathered around a chart, picking out the various landmarks. I heard them, as I was conning the ship, so I turned around and said that's so and

so. I remember Crerar looked at me and said, "It is not! That's so and so!" I said, "Yes, sir!" That struck me as either the appalling ignorance of the staff or the subservience of officers who experienced and had previously been caught saying, "No, that's not so." I couldn't believe it, I turned around and shook my head. I let them go on. That was the church tower in Courseulles or one of those things that we'd been using as a reference landmark. We'd been around there five days.

I remember now that on D-Day, there were tremendous numbers of gliders which went in. That might have been in the afternoon, I've forgotten. But they were going in and some of them were getting in all right and some were getting knocked down out of the air. It was horrible, because one would realize that each one that came tumbling down out of the sky was filled with men.

I can't remember whether we went out on patrol after we transferred the generals, I think we did and patrolled the north side of the anchorage that night. I think it was the second night that we were informed of fast little boats operated by a chap who lay on the deck of one and guided it in. They were filled with explosives and the diver who controlled them rolled off when they were well lined up with their target. I never saw those. I don't know if they actually hit *Dragon*. Remember the old cruiser *Dragon* was going to be sunk for the artificial harbour, "Mulberry." Anyway *Dragon* was positioned satisfactorily.

I remember one night, later on, I got into an argument with Peter Cock, the air defence officer, on the bridge, when he was officer of the watch. All of a sudden we were illuminated and I said, "For God's sake, push the Action Station alarm and call the captain."

"No" he said, "It's just RAF."

I was arguing with him and saying those flares are German flares because they are away brighter than ours. I said, "Go hard aport, full ahead both engines!"

If he had done that, we would have managed to just get the stern under the bomb that landed right beside us.

[Jenson: "If he had done that?"]

Yes, if he had done that it would have hit our stern.

[Jenson: "But he hadn't done that."]

Yes, the son of a bitch should have been court martialled!

[Jenson: "Why, don't we end on that note!"]

Yes, but that was the bomb that knocked Darky Lowe, our sub-lieutenant, out of his bunk. Darky had a bad back and was down in his bunk and it flipped him right out onto the deck.

[Jenson: "I don't know whether it fixed his back or not."]

Lieutenant Peter Bligh Cock, a direct descendant of the notorious Captain Bligh of the *Bounty*, was not easily pushed around, thank goodness!

Officers of HMCS Algonquin

Sub Lt Lowe   Gunner Slater   Lt Toller   Lt Knight   Lt Steele   Surg Lt Dixon   Lt Chapman
RCN   RCN   RCNVR   RCNVR   RCNVR   RCNVR   RCNVR

Lt Cock   Lt Jenson   Lt Cdr Piers   Lt Cdr (E) Lloyd   Lt Sturdy   Lt (S) Stanley
RCNVR   RCN   RCN   RCNVR   RCNVR   RCNVR

(E) Engineer (S) Supply   c. June 1944

14

Winding up the bloody war

The most hazardous and horrible place for naval operations was the Norwegian Arctic. Pack ice, ferocious storms, perpetual night in winter, perpetual day in summer – these were the characteristics of this area. Further threats were the always-present U-boats and the aircraft of the Luftwaffe, which operated from a gauntlet of seven airfields. Brooding in strategic bases were German heavy ships. The *Tirpitz* had moved to a base near the North Cape in January 1942, her mission to destroy convoys of ships carrying military supplies from Britain and the United States to the Russian port of Murmansk.

Tirpitz was a huge battleship, the sister ship to *Bismarck,* which had destroyed HMS *Hood* and was herself sunk by combined ships and aircraft of the Home Fleet. *Tirpitz* had been laid down in 1936 and completed in 1941. Her main armament consisted of eight 15-inch, twelve 9.9-inch and sixteen 4.1-inch guns. She certainly was respected by the Royal Navy, and every possible effort was made to destroy her. In September 1943, the British towed, by submarine,

midget submarines and released them off Alten Fjord, *Tirpitz*'s base. Two midget submarines got through the various barriers and one managed to place explosives beneath the battleship's hull. Many years later I attended a talk by one of the British officers involved in this extraordinary and brave action. This gentleman, who now lives in Nova Scotia, described how he and his colleagues surfaced and were brought aboard *Tirpitz*. They stood on the quarterdeck being interrogated by the Germans and apprehensively waiting for the charges to explode. Explode they did and put *Tirpitz* out of action until March 1944. In April 1944 carrier aircraft attacked her and put her out of action for three more months. This was an action in which *Algonquin* was one of the screening destroyers.

On 1 July 1944, accompanied by HMS *Vigilance*, we left the invasion theatre and sailed up the Irish Sea, escorting the cruiser HMS *Arethusa* as far as the Clyde. We then carried on around Cape Wrath and down the east

OUR FLOTILLA LEAVING SCAPA FLOW

coast of Scotland to Rosyth. This brought back fond memories of days in *Renown*, *Matabele* and *Hood*. We were there for a boiler clean and to repair various minor defects. We also were fumigated to get rid of a large rat population.

I had been cultivating a beard but it did not appear to have any hope of making me look like King George V. I looked more like Fu Manchu, and when a barmaid said, "I suppose you think you look good with a beard – you

don't," I agreed, returned to the ship and shaved off the wretched thing. My chin and upper lip were so sore from my pulling and tugging at the whiskers as I read, it was quite a relief.

We sailed at 0830 one forenoon and were home in Scapa Flow 10 hours later to rejoin the 26th Flotilla, which sailed three days later on Operation MASCOT. Our duties were to screen aircraft carriers whose planes were to attack the German battleship *Tirpitz* still in Alten Fjord near North Cape in Norway. When the planes arrived over their target, she was enveloped in a smoke screen. They bombed through the smoke, apparently without success, and returned to the carriers. Fog prevented a second attack and we returned to Scapa. For the rest of the month we screened fleet units and conducted exercises. This was the time of the midnight sun. One could read a newspaper on the bridge at 2400, but it was wise to be alert for an enemy who, of course, had excellent visibility.

On 1 August we carried out dive bombing exercises with fighter aircraft, followed by a blind full-calibre shoot at a battle practice target using radar and plotting. Our fall of shot was quite satisfactory. We next acted as escort to HMS *Nabob*, a Canadian-manned aircraft carrier, for two days while she carried out flying exercises.

Operation OFFSPRING with the carriers *Indefatigable*, *Trumpeter* and *Nabob* and cruisers *Devonshire* and *Kent* screened by our flotilla took off on 8 August from Scapa. The object was to mine the Norwegian Leads from the air

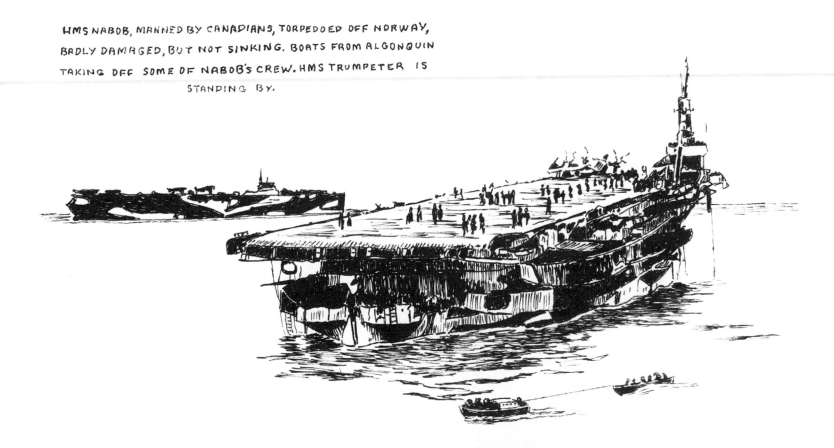

HMS NABOB, MANNED BY CANADIANS, TORPEDOED OFF NORWAY, BADLY DAMAGED, BUT NOT SINKING. BOATS FROM ALGONQUIN TAKING OFF SOME OF NABOB'S CREW. HMS TRUMPETER IS STANDING BY.

and to carry out air attacks on shipping and coastal installations. We were back home in Scapa on the 11th. A few days later we practised fuelling by the trough method from a carrier. This method, which I had first seen in *Renown*, involves steaming close alongside the fuelling vessel which then hoists the fuel pipe suspended in a trough or stirrup from a crane amidships. The recipient takes the end of the hose, secures it to a deck connection and accepts the fuel pumped aboard.

We next sailed as part of the screen for two escort carriers and a cruiser for Operation GOODWOOD. Our hope was to bomb *Tirpitz*, while covering the passage of two convoys to and from Russia. Near the Faeroe Islands, we were detached to fuel in Skaalefjord. This done, we rendezvoused with major fleet units, the battleship *Duke of York*, the fleet carriers *Formidable* and *Furious* and the cruisers *Berwick*, *Devonshire* and *Kent* with a screen of 13 fleet destroyers. The escort carriers *Trumpeter* and *Nabob* with five Captain class frigates formed another force which was to lay mines in the vicinity of *Tirpitz*. The attack was postponed a day because of unfavourable weather in the target area. We fuelled from *Devonshire* and the next day the first air attack was made on *Tirpitz*. I do not believe this attack caused much damage.

That afternoon *Algonquin* was ordered to close *Nabob* 15 miles to the west. We saw HMS *Bickerton* sinking near *Nabob*, which also had been torpedoed and was listing quite heavily. We took off 205 of *Nabob's* crew who were not necessary at this stage for steaming and fighting the ship. We proceeded to the Faeroes with her, and trans-

ferred *Nabob's* people to HMS *Zest*, a relieving destroyer which took the Nabobs back to Scapa. *Nabob* pressed on for Scapa at 10 knots in rough seas and arrived safely. She was later scrapped. Among the Nabobs we had was a sailor with tertiary syphilis. As can be imagined the ship was pretty crowded, but this man in his hammock in the cross passage at the break of the foc'sle had tons of room! We went on into Skaalefjord to fuel from a tanker. Later that evening *Duke of York* and other units arrived to fuel as well.

The next day, 27 August, we rendezvoused with the flagship and her force and went north at high speed to carry out a third attack on *Tirpitz*. The second attack had taken place after we were sent off to assist *Nabob*. In any case, *Tirpitz* was found covered by smoke and bombing results were uncertain. We were then detached to screen *Indefatigable* and proceed back to Scapa, arriving 1 September.

After we had fuelled in Skaalefjord, a number of officers and men went to a dance ashore at the community hall, a novel occasion. Between dances it was the custom for the men to be on one side of the hall and the ladies on the other. I think we must have brought some liquor ashore with us, but in any case there was a lot of alcohol consumed. The language of the Faeroe Islanders is close to a type of ancient Viking and the name on the ladies' room was "Genta," which is Viking for "Ladies." The confusion of the Canadian sailors, lacking of knowledge of ancient Viking and befuddled with rum and/or Nordic firewater, can be imagined.

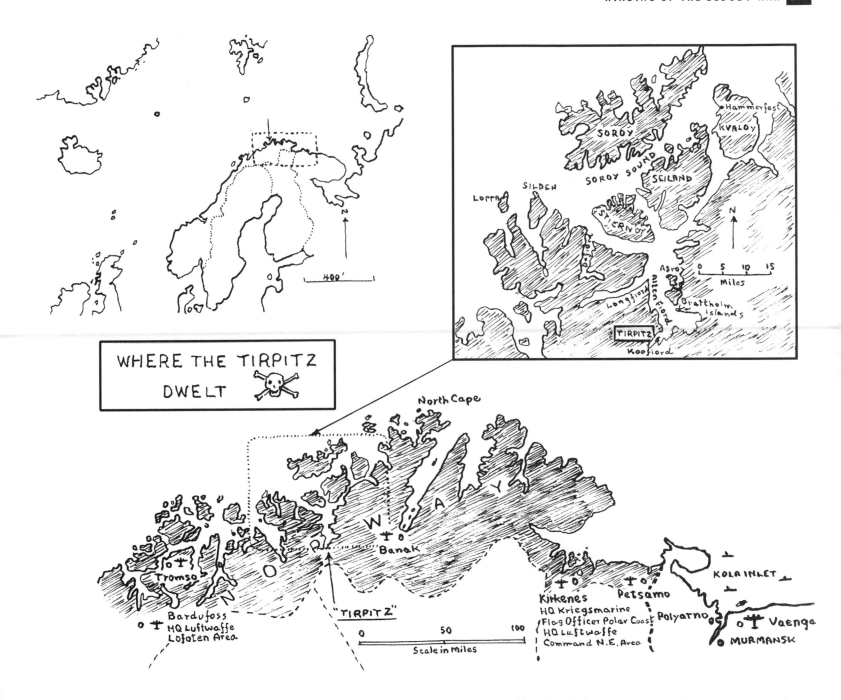

WHERE THE TIRPITZ
DWELT

SOROY
KVALOY
Hammerfest
SILDEN
SOROY SOUND
SEILAND
LOPPA
STJERNOY
N
Asroy
Allen Fiord
Longfiord
Bratholm islands
0 5 10 15
Miles
TIRPITZ
Koofiord

North Cape
W A Y
Banak
N O R
Tromso
KOLA INLET
Bardufoss
HQ Luftwaffe
Lofoten Area.
Kirkenes
Petsamo
Vaenga
Polyarno
MURMANSK
HQ Kriegsmarine
Flag Officer Polar Coast
HQ Luftwaffe
Command N.E. Area
"TIRPITZ"
0   50   100
Scale in Miles

400'

Tirpitz was repeatedly attacked in June and September 1944 from RN aircraft carriers. In November she was moved to the Tromsø area, where on 12 September she was attacked by the RAF, suffered several hits, was badly damaged and capsized.

When it was time to return to our ship, the trip down the mountain to the little jetty was a nightmare. It was pitch dark and very steep, with great boulders here and there in the brambles and heather. There was a cold, steady rain. It is true that Satan looks after his own. No one fell down the mountain and we were all on the little jetty, sitting, standing, lying down, being ill and so on. Our motor cutter arrived, loaded up, went to the ship and returned for another load. The next morning before we sailed at 0600 or so, I reported to the captain that all hands were aboard. As we steamed down the fjord to the sea, a small rowboat left shore and rowed after us. It was a member of the engineering branch who had been left asleep by the jetty. I had to lower the cutter, get our man, tow his boat back to the shore, return to the ship and be hoisted aboard. We were not delayed. All's well that ends well.

At the beginning of September, we went down to Rosyth for another boiler clean. This time I had the pleasure of meeting a lady I had first known as a midshipman and with whom I had corresponded for a number of years. It was wonderful to enjoy female company again, if only for a couple of days. She was a sergeant in the ATS, and her brother was Captain (Destroyers) in Greenock. Alas! Back to sea again, this time for Operation BEGONIA with carriers *Furious* and *Trumpeter* and cruiser *Devonshire*. Our object was to lay mines by air in the Norwegian Leads and then to beat up German installations and shipping. *Algonquin's* part was air-sea rescue and on our way to our station we encountered two large merchantmen, *Grottingholm*, Swedish, and *Arundel Castle*, British, carrying repatriated prisoners of war to the United Kingdom.

A few days later we sailed to the Faeroes to rendezvous with Russian Convoy JW60. Seven days later we arrived at Kola Inlet, where we fuelled. Then we went to the Russian base at Polyarno, where we were able to berth alongside with eight of our British friends. For some time I had been reading Tolstoy's *War and Peace* but the part of

Russia where we were was not like the country described by him. Russian Lapland looked rather like northern Canada, with even a few log cabins. The naval base had been developed by Stalin and must have been reasonably satisfactory for the Russians. There were sports facilities which we used for a track and field meet, won by Algonquins by one point. The German lines in Norway were 12 miles away so Russian security was at a high level.

Hal Lawrence from *Sioux* and I went walking together. The weather was lovely and mild, making walking delightful. We noted with interest Laplanders in native costume, little men walking with reindeer. There were limits beyond which we could not pass. One of the first lieutenants in our flotilla walked beyond the limits and was fired upon by machine gun, the bullets kicking up the dust around his feet. I did not see any trees, and the whole area appeared wild and desolate. Children begging for cigarettes were everywhere. One 10-year-old gave me 500 roubles for a package of cigarettes.

After three days alongside we sailed and picked up the White Sea section of the convoy homeward bound. We were examined by German aircraft and attacked by submarines, losing two merchantmen torpedoed. We attacked many contacts but as far as we could tell we had no success. There were at least six U-boats in contact with the convoy, but to the best of our knowledge they did not carry out further attacks. The convoy reached the Minches, by the Hebrides, on 4 of October, where we left them and went home to Scapa Flow, a few hours away.

On 13 October, we sailed as part of the screen for the cruiser *Euryalus* and escort carriers *Fencer* and *Trumpeter* for Operation LYCIDAS. The object was again to drop mines in the Norwegian Leads and attack shipping. The aircraft had the more exciting task of dropping the mines and strafing enemy shipping. We had the dull task of always keeping ahead of the carriers on passage and on takeoffs and landings. One never sees the results, if any, of one's work. The operation lasted four and a half days and a number of German ships were sunk.

The day after we returned to Scapa, we sailed to the gunnery range for a full-calibre surface shoot using radar control. This was followed by anti-aircraft practice against very realistic dive bomber attacks by fighters. A few days later we took part in a night exercise with three County Class cruisers. We practised starshell, and "star" torpedo attacks, that is, destroyers attacking a ship from every direction as from the points of a star. Three attacks were controlled from the plot, using blind radar firing. Invaluable experience was gained in night action communications and torpedo attacks at night.

These constant forays and exercises in every variety of fighting at sea gave the Royal Navy great advantage over the Germans. We were at sea constantly and had no limitations imposed on us by shortages of fuel. Our officers and men working with other ships to exercise difficult and exacting tactics tried their best to be proficient in every way, if only from national pride. Because of fuel shortage, the Germans were not accustomed to being at sea and suffered from the usual malfunctions of material, sea sickness and so on whenever they went out of harbour and were not able to settle down like real sea dogs. One thinks of Nelson's sea dogs at Trafalgar, the "far distant ships," always at sea.

Every evening at sea the first lieutenant of a destroyer had the duty of inspecting the whole ship, and in a gale this could be a precarious task. The first lieutenant of the Canadian Tribal HMCS *Iroquois*, Lieutenant Commander Tony Coughlin, was doing his rounds one night at sea when a huge wave smashed him against the after canopy or deck house and killed him. He was buried in the naval cemetery in Scapa that month. He was a popular and brave officer, a sad loss.

On 24 October we sailed with our flotilla to screen the carrier *Implacable* flying the flag of the Commander-in-Chief Home Fleet. Her aircraft attacked enemy shipping and shore installations along the Norwegian coast. Two strikes a day were carried out for three days and considerable damage and disruption to the enemy was reported. On our way home we were shadowed by enemy aircraft, but no attack developed. What a change all this was from my first days in the Norwegian Sea in 1940 when it seemed that we knew nothing but defeat. In Scapa we went alongside our depot ship *Greenwich* for a boiler clean.

I have mentioned the Wrens of Scapa Flow. It is not possible to say enough about these wonderful young women. They came to sea with us on many occasions, observing and helping with our training in gunnery, torpedo and operations exercises. In the most appalling weather, even when they were seasick, they did their duty and remained bright and cheerful at all times. On several occasions the wardroom held picnics on the shores of the Flow, all of us in plain clothes. What pleasant, innocent, friendly times these were, and I fancy they were treasured and appreciated by the Wrens as much as they were by our officers. Looking back on those times of dreadful danger and discomfort, it seems to me that the men and women of the United Kingdom and of the dominions and colonies stationed there were more bound together in unselfish devotion to a noble cause than ever before or since. It truly was a time of good against the forces of evil.

Operation Counterblast

On 8 November we sailed as part of a surface force attacking enemy shipping off the southwest coast of Norway. We carried out a night shoot at Stack Skerry, west of the Orkneys, and then headed north towards the Shetlands. However, the weather blew up to full gale force which would interfere with our shooting and torpedoing, so we turned back to Scapa Flow. We sailed again on 11 November and carried out Operation COUNTERBLAST the following night. Because of enemy minefields and other hazards, no similar operation off Norway had been undertaken for nearly four years. The actions in which we were engaged in *Matabele* would have been those previous actions.

Our force consisted of the cruiser *Kent* (Flag) and *Bellona* and destroyers *Myngs*, *Verulam*, *Zambesi* and ourselves, *Algonquin*. We sailed at 2100 on 11 November and again carried out a night shoot at Stack Skerry, employing the same tactics to be used against the enemy. At 2000 on the 12th we arrived off the Norwegian coast near Stavanger. The weather was moderately calm and clear and we formed in a loose line ahead in open order and began to sweep down the coast about seven miles offshore. The order was *Kent, Bellona, Myngs, Algonquin, Verulam* and *Zambesi*. At 2300 our radar indicated a convoy of five merchant ships and three escorts coming up the coast and closing. Another three ships appeared to be to the south.

The force opened fire when the enemy was two or three miles distant. *Algonquin* selected an escort vessel as target, hitting it with our first salvo. Other destroyers also fired and the ship burst into flames within a minute. We next took aim at a merchant ship at four miles, illuminating her with starshell from B gun and engaging her with our forward and after 4.7-inch guns. She too burst into flames. The merchant ships tried to close the coast to get under the protection of the shore batteries, but the escorts turned towards us, firing all their weapons with great determination. Several shells of all sizes landed near us, some being about 4-inch. Within the first five minutes at least six enemy ships were on fire and sinking. We then found an escort at a mile and a half and engaged her, and soon she was on fire and sinking. A gun on her stern, probably an Oerlikon, continued to fire at us, even though surrounded by flames, until the ship sank.

At 2325 the shore batteries opened fire and we were near-missed and straddled several times but not hit. Every enemy ship we had sighted was either sunk or set ablaze.

At midnight the destroyers were ordered to "finish off the enemy" and we returned to the scene of action. Three enemy ships remained. One was aground and burning. The other two burning ships blew up and sank. All the while the shore batteries were landing shells near us. We withdrew to the northwest and returned to Scapa Flow.

Our ammunition expenditure was more than 400 4.7-inch shells and 160 rounds of Bofors. We had only two scars: an Oerlikon bullet dented the chase of Y gun and another struck under the forward torpedo tubes. No one was wounded or hurt although several people claimed that shells and bullets passed between their legs or very close to them. Our torpedo gunner's mate, Jay Crotty, was standing by the tubes and was nicked by a bullet which ripped his shirt. All our radar, guns and machinery performed without fault.

"He also serves who stands and waits" describes my duties during this interesting activity. My job was to be where the captain was not, in case he was killed or badly wounded. In such a case I would automatically assume command. I took my place at the after end of the ship, by the emergency steering position atop the forward end of the after canopy. The noise of our guns firing was intense and I have to say that I felt a sort of ecstasy. It was a delight to see Germans getting their own richly deserved medicine. Our twin Bofors amidships, carried away in the heat of battle, started to engage a German lifeboat illuminated by starshell, and full of survivors, but was checked immediately. I don't think I have seen a happier or more proud ship's company than we were when we returned home.

252 HATS, OILSKINS & SEABOOTS

From where I was during the action I had no idea what was going on, just a lot of shooting. When I reflect on it, I was taking things for granted by not having more detailed knowledge of our position. If the captain and navigator had been killed, I would have had to depend on our other ships for guidance home. One thing that struck me as being most useful in those actions was the use of fighting lights on the foremast yard. All our ships had turned them on and they were very visible. In mêlées it is easy to get mixed up and it would have been a catastrophe to engage one of our own ships. *Verulam* and *Kent* each were hit by Oerlikon and *Kent* by a 3-inch shell as well. Both had a couple of wounded men.

It is a weird world. The communications officer for the German shore batteries was Lieutenant Niels Jannasch. In later years he became the director of the Maritime Museum of the Atlantic in Halifax.

On the way down the Norwegian coast, a submarine was sighted about a mile away peacefully proceeding on the surface. "We won't bother with that," said the captain. "We have other game to pursue." When I was at the NATO Defence College in 1957, there were a number of German officers and civilians, and it turned out that one civilian gentleman, G. Schaar, had been a lieutenant commander, a U-boat captain, and had been at that particular point at that particular time. He had seen us going by but thought we were Germans so didn't bother submerging. The Paris newspapers carried the amusing story about two people who narrowly missed one another during the war.

Memories of Counterblast

I was always busy with housekeeping in the ship. The captain and navigator took care of such things as tactics and strategy. In June 1995, I asked Captain R.M. Steele, our navigation officer at the time, what his recollections were of Operation COUNTERBLAST. This is a transcript of his reply:

… My memories of it go back to initially reading the operation order and later going to the briefing by Rear Admiral McGrigor. At the briefing, he explained exactly what we were going to do. He said that the reason we were striking was that we had information that a convoy was coming up the Norwegian coast with a number of ships and was picking up German forces from places along the coast with the object of taking them back to Germany for Christmas leave. This was early November 1944. The task force was to consist of two cruisers, HMS *Bellona* and HMS *Kent*, with the destroyers, HM Ships *Mygns*, *Verulam*, *Zambesi* and *Algonquin*. The first job of the cruisers would be to illuminate the convoy by firing starshell. The destroyers would be used in close action.

At the end of the briefing he explained that our submarines had plotted the courses that the German ships took down the coast repeatedly, so we knew where the swept channel was. We were going into the swept channel and keep right on the swept channel until we intercepted the convoy. He asked if there were any queries on this. I said to him that when we had been off the Norwegian coast on two occasions, we could see the German radars pick us up in their sweep. They would then stop and hold us and seemed to be plotting us. If we were going down the channel and came to one of these stations that was near a battery, would we switch on our jamming gear? We had jamming gear installed that could blank out their radar.

He said, "No, just ignore it."

I said, "They would have a very accurate range when they opened fire on us."

He said, "Well, if you were a young officer up here in the Shetlands and Orkneys and you had six ships coming down a swept channel, keeping right to the channel, coming down at a reasonable speed, what would you do? If you were a conscientious officer, you would say where is the message on these six ships coming down here? I don't have it! If you were very conscientious, you would immediately call up the Admiral Commanding Orkneys and Shetlands Operations Room and say, we've got six ships coming right down the swept channel. Who are they? And they'd say, 'Wait.'"

He added that you'd never get an answer and it would be the same with them. So we did the same and when we were coming down the channel several times we were picked up by the German radar and they held us. Then they continued their sweep and we went right on by.

As you remember when we intercepted the convoy, *Bellona* was with us and her task was to open fire and get 54 starshells in the air over the convoy immediately. That left all the other ships' armaments free to engage the enemy.

I remember at the briefing that McGrigor said that his experience was that if the fighting lasted very long, there was a tendency for the ships to get displaced. You are liable to not know which the enemy is and who are your own forces. If that happened, or seemed to be happening, he would order, "Switch on fighting lights." We had never done that in previous actions. The fighting lights, as you remember, were a line of green and red lights on the yards. That would give us not only our own ships' positions, but also inclination so that you would know where they're heading and what they're doing too.

When we intercepted the convoy and *Bellona* opened fire, the admiral altered not outboard but inboard into shallow water which surprised me. He then reduced us to six knots and we fought the action at six knots. We were right in front of the big batteries on the coast. When they opened fire they must have had all of us on radar and presumed that the outboard ones were the enemy because they fired over our heads all the time. I could hear them rattling over us. When the admiral finally ordered, "Switch on fighting lights," I switched them on and crouched down on the bridge but all the firing stopped.

Later on, after the war was over, I was talking with one of the Germans. He said they had an emergency recognition system of switching on red and green lights and they must have mistaken our switching on fighting lights for the identity of their own forces coming up. When we withdrew, we headed straight for Scapa, running right out until we came to our own big minefield and were out of radar range. We then went north and around the minefield and back into Scapa Flow. I believe it was two of their destroyers that came out on the same course that we set out on. I remember getting some information from somebody that they ran into the minefield and one was damaged. I believe that we sank 10 out of 11 ships in the convoy. That should all be in the record on COUNTERBLAST explaining this whole thing. ....

Within a couple of days we were back at sea screening the carrier *Implacable* during flying exercises. Flotilla 26 left Scapa for the Far East war against Japan, and *Algonquin* and *Sioux* were transferred to Flotilla 23. Our next operation was "Provident," sailing on 22 November. *Implacable*, two escort carriers, the cruiser *Dido* and screening destroyers made up the force, whose object was to lay mines and attack shipping off the Norwegian coast. The two escort carriers were damaged by heavy weather and had to return. The weather continued bad until 26 November when the gales abated. A heavy air strike was launched the next day, claiming much damage. The weather deteriorated again and we headed back for Scapa arriving on 29 November. We had suffered a lot of superficial damage and went to *Greenwich*, our depot ship, for minor repairs.

On one of our adventures into the Arctic Ocean, we had a passenger, Walter Gilhooly, the sports reporter for an Ottawa newspaper. Much older than us, he fitted in well and was an amiable and amusing gentleman. Most of us had never met anyone with the wonderful name of Gilhooly and soon he was incorporated into one of our wardroom songs, "Gilhooly, hooly, hooly, Gilhooly almighty!"

The consistent bad weather, the cold, the long periods of darkness and the brief periods of daylight were hard on everyone. A silly rumour spread among the sailors in the ship that the British were paying Canada rent for the use of *Algonquin* and *Sioux,* and by God they were going to get their money's worth. I don't think the captain heard this, but I passed the word to the coxswain and many others that the idea was rubbish; I had served in the Royal Navy and their treatment of their own ships was just as tough, or tougher. Such rumours can be dangerous. I think that the fact that I had served in RN ships gave me some credibility.

As for my personal feelings at this time, I was beginning to despair that there was any other kind of life and that the war might never end. I was sick of wondering when I would be killed. It had to be only a matter of time – my luck couldn't last forever. One enemy shell, torpedo or bomb could send us sky high. Then in Scapa, lying at a buoy in Gutter Sound, looking up at Ward Hill and wishing that someday I would have the energy to get to the top of that hill, I would be overcome with a sense of history. These were momentous times, quite the equivalent of the days of the Armada and Trafalgar, and it was an honour to be part of the struggle. I imagine that almost everyone aboard that great fleet of ships in that huge, lonely anchorage felt as I did from time to time. The fact that most of us believed that our martial conduct was totally honourable and above reproach was a source of moral strength, and we gained comfort from our weekly divine service, whether or not we were deeply religious.

JUNKERS Ju 88
TORPEDO BOMBER

On 5 December, *Algonquin* was off again, screening the battleship *Rodney* and cruiser *Berwick* for day and night exercises. The next day we formed part of the screen for the carriers *Implacable*, *Trumpeter* and *Premier* and the cruiser *Diadem* for Operation URBANE. The object was the usual minelaying and attacks on coastal shipping off Norway. The mission was accomplished and we were back in Scapa on 9 December.

Back to sea on 12 December we escorted the carriers *Trumpeter* and *Premier* and the cruiser *Devonshire* on Operation LACERATE, mining two areas off Norway. On 14 December the first mining strike was completed in fine weather, but conditions began to deteriorate to fog, wind and rain after our aircraft returned to the carriers. It was getting dark and the fog was getting thicker when the radar picked up echoes of aircraft closing. The destroyer screen was formed roughly in line abreast. The aircraft were Junkers 88s, torpedo bombers, attacking in three waves.

Each time they were hotly engaged, and in the last wave our combined fire shot down one Ju 88. The aircraft were flying at masthead height and appeared large and formidable as they passed overhead. There was no damage to our force and no further attacks, but there was a further incident. Our destroyers were fitted with an ABU (auto barrage unit). Radar measured the rate-of-approach of the target. At target range of 1,500 yards, the guns would automatically fire, setting up a curtain of bursting shells ahead of the approaching aircraft. One of the other destroyers happened to hit the critical range and set an ABU off. Fortunately no ships were damaged. The weather steadily worsened to a full gale. We got back to Scapa in the dark on 16 December, anchoring for the night in the Flow to ride out the gale instead of going to our buoy in Gutter Sound.

Seven tubes in our port condenser had worked loose and the boiler water was contaminated. We went alongside the repair ship, *Vindictive*, for a boiler clean and repairs. This was my original sea training ship. Now our studies on the upper deck had been converted into machine shops for ship repairs. On Christmas morning the captain asked me to take the ship into the floating drydock for repairs to the Asdic dome. This was one year in which we were permitted to enjoy our Christmas dinner in peace and a mild alcoholic haze, and everyone behaved quite reasonably. Such was not always the case.

Commander Ian A. Macpherson, CD, RCN (Rtd) was present for Operation LACERATE as a midshipman in the cruiser HMS *Devonshire*. He has kindly has given me permission to include relevant pages from his midshipman's journal:

HMS *Devonshire,* Operation LACERATE, from Scapa Flow, 10 December 1944

Divisions were held this morning, followed by prayers on the Quarterdeck. After the terrific wind that was blowing all yesterday, today was a perfectly flat calm. We haven't had such a nice day up here for quite some time.

During the dog watches Midshipmen Keester, Heitzberg, MacLean and myself went to *Norfolk* to visit the two Canadian midshipmen in her. We stayed for dinner and also the film afterwards, *The Song of Bernadette. Norfolk* is still in the throes of working-up and is in a trifle of a dirty state. She doesn't differ much from *Devonshire* except that she has a DCT and much more up-to-date radar installations.

11 December

At 0805 today we took over AA Lookout from *Berwick,* which sailed. I had the forenoon watch in the ADP [Air Defence Position] and it was rather cold, as usual, on such days. Exercise Chutney, which was scheduled for 1030, was cancelled owing to the weather.

Implacable sailed from Scapa Bay and *Mauritius* arrived and anchored in B2 berth.

I had a boat trip to Gibraltar Pier about 2300 because it was very dark and rough and the cox'n was inexperienced.

12 December

At 1315 hands were fallen in and commenced preparing for sea. Special Sea Duty Men closed up at 1335 and at 1355 we weighed anchor and proceeded out of the Flow, passing Hoxa Gate at 1440. We formed up in Order I, *Devonshire, Premier* and *Trumpeter. Diadem* also sailed about the same time, but went to the practise area for exercises with *Mauritius* and *Berwick.*

Our destroyer screen consisted of *Zealous* (S.O. [Senior Officer]), *Zephyr, Savage, Serapis, Algonquin* and *Sioux.* Course out of Hoxa was 190 at 17 kns. At 1610 we were on course 325, doing 16 kns. We commenced ZZ #15.

The ship exercised Action Stations at 1630 and secured soon after. We were on course 012 until 0400 when we altered to 055.

The Commander spoke over the SRE [Sound Reproduction Equipment] telling us that we were off to Norway again on a minelaying operation. He hinted that we may have some excitement, in that he stressed the importance of knowing where fire extinguishers, hoses, etc. were and what to do if damage was received.

13 December

At 0855 *Trumpeter* flew off one Avenger for A/S patrol. We continued on a northerly course all day keeping up the ZZ [zigzag] #15, and with a CAP (Combat Air Patrol) of 2 Wildcats, and an A/S patrol of 1 Avenger flying until dark.

Between 1035 and 1150 we tested close range weapons, as did other ships in the force.

Most of the afternoon was spent doing emergency turns because the screen had A/S contacts. At one time *Savage* dropped a five-charge pattern and she and another destroyer sat on top of the position for about a half-hour, before rejoining the screen.

At 2135 we altered course to 098 degrees, heading straight for the region of Trondheim, which was to be the object of this operation.

14 December. With Force 2 on Operation LACERATE

With us on this trip we have a number of specialist wireless officers and one RAF Sergeant. They proved to be invaluable in giving and receiving enemy reports.

At 0900 today we went to 2nd degree of AA readiness, because we were only about 40 or 50 miles from the target area. At 1000 we ceased zig-zagging and altered course into the wind, preparatory to flying off the strike. The weather was perfect for flying operations, the sea being a flat calm, with a cloudless sky and practically unlimited visibility. At 1030 *Premier* and *Trumpeter* flew off 6 Avengers and 8 Wildcats each. These A/C formed the strike, which soon disappeared towards the target area. The *Algonquin* was detached to guide them back if necessary. After flying off we continued on a course of 000 until 1208 when all the strike was landed on. At 1237 we altered course to 200 and increased to 18 kns., and at 1243 we altered to 280 and reduced to 17 kns. About 1300 we recommenced zig-zag #15.

The special wireless people aboard told us that a general air-raid warning had been sounded on the coast in the Trondheim area. About 1400 a single aircraft was picked up low on the horizon. It commenced shadowing the force, flying all around from beam to beam and then disappeared. It was believed to be a Ju 88. *Trumpeter* flew off 2 Wildcats to try and intercept it but they confused it with our own A/S patrol and so failed to find it. We heard by W/T that the shadower had reported us and so we were put on our guard. We also knew that Ju88 torpedo-carrying bombers were in force at Trondheim.

By this time the wind had commenced to increase and by the time it was twilight and the time had come to land on our patrolling aircraft, the wind was up to about force 4. All our aircraft were landed on at 1510.

About 1615 radar reported a group of aircraft coming up from astern, some 12-15 miles away. We went to 1st degree of AA readiness and with the aircraft closing rapidly, it wasn't long before attack was imminent.

The attacking aircraft split into two groups about 6 miles off and went up the sides of the force and turned in to attack on the bows. One of the screen fired a burst of Bofors at them as they went over, which gave us the tip to stand by. The starboard side opened up first, putting up a terrific close range barrage. Two torpedoes were dropped during this attack but they went by the stern. *Premier* was giving good radar reports all the time, enabling us to get a good plot.

The next time fire was opened was on the port side. #2 pom-pom saw an aircraft coming around the quarter, which seemed to be close in and low. We opened up, followed by the port side close-range weapons. #2 pom-pom continued sweeping with type 282 and soon picked up an echo on the port bow about 4000 yards distant. We opened up at about 2500 yards and again the port side fired its close-range weapons.

Aircraft were reported closing from the starboard side and I'm sure it (or they) must have been surprised when the whole of the starboard side HA armament put up such a terrific barrage. S1 and S2 fired 30 rounds, fused to 1600 yards in a very short space of time and even "Y" turret chimed in with one gun firing a round of short fused 8" H.E. (High Explosive). Perhaps it did the trick of scaring the others off, or else the enemy thought we were hit when they saw the flash of the 8". The one thing wrong with this was that it ruined the starboard side's night vision for about 10 minutes besides nearly knocking out the two Oerlikon gunners on top of "Y" turret, who weren't prepared for it.

However, the enemy did not attack again, and we claimed one JU88 shot down, and possibly another one. The "Y" people said they heard a pilot saying he would have to ditch, over the sea. All during the attack the ship manoeuvred, increasing or decreasing speed and turning all the time at the right times.

At 1747 we altered course to 290 degrees and at 1823 we commenced zig-zag #15 on a MLA (Mean Line of Advance) of 285 doing 15 knots. At 1855 we reverted to 2nd degree and at 2030 Night Defence Stations closed up, without the Torpedo Armament. At 2200 we altered the MLA to 215 and changed to ZZ#10 at 2245 doing 12 knots. Speed had to be continually reduced and finally we ceased zig-zagging in order that the carriers might keep up, not be beaten so hard by the sea which was up greatly, due to a Force 8 gale. At 2341 we altered course to 230.

The Commander spoke, telling us the results of the strike, the attack, and that we were now returning to Scapa Flow.

15 December

The force continued on the southerly course all day, with the wind on the port bow. A gale of force 8-9 was blowing and the carriers were making heavy weather of it all. At 1055 the ship altered course to be clear of the screen and fired an 8" broadside to clear the guns. Speed was reduced to 10 knots by this time. No more strikes were to be flown off. I had the first watch on the compass platform.

16 December

On the southerly course we soon got into the lee of the land and speed was increased to 16 knots. At 1700 we assumed open order on course 090, and at 1735 we altered to 060.

Special sea duty men and cable party were closed up soon, and we passed through Hoxa gate at 1802. The weather, even inside the Flow, was very dirty, with a high wind and heavy sea. In attempting to get to A2 berth to anchor, we fouled FG baffle in manoeuvring the engines to get back on our anchoring course of 129, the strong wind having blown us off. The starboard side aft was right against the baffle and we were being blown on it harder. The nets fouled the starboard inner screw and the rudder, so it was useless to try to get off that night. The port anchor was let go underfoot and later cable was veered to 4-1/2 shackles. A signal for assistance was sent. Anchor watches were set with an OOW on the bridge, an officer on the fo'c's'le and the MOW (Midshipman of the Watch) aft on the quarterdeck.

The two carriers anchored in the Flow.

17 December

The wind was still up and reached its highest velocity during the forenoon today. Two boom defence vessels came alongside. The salvage drifter also came alongside and the salvage officer came aboard. It was still too windy to do anything today, and anchor watches were still set. The film in the Wardroom after dinner was *Jack London*, which was quite good.

Ships in company are *Rodney, Diadem, Norfolk, Newfoundland, Uganda, Mauritius*, with *Kent, Trumpeter* and *Premier* in the Flow. Both the latter two received damage by the weather on the last operation.

18 December

The wind had gone right down during the night and today there is a flat calm, ideal for the work that has to be done. Two or three boom defence vessels commenced working, during the forenoon, to clear away some of the buoys and nets. By the dog watches both sides of the ship were clear, but the starboard inner screw and the rudder were still tangled. Two divers were working during the day.

At 1715 Special Sea Duty Men closed up, the anchor was weighed and we were taken in tow by two tugs, one ahead, the other on the port side. Without using our screws we were assisted to A2 berth where we let go the port anchor. At 1805 we came to with 8 shackles on the port anchor in 17 fathoms.

The Murmansk convoys in the final months of the war are a relatively forgotten part of the conflict with the German navy. Many people probably thought the conclusion of the war was now a certainty, but this was not so. The Germans were building fast new submarines which would be difficult to attack and destroy, and as far as I could see there was a possibility the war would last forever. Captain U-boats Northern Waters obviously had lots of fight left in him, and I shudder to think what would have happened if he had acquired a number of Type 21 or Type 23 submarines, which were very fast and more difficult to

POLYARNO, NAVAL BASE FOR MURMANSK
NORTH RUSSIA 1944
BARRACKS, WIRELESS MASTS, SUBMARINES (EX ROYAL NAVY)
10 MILES FROM THE GERMAN LINES

detect. They could have destroyed all Atlantic sea traffic. It was a close-run thing.

HMC Ships *Algonquin, Sioux, Haida, Iroquois* and *Huron* were involved in Murmansk convoy duties. I asked Captain Steele, *Algonquin*'s navigation officer, what his memories were of Kola Inlet and why the U-boats were a special menace in that area. It was subject to Russian air patrol, which should have kept the submarines down. Steele replied that we used to come down from south of Spitzbergen, and sometimes nearly over to Novaya Zemlya, then head for Kola Inlet. The coastal waters here were shallow and turbulent, making for difficult sonar conditions. Ap-

proaching the entrance to the inlet, Steele said, we dropped a depth charge every minute to discourage U-boats. I don't remember that, probably being fully occupied as executive officer.

Polyarno was a relatively small cove on the right of the entrance to Kola Inlet. Further inside Kola Inlet was a bay where we fuelled from a tanker at anchor. About 20 or so miles up the inlet was the city of Murmansk, a scattering of low, dark buildings. There was no boom or gate such as in Scapa, Halifax or St. John's. Instead there was a channel down the inlet with submerged nets either side to which explosives were fitted making, navigation exciting.

We undocked on 27 December and soon were screening the carrier *Vindex* and cruiser *Diadem* en route to join Convoy JW63 bound for North Russia. We met the convoy at noon on New Year's Day 1945. Happily we had good weather and were able to keep to the north, at one time actually being well north of Bear Island. Calm in the Arctic Ocean is quite remarkable. The sea is like a sheet of glass and often there are mirages. I have seen whole convoys appearing above the horizon, sailing along upside down. This time we were not bothered by the enemy, surface or air. Ships of the Soviet navy met us off Kola Inlet. They were in an irregular formation and were quite slack in our eyes. I think it was just their way of doing things; as the saying goes: "Different ships, different cap ribbons." We had hoped for some kind of air cover but we only saw one Soviet plane and that was when we were two or three miles off Kola Inlet. This was 7 January. We had to navigate up the inlet to Vaenga Bay in dense fog to fuel at the oiler. People told us that tanks and supplies brought by our ships had accumulated at Murmansk and were not being used as quickly as we had been led to believe. We returned to Polyarno to await a returning convoy.

There was a most embarrassing incident. It was after lunch and the captain was resting. The officer of the day reported to me that two Russian naval officers had to see the captain. It turned out that they thought there was a Russian woman on board. I got the coxswain and we searched the ship. We finally found out what the problem was. Two or three Russian naval officers had been visiting aboard and had discovered our gunnery officer, Lieutenant Knight, actually was of Russian birth. His father, Count Nicolas Michael Karetsky, had been a lieutenant commander in the Imperial Russian Navy and was a son of the governor of Kamchatka in Siberia. Knight's father and mother left Russia in 1918 from Vladivostok and came to live in Nova Scotia. The Russian officers were curious about an ikon which Knight had with him and he took them down to his cabin to show it to them. It was a double cabin which Knight shared with Lieutenant Toller, our Asdic officer. Toller's hair was quite long on top and he was

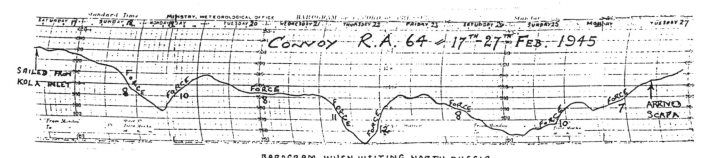

BARDGRAM WHEN VISITING NORTH RUSSIA

| FORCE 7 28-33 KNOTS - HALF A GALE | FORCE 8 34-40 KNOTS - FRESH GALE |
| FORCE 9 41-47 KNOTS - STRONG GALE | FORCE 10 48-55 KNOTS - WHOLE GALE |

asleep in the upper bunk, his hair spread over the pillow. Beside the lower bunk was a photograph of Knight's wife, a lovely blonde lady. "Who is that?" asked one of the Russians. "Oh, that's my girl friend" said Knight without looking. He thought they were asking about the photograph. They thought he was talking about the person in the top bunk. I don't think we ever managed to convince the Russians that we did not have a woman aboard.

Lieutenant Karetsky and his fiancée had selected his new name, Knight, one evening when they saw the name Knight in *Saturday Evening Post*. Knight had first gone to Russia from Halifax as liaison officer with the submarine squadron that *Niagara* had entertained in Halifax. He didn't like the Soviet Union and remarked bitterly to us that they had a file on him.

The Russians challenged our sailors to a game of hockey, a challenge that was relished by our red blooded Canucks, most of whom hadn't been on ice for three or four years. The game, which took place at an open air rink, started off in a reasonable manner, but our sailors had the idea that the Russians couldn't know much about Canada's national game. Well they did, and I am sorry to say our people did not take being mopped up in a gracious, reasonable manner and the game dissolved in a shambles. In fact, I think our people went crazy.

One afternoon I went for a walk by myself and came across a platoon of Russians engaged in arms drill. They were shouldering and presenting arms, fixing and unfixing bayonets, trailing arms and all the other standard exercises. I was impressed with their smart appearance and their obvious efforts to become absolutely perfect. When they were told to "stand easy," many of them continued to practice their rifle drill with a comrade. I couldn't imagine our own people being as unsmilingly conscientious as these people, but our homeland was not under siege.

Our officers and men were invited to a concert in a large hall. All who were not required on board were there, including Hairless Joe, a good-humoured, irrepressible dog of unknown ancestry and slovenly appearance, a street dog from Portsmouth, where our gunners had gone to school on Whale Island. It was an impressive concert, with artists from the Red Army Chorus and the Bolshoi Theatre in Moscow. The singing was fantastic and the dancing quite outside the experience of our people. I wish we had known more and behaved better. Our people enthusiastically whistled at the performers, not knowing that this is the Russian equivalent to booing and could be considered insulting. The worst thing that happened was that at the height of the performance our Hairless Joe, looking more awful than ever, wandered on to the stage, cocked his leg and made himself right at home, much to the amusement of our ignoramus crew.

The Red Navy invited us to use their officers' club, an imposing building with marble columns at the top of a hill overlooking the little harbour. One evening after dinner the captain suggested that he and I go up for a little refreshment and to see what sort of place it was. Russian cigarettes were quite long, with little tobacco but a lot of cardboard tube filled with a cotton batten plug to filter the smoke. The smell was pungent, reminding me of an English tobacco called Balkan Sobranie, and permeated every place where Russians gathered. An impressive staircase led to the dining and drinking area. At the first landing was a three-metre white alabaster statue of a genial Joseph Stalin. He was smiling, one hand holding his pipe and the other in his pocket.

The captain and I sat down to enjoy a glass of vodka, a thick yellowish liquid which the Russians called Junkers 88 fuel. A number of serious Russian officers with respectable-looking ladies were eating at small round tables. Behind us were a number of our own officers, quietly talking. Two or three, however, were attracting considerable interest. A head of department (name withheld) was attempting to demonstrate how dishes would remain in place if the cloth under them was yanked away smartly and firmly. He placed a table cloth over the head of his assistant head of department and set a stack of three or four plates on the cloth. He gave a good yank and all the dishes fell to the floor, smashing to bits.

"You had better get him home," said the captain to me.

He came quietly as I helped him down the stairs. He stopped by Stalin, saying, "The poor guy's pipe is out," pulled out a box of matches, striking one on Stalin's backside and holding the flame to the pipe. This was extremely embarrassing, perhaps dangerous, and I finally got him to the door. He started down the steps, slipped on the ice and took off on his behind down the hill of ice and snow and headed for the ship. The British Flag Officer, North Russia, had announced that anyone who committed an offence there would be turned over to the Russians. Each time Russian soldiers marched near our ship, there was one officer who would quietly vanish down the engine room hatch.

I was impressed with the manner and deportment of the Russian officers. Their shortages were dreadful: for example, they had little soap for washing. Their hands were clean but above the wrists their arms were grey with dirt. Windows in their quarters were taped over with newspapers to retain the heat. All whom we met were friendly, good humoured and ready to discuss any subject. Many of the officers and men had some knowledge of English, and some were excellent. I asked one of their sailors where he had learned to be so fluent. He replied that he had learned English in school and I was the first English-speaking person he had ever spoken to.

We sailed for Britain with Convoy RA63 on 11 January 1945. We had a peaceful trip for five days and then were struck by an 85-knot northerly gale. The convoy was dispersed by the weather, some ships heaving to. The commodore decided to run before the gale and *Algonquin* stayed with him. A following sea demolished our whaler completely. The convoy reformed off the Faeroes in continuing heavy seas accompanied by snow squalls. We stayed with the convoy until the Minches, when we returned to Scapa.

We were off to sea again on 27 January as part of the screen for the cruiser *Berwick* and the escort carriers *Nairana*, *Premier* and *Campania* on Operation WINDED. Our object was aerial attacks at night on shipping in the Norwegian Leads. We found good targets, attacked them with no aircraft losses and were back in Scapa on 29 January.

Algonquin's Song, 1944, sung to the tune of "Lili Marlene."

THE TWENTY-THIRD FLOTILLA

Up to Kola Inlet, back to Scapa Flow,
Soon we shall be calling for oil at Petsamo.
Why does it always seem to be Flotilla No. 23
Who plough the Arctic Ocean and thrash the Barents Sea?

Now and then we get a slightly different job,
But it's always screening around the same old mob,
Watching the "A" boys prang the Hun,
With never a chance to fire a gun.
      Up in *etc.*

When we get to Scapa do we get a rest?
All we have is signals invariably addresses:
Dear Algonquin with love from "D,"
Why are you here? Get back to sea.
      Back to *etc.*

Once we were in harbour, swinging around the buoy,
Waiting for a drifter, but still we got no joy.
In came a signal, "Weigh, proceed,
At your best speed, great is our need."
      Up in *etc.*

Battleships and cruisers, lying around in state,
Watching poor destroyers passing Switha Gate,
Those ships the papers call the fleet,
They look so sweet, but have no beat.
      Inside the *etc.*

Over in our mileage, due for boiler clean,
When we're not with convoys, there's practice in between.
Now as you will surely have guessed,
We do our best but need a rest.
      Out of *etc.*

What it is to have a crazy Number 1, all the rest are chocker,
Though some have just begun, the wretched pilot sits and drinks,
The captain thinks the whole thing stinks.
      We hate *etc.*

Back to Canada

We finally were recalled to Canada in early 1945, much to the delight of the whole ship. It looked as if the war was coming to a conclusion, finally our forces were fighting on German soil, and the Russians were advancing toward Berlin. Germany was in ruins with many of her great cities such as Hamburg, Cologne and Dresden largely destroyed and Berlin on the verge of total destruction. The terrible miseries, unspeakable atrocities and devastation that these people, gripped in evil, had inflicted without valid cause on their fellow Europeans, helpless and unprepared, had been repaid in kind, pressed down and brimming over. Now the full fury of the Allies was to be turned on the Japanese, whose barbaric conduct was to be repaid in such a ghastly, total manner that we ourselves would be as appalled as our enemies.

Algonquin was to be refitted in Halifax and alterations and additions made for service in tropical waters in the Far East. Officers and men were required by the Canadian government to state whether they would volunteer for service against the Japanese. One hundred per cent of Algonquins volunteered! Many of us believed that it was understood that we already had offered our services against our country's enemies but we volunteered again anyway.

We sailed from Scapa Flow to the Tail of the Bank off Glasgow, where we anchored. Spike Morris, my term mate, now a lieutenant (engineering) and a naval pilot, visited us for lunch. Soon afterwards, he made all the newspapers with a daring flight under a bridge. Was it our lunch?

While we were fuelling for our passage to Canada, we

noticed some ex-American destroyers, four-stackers, being fitted out for transfer to the Russian navy. Evidently this was not a trouble-free transfer as the Russians, fearing God knows what, kept taking the sonar apart, checking it, then putting it back together again incorrectly. Maybe it was a way of lengthening their stay near Glasgow.

For some time the wardroom had sat 13 officers at table, which, in view of our dangerous trade, made us uneasy. An imaginary officer was invented and out of nowhere his name became Lieutenant Murgatroyd. The stewards, who shared whatever would be our fate, happily also shared our feelings, and at each meal where we were likely to be 13, a place was laid for Mr. Murgatroyd and soup, meat and sweet were provided. As can be imagined Murgatroyd's various characteristics were discussed at length. He even acquired an imaginary dog called Butch, whose leash hung in the wardroom for anyone who wished to take him for a walk, which some did. It will be concluded that our return to Canada was becoming timely. The morning we left a drifter came alongside and a lieutenant, with all his gear, clambered on board for passage to Canada. I introduced myself and he did the same. "Name's Murgatroyd," he claimed. We went up to the wardroom, where breakfast was under way, and I introduced him, but no one believed me.

We returned to North America at 20 knots, arriving at St. John's in about four days. When we came up to the jetty there appeared to be no one to take our lines. We then noticed an army officer, who took our bow line and secured it. It was my father, who was Transportation Officer for Newfoundland and, of course, was aware of our arrival. Soon Dad was in my cabin, where we had a pleasant reunion. Later we had lunch up in his mess and I was able to see his office and the army headquarters in Newfoundland. *Algonquin* fuelled, took on provisions and sailed for Halifax.

Halifax was crowded with service personnel and was quite a contrast to the places where we had been. It seemed to me that there was an unpleasant atmosphere about the city. Our sailors got into trouble the first night ashore. I was told that the shore patrols were made up of Toronto policemen in naval uniform and they were looking for trouble. In all the ports *Algonquin* had visited during her commission we never had experienced any trouble. Now it seemed that their conduct changed overnight.

Leave, as well as de-ammunitioning, was delayed a week or so for our people until the Flag Officer Atlantic Coast found it convenient to look us over. He walked through our ranks saying not a word to anyone, unsmiling, perhaps even hostile. Then he spoke to us. First he was glad that he found only one man wearing a suit made of diagonal serge, whatever that was. Anyway, it was against regulations, he said. Next he cautioned us against boastful behaviour and informed us that people on this side of the Atlantic had a role every bit as important as our own had been. Lastly, this person told us that if any one of us, because of our experience, behaved inappropriately, he would be punished to the full extent. I believe it was the most stupid speech to a ship's company that I have ever heard! Anyone in authority who had such an attitude was asking for trouble. It was no surprise to me that when Victory in Europe Day occurred a few weeks later, Halifax suffered a riot and destruction by the navy and civilians such as no other city in the British Empire experienced. The admiral left the service and went to live in England.

The Battle of the Atlantic was the hardest fought battle in the entire history of the Royal Navy and its Allies. It is noteworthy that the Royal Navy lost 9.7 per cent of its total manpower during the Second World War. The Merchant Service losses were 17 per cent. 153 British destroyers alone were sunk. 33,000 British naval and merchant seamen lost their lives, the worst toll being in the Battle of the Atlantic. Drowning, burning alive, freezing to death or starving to death on rafts or in open boats were the fates which awaited many of us. The cruel sea strained stamina and morale to the utmost. As a measure of our battle, British air force losses were 9 per cent and army losses 6 per cent.

As I conclude these reminiscences and reflections on my naval experiences from 1938 to the end of the Second World War, I think of my old shipmates. My term of naval cadets keep in touch with each other, as do some Renowns. All the Matabeles perished off North Cape. Officers and men who served in *Hood* at one time have the HMS *Hood* Association, which is active and even meets from time to time with survivors of *Bismarck*. Many of the survivors of *Ottawa* meet and correspond, particularly through the Canadian Naval Association reunions. Old Algonquins have a very strong association right across Canada. All our numbers now are gradually diminishing. Soon we shall be history. It has been an honour to have served with all these gentlemen.

One last thought… Of all the ships in which I have ever served, HMCS *Algonquin*, of the V and W destroyer class, seems to me to have been the ultimate in design and performance. Just as the old clipper ships represented the final triumph of the age of sail, so the V's and W's were the culmination of the conventional destroyer.

Algonquin was the fairest of my loves.

After Divisions

Button for Flag Officers
1812–1825

15

A compendium of naval uniforms, insignia, badges, lore and practice

SACRED TO THE
MEMORY
Of Mr John Samwell
Midshipman of HMS
Shannon who died at the
Navel hospital on the 13 of
June 1815 Aged 18 years Also
Mr William Stevens boats in
Of the Same Ship who died
There on the 19 of June 1813
Aged 36 years Those brave
Officers Clos'd their career
In Consequence of desperat
Wounds received in the
Gallant action between
Their own Ship and the
American frigate Chesepak
on the 1 of June 1813 which
Ended in the Capture of
the Enemy Ship in
14 Minutes

The gravestone of John
Samwell and William Stevens
in St Pauls Church, Halifax,
Nova Scotia

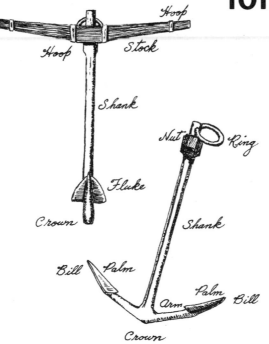

Hoop

Hoop   Stock

Shank

Nut   Ring

Crown   Fluke

Shank

Bill   Palm

Arm   Palm   Bill

Crown

An anchor and its parts

Rank badge for Captains, worn
on the epaulette strap
1812–1825

NAVAL MEMORIES 1938

Holystoning the deck
(using a sandstone block)

"Six days shalt thou labour
and do all that thou art able,
and on the seventh thou shalt
holystone the deck"
(The first holystones came from the church-
yard at St Helen's, Isle of Wight)

Tub for the mixing of grog
(rum & water)

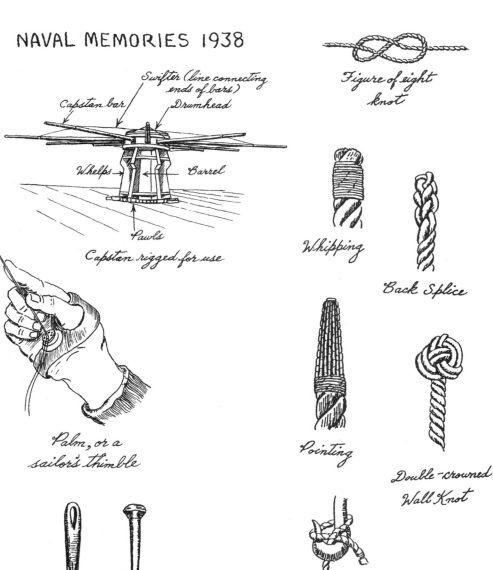

Swifter (line connecting
ends of bars)
Capstan bar
Drumhead
Whelps
Barrel
Pawls

Capstan rigged for use

Palm, or a
sailor's thimble

Figure of eight
knot

Whipping

Back Splice

Pointing

Double-crowned
Wall Knot

Midshipman's
Hitch

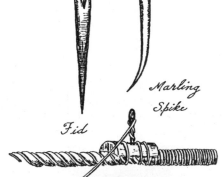

Fid

Marling
Spike

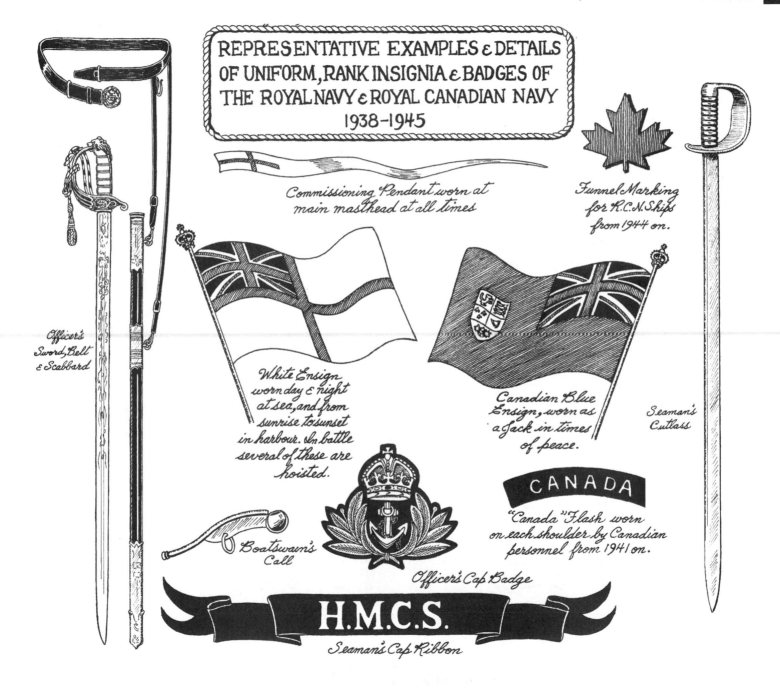

REPRESENTATIVE EXAMPLES & DETAILS OF UNIFORM, RANK INSIGNIA & BADGES OF THE ROYAL NAVY & ROYAL CANADIAN NAVY 1938-1945

Commissioning Pendant worn at main masthead at all times

Funnel Marking for R.C.N. Ships from 1944 on.

Officer's Sword, Belt & Scabbard

White Ensign worn day & night at sea, and from sunrise to sunset in harbour. In battle several of these are hoisted.

Canadian Blue Ensign, worn as a Jack in times of peace.

Seaman's Cutlass

Boatswain's Call

CANADA

"Canada" Flash worn on each shoulder by Canadian personnel from 1941 on.

Officer's Cap Badge

H.M.C.S.

Seaman's Cap Ribbon

Admiral
Gold lace on
sleeves

Admiral
Shoulder
Straps

Vice-Admiral

Vice-
Admiral

Rear-Admiral
and
Commodore
First Class

Rear-
Admiral

Commodore-
Second
Class

Commodores
First and
Second
Class

Captain

Captain
Naval
Reserve
R.N.R. or
R.C.N.R.

Commander

Commander
Volunteer
Reserve
R.N.V.R. or
R.C.N.V.R.

Lieutenant-
Commander

Lieutenant-
Commander
Naval Reserve
from the
Merchant
Service.

Lieutenant

Lieutenant-
Commander
Volunteer
Reserve

Sub-Lieutenant
& Commissioned
Officer from
Warrant Rank

Sub
Lieutenant
Air Branch

Warrant Officer.
The curl in the
gold lace faces
forward ↩

Third
Officer
Wrens
Lace is
blue.

Flag Officer's Cap with white cover for summer.

Midshipman's collar with the white patch, button & white twist.

Midshipman's sleeve of Round Jacket with 3 buttons & black twist.

Commodore, Captain and Commander's Cap

Paymaster Lieutenant, with white cloth between stripes. Colours were Engineering-purple, Medical-scarlet, Instructor-light blue, Shipwright-silver gray Electrical-dark green, Ordnance-blue.

Pilot's insignia worn on left sleeve above curl

Naval Cadet's collar with white twist & button.

Officer's Cap

Good Shooting Badge, worn on right cuff.

Chief Petty Officer, both sleeves on blue or on white uniforms

Chief & Petty Officers' Cap with Petty Officer's Badge

Bugler, worn by Boys or Seamen without a specialty on the right cuff.

Observer's insignia worn on left sleeve above curl.

Petty Officer, upper left sleeve

Wren Officer's Hat

Combined Operations, worn by all Ratings so trained on right cuff.

Leading Seaman, upper left sleeve

Button for Commodores First Class and above. Canadian buttons were altered as shown below for Commodores & below.

Button for Canadian Officers. The Royal Navy buttons were patterned with the full anchor as shown on the other buttons.

Button for C.P.O.'s & P.O.'s

Black horn button for Leading Rates and below.

Chief Petty Officer's Cap Badge in gold

▶ Petty Officer's Cap Badge in gold.

▶ Miscellaneous Junior Ratings Cap Badge in Red

Good Conduct Badges, worn by Petty Officers & below. One for 4 years Two for 8 years Three for 12 years

Petty Officer, sleeves of blue uniform. Miscellaneous junior ratings wear black horn buttons instead of gilt buttons.

Master-at-Arms

Regulating Petty Officer

Chief Petty Officers wear badges in pairs on collars of blue uniforms, or on the right cuff of white uniforms.

Torpedo Coxswain

Petty Officers & below wear trade badges on right upper arm.

Yeoman of Signals Visual Signalman 1st Class

Visual Signalman 2nd Class

Visual Signalman 3rd Class

Trained Operator Visual Signalman

Gunner's Mate

Rangetaker 1st Class

 ◀ *Chief Sailmaker*

▶ *Physical & Recreational Training Instructor 1st Class*

Layer Rating 1st Class

Miscellaneous Junior Ratings Cap with white cap cover for summer.

Torpedo Gunner's Mate

Chief Shipwright

Quarters Rating 2nd Class

Seaman's Blue Cap for winter

Submarine Detector Instructor

Chief Motor Mechanic

Naval Service of Canada

Control Rating 3rd Class

Steel Helmet

Wireless Telegraphist 1st Class

Supply Rating

Cook

Writer

▶ *Some Blue Badges for White Uniforms* ▼

Leading Torpedoman

Seaman's White Cap for summer

Chief Stoker & Stoker Petty Officer

Sick Berth Attendant

Diver, worn on the right cuff.

Seaman Torpedoman

Wren's Blue Cap

Uniforms and dress in the Royal Navy and Royal Canadian Navy, 1938–1945

In spite of the many drawings and paintings of naval battles and life aboard ships in the past, it is difficult to reconstruct scenes showing officers and men as they actually dressed at a particular point in history. With the advent of photography, historical recording improved, but it remains difficult to sort out precisely what type of dress was worn at what time under varying conditions.

Dress regulations were contained in the Appendix to the Navy List and in the Uniform Regulations for Officers of the Fleet. They are not simple to interpret.

Over 50 years have passed since World War Two ended and in Canada the traditional naval uniforms are no longer worn. In the Royal Navy the uniforms have undergone modifications. In the civilian world there has been a revolution in clothing styles, hair dress and manners, and the younger generation would strain at many of the customs and styles regarded as being quite ordinary and acceptable years ago.

My object is to record details of naval uniforms and dress and a few customs during World War Two which otherwise might be forgotten. Some will be so familiar to ex-naval readers that they may wonder why anyone would bother writing them down. I think that a great deal of history has been lost to us just because many things were so familiar that it seemed pointless to record them.

I cannot swear to the truth of some of my anecdotes, but I think most are true.

Royal Navy and Royal Canadian Navy uniforms

Uniforms of the Royal Canadian Navy were identical to those of the Royal Navy except for the buttons which bore CANADA superimposed on the crown and anchor. Sometime about 1942 members of the RCN were ordered to wear a CANADA badge on each uniform shoulder. This was not popular at the time. A great many brave men were in British uniforms with POLAND, NORWAY, etc. on their shoulders at the time, but Canada was not in the same category as their unfortunate homelands.

Because Canadian permanent force officers did their initial training in the RN, most purchased their uniforms from Gieves of 21 Old Bond Street, London. Although nicknamed "Gieves the thieves," this centuries-old firm treated customers as if they were young royalty. Men were issued uniforms but they also purchased "tiddlies" (best uniforms) from long-established firms of naval tailors. Officers received an initial "uniform allowance"; men received a "kit upkeep allowance" on a continuing basis with their pay. Each uniform dress was numbered so that "dress of the day" could be ordered or signalled easily.

Officers' blue uniforms

The basic officers' uniform was No. 5's or "Undress" as shown for the rear admiral.

The dark blue "monkey jacket," trousers, cap and black boots or shoes were comfortable for the North Sea and temperate Europe most of the time, but

*Rear Admiral
Undress Blue Uniform*

were too hot for North American summers. The cloth was superfine for best uniforms and fine serge for second best. A lighter cloth, gabardine, could be used for a summer uniform. "Undress" was worn ashore and afloat; one wore the oldest uniform for watchkeeping and bad weather.

Gold lace on the sleeves was 1¾ inches wide for the flag officer's broad stripe. The width of the ordinary stripe was $\frac{9}{16}$ inch, and for the lieutenant commander's half-stripe and the warrant officer's stripe it was ¼ inch. After 1942, lace became scarce and it was authorized that sleeves might be laced only half way around. Stripes were ¼ inch apart. Non-executive officers wore cloth of different colours between stripes, or in the case of one stripe, beneath. The colours were: engineers – purple, medical – scarlet, paymaster – white, instructor – light blue, wardmaster – maroon, ordnance – dark blue, dental – orange, shipwright – silver grey, electrical – dark green.

Waistcoats, as shown in the drawing of the Midshipman, were worn if desired. They were required with the Midshipman's round jacket, giving a railway conductor appearance.

Trousers were held up with braces, never with belts. Flies were buttoned. Zipper flies had been invented but were regarded with dark suspicion.

Shirts were of white linen with detachable starched stiff collars and starched single attached cuffs with cuff links. Shirt tails were ample, reaching nearly to the knees. Ties were plain black silk or satin. Some older officers continued to wear wing collars with plain ties, a mark of individuality which drew a second glance. **Medal ribbons** were sewn on. **Brown leather gloves** were worn or carried most of the time.

Caps were dark blue, made of superfine cloth with a chin-stay and a patent leather peak. Commanders, captains and commodores had peaks with a single row of oak leaves embroidered in gold thread on felt, flag officers' brass hats had two rows. A German spy, speaking perfect English and disguised as an RN lieutenant commander, was said to have been discovered in Halifax Dockyard. He was betrayed by

Rear View of a Monkey Jacket

Officer's shirt, collar and tie

Uniform Walking Cane

his commander's cap – seemingly a small detail but it could not have been more obvious.

In summer and in warm climates, white starched ribbed cloth covers were put on caps. When ships returned to England in wintertime, the crews were permitted to continue wearing white caps for a month. This set off their bronzed and healthy appearance.

Certain customs or styles permitted a limited degree of individuality. For example, many officers wore a white handkerchief in their breast pocket, and others tucked one up their sleeve. The top button of the monkey jacket was often left undone, except for Divisions and other formal occasions. This was supposedly the "battle-cruiser" style after Admiral Beatty. The height of individuality in my view was the admiral who had lost a hand and substituted a villainous looking hook, all shiny and sharp looking. His name was "Hooky" Walker, I think.

Hair was cut short and neat at all times, unlike the Royal Air Force. Beards were common with officers and men. "Permission to discontinue shaving" (never "permission to grow a beard" as this might have been impossible for some) had to be granted by the captain. One could not go ashore until one looked respectable. Beards were to be kept trimmed to the style favoured by King George V. Moustaches were not permitted, although I believe that at one time they had been allowed for stewards. **Pencils or pens** never were carried in the breast pocket. No executive officers wore **glasses**, but the odd one sported a **monocle**.

A rather odd custom sprang up during the war for some officers to wear a small gold **earring**. This was an ancient superstition among seamen, going back to Viking days; the earring was supposed to prevent deafness. I first saw them worn by seamen of the Orkney Islands. Some officers got an infection from piercing their ears.

Tattoos were common on both officers and men; particularly fine examples were obtained on the China Station. Tattooing was respectable: King George V was tattooed, as were the kings of Denmark, Norway and Sweden. I have a nice one myself, a dragon. One petty officer had the Lord's Prayer on his bald head, this having been arranged by thoughtful friends when they were ashore one evening in Shanghai. "A Sailor's Grave," "Death Before Dishonour," "Mother," a snarling bulldog, white ensigns and union jacks, Churchill clenching a cigar and sailing ships were favourite subjects.

Walking canes were quite popular for officers when walking ashore in uniform. They were black with silver heads. Malacca walking sticks would be carried with plain clothes.

Telescopes were carried in ships in harbour by certain officers. In flagships the starboard side of the quarterdeck was reserved for the admiral, who took his exercise pacing up and down his territory with his telescope tucked under his arm. Captains and commanders of cruisers or larger ships also habitually carried telescopes, as did the officers of the watch and midshipmen of the watch. Telescopes were often tiddlied up with coach whipping, turk's heads and woven strips of blue and white canvas. One became used to carrying a telescope and it was supposed that a special telescope muscle developed in the left armpit. The officer of the watch in harbour also wore a sword belt. In smaller ships, such as destroyers, telescopes were not affected but the officer of the day (such ships could not afford officers of the watch) did wear a sword belt.

Certain other customs come to mind. The starboard side of the quarterdeck was the senior side and, therefore, the accommodation ladder for officers was on that side. Liberty boats, provision boats etc. used the port side. Port used to be called "larboard" (Danish *laar-* empty, i.e. no steersman) but this was too easily confused with starboard, so the name was changed. In any case it was dangerous for a midshipman to stroll on the starboard side of the AX (after-castle or quarterdeck; FX stood for forecastle or fo'c's'le). It also was dangerous to speak first to a more senior officer.

In most wardrooms ordinary conversation at breakfast was discouraged. People munched, growled and read old newspapers. A young Canadian sub-lieutenant RCNVR joined an RN destroyer in which I was serving. He bounced into the wardroom crying out, "Hiya fellows, great morning eh?" Several officers went purple, however nothing was said and the sub soon learned to enjoy breakfast in grim, bad-tempered silence, as was only right and proper.

Officers' white uniforms

White tunic and long white trousers was the normal uniform on duty aboard or on shore in warm or tropical climates. It was extremely comfortable but was easily soiled and a

Commander White Uniform.

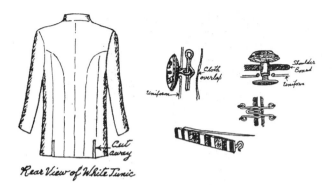

Rear View of White Tunic

nuisance to prepare for wearing. The **buttons** were detachable, the ring of the button passing through a grommet in the uniform to be secured with a brass clip. The **shoulder boards** were secured to the uniform at the top by a screw-in button and at the base by two laces which rove through two grommets in the uniform and tied with a bow inside. The **neck** was closed with three metal hooks and eyes sewn in place.

Medal ribbons were sewn on brass clasps which pinned on, or passed through tight thread loops.

Trousers had white metal button flies. Braces were worn. There were side pockets but no hip pockets. It was essential that all pieces of metal used in and about uniforms were nonmagnetic so that magnetic compasses would not be deflected.

Shoes were white buckskin with brown leather soles.
Socks were white.

Officers' tropical dress

Without doubt the tropical dress was the most comfortable uniform that could be devised for hot climates. It is amusing to reflect that during the Second World War, North American males regarded tropical shorts with scorn, an unmanly outfit reminiscent of boy scouts. Times have changed.

The cork sun helmet, "solar bowler," was cool but awkward to wear around and about a ship, particularly when climbing up and down Jacob's ladders on booms to get in and out of picket boats. There was a belief at the time that exposure of the bare head to the tropic sun was dangerous to health. Of course, this was disproved later when great armies of white men fought in the tropics and survived without sun helmets.

Aboard ship, white caps usually were worn with tropical dress.

Lieutenant Tropical Dress

Mess dress

One is inclined to smile at the thought of men in wild and remote places "dressing" for dinner and other such formalities. However, we have ample proof of how thin is the veneer of civilization and how easy it is to revert to barbarism. The nature of war often necessitates periods of monotony and it was a pleasant relief to dine formally, even if the meal consisted of corned beef with duff for dessert. Mess dress was not required during the war, but some officers dined from time to time in **mess undress**. This was similar to the Mess Dress which is shown in the illustration, except that trousers were plain, the waistcoat was blue instead of white and miniature medal bars were worn instead of miniature medals. As time went on, the proportion of wartime officers greatly outnumbered permanent force and the occasional "dressing" for dinner consisted of wearing a wing collar and bow tie with one's best No. 5's. In desolate, rock-bound anchorages in Iceland, the Faeroe Is-

Rear View of Mess Jacket

Blue Waistcoat

Half-Wellingtons

Lieutenant Commander
Mess Dress

lands, the Orkneys, the port was passed and the King's health drunk with as much formality as at a great banquet, and followed with good-humoured horseplay and pleasant conversation.

To return to Mess Dress, the "tin pants" were gold-laced 1¼ inches wide the whole length. There were no trouser pockets. Half-Wellington boots were worn,.

Battle dress

About 1941, at sea in smaller ships such as destroyers and corvettes, some officers began to wear a blue-dyed version of the khaki army battle dress. This supplemented the normal dress at sea, which was one's oldest blue uniform. In bad weather and at night a turtleneck sweater was worn, but a collar and tie were worn at meals and for duties other than bridge watchkeeping. By 1941 there were many new officers who did not have old uniforms. Also quite a number of experienced officers had lost all their kit in action and did not have older uniforms either. Soon private tailors were producing naval battle dress in blue serge. Rank was indicated on the shoulder straps, which were sewn on. Battle dress had the disadvantage of being cold in the small of the back.

Woollens, that is, turtle-neck sweaters, scarves, mittens, heavy socks and balaclavas, generally were not issued but were obtained from "ditty bags" sent as Christmas as gifts by organizations of mothers, wives, girlfriends and other wonderful ladies at home. Sometimes charming and touching little notes were enclosed. About 1944 heavy white sweaters, long heavy woollen stockings, mittens and other winter clothing were issued in ships engaged in Arctic operations. These were well designed and well made and I don't think they could have been improved upon.

Leather seaboots seemed to be prewar "pusser's stores." Rubber seaboots were the main footwear issued to upper-deck watchkeepers. If you landed

Lieutenant Battledress

in the ocean for any reason, it was advisable to kick off the heavy seaboots; otherwise swimming was impossible.

Peaked caps came fitted with a whalebone or cane grommet to stiffen the rim of the crown. Sometimes this was removed to present a more weather-beaten appearance. New cap badges could be soaked in sea water to make them faded and green. Some thought the net result was a "salty" appearance. Others thought the net result was similar to the appearance of an untidy taxi driver.

Identification tags, "dog tags," were made of a dark red or black, hard rubber composition and were worn on a string around the neck. Many people wore a silver identification bracelet on their wrist. In this connection relatively few naval personnel were wounded, dismembered or mutilated beyond recognition in comparison with the numbers lost by drowning, their bodies never being recovered.

Identification tags, "dog tags"

NAME
NUMBER
RELIGION

Lifebelts at the beginning of the war were bulky waistcoats made up of blocks of cork sewn in canvas. They were kept in lockers on the upper deck, where in the course of time they became sodden and rotten. Soon, however, the "Mae West," so named after a popular movie star with a large bust, was issued. It con-

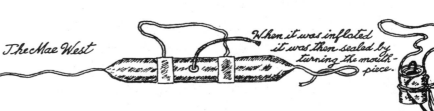

The Mae West

When it was inflated it was then sealed by turning the mouthpiece.

sisted of a rubber belt with a tube and mouthpiece for inflation when required. It was bound in white cotton with ties and a neck loop. It could be rolled up compactly and slung over the shoulder. It was carried at sea at all times. The Mae West certainly saved my life when HMCS *Ottawa* was torpedoed and sunk at night.

Later on in the war, Mae Wests were replaced by heavy jacket types. These were fitted with a collar to keep the head of an unconscious man clear of the water. Attached were a whistle to attract attention, a lanyard with a hook to catch on to a floating object and a waterproof, battery-powered blinking red light so that it could be seen in dark water. Everyone was supposed to carry a knife at all times, as it might be needed to cut oneself clear. Also attached to the jacket was a pad to protect the groin and to reduce internal injuries from the concussion of underwater explosions of depth charges dropped nearby.

Dress in action

The most constant and insidious enemy in the North Atlantic and Arctic Oceans, summer and winter, was the cold. Watchkeeping on the bridge, at the guns and at the depth charges generally entailed four hours of doing very little of a physical nature, staying more or less in one spot. In the Arctic in winter I wore underwear shorts, flannel pyjamas, serge trousers, wind-proof parka, scarf, fur hat, mittens, light socks, heavy socks and seaboots. At one time I had Eskimo sealskin mukluks from Labrador but in the warmth of my cabin they acquired a rich aroma; it was a case of me or my mukluks and they ended up over the side.

If you landed in the water, it was important to keep most of your clothing on because it lessened the chilling effect. Men who were clothed often survived while their mates who were nearly undressed perished from the chill. For this reason the men were forbidden by me to undress at sea except to change and to wash and shave daily.

When Action Stations rang, we added **anti-flash gear**, made of asbestos cloth to form a hood for the head and face, and long gloves. It had been found that exposed flesh often suffered bad burns from the flash of explosions even though no other wounds were suffered. **Steel helmets** were kept at our stations and identified in some

*Dress in Action
Russian Convoys*

manner such as that illustrated. The helmet strap seemed more comfortable worn to the back of the head. **Dark goggles** were worn for a period before going on the bridge at night so that we were not blind in the dark. Smoking was not permitted in the open at night because the glow of a cigarette might be seen at a surprising range in darkness.

Sub-lieutenant under training

After passing examinations in the fleet, midshipmen were promoted to acting sub-lieutenant and appointed to training establishments ashore at Portsmouth. The dress for training consisted of white flannel trousers, white flannel shirt and white scarf, monkey jacket, khaki gaiters and boots – a comfortable and practical outfit.

Swords were not required to be carried aboard ship during the war but they were used for ceremonial training. Sword scabbards were hooked to the sword belt when the sword was drawn and when greatcoats were worn. In this case the hilt protruded through the

*Sub-Lieutenant
Under Training*

cut in the coat behind the left side pocket. When the sword was sheathed, the scabbard hung by the straps and was carried in the left hand. An instructor told us that naval officers were not allowed to hook up their scabbards; this was an eternal punishment for a long-forgotten mutiny.

Cutlasses were carried in ships which had commissioned before the war. In some destroyers they were stowed in the wardroom, arranged in the shape of a fan in a rack secured to the deckhead.

Pistols were kept in a glass-fronted, locked cabinet in the wardroom.

Rifles and **bayonets** were kept locked in racks in flats and passageways throughout the ship. A chain was rove through the trigger guards with the lock at the end of the chain.

When men went berserk in ships, their favourite weapon was a fire axe; I never heard of any woundings, but such incidents were always exciting.

Midshipman of the Watch in harbour

The dress shown in the illustration was worn in Capital ships before the War. The round jacket or "bum freezer" was of a pattern established in Nelson's time and gave one an old-fashioned, romantic feeling. It was worn by midshipmen and naval cadets on ceremonial occasions.

*Midshipman of the Watch
in Harbour*

The short sword was a midshipman's dirk. The greatest prize to be won by a naval cadet for outstanding ability was the King's Dirk. Midshipmen were known as "snotties" and the three buttons on each sleeve were supposed to encourage young gentlemen to wipe their noses on handkerchiefs. Snotties lived in gunrooms and could be disciplined by being caned by the sub-lieutenant of the gunroom.

Outer wear

Great coats were very warm, heavy and expensive. In addition they took up a good deal of space in the limited stowage afforded in a locker. Although they were worn infrequently by seagoing personnel, they were required kit and now and again were needed for cer-emonial occasions ashore. I did not bother replacing the first great coat I lost, but when I was kitting up after my second loss, a lady sold me her son's great coat, and it served me well enough for many years. After I retired, cast-off military uniforms became quite stylish for the young and my son cut it down for his own use.

The watch coat, a type of short great coat, was optional gear.

Chief and petty officers' great coats had gilt buttons and were similar to those of officers but without the slot for the sword hilt. **Leading seamen and below** wore black horn crown and anchor buttons on their great coats. **Petty officers and leading seamen** wore their red rank badges on the left arms of their coats above the elbow.

Waterproof coats for officers were plain blue burberries. Rank was not indicated so this coat was referred to by some as "the great equalizer." **Men's water-**

Lieutenant Greatcoat

Rear View of Great Coat

Note slot for sword hilt in rear of great coat and watch coat

Watch Coat

Tail cut was 14 inches Coat terminated at the knees

Plain black buttons
Black lining
Buttons not visible when done up
Officer's Burberry

proof coats also were without rank markings. Belts were fitted and the plain black buttons were exposed.

Gas Mask

Gas masks always were carried when ashore. As the possibility of gas attack seemed to become more remote, it was found that the khaki canvas container made an ideal overnight case for pyjamas, toothbrush and shaving kit.

Foul weather gear

Oilskins, sou'westers and seaboots were worn by all ranks when wind and rain so dictated. This was quite often in British waters. In fact when I reflect on my early days in the navy, a mental image appears of heavy grey skies, grey water, grey ships and grey figures in dripping oilskins.

Oilskins were dark blue-green in colour, stiff and bulky. They were awkward to stow. In some ships there was a communal oilskin locker; a dark, damp, smelly, confusing, mesh-walled compartment with mysterious objects all over the deck to trip a person up.

Four hours of watchkeeping on an open bridge with a gale of wind and

Oilskins and Sou'wester Foul Weather Gear

sheets of spray left you soaked to the skin, even with the best foul weather clothing. A heavy towel wrapped around the neck helped stem the streams down the small of the back. In bad weather heavy seas often swept along the upper decks of destroyers. In the older "boats," wardrooms and officers' cabins were situated aft, under the quarterdeck. Even with lifelines rigged it could be impossible to get from aft up to the bridge. As a consequence, many poor wretches spent a dozen or so hours without relief until the seas moderated. In later destroyers, catwalks ran fore and aft about ten feet above the upper deck, adding greatly to everyone's safety. Also the officers' quarters were moved from their traditional position aft to the vicinity of the bridge, a more efficient layout.

Arctic dress

A special issue of winter clothing was made to ships engaged in Arctic operations. The parka and trousers were made of khaki Grenfell cloth, the hood trimmed with wolf fur. Under

A Lookout Arctic Dress

Front   *Rear*   *Grenfell cloth Wool lining*
Arctic Issue Winter Cap

Blue serge with cap ribbon
RCN Winter Issue Cap

the outer parka was a grey fearnaught parka. Ordinary trousers were worn under the Grenfell trousers; this cloth was wind-resistant and water-repellent. Long underwear was issued also, as were Grenfell cloth and fearnaught mittens fitted with trigger fingers.

Sentries

When ships were alongside, armed sentries were posted on the jetty. When the sentry was armed with a revolver, the lanyard from the butt passed around the neck and under the armpit to prevent the sentry from being strangled with his own lanyard. Belt and gaiters were khaki. In one ship a captured German submarine officer found his sentry asleep. In great indignation he marched up to the bridge and reported the sentry to the captain.

Frock coat with epaulettes

Ceremonial occasions aboard a capital ship before the Second World War presented a magnificent sight. All hands in their best blue uniforms, with all

Able Seaman
Under Arms

Lieutenant Commander, Frock Coat,
Epaulettes, Cocked Hat and Sword

their badges in gold thread, were fallen in on a holystoned, clean teak quarterdeck in their divisions: fo'c's'lemen, foretopmen, maintopmen, quarterdeckmen, gunner's party, torpedomen, signalmen, wirelessmen, stokers and supply party, with officers in cocked hats, frock coats, epaulettes, white gloves and swords, stationed by their divisions. Royal Marines in blue and scarlet with white spiked helmets formed the guard and band. The most powerful guns in the world lay trained fore and aft in their gleaming turrets, and above all, against a blue sky and waving in the breeze flew a large white ensign. This scene was a manifestation of the greatest empire the world had ever known. I cannot believe that one of us thought for even a moment that all this would come to an end during our lifetimes.

Except for State Ball Dress, this was the most formal dress worn in the navy. It was worn for visits by members of the royal family, courts martial, funerals and so on. When war broke out in 1939, officers were not required to carry this dress on board;

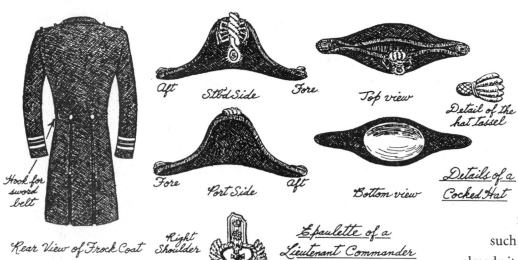

Hook for sword belt

Rear View of Frock Coat

Aft *Stb'd Side* *Fore*

Fore *Port Side* *Aft*

Top view

Bottom view

Detail of the hat tassel

Details of a Cocked Hat

Right Shoulder

Epaulette of a Lieutenant Commander

Wrens – Women's Royal Naval Service

Women served with the Royal Navy in the First World War. Nevertheless, when the Second World War began, many older officers were horrified at the thought of women in the service. My first lieutenant swore that he would resign in protest if such a thing happened, but already it was a *fait accompli* and soon these charming and efficient ladies proved their worth. In due course, the **Women's Royal Canadian Naval Service** was formed (also called Wrens), following the same format as their British counterparts.

Wren officer ranks were superintendent (captain), chief officer (commander), first officer (lieutenant commander), second officer (lieutenant) and third officer (sub-lieutenant). Their rank braid was blue with a diamond twist instead of the circular "executive curl." Hat badges were blue and of the same design as those of male officers. A light blue uniform of the same cut as the dark blue uniform also was worn but

Second Officer Wren

in fact if they did and if it were lost by enemy action, officers were not compensated for its loss by the Admiralty.

If your kit was lost or destroyed by enemy action and if you survived, you submitted a kit loss claim. Each article was listed together with its initial cost and whether it was new, half-worn or worn. The first time all my kit was destroyed, I was compensated for precisely half of my claim. The second time I donated all my gear to Father Neptune, I claimed for twice as much as I lost. Once again I received precisely half of my claim, but this time I was not so much out of pocket. For most of us who were bachelors, our ship was our home and if it sank our personal and valued possessions were lost forever.

with shoulder straps instead of the braid on the sleeves. Stockings were black.

Chief and petty officer Wrens wore the officers' tricorn hats with blue chief and petty officers' cap badges. Their uniforms had two rows of three buttons on each side instead of the four buttons on each side worn by officers. They had flaps on their jacket side pockets. White cap covers were worn by all ranks in summer.

Nursing officers wore similar uniforms to those of Wren officers but with gold cap badges, gold braid on the sleeves and the circular executive curl. On nursing duties these ladies wore white nurses' veils on their heads, light blue dresses with brass buttons in two rows and belts similar to sword belts without the slings.

Plain clothes for officers

Unlike officers of many European forces, British officers were not expected to wear uniforms when off duty ashore. Quite a common dress worn for recreation off the ship consisted of grey flannel trousers, brown shoes, a tweed jacket or blazer, soft shirt, naval tie and brown hat. In gunrooms plain clothes were referred to as "brothel creepers" or "dog robbers" but never as "civvies."

Leading Wren

Blazers were invented over a century ago by the captain of HMS *Blazer* for his boats' crews. The standard RN blazer was dark blue and had flat brass buttons cut with a naval crown. The badge on the pocket in the drawing was for the RCN, a white maple leaf bordered with red. The naval crown in the centre was embroidered in red or gold thread; this was the RN officers' badge.

When officers wore plain clothes, they were expected to wear hats or caps. To salute or return a salute in plain clothes, the hat or cap was removed.

Patterns of Naval Ties

Officer in Plain Clothes Proceeding Ashore for Recreation

Chief petty officer – dress blue uniform

The illustration shows a torpedo coxswain in his dress uniform of blue diagonal serge with gold badges and gilt buttons. The working uniform was blue serge with a single-breasted jacket with red badges. Both jackets were plain at the back with no slits.

Chief Petty Officer Blue Dress Uniform

The senior non-commissioned officer in a cruiser or battle cruiser was the Master at Arms. His formal blue dress was a frock coat and he carried a sword with a black hilt. He had his own mess.

In destroyers the senior non-commissioned officer was a torpedo coxswain. These were a select group of men of tremendous experience, both of destroyers and of human nature. With a good coxswain, chief boatswain's mate, chief gunner's mate, chief torpedo gunner's mate, chief stoker and chief engine room artificer a ship could be second to none.

The torpedo coxswain steered the ship in battle, steered her alongside and departing, and supervised all the requestmen and defaulters for the captain and the executive officer. Chief petty officers were the backbone of the service.

Chief Petty Officer White Uniform

Chief petty officer – white uniform

This uniform was similar to the officers' white uniform. Badges were blue. Petty officers and men of the miscellaneous branches (as described in the next section) also wore this type of white uniform but without the buttons on the sleeves. Badges for petty officers and below were worn on the arms above the elbow. Shoes were of white canvas with brown leather soles.

"Fore and aft rig" referred to the form of dress with a peaked cap and so on which was worn by officers, chief and petty officers and miscellaneous branches. **"Square rig"** referred to the dress of seamen, the comparison being the square blue jean collar with the square sails of a ship.

Leading rating – miscellaneous branches

Sick berth attendants, cooks, writers, supply assistants, stewards and miscellaneous tradesmen not of the seaman branch were recruited as such. They were addressed as Cook Green, Leading Sick Berth At-

Leading Sick Berth Attendant Miscellaneous Branch Uniform

tendant Black, Petty Officer Steward White, Chief Ordnance Artificer Brown and so on.

Leading ratings and below dressed in single-breasted blue serge jackets and trousers, white shirts, detachable stiff collars with rounded corners and black ties, just as for petty officers, but their buttons were black horn with crown and anchor. Cap badges were red. Arm badges were gold for best and red for working dress.

When Action Stations sounded in HMS *Renown*, the captain often startled the crew by dashing to the bridge clad in long white underwear and his steward's cap, hastily snatched up. Tall and grey-templed, he continued to look distinguished, every inch our captain.

Miscellaneous branches seemed to suffer an ambiguity in their substantive ranks; that is, although a man might be a petty officer and have authority in his own branch, his rank really had reference to his skill in his trade. For instance, a P.O. writer would be unused to taking charge of men. Sometimes there were difficulties when such petty officers had to take their turn in charge of a shore patrol.

Acting petty officer – white drill uniform

When a leading seaman was promoted, he became an acting petty officer. If satisfactory for one year, he was confirmed in rank and changed from square rig to fore and aft. The drawing shows an acting petty officer, gunlayer first class, standing by with a heaving line. He may have been the captain of the fo'c's'le, his ship about to come alongside in some tropical port. The weight of the mon-

*Acting Petty Officer
White Drill Uniform*

key's fist at the end of the heaving line would give it distance when thrown.

The **white drill uniform** jumper was fitted with a sewn-on blue jean collar. It was bound with a half-inch wide stripe of blue jean at the base and on the sleeves. The tapes for securing the silk scarf were white. This was the dress white uniform.

The **white duck uniform** was the white working dress of rough textured cotton. It was not bound with blue jean and had a plain collar.

Dress in cells was a white duck uniform stencilled with CELLS on the back of the jumper.

Able seaman – blue uniform

The seaman's blue uniform was unique; nearly every item of its composition had a long tradition. In its original form in the last century it was simple, practical and comfortable, but through the years the uniform became increasingly stylized, difficult to put on and uncomfortable. For example, the original design of the jumper was loose and free, but as time went on it became more form-fitting. Some men fitted covered zippers in the side, which made it tight and impractical for work. However, most inspecting officers made no comment. The coloured lining of sleeve cuffs also went unremarked. Red was for the left sleeve, green for starboard; some men favoured tartans. Quite often the bell-bottom trousers were belled out some inches more than the regulations allowed. Small lead weights could be inserted inside the trouser cuffs, the object being to make the bell bottoms really swing as the merry matelot marched along. Some jumpers were cut so that the "vee" practically went down to the navel. Completely unacceptable was the "dicky front" made of satin or shiny silk. "Tiddly" uniforms often were made of diagonal serge instead of the rougher blue serge.

A real "Jack ashore," cuffs rolled up and cap "flat aback," presented a sight reminiscent of engravings of the Nelson era. When such a fellow was picked up by the shore patrol, there often was an unwelcome interest in his ship by the admiral, so "Jack" became unpopular very quickly.

A seaman dressed in his best blue uniform presented a fine sight. Dress aboard ship re-

*Able Seaman
Blue Serge Uniform*

flected morale and discipline, while dress ashore represented the man's ship and his country. Men were inspected daily by their divisional officers and on Sundays formal **Divisions** were held during which the captain personally inspected each man, paying special attention to dress, cleanliness and healthy appearance.

In harbour depending on the circumstances, men off duty were allowed ashore. When **"Libertymen fall in"** was piped, the men were inspected by the officer of the watch or day and then marched to the dockyard gates, where they were dismissed. When liberty boats returned to the ship, the men were fallen in, searched to ensure they were not smuggling liquor aboard and examined for sobriety.

Gold embroidered **badges** were worn with best uniforms but as the war progressed, red badges were worn on best as well as second-best uniforms.

For weddings men were allowed to reeve white tapes in their jumpers in place of the blue tapes which secured the loop of the black silk scarf.

Unlike peak caps, **seamen's caps** were either of blue serge or white canvas, both stiffened to retain their shape. White caps were kept whitened with Blanco or "pipe clay." Chin stays kept the cap on in windy weather; when not in use chin stays were tucked inside the cap. Early in the war, the ship's name was removed from the cap ribbon and a plain "HMS" or "HMCS" substituted. Quite a few men kept odds and ends inside their caps: cigarette packages, fag ends (English parlance for cigarette butts), photographs and letters. Sometimes an officer would be quite surprised at the shower of miscellaneous objects when a defaulter

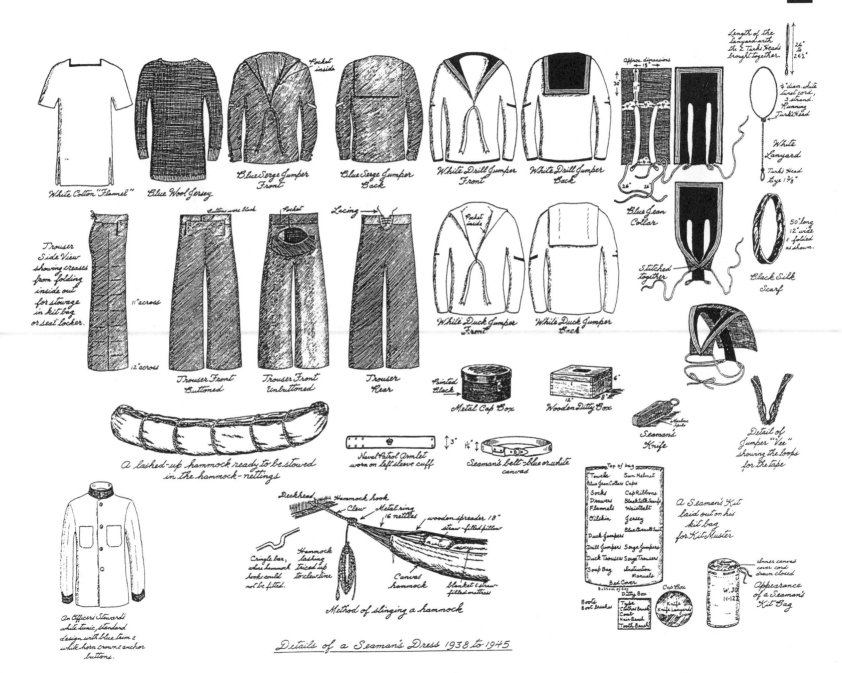

White Cotton "Flannel"

Blue Wool Jersey

Blue Serge Jumper Front

Blue Serge Jumper Back

Pocket inside

White Drill Jumper Front

White Drill Jumper Back

Approx. dimensions

Blue Jean Collar

Length of the lanyard with the 2 Turks Heads brought together.

½" diam. white twist cord, 3 strand. Running Turks Head

White Lanyard

Turks Head Eye 1⅛"

Black Silk Scarf

50" long 12" wide folded as shown.

Stitched together

Trouser Side View showing creases from folding inside out for stowage in kit bag or seat locker.

Buttons were black

Pocket

Lacing

11" across

12" across

Trouser Front Buttoned

Trouser Front Unbuttoned

Trouser Rear

Pocket inside

White Duck Jumper Front

White Duck Jumper Back

Painted Black

Metal Cap Box

Wooden Ditty Box

Seaman's Knife

Marline Spike

Detail of Jumper "Vee" showing the loops for the tape

A lashed-up hammock ready to be stowed in the hammock-nettings

Naval Patrol Armlet worn on left sleeve cuff

Seaman's belt - blue or white canvas

An Officers Stewards white tunic, standard design with blue trim & white horn crowned anchor buttons.

Deckhead

Hammock hook

Clew

Metal ring

16 nettles

wooden spreader 18"

straw-filled pillow

Cringle bar, where hammock hooks could not be fitted.

Hammock lashing triced up to clew-line

Canvas hammock

blanket & straw filled mattress

Method of slinging a hammock

Top of bag

Towels — Sun Helmet
Blue Jean Collar — Caps
Socks — Cap Ribbons
Drawers — Black Silk Scarf
Flannels — Waistbelt
Oilskin — Jersey
— Blue Overcoat Suit
Duck Jumpers
Drill Jumpers — Serge Jumpers
Duck Trousers — Serge Trousers
Soap Bag — Instruction Manuals
Bed Cover

Bottom of bag

Ditty Box

Boots — Type
Boot Brushes — Clothes Brush
Comb
Hair Brush
Tooth Brush

Cap Box

Knife
Knife Lanyards

A Seaman's Kit laid out on his kit bag for Kit Muster

inner canvas cover cord drawn closed

W. 30
14-122

Appearance of a Seaman's Kit Bag

Details of a Seaman's Dress 1938 to 1945

doffed his cap. Cap ribbons often had a Canadian or New-foundland dime or a sixpence sewn in the middle of the bow and the bow was moved around the cap over the nose.

Whenever a man was alleged to have committed an offence and when an officer investigated the case, the man removed his cap. When a man was sentenced to **punishment by warrant**, the lower deck was cleared to hear the charge and punishment. When the man's name was read, his guard ordered him to take a pace forward and as he did so, the guard took the man's cap off. The **Articles of War** were read to the ship's company every three months, and officers and men removed their caps during the reading. Of course caps were removed for church and for morning prayers.

Hands changed into **night clothing** for supper. This was an older but clean blue uniform without a blue jean collar. In some ships jumpers were optional.

Footwear usually was boots, but shoes were worn if desired.

Leading seaman – working dress (leading torpedo operator)

The normal working dress for seamen was supposed to be the oldest blue serge jumper, blue jean collar and trousers. When admirals and senior officers visited their charges for working inspections at sea or in harbour, this was the dress. When official photographs were taken, the men also were properly dressed. In real life, at least in my experience, most men wore overalls. Blue overall suits officially

Leading Seaman Working Dress

were worn by stokers, torpedo party, gunner's party and some miscellaneous parties.

From 1938 to 1945 a working dress of a practical nature, which proved agreeable to all the men, gradually evolved. The material was blue jean and it consisted of trousers, shirt and jacket. Rank and specialty badges were blue, as for white uniforms. Good conduct badges and Canada badges were not worn. It was easy to keep clean, had a neat appearance, was easy to work in and fitted in with contemporary work dress.

Aboard most ships there usually was water slopping about somewhere. Because of this and because they were easily pulled on and kicked off, rubber seaboots were popular. Often the tops were turned half way down, or just cut off. The effect was very sloppy indeed.

Every officer and man aboard ship was supposed to carry a sharp knife. The issue "pusser's (paymaster) dirk," a large clasp knife with a folding marlin spike was never popular. Pointed knives were supposed to be forbidden aboard ship because they might be used in fights, but nearly everyone, officers and men, carried one. I never heard of a stabbing incident aboard ship in all my service. Hunting knives, or often beautifully handmade knives, were carried at the belt in a sheath frequently with a separate marlin spike.

The overall, or boiler suit, although official kit, seemed to lend itself to sloppiness. Stokers often had to do messy work in very confined spaces. When appeared on the upper deck for a well-earned breather, the sight of them gave many a first lieutenant a near stroke. An innocent stoker would come up for air in his shapeless overalls, a retired cap cover on his head, laceless boots, covered with paint and grease and decorated with bits of cotton waste. Quietly enjoying a smoke and a cuppa ploo (char or tea), he would become aware of shouts from the bridge to get out of sight. How would he know the ship was looking her best to enter port!

The duffle coat

Whoever invented this coat for the service deserved the thanks of a hundred thousand mariners for its comfort and practicality. It was named after the town of Duffel in Belgium where the thick, yellowish wool cloth was first made. With a woollen scarf and other accessories, it was ideal for the North Atlantic.

Leading seaman – tropical dress

Chief and petty officers wore white stockings and white canvas shoes instead of blue stockings and black shoes as shown for the leading seaman. Their shirts were short-sleeved with collar as shown. Petty officers wore blue rank badge on their left sleeve.

Leading Seaman Tropical Dress

Detachable gilt button

North Atlantic Watchkeeper Duffle Coat and Seaboots

Scene in a destroyer messdeck

The leading seaman, hand on hip, is in winter dress as indicated by his blue cap and wool jersey. The man with his hand on the stanchion has pulled off his jumper but his blue jean collar still is tied in place; his trouser flap is partially unbuttoned. The pipe smoker wears his "flannel" beneath his jersey; the cord around his neck is for his identity tag. The seated man must be duty watch, which must have been employed in extra work as he still is clad in working dress of seaboots, heavy socks, blue-jean trousers, jersey and old white working cap. Normally he should be in "night clothing," a blue uniform without the blue jean collar. At his belt he wears a sheath knife and marlin spike.

All the men have short hair. One is bearded but his "set" is trimmed and his throat shaven so that, if necessary, he can wear a gas mask. Cigarettes are duty-free, ten cents or sixpence for a pack of 20; most men smoke. Many seamen are tattooed.

The messdeck is spartan, designed for one purpose only: fighting the ship. The first impression is of a confusion of angle irons and beams, pipes, racks and wires, ventilation trunks, wheels and valves under a low deckhead. In the scene depicted a few hammocks have been slung for the night, the first lieutenant having completed his evening rounds. When hammocks are not in use, they are lashed up and stowed in racks called "nettings." This term survives from the days when hammock stowage was nettings atop the bulwarks on the upper deck. When all the hammocks are slung in this messdeck, it will be impossible to walk erect here. Hammock hooks and bars are positioned so that every inch of slinging space can be used, 18 inches per man. Because there is so much new equipment being crammed aboard and more and more men needed, the seat lockers also are sleeping billets. Some ships are so congested that men have to climb in the still-warm bunks of the men who relieve them from their watch.

The ship is in harbour; at night for "darken ship" and always while at sea, deadlights are dropped down and screwed up tight against the scuttles (portholes). Water drips around the scuttle are caught in the "save-all," which  can be unscrewed and dumped when full. Outboard, over the scuttles of well-found ships are welded "eyebrows" to deflect water running down the ship's side. Scuttles are too small for most men to escape through. This resulted in some horrifying deaths in the past when men were trapped by wreckage or fire in messdeck exits, so large escape scuttles now are fitted in each mess.

The interiors of the ship's side and deckheads under exposed decks are coated with small particles of cork to lessen condensation. Perhaps because these are painted over, they are not effective and in cold weather the ship's inside is wet; in freezing weather it is coated with frost. In ships built in the latter part of the war, a thick asbestos insulation, smooth and painted over, covers the interiors of sides and decks. From about 3 feet above the deck, the bulkheads and deckheads are painted white. Below is painted green, blue or grey according to taste. Some decks

Scene in a Destroyer Messdeck

are covered with linoleum; some are painted red, green or grey, sometimes with a non-skid preparation containing particles to make a rough surface. Some steel decks are polished with steel wool.

In most British ships, heat is provided by electric heaters. Canadian ships have steam heat. Wartime-built British ships have a combination of electric heaters and warm air supply through the ventilation system. Some old British ships have only coal stoves in the messdecks.

Ammunition is stowed in magazines beneath the messdecks. Originally magazine hatches were flush with the deck but experience has revealed that flooding often came from the deck above down into the magazines, so hatch coamings are fitted.

Mess tables and benches are wooden with metal legs bolted to the deck; they can be struck down and folded out of the way quickly. Under the tables are stretched lines for drying dish cloths and dish towels.

Each table is a separate mess, numbered from forward to aft, odd to starboard and even to port. Each mess is under a leading seaman, the "leading hand of the mess." Every day there is a duty "cook of the mess" whose tasks include drawing water, tea, coffee and food from the galley in fannies, setting the table with utensils, salt, pepper and condiments, drawing grog for his messmates at "up spirits," washing the dishes and scrubbing the deck, table and benches. Gash (garbage) and dishwater are dumped overboard through the gash chute on the upper deck. As many an unfortunate "cook" mutters as he dumps the dishwater, "Tinkle, tinkle little spoon, knife and fork will follow soon." Floating gash is dumped at sunset so that it will disperse during darkness and not leave a trail for submarines to follow.

Personal gear is stowed in the seat lockers, uniforms being folded up inside-out in a standard manner. This accounts for the lateral creases in the leading seaman's trousers. Kit bags and cap boxes are stowed against the ship's side as shown. Someone's ditty box rests on the seat locker cushion; this is for letters and prized oddments and is respected as the one personal and private possession of a man – sacrosanct in a communal society. On the table is a pusser's dirk, an ashtray pilfered from some bar and a mug crudely marked with the mess number. Playing cards are permitted but gambling for money is forbidden, being a cause of theft and discord.

The comradeship of difficulties and danger, great self-discipline, long naval tradition and mutual respect for the privacy of each messmate enable these men to live closely together with dignity and decency despite their primitive and harsh conditions.

"Wakey wakey, Lash up and stow, Cooks to the galley, Up spirits, Action stations"
Shipboard life under the White Ensign

Naval vessels – characteristics and duties

Battleships were heavily armoured ships designed to engage other battleships and survive. A number of actions did take place, for example the destruction of the German battleship *Bismarck*. Their main employment, however, was covering and protecting convoys in particularly dangerous waters. Their major and very important duties turned out to be bombarding shore targets such as in Normandy.

Battle cruisers were similar to battleships but did not have heavy armour. This enabled them to be faster than battleships and, if required, to get into action quickly. HMS *Hood* paid dearly for this when she blew up in action with *Bismarck* and *Prinz Eugen* off Iceland.

Aircraft carriers became main components of the fleet, being able to **launch air attacks** on the enemy outside the ordinary range of land-based aircraft.

Monitors were designed solely for bombarding shore targets, for which there were plenty of opportunities.

Cruisers originally were designed to act as scouts for the main battle fleet. They were lightly armoured, well gunned and fast. They took part in many successful actions such as the destruction of the German battleship *Graf Spee*. In offshore actions they provided illumination by star shell while numbers of destroyers attacked German convoys.

Destroyers were planned to provide anti-submarine protection for the main fleet. This took place but a major task became protecting convoys. Other duties consisted of shore bombardment together with evacuations and a host of other tasks such as patrols.

Corvettes and frigates provided the backbone of convoy escorts. Canadians can feel proud of the way our ships carried out these duties in the face of submarine attacks and the ferocious weather of the North Atlantic and Arctic Oceans.

British submarines scouted enemy coasts and determined safe channels for surface ships on enemy coasts. Of course, they also torpedoed enemy ships.

Motor launches were used for patrol in more sheltered waters such as the Gulf of St. Lawrence.

Motor torpedo boats roamed the North Sea, English Channel and other European waters and earned great distinction in attacking our enemies.

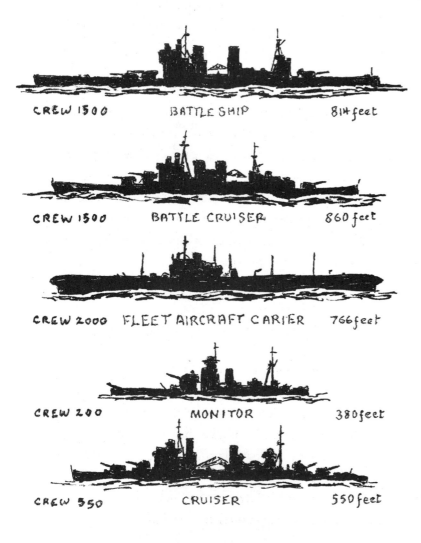

CREW 1500   BATTLE SHIP   814 feet

CREW 1500   BATTLE CRUISER   860 feet

CREW 2000   FLEET AIRCRAFT CARIER   766 feet

CREW 200   MONITOR   380 feet

CREW 550   CRUISER   550 feet

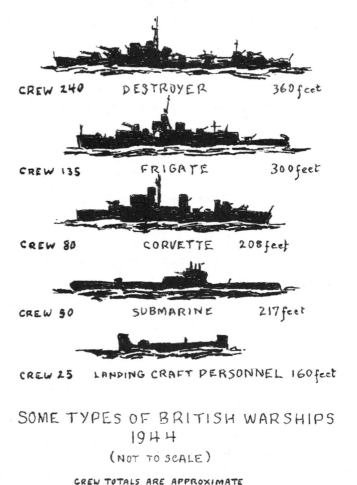

CREW 240   DESTROYER   360 feet

CREW 135   FRIGATE   300 feet

CREW 80   CORVETTE   208 feet

CREW 50   SUBMARINE   217 feet

CREW 25   LANDING CRAFT PERSONNEL   160 feet

SOME TYPES OF BRITISH WARSHIPS
1944
(NOT TO SCALE)

CREW TOTALS ARE APPROXIMATE

Officers and men – their duties and responsibilities

Naval vessels from battleships to corvettes were all organized on the same general principles. As an example a destroyer is discussed.

The **captain** is ultimately responsible for all matters connected with his ship. Whatever his rank may be he is the "Captain." The second-in-command is the **executive officer** (XO) and he takes command if the captain is killed. The XO's duties concern the discipline and good order of the crew and allocation of all duties on the watch and station bill. This bill, a large posted document, shows name, rank, action (battle) station, watches, part of ship and mess for each man and is posted on a board in the vicinity of the ship's office. The **torpedo coxswain**, who is the senior chief petty officer, keeps the bill up-to-date. The XO's other duties include supervising the cleanliness of the ship, the employment of the hands and shipboard drills. In a destroyer he is known as the "first lieutenant."

The **engineering**, **supply** and **medical** officers report directly to the captain for their departments, but the XO retains general responsibilities for discipline, appearance and domestic duties.

The **navigator** supervises the operations room and all navigation matters, generally working directly with the captain.

The **gunnery**, **torpedo**, **anti-submarine**, **radar** and **communication** officers supervise all the activities of their branch. These officers look after the seamen in the parts of the ship. Men are assigned to **parts of ship**. These are forecastlemen (FX), foretopmen (FT), maintopmen (MT) and quarterdeckmen (AX).

Communications is in two parts, visual and wireless. **Radar** personnel maintain sets, weapons, gear and offices. FX, FT, MT and AX are marked on buckets, brooms and so on and stand for forecastle, foremast, mainmast and aftercastle. The "castles" refer to the "castles" fore and aft on the old fighting ships as platforms for crossbow soldiers. **Parts of ship** look after all the gear in their areas – cleanliness, boats, brasswork, painting, and so on. The **captains of the top** are the petty officers in charge of each "top." Each part of ship has a **divisional officer** (top officer) whose duty is to look after the welfare of his men. It is the duty of the **divisional officer** to maintain records for each of his men, promotion, courses, training, conduct, appearance and so on. The divisional officer must advise his men as necessary but not be their pal.

The **gunner** is a warrant officer and his main duty is to supervise the ammunition.

The **chief bo'sun's mate**, a chief petty officer, assists the XO in his duties.

The **supply department** consists of a writer who looks after the ship's office as well as **cooks**, **officers' stewards**, and **storesmen**, whose duties need no explanation. They are known as "daymen" because they do not stand watches, being otherwise fully employed. In battle they supply ammunition, provide damage control, etc.

The **engineers** determine their own responsibilities for their machinery. **Stokers** begin at unskilled level and work their way up. **Engine room artificers** join up as highly skilled technicians starting as petty officers.

The **shipwright** is responsible for "sounding" the ship for leaks, maintaining boats, checking damage control timbers, watertight doors and other matters.

A **midshipman** is often borne to do his small ship time. Often a **chaplain** also is borne.

Standing Orders

Running a fighting ship is a complicated business and each ship should have a set of standing orders which describe the organization of the ship and the duties of officers and men in detail to meet the special nature of the particular ship. Also described in detail are the procedures, equipment and personnel required for such things as towing, fuelling at sea, boarding parties, landing parties and so on.

THE INVERGORDON MUTINY: In 1931, at the beginning of the Great Depression, ships of the Home Fleet were anchored off Invergordon near Inverness on the northeast coast of Scotland. When the ships were ordered to sea, the men refused to weigh anchor or light the boilers. The reason for the mutiny was lack of communication between officers and men. The newspapers had reported that naval pay had been reduced by 10 per cent, a terrible blow to all those who had families to support. Eventually the pay cut was restored but morale in ships was diminished badly. HMS *Hood* was one of these involved but her executive officer was replaced by Commander Rory O'Connor, a six-foot hearty Irishman and under his regime morale vastly

improved and *Hood* became a very happy ship, "Cock of the Walk".

O'Connor wrote a book, *Running a Big Ship on Ten Commandments*. His main object was to strengthen the links between officers and men and to cover in writing the main duties and activities in his ship. In my opinion this book was a wonderful guide, and when I had the responsibility, I tried to follow his example.

O'Connor's "Ten Commandments (Naval)" incorporated, in a nutshell, the principles of discipline and conduct required to make one's ship a winner.

Ten Commandments

This ship is run on the following principles. They are a guide to your conduct while serving in this ship. The observance of these instructions by each member of the ship's company is vital to the fighting efficiency and the happiness of those who serve in her.

THE SERVICE – Customs of the Service are to be observed at all times.

THE SHIP – The good name and appearance of the Ship is the responsibility of everyone on board.

THE INDIVIDUAL – Every officer and man is expected to bring credit to the Ship and the Navy by his individual bearing, dress and conduct on board and ashore.

ORDERS – All orders are to be obeyed with energy and alertness.

DUTY – Every man is personally responsible, on all occasions, for his own punctual attendance at his place of duty. Every man is invariably to ask permission before leaving his work or place of duty. Men ordered to carry out specific tasks are to report to their immediate superior on completion of the work. If through circumstances beyond their control, men are unable to continue on a task allotted to them, they shall report to their immediate superior.

COURTESY – The courtesy of making a gangway and standing to one side when an officer passes is to be shown by every man. Do not allow obscene or filthy language to become part of your natural speech, many of your shipmates find it offensive and unpleasant.

JOINING AND LEAVING – On joining and prior to leaving the ship, men are to report to the Regulating Office for instructions. Each man on joining will be given a numbered billet and deck locker or drawer. He shall not make use of any other stowage space without authority.

LEAVE – Leave will be granted for as long as possible, to as many as possible, as often as possible. If the Captain can feel confident that all of you will return from leave on time, it will be easier to grant leave up to the last possible moment. Leave breakers not only hazard their shipmates' leave, but may even impair the fighting efficiency of our ship.

WELFARE – Any man wishing to see the Executive Officer is to put in a request to his Divisional Officer. In urgent cases a request may be made through the Duty Petty Officer and Officer of the Day. Every man is entitled to state a complaint if he wishes to do so. The procedure for doing so is stated on the notice boards. Suggestions which may improve the efficiency of the ship should be discussed with your Divisional Officer and will be given the utmost consideration. Every man has a Divisional Officer whose duty is to assist him with problems of any nature.

SECURITY – Much of our equipment and activities are highly confidential and should not be mentioned or discussed in the presence of civilians. Do not imperil the security of your country.

Watchkeeping in ships

Men in a commissioned ship are divided into two watches, starboard and port. Each watch is divided into two parts, first part and second part. In addition, me are divided into three watches, red, white and blue.

Each watch is divided into parts of ship – forecastle men, foretopmen, maintopmen and quarterdeckmen. The petty officer in charge of these parts is know as the captain of the forecastle, foretop, etc. There is also a captain of the heads, a seaman who cleans the crew's toilets.

Each part of ship has a divisional officer. His duty is to look after the welfare of his men, promotions, courses and so on. If a man gets into trouble, the divisional officer is to be present at defaulters and report to the executive officer or commanding officer the conduct and character of the man.

At sea, one watch of part of a watch is always on deck night or day.

In harbour, both watches are on deck during working hours, after which the watch on board is sued for any necessary work.

All hands are in messes, usually forecastlemen, foretopmen and so on. Each mess is under the leading hand of the mess, a leading seaman which details cooks of messes to get the food and grog for their messmates, scrub the deck and wooden tables, wash the dishes, dump garbage and so on as required. Men take cook duties in turn.

All hands have their own watch and station cards and are listed on the watch and station bill. Duties at sea for seamen include lookouts, helmsmen to steer the ship, telegraphmen to relay orders to the engine room, leadsmen to take the depths of water as required, messengers for the officer of the watch, lifebuoy sentries, seaboat's crew and lowerers.

Special sea dutymen are the coxswain for steering the ship, telegraphmen for communications to the engine room, leadsmen for taking water depth (soundings), signalmen, forecastlemen to tend anchors and cables, the shipwright, and stoker for capstan.

All the above to a greater or lesser degree applies to all branches in the ship, whether it be a battleship, destroyer or corvette.

In time of war at sea, a proportion of guns, torpedoes and other stations are constantly manned to the degree required by the threat of action. The greatest threat would require watch on/watch off, port and starboard. This was the state for the first months of the war and was so de-manding that men could easily fall asleep at their posts or lack attention, which could prove fatal to everyone. The normal sea routine became three watches, red, white and blue, which was perfectly acceptable.

Passing orders – pipes and bugles

The boatswain's call, or boatswain's whistle, is an instrument by which orders can be passed around a ship. It is small, held in the palm of the hand and is blown. The frequency of the sound can be raised or lowered by opening or closing the hand. A call is illustrated at the end of this book. The call has been used for hundreds of years, since the Royal Navy was founded.

Nowadays the boatswain makes his pipe over the ship's broadcasting equipment. Normally calls are made and followed by an oral instruction, such as "clear lower decks." Some calls are made, each of special significance and following notes laid down in the seamanship manual, that are not followed by an oral order. "Pipe down" and "Hands to dinner" are examples. All hands should learn to recognize them.

When a flag officer or commanding officer comes aboard or goes ashore, the side is piped – that is, the boatswain's mate issues a long single note.

In battleships and cruisers, a Royal Marine bugler bugled "Call the hands," "Dinner," "Out pipes" and so on. What a thrill it was to hear the bugle call for action stations!

Striking bells – "time" aboard ship

A 24-hour day is divided into "watches." The "first" watch is from 2000 to 2400, the "middle" from 2400 to 0400, the "morning" from 0400 to 0800, the "forenoon" from 0800 to 1200, the "afternoon" from 1200 to 1600, the "first dog" from 1600 to 1800 and the "last" or "second dog" from 1800 to 2000.

Half hours are marked by "bells." 2400 is 8 bells; 0300 is 1 bell; 0100 is 2 bells; 0130 is 3 bells; and so on up to 8 bells at 0400 when the process begins again. The bells are struck on the ship's bell.

Fighting the ship

For the first years of the war, the captain with the appropriate officers in an action remained on the open bridge, where he could see the enemy ships or planes. Submarine

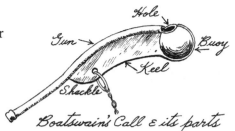

Boatswain's Call & its parts

Holding the boatswain's call

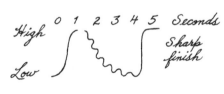

Boatswain's call "music" for
AVAST HOISTING

hunts were also conducted from the bridge. Closed bridges provided protection from the weather but visibility was limited. The Asdic (sonar) submarine indicators were on the open bridge, but this position was not as unsatisfactory as it would become later in the war.

The invention of radar, particularly the 271, increased detection ranges of ships and aircraft far beyond the capabilities of the human eye. Beneath the open bridge was the plotting room, and there was a plotting table next to a PPI (Plan Position Indicator) which gave a visual presentation from the radar. In this, one's ship was in the centre and echoes appeared on the screen whenever a ship or land was in the area. The echoes could then be plotted on the plotting table, where one's own movement was tracked automatically. The course and speed of the echo could then be determined night or day, whether or not it was visible from the open bridge. Guns could be controlled from the plot, either anti-ship or anti-aircraft. Similarly a submarine could be tracked by sonar and, in due course, attacked. In *Algonquin* the 271 radar had been superseded by a most superior set, the 276.

Shipboard daily routines

a ship's lantern

*a sea-clock;
a half-hour glass*

	Harbour routine	Sea routine	Notes
6:30	Call the hands: Wakey wakey. Lash up and stow.		(a)
7:00	Hands to breakfast. Pipe dress of the day	As for harbour	(b)
7:45	Uncover guns		
7:50	Out pipes		
7:55	Hands to Divisions and prayers	Forenoon watchmen to muster	(c)
8:30		Morning watchmen to breakfast	
9:30	First Lieutenant's requestmen and defaulters		(d)
10:30	Stand easy	As for harbour	(e)
10:40	Out pipes		
11:15	Up Spirits		(f)
11:30		Afternoon watchmen to dinner	
11:45	Clear up decks, return gear		
11:50	Hands to muster for grog		(g)
	Cooks to the galley		
12:00	Hands to dinner. Pipe leave	As for harbour	(h)
13:10	Out pipes		
13:15	Hands fall in		(i)
14:30	Stand easy		
14:40	Out pipes		
15:30		First dog watchmen to muster	
15:45	Clear up decks, return gear		
16:00	Secure. Hands to evening quarters	As for harbour	(j)
16:30	Duty watch to muster		
16:40	Cooks to the galley		
17:00	Hands to supper	As for harbour	
17:30	Last dog watchmen to muster		
18:00	Hands to clean into night clothing	As for harbour	(k)
19:30		First watchmen to muster	
20:25	Return all keys to the keyboard	Last dog watchmen to supper	(l)
20:30	Duty watch to muster. Clean up messdecks and flats for rounds		
20:55	Duty watch fall in		
21:00	Rounds	As for harbour	(m)
21:30		Pipe down	
23:00	Pipe down (lights out)		
23:30		Call the middle watchmen	
23:50		Middle watchmen to muster	
03:30		Call the morning watchmen	
03:50		Morning watchmen to muster	

Notes on Routines

When hands normally work before breakfast and the day is stormy "Guard and Steerage" (from the old days) permits hands to sleep in. What a pleasure!

(a) "Lash up and stow" means that hands put seven turns of a rope lashing around the hammock (one turn for each of the seven seas) and then put the lashed up hammock in the "hammock netting" (place of stowage in each mess) with the other hammocks. "Netting" refers to the days of sail when hammocks were placed in a long net on the bulwark (rail) to absorb shot and shrapnel.

(b) "Dress of the day" normally was an old working dress uniform, but it could be sea boots and oilskins or best uniform.

(c) "Divisions and prayers" means all hands fall in (line up) by their part of ship or specialty. The divisional officer inspects his men (are all hands accounted for?) And checks for haircuts, shaving, uniforms, cleanliness, etc. and reports this to the executive officer. Roman Catholics are ordered to fall out (go to another designated area). The remainder then "off caps" and prayers are said; then "on caps", the RC's return and hands are detailed off for the forenoon's work. In cruisers and larger ships the Royal Marine band paraded.

(d) Requestmen and defaulters are paraded before the executive officer. He considers all the requests, granting, declining or passing them on for the captain's consideration. Defaulters, men who may have committed some offence, are paraded one by one before the XO, their caps are taken off and the charge is heard and discussed. The man's divisional officer is present to comment on character. The XO dismisses the case, pronounces punishment, or passes the case on to the captain for action, and the man puts his hat back on.

(e) "Stand easy" means stop work for a rest and smoke if desired. "Out pipes means stop smoking and return to one's duties.

(f) "Up spirits" means that the coxswain and supply person proceed to the Spirit Room, pump up the required amount of rum for the ship's company and bring it to the place of issue.

(g) The standard routine is for each cook of a mess to go to the place of issue with a "fanny" (container) and draw the right amount of grog (one part rum and two parts water) for his messmates.

(h) Leave is piped for watches off duty. Hours are stated in the pipe.

(i) Hands fall in as for Divisions but without inspection and are detailed off for their duties in the afternoon.

(j) "Evening quarters." Hands are mustered and dismissed to carry on off-duty activities.

(k) "Clean into night clothing" means removing working clothes and putting on a clean uniform without a collar. (The collar with the three rows of piping represented Admiral Nelson's battles of Trafalgar, the Nile and Copenhagen.)

(l) This is to ensure that all stores are locked up for the night.

(m) An inspection of the whole ship is carried out by the officer of the day in harbour and by the executive officer at sea.

(n) A "make and mend" is an afternoon off. In the old days, this was a time to make and men clothing. Sewing was called "jewing."

Glossary of some expressions used in the RN and RCN

AB – Able seaman

Action Stations – Men at station when ship is ready for action

Adrift – Absent without leave or returning late from leave

Aggie Weston – Sailors' hostel established by Dame Agnes Weston. Economic accommodation in main naval ports.

Asdic – Sonar, submarine detection gear

Banyan party – A general party ashore

Barrack stanchion – One who manages a berth in barracks and who seems immoveable

Battlewagon – Battleship

Belay – Stop

Bird – Someone often in trouble

Blast or bottle – A reprimand

Block – A large pulley

Boats – Destroyers (Give me the boats)

Brightwork – Brass or bronze

Bubbly – Rum

Buffer – Chief boatswain's mate. The chief or petty officer under the first lieutenant in charge of the day-to-day employment of the seamen.

Bulkheads – walls in a ship

Bunting tosser – Signalman

Buzz – Rumour

CPO – Chief petty officer

Carley float – A design of life raft

Char – Tea

Chats – Chatham (British naval base)

Chatty – Lousey (chatty but happy)

Chocka – Fed up (from chock-a-block, when a rope is block to block)

Chokey – detention in a naval prison

Coxswain (cox'n) – The senior seaman CPO in the ship

Crusher – Regulating petty officer. In cruisers and above only. Assists the Master-at-Arms in matters of discipline.

Deckhead – Ceiling in a ship

Dhobi – Washing, laundry

Dickey – False white front laced at the sides, worn in summer and in tropics

Ditty box – Small wooden box. Sailor's personal, private container for odds and ends

Divisions – A muster of ship's company

Dockyard matey – A dockyard worker

Duff – Pudding

ERA – Engine room artificer

ETA – Estimated time of arrival

Fanny – Oblong steel mess can

Fo'c's'le – Forward part of the ship where the seamen live

Galley – Ship's kitchen

Gash – Rubbish

Gash shute – For putting gash into the ocean

Grog – Daily issue of rum mixed with 2 parts water, so ordered by Admiral Vernon because too many men were falling out of the rigging.

Guz – Devonport (British naval base)

HO – Hostilities Only men

Hawspipe – The hole on the fo'c's'le through which the anchor and cable pass. An officer promoted from lower deck was said to have come through the hawspipe.

Heads – Ship's toilets

Hooky – Leading seaman (from his arm badge of an anchor)

Hot bunk – Because of crowded conditions, someone coming off watch would get into the billet of someone going on watch.

Jacob's ladder – A ladder from a boom suspended over the ship's side for climbing in and out of boats

Jimmy the One – The executive officer, first lieutenant

KR&AI – King's Regulations and Admiralty Instructions

Killick – (Hooky) leading seaman. His rank was shown by a single anchor on the left sleeve. Killick is an old Norse term for a small anchor.

Kye – Ship's cocoa (which came in large blocks)

LS – Leading seaman

LSBA – Leading sick berth attendant

LTO – Leading torpedo operator

Liberty boat – Boat to take men ashore and return

Liberty ship – Merchant ships mass produced in Canada and U.S.A.

Libertymen – Men granted shore leave

Lid – Cap. "Off cap" to stand accused before an officer for an offence.

Make and mend – An afternoon off. Originally for making and mending clothes.

Matelot – RN and RCN rating. An honourable term adopted from the French.

Nackers – Balls or testicles

Nelson's blood – Rum. After he died Admiral Nelson's body was placed in a barrel of rum and sent back to Plymouth in the frigate HMS *Pickle*. En route *Pickle*'s matelots tapped the barrel and drank the rum.

Newfie – Newfoundland

Number … – Uniforms in descending order of quality. Punishments in descending order of severity.

Nutty – Chocolate bar

OA – Ordnance artificer

OD – Ordinary seaman

OOD – Officer of the day

OOW – Officer of the watch

Old Man – the captain

Oppo – A chum (opposite number)

PO – Petty officer

PTI – Physical training instructor

Party – Regular girl friend, etc.

Pierhead jump – A last minute draft to a ship about to sail

Pipe – An order passed by the boatswain's mate. "Out Pipes," the end of "Stand Easy"

Pipe down – Turn in to sleep

Pompy – Portsmouth (naval base)

Pongo – Soldier

Prick – Tobacco. Duty free loose tobacco leaves rolled up very tightly in cigar shaped bundle and soaked in rum. A favourite of stripeys.

Pump ship – To urinate

Punka louvres – Controlled openings for ventilation of living spaces

Pusser – Anything provided by Admiralty

Quarterdeck – The after end deck which was always saluted in memory of a crucifix fitted there.

Rattle – "In the rattle" — under punishment

Ringer – Officers' gold braid rings on their sleeve cuffs. A lieutenant commander is a two and a half ringer, etc.

Round turn and two half hitches – To come to your senses

Salt horse – Officer who did not have a long-course specialty

Scran bag – Lost and found articles or a very untidy person

Scribe – A writer (ship's office)

Scuttle – A port hole

Sick berth tiffy – Sick berth attendant

Sippers – Sharing one's rum ration

Slackers – Halifax (naval base)

Son of a gun – In the old days womenfolk lived with their men in ships between the cannons. Male babies were termed "sons of guns."

Sparker – Wireless operator

Splice the main brace – A double issue of rum on special occasions

Stand easy – A 10-minute pause from work in the forenoon and afternoon. "Out pipes" terminated this.

Station cards – Identity document

Stripey – A man with two or three good conduct badges and still an able seaman

Subby – Sub-lieutenant

Swinging the lead – To be idle from work

Tally – A name. Cap tally showed name of ship

Tapes – Ribbons on uniform jackets

Ticklers – Duty-free cigarettes

Tiddly – Shipshape

Tiddlies – Best uniform

Tiffy – Engine room artificer

Tin fish -Torpedo

Tot – Daily issue of rum. Men could be Temperance if they wished and receive money instead

Watch on / Watch off – On duty 4 hours on and 4 hours off

Winger – A special friend

Index

ILLUSTRATIONS (in order of appearance)